religion and violence

VOLUME 1

religion and violence

An Encyclopedia of Faith and Conflict from Antiquity to the Present

VOLUME 1

JEFFREY IAN ROSS, EDITOR

M.E.Sharpe
Armonk, New York
London, England

The EuroSlavic and Transroman fonts used to create this work are © 1986–2010
Payne Loving Trust. EuroSlavic and Transroman are available
from Linguist's Software, Inc., www.linguistsoftware.com
P.O. Box 580, Edmonds, WA 98020-0580 USA, tel. (425) 775-1130.

Cover photos provided by Getty Images (clockwise from upper left): Thopson/AFP;
Spencer Platt; Choo Youn-Kong/AFP; Robert Nickelsberg; Tim Boyle.

Library of Congress Cataloging-in-Publication Data

Religion and violence : an encyclopedia of faith and conflict from antiquity to the present / Jeffrey Ian Ross,
editor.
    p. cm.
Includes bibliographical references and index.
  ISBN 978-0-7656-2048-4 (hardcover : alk. paper)
  1. Violence—Religious aspects—Encyclopedias. 2. Religions—History—Encyclopedias. 3. Violence—
History—Encyclopedias. I. Ross, Jeffrey Ian.

BL65.V55R45555 2011
201′.7633203—dc22
                                                              2010039628

Printed in the United States of America

To Ted Robert Gurr, PhD,

scholar and mentor

Contents

Volume 3

Foreword

The preparation of an encyclopedia is a huge task in the very nature of the term. To produce such a work that contains a unique blend of talent, character and vision, is a yet larger effort. Jeffrey Ian Ross has performed a valuable, if admittedly contentious service in this collective portrait of *Religion and Violence.* Indeed, it will irritate those who believe that a particular faith embodies only goodness, and that violence is a deviation from its stated goals. The work emphatically says, and with reference to a full panoply of faiths, that conflict is endemic to all notions of superiority, perfection, and divine revelation. This encyclopedia does not settle matters, but it rather raises twenty-first-century issues of relativism and absolutism, positivism, and mysticism. Above all, it reminds us, or it should, that the issue of religion involves a struggle—sometimes brutal and activist—between visions of the good versus other goods. The study of evil pales in comparison to the faith and conflict in the behavior of everyday life.

Irving Louis Horowitz

Acknowledgments

The process of developing, researching, inviting contributors, and editing this encyclopedia has been an especially long but rewarding journey. In any given project, however, there are many people to thank, and this one is no different. I extend my appreciation to my entry writers, who demonstrated considerable patience through all stages of the project and maintained confidence that this manuscript would eventually make its way into print.

Thanks to the folks at M.E. Sharpe, including former Acquisitions Editor Todd Hallman, Assistant Editor Alison Morretta, Managing Editor Angela Piliouras, and Vice President of New Product Development Donna Sanzone, for stepping up to the plate to ask the tougher editorial and production questions.

Deep-felt thanks to Irving Louis Horowitz—friend, mentor, and colleague—for writing an excellent foreword to the encyclopedia, and to Keanu and Dakota Ross-Cabrera for providing extraordinary research assistance.

Namaste to Owen Anderson, Steven Leonard Jacobs, Dawn L. Rothe, James D. Sellmann, Cécile Van de Voorde, and Aaron Z. Winter, who acted as an informal-virtual advisory board of sorts. These scholar colleagues helped me navigate some of the intellectual, historical, ideological, and practical issues I confronted along the way, and for this I am grateful.

Last, but certainly not least, I extend my never-ending gratitude to my wonderful family. I thank Natasha J. Cabrera, my wife and fellow scholar, for providing encouragement and feedback at several critical times, serving as a sounding board for my ideas, and trying her best to keep me focused. I also recognize Keanu and Dakota, our children, who are a constant source of inspiration and joy.

Editor

Jeffrey Ian Ross
University of Baltimore

Contributors

Jonathan M. Acuff
University of Washington

Göran Adamson
Independent Scholar

J. Keith Akins
New Mexico State University

Owen Anderson
Arizona State University

Kelly J. Baker
Florida State University

James David Ballard
*California State University,
Northridge*

Paolo Barbaro
École Pratique des Hautes Études

Johannes Botes
University of Baltimore

Wendell S. Broadwell, Jr.
Georgia Perimeter College

Christopher Brock
London Metropolitan University

Richard Butler
Brookdale Community College

Cenap Çakmak
*Eskişehir Osmangazi University,
Turkey*

Matthew Cannon
University of Limerick, Ireland

Tammy Castle
James Madison University

Daniele Conversi
University of Lincoln

Ana Cornwell
University of Guam

Angela West Crews
Washburn University

Gordon A. Crews
Washburn University

Gerald Cromer
Bar Ilan University

Brandon M. Crowe
Arizona State University

Jeffrey D. Dailey
Texas A&M University-Commerce

Claire Delisle
University of Ottawa

M. George Eichenberg
Tarleton State University

Courtney Erwin
Cordoba Initiative

Stefano Fait
*University of St. Andrews,
Scotland*

Sean Farrell
Northern Illinois University

Glen Feder
The Washington Center

Laura Finley
Independent Scholar

Larry French
University of New Hampshire

Michel Jacques Gagné
Champlain College-Saint Lambert

Carolyn Gallaher
American University

Venessa Garcia
Kean University

Fiore Geelhoed
Erasmus University, Rotterdam

Jeffry R. Halverson
Arizona State University

Daniel Haynes
Independent Scholar

Keith Hayward
University of Kent

Christopher Hrynkow
University of Manitoba

Stephen Leonard Jacobs
University of Alabama

Sara Johnsdotter
Malmö University, Sweden

Kirk Johnson
University of Guam

David M. Jones
University of Wisconsin, Oshkosh

James R. King
Columbia University

James T. Kirkhope
Terrorism Studies Group

Lucian N. Leustean
London School of Economics and Political Science

Edith Linn
Berkeley College

Craig T. Love
Westat

Brenda J. Lutz
Indiana University-Purdue University, Fort Wayne

James M. Lutz
Indiana University-Purdue University, Fort Wayne

Joshua Martin
Cordoba Initiative

George Michael
University of Virginia at Wise

James F. Moore
Valparaiso University

Christopher W. Mullins
University of Northern Iowa

Nathaniel Samuel Murrell
University of North Carolina, Wilmington

Aisha Musa
Florida International University

Kenneth Omeje
University of Bradford

I.D. Onwudiwe
Texas Southern University

Nadia Suhaila Oweidat
Oxford University

George Palermo
University of Nevada

Arie Perliger
State University of New York, Stony Brook

Patricia Power
Arizona State University

William Raffel
Buffalo State College

Kilby Raptopoulos
University of Arkansas at Little Rock

Hussein Rashid
Harvard University

Carlo Rossetti
University of Parma, Italy

Dawn L. Rothe
University of Northern Iowa

Jarem Sawatsky
Canadian Mennonite University

Len Sawatsky
Canadian Mennonite University

Beau Seegmiller
Arizona State University

James D. Sellmann
University of Guam

Michael Shank
George Mason University

Julie Shedd
George Mason University

Thomas Shevory
Ithaca College

Paul E. Sigmund
Princeton University

Raghu N. Singh
Texas A&M University-Commerce

Kim Skoog
University of Guam

Yushau Sodiq
Texas Christian University

Hakki Tas
Bilkent University

Nicholas ten Bensel
University of Arkansas at Little Rock

N. Prabha Unnithan
Colorado State University

Cécile Van de Voorde
John Jay College of Criminal Justice

Anicée Van Engeland
European University Institute

Sebastien Viguier
Princeton University

Michael S. Waltman
University of North Carolina at Chapel Hill

Michael Winkelman
Independent Scholar

Aaron Winter
University of Abertay, Dundee

Tusty Zohra
University of Nebraska, Omaha

Introduction

Daily newspaper headlines, talk radio and cable television broadcasts, and Internet news Web sites continuously highlight the relationship between religion and violence. These media contain stories about such diverse incidents as suicide attacks by Islamic fundamentalists in Afghanistan, Iraq, Israel, Pakistan, and elsewhere, and assassinations of doctors who perform abortions by white American Christian true believers in the United States.

How does one make sense of the role of religion in violence, and of perpetrators of violence who cite religion as a motivation? Although a number of publishers have developed encyclopedias on religion or on different facets of religion, no English-language press has produced an encyclopedia specifically on the subject of religion and violence. It is with this in mind that I have assembled and edited *Religion and Violence: An Encyclopedia of Faith and Conflict from Antiquity to the Present* (hereafter *Religion and Violence*). This reference work, consisting of 130 entries, is designed to answer both basic and relatively complex questions regarding the intersection of religion and violence.

In order to accomplish this goal, I have included entries focusing on well-known acts of religious violence that have occurred in different countries or regions, as well as well-known individuals and groups who have not only advocated, but committed this form of criminal and/or political violence. The entries summarize key concepts and, where appropriate, include tables and photographs illustrating these themes. The strength of this encyclopedia is its comprehensive, and concise, approach to explaining the most important individuals, concepts, groups, practices, and movements in the field of religion and violence, as well as their causes and effects. It also includes a number of in-depth case studies.

Religion and Violence has been a massive undertaking, occupying no less than four years of my professional life. I have approached the subject matter in as comprehensive a manner as possible, looking at all the possible vagaries of the topic. The encyclopedia includes a wide range of entries: biographies of key figures, historical events, religious groups, countries and regions where religion and violence have intersected, and practices, rituals, and processes of religious violence.

Editorially, the treatment of entries (depth of analysis or length) may vary depending upon a topic's relative importance to overall coverage. The contributors are truly interdisciplinary in their training and research. They come from a variety of disciplines in the social sciences, including conflict analysis and resolution, criminology, criminal justice, geography, government, history, peace studies, political science, religious studies, and sociology. Others have backgrounds in the humanities, such as communication, education, law, and philosophy, or the sciences, such as medicine and psychiatry. Still other writers are area studies experts (e.g., Asian studies, Judaic studies).

It must be noted that a distinction exists between psychological/structural and physical violence. Psychological violence (or trauma) is often a precursor to and/or the effect of physical violence. The first affects individuals' mental states and often leads to anger, cynicism, depression, and resistance to authority. Physical violence affects people's bodies and eventually their minds. This encyclopedia primarily deals with the latter.

Literature Review

Despite mass media attention and the occasional scholarly treatment of religion and violence, including academic conferences devoted to the subject, few academics have specifically examined the nexus of religion and violence. Furthermore, the majority of this research lies in numerous case studies of particular incidents, individual actors, groups, and campaigns, sometimes brought together as edited books. In other words, very few integrative analyses on the role of religion and violence have been produced. There are some exceptions, which are reviewed below.

Girard (1972/1977) is the author of one of the best known and most cited pieces of scholarship on religion and violence. In his book *Violence and the Sacred*, he claims that all religions begin with human sacrifice and that the purpose of ritual is to minimize this kind of group hurt. Girard highlights how states evolve when religion can no longer achieve the goals of the community. He suggests that mimetic desire (the need to have things that others have just for the sake of having them) breeds violence and that this pattern is placated by religion, which encompasses the dual processes of scapegoating and sacrifice. For Girard, mimetic desire is at the heart of all religious violence.

Building on and critiquing Girard's work, Rapoport (1991) competently outlines how, at different points in history, the major religions have exhibited both a side that advocates nonviolence and another side that encourages followers to engage in violence. Rapoport identifies six areas in which religion and violence are linked; these follow a progression from areas that are the most obvious and least controversial to linkages that are subtle and barely detectable but highly controversial. For Rapoport, religion has the ability to "inspire ultimate commitment"—it provides methods of communicating violence, violence is intimately connected to "the origin and/or purpose of religion," and religious revivals often include violence. While Rapoport can be insightful, some of the evidence he presents (e.g., passages from the Bible and popular interpretations of religious events) is open to multiple interpretations. Meanwhile, other statements can be criticized because the evidence he presents is not substantiated.

Another treatment that sheds light on this subject is that of Wellman and Tokuno (2004). They state, "[t]he symbolic and social boundaries of religion (no matter how fluid or porous) mobilize individual and group identity in conflict, and sometimes violence, within and between groups." They add, "[c]onflict tends to galvanize religious communities rather than subdue them." Among their numerous insights, Wellman and Tokuno note, "[w]e believe it is folly to assert that true religion seeks peace; or that religion is somehow hijacked when it becomes implicated in conflict or even violence. Indeed, religion does produce conflict, and, less frequently, violence." They conclude their thoughtful article by asking the question: Is violence in connection with religion inevitable? They answer this provocative question by stating, "[r]eligious conflict is predictable and should be expected. Because religion is often an independent cultural force in society, it has the tendency to become a threat to other cultural and political powers. Religious violence, we would argue, may not be inevitable, but it should surprise no one."

One of the most classic and accessible books on the topic at hand is McAfee Brown's *Religion and Violence*, already in its second edition (1973/1987). In the second edition, Brown identifies seven concerns that are more prominent since the publication of the first edition: nuclear weapons, terrorism, the death penalty, sexual violence, the drug culture, disinformation, and revolution. Brown's is a straightforward explanation of the multiple connections between religion and war. He carefully defines his terms and addresses such subjects as war and religion, concluding his book with a discussion of alternatives to violence. The majority of his examples stem from American history.

Major Themes in the Encyclopedia

As mentioned above, the entries cover five major themes: biographies of important figures; historical events; country and regional studies; religious groups; and practices, rituals, and process of religious violence. Below is a review of these categories.

Biographies/Important Figures

Through my research, I identified individuals who are pivotal to the subject of religion and violence. These are well-known people throughout history who have advocated and/or participated in violence in connection with religion or religious campaigns. The list also includes individuals who have argued against the use of violence in a religious context or citing religious motives. Most are charismatic figures with excellent writing, oratory, and leadership skills. They are also leaders of groups and typically have very competent organizing skills.

These biographies represent individuals from a variety of religions and time periods: from Gerry Adams, as the leader of the Sinn Féin (the political arm of the terrorist Provisional Irish Republican Army, or PIRA), Bobby Sands (the famous PIRA hunger striker), and Ian Paisley (one of the most prominent Unionists in Northern Ireland)—all associated with the Northern Irish "Troubles" (i.e., the decades-long conflict between Protestants and Catholics)—to Louis Beam, Jr., Robert Jay Mathews, and Randy Weaver (all members of America's shadowy extreme right, who drew inspiration from their racist and Christian Identity beliefs), to Mohandas K. Gandhi (the father of modern India, who stood up to nearly a century of British colonial rule through creative nonviolence and ushered in a new state founded on the principles of religious freedom and democratic participation).

Also included are Muslim fundamentalists such as Sayyid Qutb and Osama bin Laden, both of whom preached against so-called Western "infidels." There is an entry on Mehmet Ali Ağca, the young Turkish citizen who in 1981 attempted to assassinate Pope John Paul II in St. Peter's Square, Rome. Other individuals throughout history who have resorted to violence do not have separate entries, but are mentioned in various entries.

Historical Events

Numerous events have shaped the history of religion and violence in the world. After reviewing the literature and consulting with colleagues, I selected the most noteworthy topics. Some of these have been one-time incidents like the 9/11 terrorist attacks, which resulted in the deaths of almost 3,000 individuals and injured some 6,300 others. Other events in the history of religion and violence are Bloody Sunday (January 30, 1972), when British soldiers opened fire during a peaceful Republican protest through the streets of Derry, Northern Ireland. Some historical events were lengthy campaigns like the Crusades, and relatively short genocides like the one that took place in Rwanda (1994), perpetrated by the Hutus, who were disproportionately Christian, against the minority Tutsis. In this conflict, the local Roman Catholic and Seventh Day Adventist churches, because of their authority, power, and legitimacy, took an active part in advocating violence.

Undoubtedly, one way to measure the significance of historical events involving religion and violence is by their duration or by the destruction left in their wake, including the number of people injured and killed. Therefore, events with significant death tolls have been included in the encyclopedia. But in addition, articles are also included that analyze the threat of violence, such as the Danish cartoon crisis and the numerous fatwas (religious edicts) issued against prominent people like Nobel Prize–winning author Salman Rushdie.

Country and Regional Studies

Articles on countries that have been historically marked by religious violence include discussions of Israel and Northern Ireland, for example. Entries cover contemporary religious violence in all the major regions of the world, ranging from South America to North America; from Central Asia to the Middle East. This approach promotes a global approach to contemporary religious violence.

Religious Groups

Approximately one-quarter of the encyclopedia deals with groups, organizations, and movements that may not normally be considered a religion in and of themselves. Although these entities, sometimes called cults or new religious movements, may practice a form of religion or advocate a religion, they are not normally considered to be major religions themselves. They may also be the victims of religious persecution. A major editorial criterion for the selection of groups was whether there has been sufficient news media and scholarly discussion about them over the past quarter of a century. Thus, we find entries that range from Aum Shinrikyo to the Jewish Defense League. The groups included also may be offshoots of major religions or religious practices (e.g., Hamas or Hizballah).

Major Religions

The major religions of the world are so reviewed because they either had a profound and lasting historical influence (Judaism) or they presently command a very large number of followers (Islam or Daoism). Numerous religions exist, but not all can be considered major. That is why there is a concentrated focus on essays that analyze the world's major religions and their connection to violence. From African traditional religions to Unitarian Universalism, these entries examine the major players and historical events that have shaped religious violence. Almost every religion and religious offshoot has some sort of manifesto, bible, or statement of purpose that members and outsiders can refer to. Much of this is derivative of the major religions. Others, like cults, sects, and new religious movements, seem to simply be made up based on the whims of their leaders.

Religious Practices, Rituals, and Processes

The majority of this encyclopedia contains entries that describe and analyze religious practices, rituals, and processes that contain violence. This ranges from cults whose members use or are subjected to violence to the worlds' major religions (e.g., Judaism, Catholicism) that have used or justified violence in their name. It includes periods of intense violence and ones in which violence was shunned (e.g., conscientious objection). Also in the encyclopedia are cross-cutting essays that look at phenomena like the Internet and religious violence, philosophy and religious violence, as well as ethnicity and violence.

Readers may wish to know if religious violence is increasing and whether there are more groups resorting to violence in order to achieve their objectives. Neither of these questions can be answered unequivocally. No comprehensive and scholarly analysis has been done to track this. However, one thing is certain, and that is the impact of the so-called crisis of modernity on religion, in which a religion's inability to justify itself in the face of secular challenges has been a historically unique problem that has resulted in new forms of religious violence.

Distinctive Features of This Work

There are several significant and interrelated features of this encyclopedia that the reader will find helpful in navigating the information contained within.

Comparative and International Connections. Given the comparative and international nature of the subject matter, *Religion and Violence* is sensitive to the global ramifications of both religious violence and the study of religion and violence.

Realism Rather Than Sensationalism. With a subject that deals with the connections between religion and violence, it is sometimes difficult to avoid sensational issues—especially when they have received ample media coverage. *Religion and Violence* tries to minimize the sensational aspects and take an objective, analytic approach.

Comprehensiveness. *Religion and Violence* offers a relatively comprehensive understanding not only of the multitudinous examples of its subject matter, but also of the history and the causes and effects of religious violence.

Current, Scholarly, Multidisciplinary. The encyclopedia integrates scholarly analysis with current events by relying not only on academic research but also on recent media accounts and information gathered by respectable news outlets. It is both interdisciplinary and transdisciplinary. All entries were written by recognized scholars from different disciplines.

Balance. Every effort has been made to present the topics at hand in a balanced, neutral manner. At the same time, it is recognized that a field as contentious as religion and violence may engender competing interpretations.

Conclusion

The connection between religion and violence is pervasive and undeniable. Under the premise that more knowledge is power, this encyclopedia should be an essential source for those seeking a better understanding of this subject.

Jeffrey Ian Ross, PhD

Acknowledgments

Special thanks to Owen Anderson, Steven Leonard Jacobs, Dawn L. Rothe, Donna Sanzone, James D. Sellmann, Cécile Van de Voorde, and Aaron Z. Winter for comments.

Further Reading

Bromley, D.G., and J.G. Melton, eds. *Cults, Religion and Violence.* Cambridge, UK: Cambridge University Press, 2002.

Brown, Robert McAfee. *Religion and Violence.* 2nd ed. Philadelphia: Westminster Press, 1987.

Crockett, Clayton, ed. *Religion and Violence in a Secular World: Toward a New Political Theory.* Charlottesville: University of Virginia Press, 2006.

De Vries, Hent. *Religion and Violence: Philosophical Perspectives from Kant to Derrida.* Baltimore: Johns Hopkins University Press, 2001.

Galtung, Johan. "A Structural Theory of Aggression." *Journal of Peace Research* 1:2 (1964): 95–119.

Girard, Rene. *Violence and the Sacred,* trans. Patrick Gregory. Baltimore: Johns Hopkins University Press, [1972] 1977.

Isherwood, Lisa, and Rosemary Radford Ruether, eds. *Weep Not for Your Children: Essays on Religion and Violence.* London: Equinox, 2008.

Juregensmeyer, M. *Terror in the Mind of God: The Global Rise of Religious Violence.* Berkeley: University of California Press, 2000.

Rapoport, David C. "Some General Observations on Religion and Violence." *Terrorism and Political Violence* 3:3 (Autumn 1991): 118–140.

Stark, Rodney. *One True God: Historical Consequences of Monotheism.* Princeton, NJ: Princeton University Press, 2001.

Wellman, James K., Jr., and Kyoko Tokuno. "Is Religious Violence Inevitable?" *Journal for the Scientific Study of Religion* 43:3 (2004): 291–296.

religion and violence

VOLUME 1

Adams, Gerry (1948–)

Gerry Adams is the president of Sinn Féin, the political party representing the Irish Republican Movement in Northern Ireland. He was first elected to this position in 1983. Adams is the Westminster member of Parliament for West Belfast but has not taken his seat because of Sinn Féin's abstentionist stance in British government. He is also an elected member of the Northern Ireland Assembly, which sits in Stormont. Republicanism is a nationalist political orientation, the long-term goal of which is to reunify the six counties of Northern Ireland with the Republic of Ireland. In the short term, it aims to end the British presence in the North by encouraging the devolution of powers from London to Belfast and to replace it with a democratic form of governance involving the parties in the Northern Ireland Assembly.

A Controversial Figure

Adams is a controversial political figure, and many associate him with the Provisional Irish Republican Army (IRA), the formerly armed organization of the Republican Movement, dedicated to the removal of British troops in Northern Ireland, a charge that he has always vehemently denied. He is considered by his adversaries to be a dangerous terrorist. For many years, there was a media voice ban on Adams both in Ireland and in Britain; although his image could be displayed on television, his words were dubbed in by another person. Moreover, until 1993, he was not permitted to travel to Britain, even though he is a citizen of the United Kingdom; nor was he allowed into the United States until 1994.

Sinn Féin president Gerry Adams, speaking at a news conference in Belfast on April 6, 2005, urged the IRA to renounce the armed struggle in favor of a nonviolent, political approach to the peace process. (*Paul McErlane/Getty Images*)

The Peace Initiative

Adams is best known for initiating the Irish peace process in 1993, but his work on the peace initiative can be traced back to 1987, when he wrote the discussion paper "A Scenario for Peace." It was at this time that he entered into secret talks with John Hume, then president of the Social Democratic Labour Party, the constitutionalist nationalist party in Northern Ireland. These talks were helped along by a priest from the Clonard Monastery in Belfast, Father Alex Reid, an influential backroom facilitator who acted as messenger to the Irish and British governments as well as the other political parties in the years leading to the peace talks. After twenty-three years of what is referred to as the Troubles, the Downing Street Declaration was presented on December 15, 1993, by the heads of the British and Irish governments, spelling out the framework for establishing peace talks. The ensuing negotiations, under the chairmanship of Senator George Mitchell of the United States, brought every political party to the table and resulted in the signing of the Belfast Agreement, also referred to as the Good Friday Agreement, in April 1998.

The Peace Process and the Belfast Assembly

Adams has consistently advanced the political struggle in the North, for the long-term goal of a united Ireland, an "Ireland of equals," free of a British presence. Immediate goals include getting the New Assembly reinstituted, sharing power with the Democratic Unionist Party, and making the newly reformed police service of Northern Ireland democratically accountable, responsible, and nonsectarian. The assembly was shut down for the fourth time in October 2002 because of an alleged Sinn Féin–led spying operation. This allegation was disproved when it emerged that the British were spying on Sinn Féin with the help of a highly placed agent in the party's Stormont administration, a man named Denis Donaldson.

Bringing the IRA on Board

Under Adams's leadership, the Republican Movement was able to back a peace initiative without a split in the ranks of the IRA. In fact, thanks to the political acumen of Adams and his close associates, including Martin McGuinness, Sinn Féin's chief negotiator in the peace process, the IRA was able to institute a lasting cease-fire in 1997 and to decommission all weapons in July 2005. The verification of the decommissioning of weapons was overseen by General John de Chastelain, head of the IICD (Independent International Decommissioning Commission) with the assistance of two churchmen, who witnessed the process.

It is thought that Adams's strategy to first persuade Republican prisoners to back the peace initiative enabled Sinn Féin to convince its constituents of its merits, since the prisoners are held in such high esteem by the community (Feeney 2003). Furthermore, Adams has commanded the necessary authority and respect to succeed in his endeavors to find peace despite the painstakingly slow process.

The Beginning of an Activist Career

Adams first became involved in politics as a young man, when he started to advocate for decent housing in Belfast. He participated in protests and marches and was involved during the rise of the Northern Ireland civil rights movement in the late 1960s. Nationalists who were marching peacefully to protest poor housing, unemployment, and gerrymandered electoral districts were attacked by Loyalists (those loyal to the British Crown) and the Royal Ulster Constabulary (RUC), a police force made up almost exclusively of Protestants. Adams was soon in the thick of efforts to protect the Catholic neighborhoods from being attacked by Loyalists. The attacks included the burning of Bombay Street in 1969, in which the homes of 1,500 Catholics and 300 Protestants were destroyed while the RUC remained passive. The British army was sent in to respond to the crisis, and internment was instituted. The detention of thousands of Catholics in the North combined with the Falls Road Curfew and Bloody Sunday, in which twenty-eight innocent demonstrators were killed or wounded by British army paratroopers in Derry in January 1972, drove many to join the Irish Republican Army.

The six counties of the North—Fermanagh, Armagh, Tyrone, Derry, Antrim, and Down—

were partitioned from Ireland as part of the Independence Treaty in 1921. Sectarian tension between the majority Protestants and the minority Catholics in those six counties resulted in off-and-on violence throughout the twentieth century but culminated in the Troubles, starting in 1969. In response to the violent attacks on Catholics, the Provisional Irish Republican Army first defended Catholic neighborhoods from Loyalist attacks before waging an armed offensive against the British from 1970 until the cease-fire in 1997.

Adams in Prison

First arrested on March 14, 1972, Adams was tortured by the authorities and eventually sent to the Maidstone Prison ship before being transferred to Long Kesh, an old air force base. There Republican internees were held in garage-like tin structures referred to as cages. It was in Long Kesh that Adams met up with other members of his family and many friends. His stature as a leader was already manifest during this time, as he was released to partake in a delegation of IRA leaders who were flown to England to meet with William Whitelaw, then secretary of state for Northern Ireland, in an effort to secure a truce. When the truce broke down and he was rearrested in 1973, he was tortured and interned in Long Kesh until 1977. He was reapprehended by the authorities in 1978 and charged with membership in the IRA but was released seven months later because of insufficient evidence to convict him.

During his four-year detention in the cages of Long Kesh, Adams wrote prolifically. He smuggled articles to the *Republican News* under the pen name Brownie, and his penchant for finding a political route to end the crisis could already be perceived in his writings, though he presented his arguments with subtlety. He was OC (officer commanding, part of the

IRA military command structure in prison) in the cages and was housed in the same cage as other Republican luminaries such as Brendan Hughes, Bobby Sands, Bik McFarlane, and Gerry Kelly, among others. As OC, Adams focused on democratizing the workings of the Republican Movement and encouraged debate on the struggle. His time in prison made him sympathetic to the plight of Republican prisoners, and he is credited for starting the P.O.W. department within Sinn Féin. During the 1980 and 1981 hunger strikes, he was part of a team of Sinn Féin leaders in Belfast who helped the prisoners stand firm on their demands for recognition of their status as political prisoners. Adams had not necessarily agreed with the hunger strike tactic but he understood the level of frustration of the prisoners. When hunger striker Bobby Sands was put up as a candidate in a Westminster by-election, Adams and his team campaigned on his behalf. Sands's resulting victory did not save his life (nor the lives of nine other comrades on hunger strike, subsequently), but it did catapult Sinn Feín onto the electoral scene and paved the way for a drastic change of orientation in the party.

The Rise of the Adams-McGuinness Leadership in Sinn Féin

The younger northern leadership of Sinn Féin became an efficient political machine, and the difference in both style and politics between them and the Dublin-based leadership of Ruairí O'Bradaígh and Dathaí O'Conaill became obvious. Fundamental disagreement over the latter's "Eire Nua" policy document, advocating a unitary federal Ireland, served as a catalyst for change. The old guard stepped down, and Adams and Martin McGuinness took over the leadership.

Adams and his close associates were responsible for the "armalite [machine gun] and ballot box strategy" in the early 1980s, when Adams became president of Sinn Féin. This strategy involved the continuation of the armed struggle alongside the contesting of elections (running for office, presenting candidates, etc.). The political acumen of Adams, who gingerly inched his way to a political route without alienating the "physical force tradition" of the IRA, is seen as a major element in avoiding a split in the movement between pro-peace initiative forces and the traditionally hawkish armed-struggle component. This strategy also involved doing away with an abstentionist policy in the Republic of Ireland. Until this time, elections in the South had been contested on the understanding that winners would not take their seat in the Dáil (Irish parliament).

U.S. Influence on the Peace Initiative

In 1992, during the run-up to the Democratic Convention in the United States, the Irish American lobby encouraged Bill Clinton to work toward securing peace talks for Ireland. When Clinton won the presidency, he delivered on his promise to get involved in the Irish cause. With the help of Senator Ted Kennedy and such prominent Irish Americans as Chuck Feeney and Bill Flynn and by bringing in the National Security Council staff and leaving out the State Department, Clinton began a process of bringing Adams in from the cold, granting him a visa to visit the White House in 1994. The British were furious. Clinton's backing of Adams injured the "special relationship" between the British and American administrations. Notwithstanding the diplomatic chill that descended upon him, Clinton was instrumental in getting the British and Irish governments to sign off on the Downing Street Declaration.

Adams's Republican Background

Adams comes from a large family with a strong Republican tradition. His grandfather on the maternal, Hannaway side was a union organizer who worked with James Connolly and Jim Larkin. His father, Gerry Sr., was imprisoned, and most of his uncles and brothers have been incarcerated at some time or other. His cousin Kevin Hannaway was tortured by the British authorities during internment. Adams is married to Colette McArdle, has a son, Gearóid, and is a grandfather. He was born in Belfast on October 6, 1948, and has always lived there.

Adams has spent much of his life on the run from the authorities or hiding from Loyalists who have a price on his head. In 1983, as he was coming out of a Belfast courtroom, the car he was riding in was attacked by a Loyalist gang, who riddled it with bullets, hitting Adams and the other passengers but not the driver. Adams survived the attack. In June 1993, his house was bombed. He was not there; his wife and son were but escaped unharmed.

Adams as Writer

Adams is a prolific writer. Over and above his contributions to the *Republican News* during his incarceration, he has written over fifteen books, including short stories and nonfiction. Among his works are *Falls Memories* (1994), a collection of essays; *Before the Dawn* (1996), an autobiography; and a 2003 work chronicling the peace process, *Hope and History: Making Peace in Ireland*. Those who meet him may characterize Adams as mild mannered and charming. He comes across as a humble man, and he has remained very close to his base, both in Belfast and abroad. He speaks of the plight of his people in a way that convinces the listener that he has no greater preoccupation than to find peace in Ireland.

Sinn Féin, an Electoral Force

Since 2001, Sinn Féin has been the largest nationalist party in the North, having replaced the Social Democratic and Labour Party, and the only all-Ireland party. In 2002, Sinn Féin returned five TDs (members of the Irish parliament). There had been no Sinn Féin representatives in the 1992 election and only one in 1997. However, in 2007, the party lost one seat, returning four TDs. Nonetheless, with Adams and his comrades at the helm, Sinn Féin has been a force to be reckoned with electorally in both the North and the South.

Claire Delisle

See also: Bloody Sunday; Northern Ireland; Paisley, Ian; Roman Catholicism; Sands, Bobby; Terrorism.

Further Reading

Adams, Gerry. *Before the Dawn: An Autobiography.* New York: William Morrow, 1996.
———. *Falls Memories: A Belfast Life.* Niwot, CO: Roberts, Rinehart, 1994.
———. *Hope and History: Making Peace in Ireland.* Dingle, Ireland: Brandon, 2003.
Coogan, Tim Pat. *The IRA.* New York: Palgrave, 2002.
Feeney, Brian. *Sinn Féin: A Hundred Turbulent Years.* Madison: University of Wisconsin Press, 2003.

Africa, North

Religion has been associated with some, but not all, of the political violence in the North African countries of Libya, Tunisia, Algeria, and Morocco in recent years. (While Egypt is geographically part of North Africa, it is normally considered a Middle Eastern country.) The level of violence reached its highest levels in Algeria in the 1990s, but the violence has not been limited to Algeria. There have been incidents in the other countries, and dissident groups in Algeria and Morocco have been responsible for violent attacks in Europe. It was Moroccan militants who were implicated in the bombings of the Madrid commuter trains in 2004 and Algerian dissidents who attempted to use an Air France airliner as a bomb for an attack on Paris in 1994. Citizens from all four countries served as volunteers in Afghanistan in the war against the Soviet troops (1979–1989) and the local communists that the USSR was supporting. (In 1992 the last of the communist leaders was defeated, ending the era of Marxist-Leninist government.) Algeria by far sent the most volunteers. It is estimated that more than 3,000 Algerians served in these wars, as well as 400 Tunisians, 200 Libyans, and an undetermined number of Moroccans (Reeve 1999). Later in 1992, a Pakistani count of militants in training camps in Afghanistan found 946 Algerians, 199 Libyans, 117 Tunisians, and 102 Moroccans. Many of these volunteers returned to their countries and have worked to replace the more secular regimes with more religious governments.

Libya

Libya under Muammar Gaddafi has witnessed a number of attempts at violent political change by opponents of the regime. Most of the attempts have involved actions by disgruntled members of the ruling elite or military officers. Attacks by religious militants have been rarer. Gaddafi established his version of socialism in the country, but he has never directly challenged Islam and has generally been supportive of Islam since he came to power in 1969. His background is also from the Cyrencian region of the country (as opposed to the more cosmopolitan Tripolitanian region around the capital), which was the core area of support for the Sanusi order, a religious brotherhood that appeared in the nineteenth century seeking to purify Islam of external factors. This connection might explain his acceptability to many practicing Muslims in the country. Even with his general support for Islam, religious groups have targeted the regime. The Libyan Islamic Fighting Group, made up of Libyan veterans of the wars in Afghanistan, appeared in 1995. It wants to overthrow the present regime and create an Islamic state; the group has taken credit for two failed assassination attempts against Gaddafi, in 1996 and 1998. Beyond these attempts, however, the group has been largely inactive in Libya, and the regime has not seemed to be in danger from the more extreme religious groups. When Gaddafi dies or retires, it is possible that the groups seeking to create an Islamic state could become important or could be responsible for further attempts at violent change.

Tunisia

Tunisia has always been one of the more secular states in the Arab world. Under President Habib Bourguiba (1957–1987) the government emphasized modernization and attempted to increase the level of secularization in the state and in Tunisian society. The government sought to undermine religious influences and even attempted to encourage citizens not to fast during the holy month of Ramadan because it had negative effects on productivity. Tunisia has effectively been a one-party state under Bourguiba and his successors, and the government has been able to remain in control and deal with any threats to its continuance in power. When opposition parties were permitted to form, they were faced with prohibitions against establishing parties based solely on religious appeals. Religious candidates in 1988 were allowed to run as independents. The efforts to restrict the Islamic groups combined with increases in the price of bread led to riots that challenged the government. While the government was able to contain the riots, the situation indicated that Tunisia was not immune to religious appeals.

Opposition to the regime in Tunisia has been limited, but the challenges have had a religious base. Returning veterans from the Afghan wars combined with other militants to form the Tunisian Combatant Group, which favored the creation of an Islamic state. This group has been responsible for a few attacks. One of the most notable actions by the group was against foreign tourists on the island of Djerba in 2002. A truck bomb resulted in nineteen deaths, with fourteen of the victims being European tourists. The attack may also have had additional symbolic importance, since it occurred at the oldest synagogue in the country (Gunaratna 2003). While the incident may have been principally intended to strike at representatives of the West or at the Western attitudes in the state, it had the secondary benefit of hurting the tourist sector. Attacks against the vulnerable tourist sector can reduce revenues available to the government. The reduction in resources can result in fewer programs that could undercut the appeal of the militant Islamic groups and also limit funding for the security forces. While the Islamic militants have launched relatively few incidents in Tunisia, they have been active in Europe in providing support for al-Qaeda operatives and cooperating with other Islamic militants engaged in a global jihad against the West.

Morocco

Since achieving independence in 1956, Morocco has had relatively low levels of violence related to religious controversies. There were attempted coups and attacks against the king during the long reign of Hasan II (1961–1999), but the responsible groups were opposed to the monarchy on ideological grounds. They favored a more socialist or democratic political system, not a conservative Islamic state. Morocco has also dealt with violence in the former Spanish Sahara that has been incorporated into the country, but religion has not been a factor in that conflict. There have been tensions at times that have involved differences between urban and rural sectors. Many rural areas are inhabited by Berbers, while the urban dwellers are culturally Arab, but religion has not usually been a factor in these tensions. Overall, the monarchy has been able to mobilize support from among the more conservative sectors of society, including religious elements. This support has been useful for dealing with dissent from the ideological groups opposed to the monarchy. Further, conservative support for the monarchy actually has a religious base, since in Morocco the monarch also has religious functions and the royal family is considered to be in the direct line of descent from the Prophet Muhammad—a circumstance that provides some religious legitimacy to the monarchy.

While most of the violent opposition to the monarchy has had secular roots, there have been some relatively sporadic outbreaks of violence linked to religious opponents. There were some attacks in 1994 by religious militants, but the government was able to quickly arrest the persons involved and bring them to trial. In the 1990s two new organizations appeared, the Moroccan Islamic Combatant Group and Salafiya Jihadia. These groups, like other militant organizations in the region, have included veterans of the Afghan conflicts. The second group was responsible for the May 2003 attacks against foreign targets in Casablanca that left more than forty dead and at least sixty-five others injured. In the wake of these attacks, the security forces arrested many religious militants (as well as secular ones) as part of an effort to limit any further outbreaks of violence. While the attacks themselves came as a surprise to the authorities, the efforts to prevent the spread of violence have so far been successful. Moroccan militants have been active in the broader struggle between Islam and the West in what is increasingly called the global jihadist movement. Thus, the targets in Casablanca were foreigners. The Moroccan Islamic Combatant Group developed close ties with al-Qaeda. The idea of using speedboats loaded with explosives to attack U.S. ships (and others) was first considered with the Straits of Gibraltar being the area of attack. The planning fell through when Moroccan intelligence agents arrested the al-Qaeda operative involved. Members of this group also allegedly participated in the Madrid train bombings in 2004 that killed 191 people and injured more than 1,800. While these foreign activities have not yet spilled over to the Moroccan domestic arena in any major way, that possibility does exist for the future. There is a potential for campaigns of violence against a government that is generally considered to be not Islamic enough and that has developed fairly strong ties with the West that are contrary to the beliefs of the militant groups.

Algeria

Algeria has experienced significantly more violence than the other three countries. The country underwent a long, violent national liberation struggle (1954–1962) that involved guerrilla warfare and terrorist campaigns by dissidents in the cities, who targeted officials, the police, and the French settler population in general. This struggle, however, was a national liberation struggle rather than a religious one. While the Algerians were overwhelmingly Muslim, they were mobilized against the French on the basis of nationality. Islam provided an additional cultural distinction between Algerians and the French, but it was not a defining characteristic of the struggle, particularly with the relatively secular nationalist leadership. There were significant political conflicts in the early years of the country, and occasionally violence occurred, but these conflicts did not reflect religious differences between the sides. Differences between the Berbers and Arabs and between those who fought the guerrilla war and those who were in exile during the liberation struggle appeared after independence. Policy differences led to the military coup in 1965 that overthrew Ahmed ben Bella, but neither the military nor ben Bella represented a religious viewpoint; moreover, both consistently have followed a path of secular modernization. The violence of the independence era, however, was available to suggest to later groups that such violence could be an effective way to bring about changes in the political system.

The military provided the base for the governments that ruled Algeria from 1965 into the 1990s. Presidents died and were replaced, but it was the officer corps that was the important decision-making entity in the country, not an official single party. While the government had relatively few problems in the 1970s, by the 1980s Algeria began to face economic problems. The decline in petroleum prices in 1986 led to an economic downturn and lower standards of living for most of the population, especially in the rural areas. The serious discontent that resulted was largely organized by Islamic groups. For two years there were demonstrations and riots, the riots in 1988 resulting in as many as a thousand deaths. The Islamic opposition groups were able to draw upon those who suffered from the economic downturn, including small merchants, first-generation college graduates, and civil servants. Faced with the economic problems and popular discontent, in an effort to regain popular support, the government chose to create a more democratic political system. President Chadli Bendjedid (1979–1992) hoped to revive the fortunes of the party, the regime, and the elite in general. The regime scheduled local elections and a two-stage election process for the national legislature. Opposition parties were allowed to form and present candidates in these elections. They contested the initial

rounds and won them, leading to their proscription. The government assumed that the official party (and its allies) either would be able to win an absolute majority of the seats in the national legislature or would likely be the largest party and thus essential to any coalition cabinet that might be formed.

Many parties did initially form to contest the elections, as President Bendjedid expected. The Islamic Salvation Front (FIS) was formed, however, and it was able to bring together most of the Islamic groups preparing to contest the election. The FIS was an umbrella group and was not unified on many issues beyond the desire to have a government that was less secular (or much less secular for some elements). Some groups in the FIS were relatively moderate and willing to tolerate and work with non-Islamic parties, while other FIS groups wanted to establish a theocratic state. Even with the internal divisions, the FIS managed to maintain enough unity for success in the elections. It did quite well in the local elections that came first. The government then began to harass the FIS, and a few of its leaders were arrested. The regime sought to limit the chances of the FIS by assigning more seats to districts favorable to the government and performing other types of electoral manipulation. These efforts failed, and in the first round of the elections for the national parliament, the FIS was able to capture enough seats outright to virtually guarantee that it would have an absolute majority in the parliament and be able to displace the ruling elite. Faced with the prospect of losing power, the government canceled the final round of the elections. More FIS leaders were arrested. Demonstrations against the government occurred, and the response was to ban the FIS and arrest even more of its members. President Bendjedid resigned after the failure of his plan, and a military council took over in his place.

Repression proved to be an unwise approach.

The Islamic groups had already mobilized, and there was no effective way to immediately demobilize them. The military intervention to prevent the elections discredited the moderate leaders who had relied on elections as a route to power. Further, the arrest of the FIS leaders removed the more moderate voices from the group. While not all those who were detained were moderates, many were. The balance in the Islamic forces now shifted to the hard-liners in the group, including many of the numerous veterans of the Afghan wars. These veterans not only provided numbers for the Islamic forces, additionally, they had military training and were experienced in fighting a guerrilla and terrorist campaign against government forces. These veterans and other militants were now prepared to use violence to bring about the removal of the secular elite still in power and to create an Islamic state.

While the dissidents mobilized on a religious basis, the government represented more secular groups within the society, since the government elite was more Europeanized. Government educational policies actually increased the divisions between the modern and traditional groups. At the university level, technical and scientific courses were taught in French, and it was the technical and scientific degrees that provided graduates with greater job opportunities. Other courses were taught in Arabic, but the graduates of those programs had fewer opportunities. When fighting broke out, graduates from the Arabic courses provided the Islamic groups with many recruits.

The dissident groups included the Armed Islamic Group (GIA) and the Islamic Movement Army (MIA)—linked to the FIS—among others. Faced with government repression and with the moderate leadership removed, the dissidents launched attacks against the government. The rebels ambushed military and security forces in the countryside, relying on techniques learned in Afghanistan. The Islamic dissidents also launched terror campaigns. They targeted government officials—including teachers, journalists seen as being progovernment, and foreign technicians who were important for maintaining the economy. More liberal and secular members of Algerian society became targets as well, since they were identified with the European elite and the foreign, non-Islamic influences that were seen as threatening. Women who were public figures or even women in Western dress became targets for assassination. Even schoolgirls who did not cover their heads in approved Islamic fashion were killed as a warning to others. As the fighting continued, some of the dissident groups began to launch night attacks against villages considered to be loyal to the government. They would take over the villages and massacre men, women, and children. These attacks served multiple purposes. One goal was to draw government troops to the scene in order to ambush them. The attacks were also intended to demonstrate to the villagers that the government could not protect them. The killings were intentionally violent and primitive in order to enhance and spread the fear (Laqueur 1999).

The Algerian rebels also attempted to strike at the foreign supporters of the government, especially France, beginning in the mid-1990s. They launched a bombing campaign in France that was intended to convince the French that the cost of supporting the Algerian government was too high. The French, however, were able to contain the violence relatively quickly. The security forces were able to break up the organizations that were responsible and to capture many of those responsible or the groups that were supporting them. In 1994, a team from the GIA hijacked an Air France flight and flew it to Marseilles. The hijackers apparently intended to use the plane as a bomb against Paris—probably the Eiffel Tower. (It is unclear whether this attack was a possible precursor to the attacks of September 11, 2001.) The plan failed when French commandos successfully stormed the plane while it was on the ground in Marseilles for refueling.

The civil war in Algeria between the Islamic groups and the more secular government was quite deadly. At least 100,000 persons died as a consequence of the violence. The government, however, has been able to contain the rebellion and limit the level of violence. The more moderate leaders of the FIS were released from prison, and compromises were negotiated. In 1995 reasonably free elections were held, and the president who had been leading the struggle against the dissidents turned power over to his successor. Since then the government has regained control over most of the country. Since the militants were organized into a number of different groups and relatively decentralized, it has not been possible for the government to eliminate all of the violent opposition, and pockets of resistance remain. Most of the groups are splinters from the GIA that lost support because of the village massacres, and some of them have developed links with al-Qaeda. It is thus distinctly possible that religiously based violence could break out again in the future.

Conclusion

These four countries represent different kinds of political systems: a monarchy in Morocco, where the king still has real power; a secular one-party system in Tunisia; a regime in Algeria that relied on the military as its institutional base until the recent elections; and the harder-to-classify regime of Gaddafi in Libya. Violence in Libya has involved both religious and secular groups, while in Tunisia it has been restricted to religious dissidents. In Morocco most of the violence originated with secular opposition; in Algeria, however, the civil war was rooted in religion, and violence originating from secular sources has been less.

It has been suggested that modernization and urbanization have played a role in the outbreaks of violence. The cities have attracted rural migrants who then have found themselves somewhat disoriented, out of place, and lacking a supporting social structure. Libya has urbanized most quickly but has avoided the worst problems, partially because of the availability of oil revenues to alleviate discontent. Tunisia is relatively urban as well, but the process there has been more gradual. It was the cities that provided the spark for the bread riots that were associated with Muslim groups. Morocco and Algeria are somewhat less urban. Algeria has suffered the most from violence, and the Muslim extremists have been able to draw support from the urban slums and those suffering from uncontrolled urbanization. For many years, oil revenues were available to mitigate the problems, but the drop in oil prices helped to set the stage for the violence. While the actual role of urbanization and modernization is unclear, there seem to have been at least some negative effects for the governments in power.

Religion will continue to be an important factor in the political life of these North African states. All four have experienced attacks from religious dissidents. While political stability may be present for a time, the possibility of additional outbreaks is present. Succession struggles may provide opportunities for religious militants. The current regime in Libya is probably most dependent on Gaddafi and his central role in the government. His death or removal could lead to violence. The monarchy in Morocco is somewhat dependent on the character of the individual on the throne, and a succession crisis could occur there as well. Algeria, with the military as an institutional prop, and Tunisia, with a strong ruling party, would appear to be less susceptible to a succession crisis, but one could still occur. Militancy could increase among Muslims if workers and relatives in Western Europe face increasing anti-Islamic feeling and xenophobia. If the resident North Africans in Europe become more alienated, one result could be increased anti-Western feelings and extremism among Muslims, both in Europe and North Africa. In sum, violence rooted in religion could be a problem in the future, just as it has been in the past.

Brenda J. Lutz and James M. Lutz

See also: Al-Qaeda; Islamic Fundamentalism; Muslim Brotherhood.

Further Reading

Burke, Jason. *Al-Qaeda: Casting a Shadow of Terror.* London: I.B. Tauris, 2003.

Crenshaw, Martha. "Political Violence in Algeria." *Terrorism and Political Violence* 6:3 (1994): 261–80.

Gunaratna, Rohan. "Understanding Al Qaeda and Its Network in Southeast Asia." In *After Bali: The Threat of Terrorism in Southeast Asia,* ed. Kumar Ramakrishna and See Seng Tan, pp. 117–32. Singapore: Institute of Defence and Strategic Studies and World Scientific Publishing, 2003.

Laqueur, Walter. *The New Terrorism: Fanaticism and the Arms of Mass Destruction.* New York: Oxford University Press, 1999.

Lutz, James M., and Brenda J. Lutz. "Terrorism as Economic Warfare." *Global Economy Journal* 6:2 (2006): 1–20.

Maddy-Weitzman, Bruce. "The Islamic Challenge in North Africa." In *Religious Radicalism in the Greater Middle East,* ed. Bruce Maddy-Weitzman and Efraim Inbar, pp. 171–88. London: Frank Cass, 1997.

Malley, Robert. *The Call from Algeria: Third Worldism, Revolution, and the Turn to Islam.* Berkeley: University of California Press, 1996.

Rabasa, Angel, Peter Chalk, Kim Cragin, Sara A. Daly, Heather S. Gregg, Theodore W. Karasik, Kevin O'Brien, and William Rosenau. *Beyond al-Qaeda: Part I, The Global Jihadist Movement.* Santa Monica, CA: RAND, 2006.

Reeve, Simon. *The New Jackals: Ramzi Yousef, Osama bin Laden and the Future of Terrorism.* Boston: Northeastern University Press, 1999.

Shapiro, Jeremy, and Bendecite Suzan. "The French Experience of Counter-Terrorism." *Survival* 45:1 (2003): 67–98.

Spenser, William J. *The Middle East,* 11th ed. Global Studies Series. Dubuque, IA: McGraw-Hill, 2007.

St. John, O. Peter. "Algeria: A Case Study of Insurgency in the New World Order." *Small Wars and Insurgencies* 7:2 (1996): 196–219.

Takeyh, Ray. "Islamism in Algeria: A Struggle Between Hope and Agony." *Middle East Policy* 10:2 (2003): 62–75.

Tan, Andrew T.H. *The Politics of Terrorism: A Survey.* London: Routledge, 2006.

Testas, Abdelaziz. "The Roots of Algeria's Religious and Ethnic Violence." *Studies in Conflict & Terrorism* 25:3 (2002): 161–83.

Willis, Michael. *The Islamist Challenge in Algeria: A Political History.* New York: New York University Press, 1997.

Africa, Sub-Saharan

Imperialism brought to Africa different ideologies and conditions and a multiplicity of ideas that were rooted in economic, political, and religious problems. Colonialism introduced Christian religion that was designed to achieve imperialist objectives through the use of violence.

Religion played a central role in all precolonial and colonial African governments. Even apart from the motives of colonial Christianity, religion and politics have been bonded throughout African history. In precolonial Africa, rulers were thought to have divine powers that could control rainfall and crop growth. In contemporary Africa, expressions of Christian activities take the form of born-again Christianity—expressions and activities that may lead to religious uprisings against unbelievers or other religions in various communities. Such is also the case with Islam, which has seen forceful expressions of religious factions, often motivated by Muslims who have associations with the Middle East and the passion to create a new political arrangement and the Islamization of society. There is much documented evidence of the various dimensions of violence caused by these religions in different African countries, and in contemporary Africa religious violence has had and continues to have destructive effects on the populace.

Africa has witnessed violence (political Islam/Christianity), leading to butchery or annihilation of numerous people and objects of worship, all in the context of religion. The methods of violence are rooted in various forms, most notably crusades in Nigerian history, civil wars in Sudan and Darfur, and genocide in Rwanda. Other modus operandi may take the form of terrorism, martyrdoms, and sacrifices. While there are other religions that may cause havoc in the world today, such as Buddhism and Hinduism in Sri Lanka, Africa generally is confronted by two major religions, Christianity and Islam. Sudan, however, presents a different scenario, in which there is a confrontation between Islam, sometimes Christianity, and African traditional religions. Christianity and Islam are religions rooted in sacred writings and can be used to serve and justify religious killings and oppressions. In various parts of the world today, religions are in one way or another associated with warfare, and Africa is not alone in this regard. Indeed, most religious zealots believe that their actions are approved by their god and are willing to kill and die for their political causes. The attack on the World Trade Center in 2001, which claimed about 3,000 lives, was religiously motivated, and two countries in East Africa, Kenya and Tanzania, have experienced similar catastrophes based on political Islam.

East Africa and Political Islam

David Dickson, in his 2005 special report for the United States Institute of Peace points to the impartiality of Islamism and argues that it involves a desire for the recruitment of followers in order to achieve certain ideological objectives, such as the defeat of imperialism. The August 7, 1998, bombings of the U.S. embassies in Nairobi, Kenya, and Dar es-Sala'am,

Tanzania, which resulted in the deaths of 224 people and the wounding of approximately 5,000, and the 2002 attack on an Israeli-owned hotel in Mombasa, are all examples of religious violence in East Africa. These attacks on innocent citizens represent manifestations of political Islam in Africa. Historically, in East African countries such as Kenya, Tanzania, and Uganda (often Rwanda, Burundi, and Somalia are included as part of the East African nations), Africans with Islamic and Koranic education were discriminated against by Westernized political leaders. Dickson asserts that such marginalization gave rise to the spiritual and mystical Sufism that Muslims embraced and cemented their desire to adopt the reformist ideology of Wahhabism, which is sanctioned by the Saudis and described by some as a "death cult." The victimization of Muslims in the region led to tensions and agitations in East African countries. Allegedly, in an environment where Muslims felt constrained, Osama bin Laden and al-Qaeda found a fertile breeding ground to construct an infrastructural system near the coastal areas of Kenya and Zanzibar and along the Tanzanian coasts, making possible the attack on U.S. embassies and attacks and bombings on Israeli tourists in Mombasa.

Al-Qaeda's Presence in East Africa

Al-Qaeda's successful penetration of East Africa, where it conducted a terrorist campaign against the United States and its interests, may be a result of the dire economic, security, and governance dilemmas in the region. It has been reported that al-Qaeda has had some relative success in employing East African Muslims to engage in attacks with large-scale goals. In addition to the embassy and Mombasa assaults, al-Qaeda has been accused of providing support to different Muslim militant groups in East Africa, such as the Somali Islamist organization Al-Ittihad al-Islami (AIAI). The main objective of AIAI is to institute an Islamic government based on Islamic law in both Ethiopia and Somalia. The AIAI follows the dictates of Wahhabi principles, which is also the doctrine preferred by bin Laden and his al-Qaeda associates. It has also been reported that al-Qaeda has spent over $3 million to recruit and train former Afghan resistance fighters to fight in Somalia. Bin Laden has allegedly exploited the lawlessness in East Africa by establishing military training fields, where militants are schooled in guerrilla tactics and operations and sent to different parts of the world to execute attacks against U.S. interests.

It is obvious from these instances of religious violence that political Islam in East Africa has been motivated by outside influences and transnational militants who use Africa as a battleground for their separate political ideologies. The main strategy of the outsider is to utilize deprived states as training grounds to strike against U.S. interests—particularly to destabilize the U.S. economy. It must be underscored, however, that despite the al-Qaeda insistence on using East Africa as a guerrilla combat zone against the United States and despite the economic, security, and governance problems of the region, bin Laden's network poses a minor threat. Africans, in general, pay homage to their traditional beliefs, and violence and killing are not part of that general belief system (Darfur, Uganda, and Rwanda are exceptions). Populations in East Africa remain strongly tied to their ethnic and tribal roots and as a rule do not honor alien religious creeds. As a result, Africans are more likely to fiercely resist threats to their national identity than to their transnational concerns. However, the al-Qaeda doctrines of anti-Americanism are strong and have won some East African converts and sympathizers. Therefore, Al-Qaeda still poses a threat, no matter how small, not only in East Africa but also in the Horn.

The Horn of Africa

The Horn of Africa encompasses the easternmost projection of the African continent, containing the region that includes Djibouti, Ethiopia, Eritrea, Somalia, and Sudan. The 2010 *World Factbook* also includes Rwanda, Tanzania, Uganda, Kenya, and Burundi in its survey. The long-standing turmoil and lawlessness in the area has given rise to violent forms of political Islamic extremism. According to the Central Intelligence Agency's 2010 estimates, there are approximately 91.9 million Muslims in the greater Horn of Africa.

As reported by the survey, Somalia and Djibouti are principally Muslim nations, although Ethiopia and Eritrea account for about 45 to 50 percent of the Muslim population. Historically, Islamic movements in the region deeply opposed colonial occupation and the British governance in Somaliland in the early twentieth century. The Ethiopian hegemony in the region has also been fiercely challenged by the Muslim League in Eritrea and by the Muslim-dominated Eritrean Liberation Front and Somalian warlords.

At the end of 2006, Ethiopia went to war with Somalia's Islamic militants by bombing targets into Somalia and introducing Ethiopian ground troops into Somaliland. This form of military escalation could again cause a violent religious confrontation that may plunge the Horn of Africa into a major battle. Ethiopia, which commands the strongest military in the Horn, claimed that its forces were in Somalia to protect the sovereignty of the nation, support the internationally recognized Somalian transitional government, and protect Ethiopia itself from the Islamists and that it had no intention of meddling in the internal affairs of Somalia. Ethiopian involvement caused some riots in the Somalian capital of Mogadishu, as

Regional Muslim and Christian Populations

Approximately 156.3 million Muslims in West Sahel

Country	Total Population	Muslim Population in 1,000s	Percent of Muslims	Percent of Christians
Benin	8,791,832	2,110	24	43
Burkina Faso	15,746,232	7,873	50	10
Chad	10,329,208	5,474	53	20
Côte d'Ivoire	20,617,068	8,041	39	33
Ghana	23,887,812	3,822	16	69
Republic of Guinea	10,057,975	8,549	85	8
Guinea Bissau	1,533,964	767	50	10
Liberia	3,441,790	413	12	86
Mali	13,443,225	12,099	90	1
Mauritania	3,129,486	3,129	100	1
Niger	15,306,252	12,245	80	—
Nigeria	149,229,090	74,615	50	40
Senegal	13,711,597	12,889	94	5
Sierra Leone	5,132,138	3,079	60	10
Togo	6,031,808	1,206	20	29

Approximately 91.9 million Muslims in the Greater Horn of Africa

Country	Total Population	Muslim Population in 1,000s	Percent of Muslims	Percent of Christians
Burundi	9,511,330	951	10	67
Djibouti	724,622	681	94	6
Eritrea	5,647,168	—	—	—
Ethiopia	85,237,338	28,981	34	—
Kenya	39,002,772	3,900	10	78
Rwanda	10,746,311	537	5	94
Somalia	9,832,017	9,832	100	0
Sudan	41,087,825	28,761	70	5
Tanzania	41,048,532	14,366	35	30
Uganda	32,369,558	3,884	12	84

Source: Central Intelligence Agency, *The World Factbook 2010*. Online. Available: https://www.cia.gov/library/publications/the-world-factbook/index.html. (Accessed October 8, 2010)

well as bringing some elation to the citizens who support their government and are opposed to the militants. The tragedy occurred when Islamic leaders declared Somalia open to Muslim fighters who wished to wage a jihad against Ethiopia, a government with a long Christian identity. Since 1991, when the central government collapsed, Somalia has been in a state of anarchy, leading to a warlord-led interclan war. After the Islamists defeated the warlords in 2006, they threatened to liberate Somali-speaking areas of Ethiopia and to provoke the Ethiopian Muslim population. This may be a cause of the contemporary violence between the Ethiopian government and the Somalian Islamists. Although Somalia has served as a "passage path" (an avenue or access for spreading extreme ideologies) for fanatics, most notably al-Qaeda, Wahhabism has not necessarily succeeded in radicalizing Muslims in the Horn of Africa. In reality, Wahhabis have been allegedly connected only to the burning of mosques and the provocation of some problems among Islamic groups in Ethiopia; while in Somalia, the Islamic al Ittihad al Islami has roots in Wahhabi doctrines. In

Djibouti, however, resentments among local religious groups have hindered the spread of Islamic militancy.

Influence of Wahhabi Ideology in Sudan

In Sudan, the condition is very different, and political Islam has deep ideological roots in Wahhabi doctrines. For example, in 1985, Hassan al-Turabi established the National Islamic Front—which later was transformed into the Popular National Congress—and cemented his role as the speaker of the National Assembly in the Islamic Fundamentalist Government. Additionally, Sudan also hosted Osama bin Laden from 1991 to 1996 before normalizing its relations with the West in 2000. The country is currently ravaged with overwhelming disaster. In contemporary southern Sudan, the Sudanese People's Liberation Army (SPLA) has been fighting a war since 1983 in order to wrest power from the Islamic-controlled government in the capital city of Khartoum. While the desire of the South is to secede from the northern-dominated government, the cardinal policy of SPLA is to liberate Sudan from tyranny and to institute a democratic, secular state. The killings and violence in Sudan have become so widespread that the Nuer civilian populations in the area have come to refer to it as a "curse from God." The United Nations has labeled the conflicts as the "world's worst humanitarian crisis," and the United States government classifies the conflict as genocide. Due to the split of the SPLA into warring factions, children, women, and the elderly have suffered untold hardships. Food is scarce, sanitary conditions terrible, and the government creates obstacles for humanitarian efforts in Darfur.

The village of Tundubai in Sudan's Darfur region is pictured after being burned by Arab Janjaweed militias. The Sudanese government has been accused of backing and arming the militias in their campaign against Darfur's "black African" population—the indigenous ethnic minorities who are considered non-Muslim and inferior. (Desirey Minkoh/AFP/Getty Images)

In Darfur it became commonplace for the government-backed Janjaweed militias to rape women in a systematic fashion and with impunity. Because of the regime's complicity with the civil militias, hundreds of thousands of Darfurians who escaped the killings, rapes, and pillage were unable to return to their homes. Amnesty International reports show that about 200,000 people died and another 2.5 million were internally dislocated by the end of 2006. This brand of violence, utilized by the government and by the rebel groups, continues to destabilize the fabric of the continent. Indeed, Chad and Sudan indirectly fight a war by supporting each other's rebels on both sides of their common frontier. This type of war is facilitated by the fact that tribes in the Saharan region cut across state boundaries. Though direct government involvement in human rights violations has decreased, systematic human rights abuses continue to happen under the auspices of the Janjaweed militia. According to a 2007 Amnesty International report, refugees continued to be targets of Janjaweed and Darfur rebel group activities in both the Darfur region and eastern Chad.

The contemporary Darfur crisis is not rooted in ethnicity caused by clan conflict, as is often claimed by the government; nor is it an unfortunate problem caused by nature (drought and desertification) or even a coup by enemies of the Khartoum administration. The historical and religious explanation is rooted in racism, claims of Muslim authenticity, discrimination, and economic greed. Colonial Britain annexed Darfur in 1916 and later abandoned the territory. Sudan, like other African states that regained independence from Europe, also experienced the crisis of imperialism. Imperialism left these countries with many problems, such as the dilemma in Darfur today. Darfur was generally inhabited by sedentary African tribes and Arab nomads. The government in Khartoum since independence has been occupied by Nile Valley Arabs who claim to be superior and proudly describe themselves as *awlad al-beled* (sons of the land). These ruling elites, who are a mixed-blood population of Cushitic, Semitic, and Nilotic, are looked upon as *Abd* (slaves) when they travel abroad and intermingle with "true" Arabs (Prunier 2006).

By the 1970s, the trouble between the awlad al-beled and other Arabs began to escalate since the ruling elites describe the black African Christians and other Arabs of the South as darker-colored, illegitimate, backward, and inferior. By constructing Sudan both as Islamic and as Arab, the Nile Valley or northern elites excluded not only southerners but other peripheral kinfolks—such as the Fur, the Beja, and the Nupians in the west, east, and north of the country, respectively—from the affairs of the nation. Following the military regime's ascent to power in 1989, the new government—fully supported by the Islamist National Islamic Front—immediately decreed Darfur the least Islamized region after the South. This Islamic decree worried all Darfurians (nomads and sedentary farmers) and other peripheral groups like the Fur, who viewed the proclamation as racist. The minority groups, who are also nomads and sedentary workers, joined rebel groups now that they had been described as black Africans, a label that suggests that they are inferior and non-Muslims. In 1981, the Darfur people regrouped and demanded parity with other regions in Sudan. In this new dispensation, the African tribes, who are also Arabs and Muslims, became a threat to the center. The powerful Arabs in Khartoum sought to stop the situation and recruited their Darfurian associates to fight in the southern war. All accounts report that the Janjaweed was recruited and sponsored by Khartoum to inflict atrocities against their own brothers and sisters, a situation as deplorable as the genocide in Rwanda.

Genocide in Rwanda

In 1959, prior to gaining political independence from Belgium on July 1, 1962 (primarily due to Hutu political agitation), the majority Hutu ethnic group overthrew the Tutsi ruling king. Subsequently, thousands of Tutsis were murdered, forcing about 150,000 to flee into neighboring countries. The war exacerbated ethnic tensions and culminated in the 1994 genocide, which claimed the lives of about 800,000 Tutsis and moderate Hutus. Subsequently, the Tutsi rebels defeated the Hutu regime and ended the massacre in July 1994. Rwanda was a peaceful nation prior to colonial dominion; the Hutus and Tutsis lived in harmony and even intermarried without problems until the introduction by Europeans of Christianizing missions into the hearts of the natives. The first recorded missionary sites were established in 1900 by the Society of Our Lady of Africa, generally known as the White Fathers. Some claim there is evidence that both the Catholic and the Protestant churches in Rwanda were either directly or indirectly involved in the 1994 genocide (Longman 2001). The actions of the missionaries in Rwanda, as in other colonized African nations, contributed to conflicts and ethnic mayhem today.

Missionaries in Rwanda played a pivotal role in creating and sustaining ethnic ideologies and myths that helped to interpret Rwandan social arrangements in ways that benefited the interests of the Belgian and German colonial administrators. Both the Catholic and Protestant churches in Rwanda are multinational, and the genocide that occurred happened among ethnic groups. In some cases, Rwandan Tutsis who ran into a Catholic church for refuge were killed by their fellow parishioners—some by priests and pastors (Longman 2001). The churches' intrusion in Rwandan internal affairs contributed significantly to the genocide. The priests pacified the leaders and preached obedience to the rulers, regardless of oppressive behaviors or terrorizing tendencies toward the populace by the ruling class. In this way, the churches gained favor and the approval of the rulers. Additionally, the so-called progressive Catholic priests preached against the minority Tutsi and their dominance in Rwandan ruling elites. The priests engineered the hatred against the Tutsis by the Hutu majority, which ultimately resulted in the genocide. The church was tainted by its involvement in the genocide, as both Catholic and Protestant church employees—including priests and pastors—were active participants in the slaughter.

West Africa: The Case of Nigeria

While the conflict in Rwanda was between Christians and Christians, religious turbulence in Nigeria has usually involved Muslims and Christians, sometimes moderate Muslims and radical Muslims with roots in Sufism and the Wahhabi ideologies of Saudi Arabia. Whereas Rwanda's population has been about 95 percent Christian and 4.6 percent Muslim, Nigeria's population distribution has been relatively equal between the two major religions, Islam and Christianity. Colonialism condemned native religions, entrenching Christianity in the communities, and the delegitimization of traditional religions contributed to the contemporary religious violence in the country. An important object of the administrators was to introduce Christianity as a civilizing mission and eliminate traditional religious beliefs. The colonial authorities mandated that citizens identify their religious affiliation on official forms as either Christian or Muslim. The natives were terrified to identify themselves by their traditional religions. Images of African deities and gods were destroyed or exported abroad and at present can be found in European museums rather than in their natural African shrines. The eventual result of the civilizing mission was a struggle between Islam and Christianity. Natives were labeled pagans if they opposed Islam and Christianity. Each group endeavors to have more political and judicial influence in the affairs of the nation. The conflict led to some aspects of the Nigerian style of jihad and continuing violence.

Maitatsine Uprisings in Nigeria

The 1980 and 1982–1983 Maitatsine uprisings in northern Nigeria took place between a wing of Muslim militants and the Nigerian police and posed a major threat to Nigerian security. The Maitatsine instability has its origins in traditional Islam, a northern state religion that began in the fifteenth century. During that era, most Hausa rulers in the north of Nigeria were converted Muslims. Between 1804 and 1808, Nigeria experienced the jihad of Usman dan Fodio of Sokoto caliphate. Usman dan Fodio was a devout Fulani philosopher, a venerated Islamic scholar, and an avant-garde reformer. During his era, he was very popular and had a large following, and his jihad, unlike the religious uprising of Maitatsine, was aimed at the purification of Islam, not the killing of unbelievers. As a religious and political leader, he created a new Muslim state in northern Nigeria, known as the Fulani Empire, which was grounded in Islamic law. The Fulani Empire stretched across most of northern Nigeria and wielded great political power and influence in Nigeria and over the colonial administrators.

After Nigerian independence in 1960, the powerful northern Muslim elites still controlled political, military, and economic power in the country. In 1966, Sir Ahmadu Bello, former premier of the region and the sardauna (sultan) of Sokoto, who was a devoted Muslim leader with genealogical affiliation to Usman dan Fodio, was assassinated in a military coup. That assassination and the subsequent military rule in the nation set in motion the events that resulted in the 1980 and 1982 religious riots. The Muslim elites' powers were reduced, and the new military president, General Yakubu Gowon, was a devout Christian. Moreover, the new constitution provided for the freedom of religion. This did not augur well with some Muslim prophets in the North who wanted to establish a firm Islamic state in the country. Alhaji Muhammadu Maroua, popularly known as Maitatsine ("He who curses others" in Hausa), incited his Isala faction to perpetrate acts of violence in Kano. This ultimately led to his death and also claimed the lives of 5,000 of his supporters in 1980.

It took the combined efforts of the Nigerian army and air force to quell the violence. Subsequently, in 1982, in Maiduguri, Nigeria, the police and the disciples of Maitatsine once again engaged in a fierce battle when police tried to arrest the disciples and remaining leaders of the Maitatsine movement. This bloody encounter led to the death of hundreds of Maitatsine supporters. The Maitatsine movement still poses a serious threat in Nigeria and must not be ignored, because adherents of the uprising not only resist political changes in the country but also are eager to use violence against moderate Muslims. In short, they dislike Western education and technological advancements, and the contamination of Islam in a worldly Nigeria. These two accounts, of the jihad of Usman dan Fodio and the religious violence of Maitatsine and his cohorts demonstrate that Nigeria is still a volatile society, as also evidenced by recent acts of religious violence in Africa's most populated nation.

The Sharia Issue

Today, sharia (Islamic law) has been introduced in twelve of the thirty-six states of Nigeria.

Additionally, sharia also has been made part of the Nigerian constitution, which now permits a sharia Court of Appeals in the Nigerian polity. The spread of sharia in Nigeria may be a product of Nigerian Muslims' desire to reassert their political power in response to Christian political ascendancy. On the other hand, the Christians and mixed religious states view sharia as an alien religious and cultural imposition. Although sharia exists in twelve states, its strong adherents will not rest until it has engulfed the whole of Nigeria and beyond. The angry resistance to the spread of sharia in Nigeria is a major cause of tension and violence in the country.

In February and May of 2000, communal religious violence claimed the lives of 2,000 Nigerians in Kaduna City. In 2002, a newspaper article considered to be offensive to the Prophet Muhammad led to another round of violence in Kaduna, which claimed the lives of 200 people. Christian opposition to sharia practices in the North will continue to elevate tensions in Nigeria. Sharia may be an excuse, however, and not the root problem in an oil-rich nation with severe economic disasters and massive unemployment among the youth. Nigeria will continue to experience violence, whether from Islamic militants or from Christian fanatics, as long as there is growing economic marginalization of the masses and continued presence of massive poverty. Violence on the scale of terrorism may also escalate in Nigeria as a result of the infusion of radical religious ideologies in the minds of depressed citizens. This reality is a source of worry not only in Nigeria but also in the international community. Christianity and Islam can work hand in hand without constant threats and violence even though the Nigerian population is equally divided between the two religions. Such is not the case in Senegal, a country of 11 million people in West Africa.

Indeed, 94 percent of the Senegalese population is Muslim, and the country has in place a rough equilibrium between Islam, a secular state, and modernization. As is true for their African counterparts, the conviviality between political and Muslim leaders has its origins in colonial administration. The French deferred to Muslim leaders in exchange for acceptance of colonial control and imposition of taxation. The French feared any form of jihad in their acquired territories. Although Senegal still provides sanctuary to a minority of Islamist radicals and militants encouraged by the Iranian revolution, the fact remains that only 40 percent of Muslim leaders subscribe to the sharia policy.

Conclusion

Sub-Saharan Africa remains a volatile region, ripe for potential fundamentalist eruption into violence, whether from political Islam with its roots in the Middle East or from Christian movements in the form of born-again radicals. Nigeria is especially important in the whole phenomenon of religious and political violence because it typifies Africa and is a country that possesses the resources and military force to control crises in the region. It is important to understand the historical connections of violence in the region as well as the region's political, economic, social, and religious dynamics. Because Muslims and Christians coexisted in peace and traded peacefully prior to colonial control, the influence of Osama bin Laden and his terror network should not be used as a diversion in the demonization of Muslims and radical Christians in Africa. The contemporary wave of religious turbulence in sub-Saharan Africa could be averted by sound economic and political reforms. Most importantly, educational and employment initiatives must be targeted at the poor masses whether they are Muslims or Christians. Economically depressed and educationally marginalized people should not be required to pay allegiance to any particular religion. Poor and depressed citizens of Africa, and Nigeria in particular, could be vulnerable to the ideologies of the terror groups and volatile if converted. This is as true in virtually every region of Africa as it is in Sudan, Somalia, and Nigeria.

I.D. Onwudiwe

See also: African Traditional Religion; Lord's Resistance Army; Rwandan Genocide; Terrorism.

Further Reading

Dickson, D. "Political Islam in Sub-Saharan Africa." *U.S. Institute of Peace: Special Report* 140 (May 2005): 1–12.

Dundas, P. *The Jains.* London: Routledge, 1992.

Ellis, S., and G.T. Harr. "Religion and Politics in Sub-Saharan Africa." *Journal of Modern African Studies* 36:2 (1998): 175–201.

Gettleman, J. "Ethiopia Makes War on Islamists in Somalia: Religious Violence Is Escalating in the Horn of Africa." *New York Times*, December 25, 2006.

Hickey, R. "The 1982 Maitatsine Uprisings in Nigeria: A Note." *African Affairs* 83:331 (April 1984): 251–56.

Hutchinson, S.E. "A Curse from God? Religious and Political Dimensions of the Post-1991 Rise of Ethnic Violence in South Sudan." *Journal of Modern African Studies* 39:2 (June 2001): 307–31.

Longman, T. "Christian Churches and Genocide in Rwanda." In *In God's Name: Genocide and Religion in the Twentieth Century*, ed. O. Bartov and P. Mack, pp. 140–60. New York: Berhahn Books, 2001.

Mahmood, Y. *Sharia Law Reports of Nigeria.* Owerri, Nigeria: Spectrum Law Series, 1993.

Onwudiwe, I.D. "A Critical Theoretical Analysis of Old and New Terrorism: Implications for the Third-World." *International Journal of African Studies* 5:2 (2006): 85–118.

———. *The Globalization of Terrorism.* London: Ashgate, 2001.

Prunier, G. *Darfur's Sudan Problem.* Open Democracy, 2006. Available: http://www.opendemocracy.net/democracy-africa_democracy/darfur_conflict_3909.jsp.

Schwartz, S. *The Two Faces of Islam: Saudi Fundamentalism and Its Role in Terrorism.* New York: Anchor Books, 2003.

The State of the World's Human Rights: Africa. Amnesty International, 2009. Available: http://thereport.amnesty.org/Regions/Africa.

Tanner, R.E.S., and C.J. Pawson. "Contemporary Religious Violence and the Environment: Some Tentative Observations and Assessments." *Journal of Human Ecology* 15:2 (2004): 119–27.

Vail, L. "Introduction: Ethnicity in Southern African History." In *The Creation of Tribalism in Southern Africa*, ed. L. Vail, pp. 1–19. Berkeley: University of California Press, 1989.

The World Factbook. Langley, VA: Central Intelligence Agency. Available: https://www.cia.gov/library/publications/the-world-factbook/index.html.

African Traditional Religion

Adherents of African traditional religion (ATR) have historically tapped into the spiritist powers and forces presumably underpinning ATR to enhance their individual and collective defense against adversarial forces, as well as their capacity to prosecute wars and violent conflicts. This driving objective can be quite easily misconstrued to reinforce the negative and pathological slant that has largely characterized discourses about ATR dating back to Western expeditions to Africa in both precolonial and colonial history. Western occidental civilization and the Judeo-Christian faith have historically demonized and antagonized ATR as evil, primitive, barbaric, and occultic, leading to the self-appointed mission to obliterate ATR and convert its adherents to the supposedly superior Judeo-Christian religion and civilization. African colonial and postcolonial history is dotted with many instances of spirited attempts to eradicate ATR by Christian missionaries—sometimes with obvert or tacit support of the state—through the infliction of violence.

For a similar reason, mainstream Islam is equally guilty of this anti-ATR missionary crusade, which historically has been promoted through a combination of force, choice, proselytization, dialogue, and incentives in the form of creation of diverse opportunities within Islamic systems and political establishments (caliphates, sultanates, and emirates). In fact, the Middle Eastern Arab military/jihadic conquest of North Africa from the mid-seventh through the eleventh centuries C.E. was not only decisive, but quickly followed by the Arabization (that is, the introduction of Arabic language and cultural patterns) of the local cultures and populations, the establishment of Islamic sultanates and state structures in various regions, the domination of local commerce by Arab traders, and the gradual expansion of Islamic faith to the local population through the activities of Arab merchants over the coming centuries.

To be sure, African traditional religion, like every other religion, is fundamentally not about violence but about what religion broadly represents: "belief in the existence of an invisible world, distinct but not separate from the visible one, that is home to spiritual beings with effective power over the material world" (Ellis and Ter Haar 2004). The capacity to descend or resort to violence, whether defensive or offensive, resistant or schismatic, discursive or coercive, is a potential feature—sometimes an externality—of virtually all religions, and ATR is not an exception. Even though African traditional religion is not fundamentally about violence, it is evident that ATR, like many other religions, underpins a profound nexus of structural violence.

African Traditional Religion: Nature, Context, and Structure

ATR broadly subsumes a hierarchy of African deities, deified objects, and spiritual forces that in various ways connect the people to the conceivably more decisive supernatural realm. Some of the spiritual forces and gods are believed to inhabit the cosmic system or some natural forces and creatures, including the sun, moon, virgin forests, mountains, rivers, lakes, caves, and totems. There are also spirit forces associated with the deification of some dead legendary ancestors or fictive progenitors. From the perspective of adherents and worshippers (both "prehistoric" and present-day), ATR serves to support a wide range of spiritual, secular, and mundane concerns, including reverential worship and fellowship, individual and collective protection and security, material prosperity, therapeutic healing, explanation of the unknown, and control of present and impending adversities. The empirical content of ATR varies from one culture or community to another. One can identify some of the defining structural and empirical characteristics of ATR as follows.

A main component of ATR is the belief in structural polytheism—a plurality of deities and gods. Africans are a religious people, and the individual peoples of Africa have their own system of religious beliefs and practices. Religion is so fully present in all aspects of life that it cannot be isolated. In sub-Saharan Africa there is widespread belief that the immaterial forces perceived to be operating in the material world consist of or are controlled by individual spirits. Some refer to ATR in the plural (ATRs) because the tribal system is the operational framework for ATRs, and each tribe has a particular and distinct religious system. However, there is also a mosaic of subtribal—or perhaps more appropriately subethnic—and transethnic deities in various communities of sub-Saharan Africa.

Adherents of ATR take a holistic approach to reality, in which the spiritual and physical worlds are inseparable, the former preceding the latter. In African traditional religion and cosmology, the structural distinction between the sacred and the secular, the religious and nonreligious, as well as the spiritual and material areas of life found in Judeo-Christian civilization, is completely blurred. This so-called structural separation between the sacred and secular reflects the specific historical experience of Europe but not necessarily the rest of the world, not least Africa (Ellis and Ter Haar 2007). The African holistic approach to reality and preeminence of religious discourse can be attributed to the fact that religion permeates all spheres of life in Africa—beliefs and worldview; farming, harvest, and crop yield; marriage and childbearing; stages and rituals of community socialization; death and burial; personal and collective security; defense and warfare; environment and natural disaster.

ATR is a community-centered and community-driven religion, implying that the individual is religious by virtue of membership in a closely knit, multifunctional community. In the traditional African societies, especially in precolonial history, everybody was so deeply and communally religious that there was no space for atheism or agnosticism. The advent of the two main Abrahamic religions (Christianity and Islam) has significantly vitiated the community spirit of ATR, especially in many urban areas, where either ATR has to a large extent been displaced or some measure of syncretism prevails. It is noteworthy that among many Africans oriented to syncretism (i.e., adhering to two or more religions—in most cases, ATR and one of the two dominant Abrahamic religions) there is a tendency to conceal the involvement in and practice of ATR. This is most common among the educated elites and urban dwellers, and the reason is clearly because of the legacy of demonization that ATR inherited from colonial times. With regard to the tendency of many Africans toward syncretism, it has been noted that "unless Christianity and Islam fully

occupy the whole person as much as, if not more than, traditional religions do, most converts to these faiths will continue to revert to their old beliefs and practices for perhaps six days a week, and certainly in times of emergency and crisis" (Mbiti 1969). Many also attribute the present and growing religious revival in many parts of Africa (of radical Islam, neopentecostalism, and neotraditionalism) to deepening economic hardship, state failure, and the impact of globalization.

ATR is rooted in a belief in the human embodiment of religious codes and does not rely on scripture. ATR's codes are largely embodied by powerful personages and adherents, albeit the codes are believed to be inspired and sanctioned by the applicable god(s). There is an evident lack of codification and scripturalization of the religion into sacred texts. "Religion in African societies is written not on paper but in people's hearts, minds, oral history, rituals and religious personages like priests, rainmakers, officiating elders and even kings. . . . [Hence], to study ATRs, one has to, of necessity, study the people that embody the religion" (Mbiti 1969). Some critics have argued that the lack of sacred scriptures disposes ATR to the arbitrary manipulation of officiating priests and other powerful intermediaries. This is further seen as an indication of how underdeveloped ATR is as a religion. But it is evident that twisting of religious codes occurs in all religions and is a phenomenon associated with the susceptibility of the belief systems (written or unwritten) to multiple subjective interpretations.

African traditional religion is one based on self-containment, nonproselytization, and this-world utility: It does not have missionaries for the purpose of winning converts to expand its territorial reach. Adherents of ATR believe that one is born into one's religion, and thus they do not preach or attempt to convert others. This is a belief that ATR shares with some Asian religions, such as Hinduism and Confucianism. Similarly, the religion lacks messianic pillars and founders comparable to Jesus Christ in Christianity and Muhammad in Islam, although many traditions of ATR incorporate certain legendary figures (in some cases, symbols of ancestor worship) into their belief systems. By and large, ATR has a this-world utilitarian approach to gods and deities. There is a great orientation of the religion to how divinity can help maintain or achieve a harmonious social order and how spiritual power can be harnessed to solve real-life existential problems, including combating diverse threats to security and social order. Without doubt, as in most religions, human intermediaries often exploit and abuse these processes. The mystical and eschatological dimensions of ATR essentially help in explaining, rationalizing, and engaging the unknown and the seemingly mysterious. These include issues like unraveling past retributive atrocities, getting a handle on complex oddities of the present, and foretelling the future, as well as issues of after-death, incarnation, and eternity.

ATR and Violence

One can identify three major types of violence or conflict associated with ATR and its adherents, which are by no means mutually exclusive: conflict of self-preservation; clash of civilizations; and instrumental conflict of diverse motives—notably offense, defense, and reestablishment of social order.

Conflict of Self-Preservation

Conflict of self-preservation is arguably the oldest and most ruthless form of conflict ATR has historically faced and continues to face. It is a conflict associated with the age-old construction of ATR as a pathological phenomenon exclusively promoting sinister activities such as witchcraft, ritual murder, fetish cults, and can-

nibalism, and therefore must be exterminated. Precolonial and colonial missionaries, the colonial establishment, and mainstream Victorian anthropologists were some of the chief proponents of this viewpoint. Most colonial anthropologists of the evolutionist tradition conflated and castigated ATR as animism, which they described as the most primitive or rudimentary stage in the spiritual evolution of a people. With the combined advantages of commanding discursive and political power, the colonial missionaries and government (often working in partnership but also independently) set out in various places to forcibly outlaw, abolish, and eradicate some African religious practices and community deities. In many cases, the real reason for the prohibition or destruction of some of ATR's oracular shrines and deities was that the local people used them as rallying points to mobilize for opposition and resistance against colonial conquest and Western missionary activities. Reenactments of this "civilizing mission" of the church and state have also played out in postcolonial history in different countries. It is a form of organized violence that almost invariably has put ATR on the defensive, fighting a resistance battle and a war of self-preservation.

One of the classic examples of colonial violence against ATR and local adherents' war of self-preservation was the British colonial military expedition of 1901–1902, carried out to destroy the oracular shrine and temple of Ibin Ukpabi (popularly branded the Long Juju of Arochukwu by colonialists), located in Arochukwu in the Igbo heartland of southeastern Nigeria. Ibin Ukpabi was an influential god and bulwark of the Aro people (those that trace their ancestry to Arochukwu) and of their imperial domination and governance of many tributary communities in the surrounding region. Prior to colonial rule, Ibin Ukpabi maintained subsidiary oracular shrines in different parts of

Igboland, from where tributary chiefs and the Aro diaspora referred appellant litigations to the headquarters' shrine and officiating high priests in Arochukwu. During the transatlantic slave trade of the seventeenth to nineteenth centuries, the Ibin Ukpabi and its oracular shrines and priests in tributary communities played an active role in conscripting slaves using divination, blackmail, and various sorts of deception and handing them over to European slave traders for a ransom. However, the continuation of Ibin Ukpabi's oracular imperium during the transition from slave trade to colonialism was perceived by the colonialists as antithetical to the ambitious imperial project of the British Crown. Hence, in the military expedition of 1901–1902 the Ibin Ukpabi principal shrine was reportedly obliterated. The Aro nation fought back the colonial invaders using a combination of locally crafted weaponry and supernatural ammunition (the projection of psychic missiles and spells, oracular divination, offensive magical charms) but lost to the superior firepower of the colonial army. A significant number of traditionalists in the Arochukwu community and beyond believe that the destruction of the Long Juju's shrine in 1902 by no means obliterated the god, being a supernatural deity, or the potency of its powers. Thus, pockets of worshippers, priests, and adherents of Ibin Ukpabi still exist among Aro indigenes and the Aro diaspora.

The strong voodoo religious tradition of the Fon ethnic group in Benin Republic, which centered on the worship of the Mawu deity (also called Nana Buluku), was for several decades the object of violent assault by colonial missionaries and the self-styled Marxist-Leninist regime of Mathieu Kérékou (1972–1989). Mawu priests were repeatedly stigmatized and persecuted for allegedly initiating large numbers of community members and worshippers into a vicious, exploitative, and oppressive cult system (Vodun) with strict codes of conduct and ruthless sanc-

tions against transgression. More significantly, the activities of the Vodun cult priests were perceived as jeopardizing allegiance of the populace to the state and the state's monopoly of the legitimate use of force. Traditional sanctions of the Vodun cult among the Fon could be invoked by cult priests against adversaries. These sanctions included dangerous diseases like smallpox and leprosy; destruction by thunder and lightning; birth of deformed or monstrous babies; devastation of farm crops by pests, birds, and wild beasts; and banishment and forcible expropriation of property. The general belief that Mawu was capable of inflicting these havocs and sanctions on transgressors and adversaries through its intermediary Vodun spirits and cults made the cults and cult priests highly dreaded by local people. The seventeen years of Marxist-Leninist dictatorship and antireligious witch hunts (mostly Vodun) significantly diminished the influence of the voodoo tradition. As in many state-masterminded crackdowns of traditional religious practices, the magical warfare and struggle for self-preservation waged by the Vodun cult system were no match for the superior military power of the state. Neotraditionalism has noticeably revived and bolstered the Vodun institution since the emergence of liberal democracy in Benin in 1991.

Elsewhere, in South Africa, Cameroon, Ghana, Uganda, Kenya, Ethiopia, and Djibouti there have been various instances of violence associated with attempts to exterminate different aspects of ATR in colonial and postcolonial history over allegations and issues such as degradation and violence against women, cult slavery, ritual murder, and celebration of traditional festivals considered obnoxious or offensive to modern sensibilities. A large proportion of the alleged violations in various countries have been reported among syncretic (hybrid) sects in which ATR incorporates elements of Islamic or Christian traditions.

Clash of Civilizations

In his famous "clash of civilizations" thesis (1993), in which cultural entities (notably, religions) were depicted as most likely to shape civilization identity and provide a fault line for conflict, Samuel Huntington developed a sevenfold classification of world major civilizations but was uncertain whether there remained an African civilization in contemporary postcolonial history. He classified North Africa as part of the Arab civilization and treated sub-Saharan Africa as mainly a subdivision or appendage of Western (European) civilization as a result of its colonial history. Paradoxically, Huntington identified Latin America as a distinct civilization, not minding its colonial history and European religious and cultural heritage. Huntington seems to have presumed that sub-Saharan African civilization was obliterated and replaced by Western civilization, but that assumption is incorrect. If civilizations do clash, sub-Saharan Africa remains a major theater for the patterns of religious and cultural conflict described by Huntington. As discussed above, the conflict of self-preservation that pits the entire paraphernalia of the Western modernization project in Africa against African traditional religion is fundamentally a clash of civilizations. The civilizations conflict did not end with colonial and Cold War history in sub-Saharan Africa but has continued in more contemporary history.

There have been a number of recent incidents of sexual exploitation of cult women and girls, otherwise known as religious cult prostitution, among some local communities of the Igbo ethnic group in Nigeria, the Ewe communities of southern Togo and Ghana, and different autochthonous cultures in Ethiopia. Under this tradition, young girls and women dedicated to fetish gods are importuned by fetish priests and some of the local men to gain sexual, marital, and other vital privileges, including subjection to forced farm labor. As a general tendency, the tradition thrives on a caste stratification that subjugates and dehumanizes the cult women, who are offered to the idols by their families as reparation for some wrong allegedly committed by their ancestors. It is generally the belief of local practitioners that such human reparation will stem the tide of misfortune and bad luck, which the idols presumably unleash on the "culpable" families. Despite being outlawed by the subnational governments and despite the destruction of the oracular shrines of the cults by the combined forces of the state and church and other civic groups, religious cult prostitution has often thrived underground in the affected communities. Even though this tradition is linked to ATR, it is important to note that there are similar traditions of sexual exploitation of girls and women elsewhere in the Middle East, Asia, North Africa, and the United States, both within and outside organized religion.

Beyond the sexual exploitation of cult women, another area where aspects of ATR may precipitate violence is necromancy and witchcraft. In many village communities and local districts of South Africa, the Democratic Republic of the Congo, Cameroon, Nigeria, Gabon, Zambia, Zimbabwe, Lesotho, and Swaziland, several incidents of witchcraft-related violence have led to fragmentation of community social structures and heavy-handed victimization of alleged culprits or witches. The case of Cameroon, one of the few countries in the world that has antiwitchcraft legislation, is particularly instructive because of the extraordinary politicization of witchcraft there. Section 251 of the Cameroonian penal code considers the practice of witchcraft a key obstacle to progress, punishable by two to ten years imprisonment or a fine of 5,000 to 100,000 Central African francs if proven in court. In both theory and practice, the judicial proof is supposedly based on evidence supplied by witch doctors as expert witnesses. Since witchcraft can hardly be proved empirically, witch doctors, law enforcement agents, and state politicians exploit the antiwitchcraft legislation to blackmail and persecute their vulnerable subjects and opponents. Cameroon's president, Paul Biya, who has faced relentless opposition for recently changing the country's constitution to further lenghthen his twenty-seven-year reign, has intensified his crackdown on opposition politicians and civil society activists whom he labels "apprentice sorcerers." From the perspective of the state, the label "sorcerer" and the allegation of sorcery were sufficient justification for brutality and indefinite incarceration of the president's opponents.

Beyond the vicious instance of politicization, those accused of having and operating the spirit of witchcraft are usually poor rural women and girls. The extent to which traditional witchcraft in Africa is linked to ATR is debatable, even though it is apparent that individuals accused of operating witchcraft spirits are too often adherents of ATR. It is hardly in doubt, however, that divination and necromancy aimed at establishing the source and masterminds of witchcraft are integral to ATR.

Instrumental Conflict

ATR has been, both historically and in more contemporary times, associated with various forms of "instrumental conflict"—conflict as a means for goal attainment. As this tendency seems to have increased with deepening political crises and economic hardship on the African continent, many scholars attribute neotraditionalism to worsening political and economic conditions. During the first postindependence decade of Zimbabwe, mediums ordered many squatters to move onto alienated land in the north of Mashonaland so as to reclaim ancestral territories; the Zimbabwean government responded by having mediums placed under

house arrest and squatters forcibly removed from occupied land. There are diverse examples of incidents and allegations of ritual killings linked to the use of offensive and defensive juju (a fetish object to which supernatural powers are ascribed), as well as internment of occult dignitaries in various African countries (e.g., Côte d'Ivoire, Kenya, Guinea, Togo, Zambia, Gabon, DRC, and Nigeria), in which many top political leaders and traditional rulers were implicated.

One stunning example of high-profile ritual killings in modern African history is the case of the Ogwugwu shrines in the remote Igbo village of Okija, a mini-Mecca to many top Nigerian politicians and business tycoons, which was raided on August 3–4, 2004, by a team of about 500 policemen. More than twenty human skulls and fifty corpses at different stages of decomposition, supposedly slaughtered for ritual purposes, were discovered during the raid, in which some thirty-one priests of the deity were arrested. Further evidence following the discovery of the Ogwugwu ritual killings revealed that among regular visitors to the shrines were a number of federal and state government legislators and state governors who frequented the oracular deity for personal talismanic protection, good-faith and loyalty-related oath taking, and settlement of disputes. The federal government immediately directed the police to carry out a detailed investigation of the Ogwugwu cult with a view to prosecuting the culprits. The police inquiry amounted to nothing, however, as the powerful politicians implicated in the infamous occult saga used their influence to stifle the investigation and any possible judicial proceedings.

Similarly, a large number of combatant groups (rebels, militias, and state security forces) in various African civil wars and political insurgencies have been associated with the use of occult power derivable from ATR to reinforce their military capabilities. The Egbesu and Bakassi Boys and the Oodua People's Congress (OPC) are major Nigerian ethnic militia groups noted for use of the famous "bulletproof magical charms" to reinforce their defensive and combatant capabilities in their war against uncompromising adversaries. These adversaries are the government security forces, in the case of the Egbesu Boys, of the oil-rich Niger Delta region; notorious armed robbers that menace public order, in the case of the Bakassi Boys of the ethnic Igbo major commercial towns; and rival ethnic groups and government security forces, in the case of the ethnic Yoruba-led OPC.

There have been various incidents and allegations pertaining to the religious components of the civil wars in Africa. This is especially true in Liberia, where many of the atrocities committed in war are associated with belief in the juju spirits. In neighboring Sierra Leone, the link between ATR and violence is also evident. As Robert Kaplan reported in *Atlantic Monthly* (1994), "Rebels were said to have a young woman with them who would go to the front naked, always walking backwards and looking in a mirror to see where she was going. This made her invisible, so that she could cross to the army's positions and there bury charms . . . to improve the rebels' chances of success."

Additionally, the religious repertoire of Liberian and other African civil wars has been reported to include combatants who used shamanistic charms and other animist protection in the belief that such magical devices would protect them from the enemy's bullets and fighters who ate body parts and drank the blood of their slain enemies and used their enemy's skull as a drinking bowl—all based on the superstition that such practices reinforce combat bravery. These barbaric incidents associated with political violence and plunder in Liberia are part of a historical tradition that goes back to Liberia's turbulent past. For scholars like

Patrick Chabal and Jean-Pascal Daloz (1999) these events, barbaric as they might seem, have embedded instrumental value—being "how Africa works"—as disorder and retraditionalization of society are strong political instruments in Africa.

In spite of the efforts by the international community to humanize war, wars remain inherently and largely uncivil. Mind-boggling monstrosities of various shades are rampant in wars and political violence and are by no means peculiar to Africa or its traditional religions. To focus on the episodes of neobarbaric violence in African wars, whether religiously motivated or not, is to ignore the underlying causality of these armed conflicts: the collapse of the fragile neopatrimonial state that succeeded the colonial state.

Kenneth Omeje

See also: Africa, Sub-Saharan; Islam; Sacrifice (Animal).

Further Reading

Adekunkle, Julius, ed. *Religion in Politics: Secularism and National Integration in Modern Nigeria.* Trenton, NJ: Africa World Press, 2009.

Alie, Joe A.D. "The Kamajor Militia in Sierra Leone: Liberators or Nihilists?" In *Civil Militias: Africa's Intractable Security Menace?* ed. D.J. Francis, pp. 51–70. Aldershot, UK: Ashgate, 2005.

Chabal, Patrick, and Jean-Pascal Daloz. *Africa Works: Disorder as Political Instrument.* Oxford: James Currey, 1999.

Ellis, Stephen. "Liberia 1989–1995: A Study of Ethnic and Spiritual Violence." *African Affairs* 94:375 (1995): 165–97.

———. *The Mask of Anarchy: The Destruction of Liberia and the Religious Dimension of an African Civil War.* London: Hurst, 1999.

Ellis, Stephen, and G. Ter Haar. "Religion & Politics: Taking African Epistemologies Seriously." *Journal of Modern African Studies* 34:3 (2007): 385–424.

———. *Worlds of Power: Religious Thought and Political Practice in Africa.* London: Hurst, 2004.

Huntington, Samuel P. "The Clash of Civilizations?" *Foreign Affairs* (Summer 1993): 22–49.

Isichei, Elizabeth. *A History of the Igbo People.* New York: Palgrave Macmillan, 1976.

Kaplan, Robert D. "The Coming Anarchy." *Atlantic Monthly* 273:2 (1994): 44–76.

Kohnert, D. "Witchcraft and Transnational Social Space: Witchcraft Violence, Reconciliation and Development in South Africa's Transition Process." *Journal of Modern African Studies* 41:2 (2003): 217–45.

Mbiti, John S. *African Religions and Philosophy.* Oxford: Heinemann, 1969.

Møller, Bjørn. *Religion and Conflict in Africa with a Special Focus on East Africa.* Danish Institute for International Studies Report 2006:6. http://www.diis.dk/sw24555.asp.

Olaoba, O.B. "Ancestral Focus and the Process of Conflict Resolution in Traditional African Societies." In *Perspectives on Peace and Conflict in Africa,* ed. Isaac Olawale Albert. Ibadan, Nigeria: University of Ibadan, Institute for Peace and Conflict Studies Programme, 2005.

Omeje, K. "The Egbesu and Bakassi Boys: African Spiritism and the Mystical Re-traditionalisation of Security." In *Civil Militias: Africa's Intractable Security Menace?* ed. D.J. Francis, pp. 71–88. Aldershot, UK: Ashgate, 2005.

———. *High Stakes and Stakeholders: Oil Conflict and Security in Nigeria.* Aldershot, UK: Ashgate, 2006.

———. "Sexual Exploitation of Cult Women: The Challenges of Problematizing Harmful Traditional Practices in Africa from a Doctrinalist Approach." *Social & Legal Studies* 10:1 (2001): 45–61.

Paden, John N. *Faith and Politics in Nigeria: Nigeria as a Pivotal State in the Muslim World.* Pivotal State Series. Washington, DC: United States Institute of Peace, 2008.

Ras-Work, Berhane. *The Impact of Harmful Traditional Practices on the Girl Child.* United Nations Division for the Advancement of Women (DAW) / UNICEF Expert Group Meeting on Elimination of all Forms of Discrimination and Violence Against the Girl Child, Innocenti Research Centre, Florence, Italy, September 25–28, 2006. Available: http://www.un.org/womenwatch/daw.

Richards, Paul. *Fighting for the Rain Forest: War, Youth and Resources in Sierra Leone.* Oxford: James Currey, 1996.

———. "To Fight or to Farm? Agrarian Dimensions of the Mano River Conflicts (Liberia and Sierra Leone)." *African Affairs* 104:417 (2005): 571–90.

Tanto, Talla Richard, and Ndambi Isaac Akenji. "Indigenous Authority and Witchcraft Containment in Post-colonial Cameroun: The Case of the Wumbum in the Bamenda Grassfields." In *Perspectives on Peace and Conflict in Africa,* ed. Isaac Olawale Albert. Ibadan, Nigeria: University of Ibadan, Institute for Peace and Conflict Studies Programme, 2005.

Violence Against Girls in Africa: A Retrospective Survey in Ethiopia, Kenya and Uganda. African Child Policy Forum, 2006. Available: www.africanchildforum.org/Documents/Survey%20Report.pdf.

Wiredu, Kwasi. "On Decolonizing African Religions." In *The African Philosophy Reader,* 2nd ed., ed. P.H. Coetzee and A.P.J. Roux, pp. 20–34. London: Routledge, 2002.

Zinzindohoue, Barthélemy. "Traditional Religion in Africa: The Vodun Phenomenon in Benin." *African Societies* (2002). Available: http://www.afrikaworld.net/afrel/zinzindohoue.htm.

Ağca, Mehmet Ali (1958–)

In 1981, Pope John Paul II (1920–2005) was shot and wounded in Rome's St. Peter's Square by Turkish citizen Mehmet Ali Ağca, for reasons that remain unknown. The pope forgave Ağca three days after the shooting and visited him in prison shortly thereafter. In 2000, Italian president Carlo Azeglio Ciampi (1996–2006) pardoned Ağca, who had been in prison for nearly two decades. Ağca was then deported to Turkey and imprisoned for the 1979 murder of a newspaper editor and the robbery of an Istanbul factory. Ağca was released on January 18, 2010.

Ağca's Background

Mehmet Ali Ağca was born in 1958 and grew up in Yeğiltepe, Malatya, a relatively prosperous city in Anatolian Turkey. His mother was impoverished and suffered from lung cancer, and his father was an alcoholic. In his youth, Ağca was associated with the Gray Wolves, an ultranationalist and anticommunist ideological movement. As he later confessed, he had underground relationships with Turkish extremists on both the right and the left throughout the period between 1976 and 1980. More specifically, in his defense during the 1981 trial he claimed to have established secret connections with six militant organizations—Akıncılar, Ülkücüler, Emeğin Birliği, Halkın Kurtuluşu,

Attendants help Pope John Paul II into a car after he was shot and wounded by Mehmet Ali Ağca in St. Peter's Square, Rome, on May 13, 1981. Ağca served twenty years of a life sentence, though soon after his release, he was arrested and imprisoned for other crimes. The motive for his attack on the pope is still unknown. *(Keystone/Hulton Archive/Getty Images)*

THKO, and THKPC—after training to be a guerrilla in Palestine during the spring of 1977. Whereas Akıncılar and Ülkücüler are oriented to the far Right, the remaining four are leftist activist groups.

At only twenty-one, Ağca committed his first known murder. On February 1, 1979, he assassinated Abdi İpekçi, the editor of the mainstream secular daily *Milliyet*. Ağca was arrested five months later, on June 25, but he managed to escape from the Kartal-Maltepe prison on the night of November 23. For the following eighteen months, he was the subject of Interpol alerts. The role of ideological motivation in the İpekçi assassination is still debated; however, there was at least $16,000 in Ağca's bank accounts at the time he carried out the murder, and some people believe that he was hired for that assassination.

Ağca's escape occurred less than four days before Pope John Paul II's scheduled visit to Turkey, on November 27. The day after his escape, Ağca sent a letter to the offices of *Milliyet* threatening the life of the pope. At one point in the letter, he wrote, "If this visit . . . is not canceled, I will without a doubt kill the Pope-Chief. This is the sole motive for my escape from prison. Furthermore, the responsibility for the attack on Mecca, of American and Israeli origin, will not go unpunished."

Hiding underground and financed by an unknown network, Ağca traveled throughout Eastern and Western Europe in order to conceal his whereabouts. He made stops in Bulgaria, Yugoslavia, France, Great Britain, Belgium, Switzerland, Denmark, Austria, Hungary, Tunisia, and Spain. His final stop was in Italy, where he was to act upon the threat made eighteen months prior.

The Assassination Plot

On May 13, 1981, at twenty-three years of age, Ağca attempted to assassinate Pope John Paul II while he was riding in an open car across St. Peter's Square in the Vatican and had stopped to offer personal blessings to those in the crowd. From less than 20 feet (6 meters) away, Ağca shot him four times with a 9-millimeter Browning semiautomatic pistol. The pope was critically wounded; one bullet grazed his left hand and right arm, and another struck his abdomen. Ağca dropped his pistol and tried to escape but was captured immediately after a nun, Suor Letizia, knocked him to the ground. The pope was taken to the Gemelli Clinic, which had a special section for papal medical emergencies. Although his condition was critical, the bullet had missed the aorta by millimeters, and doctors operating for over five hours managed to save his life. He lost two feet (0.6 meters) of his intestines and 60 percent of his blood.

Within a month, the pope returned to work, but he never fully regained his health. In his fifth book, *Memory and Identity: Conversations at the Dawn of a Millennium* (2005), he expressed his feelings shortly after the shooting: "I had a feeling that I would survive. I was in pain, I had reason to be afraid, but I had this strange feeling of confidence." He also mentioned that before reaching the hospital, he had told his personal secretary, Stanislaw Dziwisz, that he forgave the assassin.

In the 1981 trial, Ağca was sentenced to life imprisonment. On Christmas Day in 1983, Pope John Paul II met with Ağca in the prison. Afterward, the pope stated that during their conversation Ağca revealed that he was troubled by the fact that the assassination had been unsuccessful. Ağca's main interest was the Fatima mystery, to which the pontiff credited his own survival. According to the pope, "Ali Ağca . . . understood that above his power, the power of shooting and killing, there is a greater power. He began looking for it."

In June 2000, after spending nineteen years in prison, Ağca was granted clemency at the Vatican's request. He was then transferred to Turkey to serve his sentence for Abdi İpekçi's slaying and the robbery of an Istanbul factory that same year.

Conspiracies on the Assassination Plot

The mysterious part of the would-be assassination attempt was the third secret of the prophecy of Fatima. Three shepherd children living in the rural Portuguese town of Fatima claimed to have been visited by an apparition of the Virgin Mary six times between May and October of 1917. The apparition, now famously known as Our Lady of Fatima, confided to them prophetic messages that were to be revealed later. One of them, the third secret of Fatima, foretold that an assassination attempt would be made on the pope. The secret was revealed in 2000 during the pope's visit to the shrine of Fatima, whose feast day was the day of the attack on the pope. John Paul II believed that he was saved by a miracle that he linked to the Virgin of Fatima. "One hand fired," the pope claimed, "and another hand guided the bullet." Besides these explanations, however, the pope understood that, as he said, "Ali Ağca is, as everyone says, a professional assassin. Which means that the assassination was not his own initiative, that someone else thought of it, someone else gave the order."

The identity of this "someone else" remains a mystery. According to a Vatican report, Ağca traveled to more than twenty countries between 1979 and 1981. This suggests that he was not acting alone. To date, no religious motivation has come to light in either assassination attempt.

Ağca was developing ties in many directions but none with Muslim extremists. In addition, no direct links with leaders of the ultranationalist Gray Wolves have been proven.

After further information emerged, some observers believed that the attempted assassination was ordered by the Bulgarian secret service. Information emerged that Ağca had stayed in Bulgaria on several occasions. Moreover, he was picked up on the day of the attempted assassination by a Bulgarian intelligence officer and Sergei Antonov, an airline official who was accompanied by two Bulgarian diplomats. In a report prepared by two Turkish judges who interrogated Ağca in Italy in the summer of 1983, Ağca's testimony read, "In Syria . . . we were trained by Bulgarian specialists. This training involved the use of weapons, explosives, cold war concepts, how to carry out coup d'états and related revolutionary theory."

Another theory is that the Bulgarians were simply following orders from the Soviet secret service, the KGB, which was alarmed by the Polish pope's support for the Solidarity Trade Union in Poland. Several factors could explain why the pope would have been a target of the Kremlin. First, he was Polish; second, he was the head of the Roman Catholic Church; and, third, he was an advocate of freedom and human rights. Antonio Albano, the Italian state prosecutor, also pointed out in his report that the Solidarity Movement in Poland during the summer of 1980 was the "most acute crisis for the socialist states of Eastern Europe" and a danger to their political cohesion. "And since Poland's ideological collapse was mostly due to the fervid religious faith of the population, sustained and helped above all by the first Polish Pope in history, the Polish rebellion might be greatly weakened and fragmented by his physical elimination."

Ağca confirmed these suspicions by claiming that he took the assassination order from the Soviet embassy in Sofia. In a 2001 letter, he wrote that he had the order to assassinate the pope from the Russian Intelligence Service (KGB) and pointed to his contacts with KGB member Soviet General Vlademir Kuzinski. Ferdinando Imposimato, who was in charge of the investigation, also confirmed the Ağca-Kuzinski contact. Imposimato was indeed convinced of Soviet bloc involvement. The Italian judge determined that at the time of attack, the pope was preaching a message that condemned the Communist collectivist ideology. Dismissing the theory of their involvement, the Soviets claimed that the Central Intelligence Agency (CIA) was behind the assassination and that the United States was responsible.

Shortly after the shooting, the guards found a note in Ağca's pocket stating, "I killed the pope to protest against the imperialism of the Soviet Union and the United States and against the genocides they are perpetrating in El Salvador and Afghanistan." Over the years, however, he gave conflicting reasons for writing that note. He first claimed that he acted alone. But after serving ten months in prison, he retracted his claim and argued that the Bulgarians were involved. He later changed his testimony again and claimed to be a reincarnation of Jesus Christ. In his trial in Italy, Ağca argued that the shooting was just a fulfillment of Fatima's third secret, which would be declared fourteen years later. He shouted, "I am Jesus Christ. In the name of the omnipotent God, I announce the end of the world. . . ." In his later interviews, he dropped all references he had previously made to the investigators. He said, "It's pointless to keep speculating and looking for secret plans and plots. The truth is that on that day not even I knew why I shot . . . I might have done it to make history." According to Imposimato, Ağca initially said many true things, but he changed his testimony after he was threatened by Bulgarian and KGB secret agents while in prison.

The Bulgarian connection was not proved, and the 1986 trial in Italy of six other Turkish and Bulgarian men suspected of collaborating with Ağca ended with an acquittal for lack of sufficient evidence. Ağca remained the only person punished for the assassination attempt. In 2002, John Paul II laid the issue to rest and declared that he never believed in a Bulgarian connection. In 2005, Mehmet Ali Ağca was released from prison after twenty-five years. He would have served his prison sentence until at least 2016, but a change in the law granted him amnesty. However, within a month, the decision was rejected by a higher court, and he was sent back to prison.

Hakki Tas

See also: Roman Catholicism.

Further Reading

Connolly, K. "Cheers and Petals for the Turk Who Shot the Pope." *Telegraph* (UK), January 14, 2006.

Epstein, E.J. "Papal Assassasination: Did He Act Alone?" *New York Times Book Review,* January 15, 1984.

Fetherling, G. *The Book of Assassins: A Biographical Dictionary from Ancient Times to the Present.* New York: Wiley, 2001.

Henze, P. *The Plot to Kill the Pope.* New York: Charles Scribner's Sons, 1985.

Owen, R. "Papal Bullet 'Diverted by Virgin Mary,'" *The Times* (UK), February 19, 2005.

Sterling, C. *The Time of the Assassins.* New York: Holt, Rinehart and Winston, 1983.

Al-Aqsa Martyrs Brigades

Al-Aqsa Martyrs Brigades, also known as the al-Aqsa Martyrs Battalion, Martyrs of al-Aqsa, and Brigades of Shahid Arafat, are a Palestinian militant nationalist group that emerged in 2000 at the beginning of the Second Intifada, the second Palestinian uprising against Israeli rule (the First Intifada occurred from 1987 to 1993). The al-Aqsa Martyrs Brigades (hereafter, the Brigades) have been directly linked to the Fatah (or al-Fatah) political party. The main goal of the Brigades is twofold: they endeavor to rid the West Bank, the Gaza Strip, and Jerusalem of Israeli forces and settlers by targeting Israeli citizens and interests, and they promote the creation of a Palestinian state. Furthermore, they deny the validity of the Middle East peace process.

Overview

The Brigades have been a driving force behind the Second Intifada (also known as the Oslo War or Arafat's War), which is also called the al-Aqsa Intifada in reference to the al-Aqsa Mosque in Jerusalem, the third holiest shrine of Islam, which Israel had allegedly planned to destroy. The latest wave of violence in the long-standing Arab-Israeli conflict, the al-Aqsa Intifada began in late September 2000 and has claimed the lives of 1,194 Israelis as of August 2010 and over 5,500 Palestinians (as of mid-2009). Although a truce was implemented on November 26, 2006, the conflict has not yet officially ended. Palestinians view it as a necessary war to liberate their nation from foreign (Israeli) occupation, whereas Israelis consider it a full-blown terrorist campaign purposely targeting Israeli civilians.

The Brigades originated from Fatah (Harakat al-Tahrir al-Watani al-Filastini, or Movement of Liberation of the Nation of the Palestinians), a secular nationalist party of center-left and the oldest and largest organization of the Palestine Liberation Organization (PLO). Fatah is also the dominant force within the Palestinian Authority (PA) and the Palestinian security forces. The party was founded in 1958 by members of the Palestinian diaspora, most of whom, including Yasser Arafat, had been studying in Egypt. Israeli intelligence services claim that members of the Brigades are drawn from the ranks of the loosely organized Tanzim militia, an armed faction of Fatah composed mostly of militant youth. The Tanzim militia was established in 1995 as a paramilitary unit by the Palestinian Authority, along with the Fatah leadership, in order to counterbalance the growth of Palestinian Islamist groups. The connection between the Brigades, Fatah, and Arafat remained unclear for years, as much debate surrounded the question of Arafat's involvement in and control over the Brigades and their exact relationship with Fatah. At first, the Brigades were described as a group of insurgent revolutionaries linked to Arafat's Fatah organization or at least condoned and unofficially supported by Fatah. The Brigades have since been unambiguously described as Fatah's military wing by many Palestinian officials, including former PA prime minister and Fatah leader Ahmed Qurei in July 2004. The Brigades were in fact considered to be Arafat's private militia until his death on November 11, 2004. Many Brigades fighters and leaders have since referred to their group as the Brigades of Shahid Arafat or al-Shahid Yasser Arafat Brigades.

The ideology of the Brigades is embedded in Palestinian nationalism rather than Islamic fundamentalism. The emergence of the group has been viewed as a logical step in the evolution of Fatah toward a more militant type of opposition to Israeli occupying forces. Arguably, Arafat gave a free rein to the Brigades in order to assuage the Palestinian people's plea for direct action against Israel.

According to the U.S. government, the Brigades are composed of multiple terrorist cells (the exact number of which is unknown) active in Israel, the West Bank, and the Gaza Strip. There may additionally be supporters in Palestinian refugee camps located in southern Lebanon. Since March 27, 2002, the Brigades have been designated as a Foreign Terrorist Organization (FTO) by the United States secretary of state in accordance with Section 219 of the Immigration and Nationality Act (INA) of 1952, as amended. The group has been listed as a Specially Designated Global Terrorist (SDGT) in accordance with President George W. Bush's executive order of September 2002 (EC13224). Individuals affiliated with the Brigades have been listed as Specially Designated Terrorists (SDT) pursuant to President Clinton's 1996 counterterrorism legislation. Moreover, since December 2005, the Brigades are officially considered a terrorist group by the European Union pursuant to Decision 2006/379/EC of the European Union Council.

Israel also considers the Brigades to be a terrorist group and has responded to their attacks by implementing a controversial preventive policy: targeted assassinations, which have been described as "focused foiling" by the Israel Defense Forces (IDF) and may also be defined as extrajudicial executions. Israel has employed helicopter gunships, car bombs, tanks, and snipers in attacks against Palestinian guerrillas and terrorists. The rationale behind these assassinations is that to most effectively fight terrorism, the Israelis must target the leadership and destroy the command structure of the terrorist organizations. They focus on individuals who are actively involved in the planning and coordination of terrorist attacks and who are beyond the reach of the law. Critics of this policy believe that the assassinations often lead to Palestinian revenge attacks and perpetuate the cycle of violence, effectively evolving into a second war of attrition between Israelis and Palestinians (Poland 2004).

Activities

Members of the Brigades are responsible not only for suicide bombings and shootings against Israeli civilians and military forces, both in Israel and in the Palestinian territories, but also for rocket and mortar attacks against Israel and Israeli settlements in the Gaza Strip.

They have carried out car bombings, taken hostages, and executed many Palestinians accused or suspected of collaborating with Israel. The Brigades (along with Fatah's Tanzim) have claimed responsibility for hundreds of terrorist attacks against Israeli civilians. According to Israeli authorities, however, the Brigades are responsible for thousands of attacks or attempted attacks, including car bombings, shootings, and kidnappings.

The Brigades were admittedly inspired by Hizballah's brand of violence, notably suicide bombings. However, their attempts at mimicking Hizballah's successful efforts to drive Israel out of southern Lebanon have not been successful. Where Hizballah's plan of attack was more disciplined and focused on Israeli military targets, the attacks perpetrated by the Brigades have been fairly indiscriminate. They draw no distinction between military and civilian targets or between occupied territories and the State of Israel. By choosing "soft targets" (i.e., civilians in Israel or Israeli settlers on the West Bank) and carrying out suicide bombing campaigns on Israeli soil, the attacks actually strengthened the resolve of the Israelis to continue their fight against Palestinian opposition (Poland 2004).

Suicide Bombings

Since the onset of the al-Aqsa Intifada, suicide bombings have become the most popular method of mass-casualty attack against Israel. The Brigades have industriously promoted suicide attacks, or "martyrdom operations," as heroic acts and have, in effect, turned martyrs (*shuhada*) into folk heroes, owing mostly to the massive media coverage that instantly results from such attacks. Leaflets distributed by the Brigades following a suicide attack take responsibility for it and publicly praise the martyr (*shahid*) who carried it out. Videotapes made by the bombers on the night preceding an operation have become high-demand popular-culture

items. Posters are typically hung on public walls in order to reinforce the sense of pride and achievement, as well as the newfound cult status of the martyrs, who demonstrated their unwavering faith in Allah by giving their life for the liberation of Palestine.

Between November 2001 and December 2006, the Brigades claimed responsibility for at least twenty-three suicide bombings against civilian targets in Israel and in or near the Gaza Strip, as well as on the West Bank. The Brigades have perpetrated several joint attacks with other militant groups considered terrorist by the United States, including Hamas (an Arabic acronym for Harakat Al-Muqawama Al-Islamia, or Islamic Resistance Movement—an outgrowth of the Palestinian branch of the Muslim Brotherhood), the Palestinian Islamic Jihad (or PIJ, whose leaders operate primarily from Syria), and the Popular Resistance Committees (or PRC, Gaza Strip militant Palestinian groups also springing from Fatah). The Brigades have even received limited support from Hizballah (or "Party of God," based in Lebanon).

The very first suicide attack perpetrated by the Brigades took place at the Vadi Ara Junction on November 29, 2001. It was carried out as a joint operation with the PIJ and claimed three lives. In 2002, the Brigades took responsibility for nine bombings, mostly in Jerusalem and Tel Aviv. The total death toll attributed to the Brigades between January and June 2002 was thirty-six. That year alone, they noticeably perpetrated two-thirds as many attacks as Hamas had between 1999 and 2002. They further distinguished themselves by becoming the first Palestinian group to use a female bomber, or *shahida*—a term coined by Yasser Arafat—in the January 27, 2002, Jaffna Road suicide bombing. When the Brigades realized that Hamas was becoming a more prominent actor of the Second Intifada and jeopardizing their reputation among the public by resorting to suicide bombings, they decided to upstage Hamas and thus co-opted suicide bombings in a lurid and highly sensational fashion by using adolescent girls and women as human bombs, which the Koran forbids Islamists to do.

In 2003, only two bombings were perpetrated; both occurred in Tel Aviv. The first one, on January 5, targeted the central bus station. The second one, on April 30, was a joint Brigades-Hamas operation that targeted civilians at a local club called Mike's Place. Together they killed twenty-six people.

Hamas and the Brigades collaborated more frequently in 2004, carrying out four bombings—a double operation on March 14, known as the Ashdod Port massacre, and two bombings at border-crossing points in the Gaza Strip on April 14 and 17—killing fifteen people. Three more suicide attacks were carried out by Brigades members in Jerusalem: on buses (January 29 and February 22) and at French Hill Junction (September 22), claiming twenty-one additional lives. The 2004 death toll credited to the Brigades was thirty-six—as high as in 2002.

In 2005, three suicide bombings evidenced a heavier outside involvement in Brigades operations. On January 13, 2005, a bombing at the Kharni Passage near Gaza, which was orchestrated by the Brigades with the help of Hamas and the PRC, killed six Israeli settlers. On February 25, 2005, the "Stage Club" bombing on the seaside promenade of Tel Aviv killed five people; it was the result of the renewed collaboration between the Brigades and the PIJ and the first instance of a Hizballah connection. On August 28, 2005, a bombing in Beer Shiva targeting the central bus station caused no casualties but injured dozens of people. The operation was a joint Brigades-PIJ attack. The total death toll for 2005 was eleven.

.On March 30, 2006, the Brigades continued their suicide terror campaign with a bombing in Kdumim, which killed four people. On April 17, 2006, the PIJ and the Brigades joined forces again to carry out a bombing at the Tel Aviv old central bus station that killed eleven people. On July 14, 2007, Al-Aqsa leaders agreed to a cease-fire with Israel when Israeli Prime Minister Ehud Olmert granted a conditional pardon to 178 terrorists in the Palestinian Authority territories.

Female Suicide Bombers

On January 27, 2002, Yasser Arafat addressed over a thousand Palestinian women at his Ramallah compound. His speech emphasized the significance of the role of women in the Intifada and exhorted Palestinian women to actively participate in armed resistance operations against the Israeli occupying forces. He declared, "Women and men are equal. You are my army of roses that will crush Israeli tanks! Shahida all the way to Jerusalem!" That same day, Wafa Idris, a twenty-eight-year-old divorced paramedic in the Palestinian Red Crescent Society and Fatah activist, became the first Palestinian woman to carry out a martyrdom operation, on Jaffna Road in Jerusalem. The blast killed an elderly Israeli man and wounded 131 people. Although Idris did not leave a videotaped message prior to fulfilling her mission, the Brigades claimed responsibility for the attack. Idris instantly became a heroine throughout the Arab world.

The use of female bombers demonstrated a tactical shift by those loyal to Arafat and served to increase their credibility and popularity with the general population. By creating an army of female suicide bombers during the first two years of the Second Intifada, Arafat's al-Aqsa Martyrs Brigades achieved a level of equality with the more radical religious elements that sought to depose Arafat as president of the Palestinian Authority. Arafat's Tanzim militia and the al-Aqsa Martyrs Brigades were thus able to achieve the status of martyrdom that was growing increasingly popular throughout the West Bank and Gaza (Victor 2003).

Whereas the use of women as suicide bombers is not a new phenomenon (it was first documented in Lebanon in 1985), it is not supported unanimously across the Arab world. Nonetheless, Idris and every Palestinian female bomber after her—all sponsored by the Brigades, Hamas, or the PIJ—have been idolized and hailed as role models for Palestinian women and the oppressed in general. Idris was openly celebrated by Yasser Arafat, and her self-sacrifice was celebrated by Saddam Hussein and other Arab political leaders. The Palestinian Authority even honored her through the creation of a university program titled Shahida Wafa Idris Course for Fatah Women Cadres. Forty-six women graduated from the program in 2005. Concerts were broadcast on PA television, summer camps and parades were organized as a tribute to Idris, and courses on democracy and human rights were dedicated to her at al-Quds Open University.

In 2006, the Brigades reportedly established a special suicide unit composed exclusively of women and received full support from Fatah leaders. Masked women claiming to be Fatah members held a press conference in July 2006 to announce the creation of a martyrdom unit boasting 100 members and expected to grow significantly in the near future. The women declared that they were preparing suicide attacks against IDF personnel "in retaliation for the Israeli aggression and crimes against our people in the Gaza Strip." They also openly targeted Hamas, which they accused of being responsible for the assassination of a Brigades member earlier that month.

Child Suicide Bombers

The Brigades have additionally singled themselves out by training and using child suicide bombers. Since the outbreak of the Second In-

tifada, children under the age of eighteen have been involved—directly or not—in the perpetration of over thirty successful suicide attacks. In addition, Israeli security forces have allegedly thwarted dozens of attacks by Palestinian teenagers.

The recruitment of Palestinian youths has been made easier over the years by their systematic indoctrination through government-controlled news and entertainment media, carefully devised anti-Israel curricula, and summer camp programs designed to methodically mold them and prepare them for the unavoidable armed conflict against Israel. The active recruitment and steady involvement of children in Palestinian militant actions and terrorist missions against the Israeli military and civilians have been at the center of an international debate on human rights in general and the rights of children in particular. Whereas Human Rights Watch (HRW) has reported no evidence of the systematic recruitment or use of children by the Palestinian Authority, the Coalition to Stop the Use of Child Soldiers (CSUCS), which counts HRW as a member of its steering committee, documented at least nine suicide bombings involving the use of Palestinian children as combatants between October 2000 and March 2004. Additionally, the Palestinian Human Rights Monitoring Group (PHRMG) has persistently claimed that the Brigades have recruited, trained, and used children as fighters and suicide bombers, as have Hamas, the PIJ, and the Popular Front for the Liberation of Palestine (PFLP).

Using children as civilian shields is a cruel and barbaric practice prohibited by Article 28 of the Geneva Convention. The 1989 United Nations Convention on the Rights of the Child (CRC) prohibits the recruitment and direct involvement of children under fifteen years of age in hostilities and armed conflicts. Additional treaties make the indirect involvement of children illegal as well. Many countries have raised the minimum age for involvement in armed conflict to eighteen. Nearly all the members of the United Nations have signed the CRC; Somalia and the United States have not.

Developments Since 2006

In late 2006, violence escalated not only between Palestinian militants and IDF security forces but also between competing Palestinian groups within the West Bank and Gaza Strip. In October 2006, leaflets were distributed to announce that the Brigades intended to assassinate top leaders of Hamas. On November 22, 2006, IDF shot and killed a Brigades member as they were attempting to process a PIJ commander who was arrested in Jenin. A ceasefire was imposed in Gaza on November 26.

On December 7, 2006, the Brigades formally warned Israel against attacking the al-Aqsa Mosque and threatened to retaliate should the holy shrine be targeted by IDF raids or further desecrated by Israel-led archaeological digs. According to Palestinian news reports, the Brigades "urged citizens in the area surrounding the mosque to cross the fences and pray in the mosque and do their utmost to counter Israeli attempts at Judaizing Jerusalem and reconstructing the supposed Solomon Temple." On December 14, 2006, in a refugee camp close to Nablus, elite IDF soldiers killed a Brigades commander, Mohamed Ramaha, as well as several members of the group, thus illustrating Israel's continued use of the debatable terrorism prevention method known as targeted or selective assassination.

On December 24, 2006, the Israeli prime minister, Ehud Olmert, rejected a proposal by military leaders to allow the IDF to return fire on Palestinian militants launching Qassam rockets from the Gaza Strip into nearby Israeli cities and communities. Olmert indi-

cated that he was confident that PA president Mahmoud Abbas would promptly address the rocket-launching issue and put an end to it. This approach, in effect, modified the IDF rules of engagement to better fit the framework of the cease-fire and more significantly prevented the IDF from reacting to Palestinian attacks as it used to (i.e., by ordering aerial strikes and sending in artillery units). Abu Ahmed, the Brigades leader in the northern Gaza Strip, declared that his group would respect the cease-fire ordered by President Abbas. He nevertheless added that they would uphold their right to retaliate against any type of Israeli aggression and renew their efforts to force Israel's complete withdrawal. On December 27, 2006, after two teenagers were critically injured by Palestinian rocket fire, Olmert recanted his decision and allowed Israeli forces to carry out select anti-rocket operations aimed at militants in Gaza.

Cécile Van de Voorde

See also: Al-Qaeda; Islamic Fundamentalism; Terrorism.

Further Reading

Davis, J. *Martyrs: Innocence, Vengeance, and Despair in the Middle East.* New York: Palgrave Macmillan, 2004.

Hoffman, B. *Inside Terrorism.* New York: Columbia University Press, 2006.

Julian, Hana Levi. "Female Suicide Bomber Organization Founded by Fatah." *Israel National News,* July 10, 2006.

Klein, Aaron. "Olmert Lets Army Stop Terror Rockets After Boys Critically Injured." *World Net Daily* (Jerusalem), December 27, 2006.

Martin, G. *Understanding Terrorism: Challenges, Perspectives, and Issues.* Thousand Oaks, CA: Sage, 2006.

Palestinian Human Rights Monitoring Group. www.phrmg.org/.

Palestinian Media Watch. www.palwatch.org.

Poland, J.M. *Understanding Terrorism: Groups, Strategies, and Responses,* 2nd ed. Upper Saddle River, NJ: Prentice Hall, 2004.

Shahar, Y. *The Al-Aqsa Martyrs Brigades: A Political Tool*

with an Edge. Herzliya, Israel: Institute for Counter-Terrorism, 2002.

Simonsen, C.E., and J.R. Spindlove. *Terrorism Today: The Past, the Players, the Future,* 3rd ed. Upper Saddle River, NJ: Prentice Hall, 2006.

U.S. Department of State. *Country Reports on Terrorism: Foreign Terrorist Organizations.* Washington, DC: Government Printing Office, 2005. Available: http://www.state.gov/documents/organization/65479.pdf.

Victor, B. *Army of Roses: Inside the World of Palestinian Women Suicide Bombers.* New York: Rodale Books, 2003.

Weiner, J.R. *The Use of Palestinian Children in the Al-Aqsa Intifada.* Jerusalem: Jerusalem Center for Public Affairs, 2000. Available: http://www.jcpa.org/jl/vp441.htm.

White, Jonathan R. *Terrorism and Homeland Security: An Introduction.* Belmont, CA: Wadsworth, 2005.

Al-Qaeda

Al-Qaeda means "the base, the law, or the foundation." It is also the name of a transnational armed group created in 1988 by Osama bin Laden that carries out deadly and indiscriminate terrorist attacks throughout the world. Bin Laden is a Saudi Arabian Islamist militant of Wahhabi faith and is on the Ten Most Wanted Fugitives list established by the FBI. The aim of the group created by bin Laden is to universalize Islam through jihad and defend Islamic territories against Western influences and invasions. The group resorts to deadly attacks and is known for the four simultaneous attacks carried out on American soil on September 11, 2001.

Al-Qaeda's network is extensive, as it relies upon small cells scattered around the world. It is also known under other names, such as Qa'edat al-Jihad, Maktab al Khidamat, International Islamic Front for Jihad Against Jews and Crusaders, Al-Jabhah al-Islamiyyah al-'Alamiyyah li-Qital al-Yahud wal-Salibiyyin, Group for the Preservation of Holy Sites, Islamic Army of the Liberation of Holy Places, and Islamic Army for the Liberation of Holy Shrines. The organization's militants lead a *jihad* (in this case, meaning "Islamic war") and call themselves Qa'edat al-Jihad, which means "the base for jihad."

History

The origins of the group can be traced back to the 1979 invasion of Afghanistan by Soviet troops. In 1984, the Jordanian Palestinian sheikh Doctor Abdullah Azzam, bin Laden's instructor and a preeminent figure of the Muslim Brotherhood, created in Peshawar, Pakistan, the group Maktab al Khidmat lil Mujahidin al-Arab (MAK), funded by bin Laden. Its goal was to train mujahideen and Muslim fighters to lead the jihad in Afghanistan against the Soviets who had invaded an Islamic territory. MAK hosted and trained Muslim fighters coming from around the world. It was also funded by Middle Eastern countries, the United States, and the CIA, as it was perceived as a rampart against communism. Some experts even say bin Laden himself received training from the CIA.

Soon the organization extended from a logistical and financial support to a war organization: With the end of the Soviet occupation of Afghanistan in 1989, some members of the organization wanted to carry on with the defensive jihad all over the world. The Afghan Service Bureau, the other name of the MAK, evolved. Several organizations grew from this movement, and one of them became al-Qaeda in 1988. The two leaders of MAK, bin Laden and Azzam, disagreed on what had to be done next: bin Laden wanted to lead a globalized jihad that included nonmilitary actions; Azzam wanted to focus on military actions solely. Azzam was killed with his two sons in a car explosion, leaving the path clear to bin Laden.

Besides a new name and a new organization, al-Qaeda developed a new strategy by expanding terrorist actions and the targeting of noncombatants throughout the world. Many small

A video capture from a tape collection acquired by CNN depicts a May 26, 1998, press conference held by three high-ranking al-Qaeda officials: (left to right) Ayman al-Zawahiri, Osama bin Laden, and Mohammed Atef. Other tapes in the collection show suspected members engaging in weapons training, conducting poison gas experiments, and making TNT. (*CNN via Getty Images*)

organizations were created to support al-Qaeda. Bin Laden and his new organization began looking for new war fronts to lead a jihad. At the time, bin Laden used his own funds for the movement, as he came from a wealthy family and was a businessman.

At first, al-Qaeda remained in Afghanistan to train its members, while bin Laden went back to Saudi Arabia, until he had to leave the country. Indeed, in 1990, bin Laden criticized Saudi Arabia, labeling it an infidel for inviting foreign troops onto its soil during the war in Kuwait. He left the country for Sudan with many of his followers. Al-Qaeda grew in Sudan; it had many businesses, thanks to bin Laden's contacts, and became financially stronger. The group was threatened with dissolution when in 1996 bin Laden was asked to leave Sudan,

accused of participating in Hosni Mubarak's attempted murder.

The group moved back to Afghanistan and established strong ties with the Taliban. Afghanistan was therefore a safe haven for al-Qaeda, and bin Laden reinforced its structures. From Afghanistan, its militants were sent to continue the jihad throughout the world. For example, fighters went to Bosnia during the war to defend and expand Islam. In Bosnia, al-Qaeda had the opportunity to test its fighters for the first time. It had limited success, but it was then ready to turn to the next phase: global expansion of the jihad.

Al-Qaeda carried out many terrorist acts in the world before the September 11, 2001, attacks. The United States government retaliated in vain. It was only in 2001 that the U.S.

government decided to begin a War on Terrorism to get rid of the threat. It decided to attack Afghanistan to destroy al-Qaeda bases. Most of al-Qaeda's top members were either killed or arrested, but the United States and its allies soon discovered that the organization had many cells spread throughout the world. Bin Laden could not be found.

The group has extended its reach and is present in many countries, including Iraq. Al-Qaeda militants are said to have bombed the International Committee of the Red Cross and United Nations headquarters in Iraq, in October 2003 and August 2004, respectively. Since then, al-Qaeda has claimed responsibility for many suicide bombings carried out in Iraq. The leader of the Iraqi insurgents, Abu Musab al-Zarqawi, merged his organization, Jama'at al-Tawhid wal-Jihad, with al-Qaeda in 2004. From Iraq, the movement exported violence to countries such as Morocco, Tunisia, and Jordan. It is believed that al-Qaeda was fully established in Iraq after al-Zarqawi's death in 2006.

Ideology and Aims

Al-Qaeda follows a radical branch of Sunni Islam that has a deep Wahhabist and Salafist influence. Because of its Salafist creed, al-Qaeda's disciples follow only the oldest Islamic sources and interpretations of Islam. The organization is Wahhabist in the sense that its militants and leaders believe in a pure and uncorrupted form of Islam and strive to follow the Prophet's example and to live according to interpretations hard-liners have of his life.

Al-Qaeda has become the symbol of international terrorism since the 2001 attacks. The aims of the organization are to eliminate secularism from the Arab world and foreign influences from Muslim countries, fight against the unbelievers and infidels to protect and expand Islam, and reestablish the caliphate. The caliphate is an ancient system of government based on Islamic law (sharia) under the lead of an imam or a caliph. The Taliban's Afghanistan was supposed to be the model state for the caliphate.

Al-Qaeda believes that the secular and corrupted regimes in the Arab world are the consequences of the Western world's influence. Therefore all non-Islamic regimes, including non-Muslim and Western regimes, are enemies of al-Qaeda. They believe it is their duty to lead a global jihad against Western countries. Al-Qaeda also seeks to free three holy places from foreign influences: Jerusalem, Mecca, and Medina This fight takes place on Muslim soil as well as abroad, as the so-called negative influence must be curbed and suppressed. Countries such as the United States are enemies, as they are perceived by the group as being responsible for promoting secularist theories and advocating the separation of state and church. These ideas are perceived as a threat to Islam, as is the invasion and occupation of the Arab world by foreign troops. Attacking them and killing their citizens is part of the jihad.

Al-Qaeda says it leads a defensive jihad: it fights to defend Islam and oppressed Muslims throughout the world. In that sense, the organization leads what in bin Laden's view is a defensive war, considered to be a duty for Muslims. The group draws its ideology mainly from conservative Islamist scholars who encourage offensive jihad: al-Qaeda abides by Qutbism, an ideology inspired by Sayyid Qutb. Qutb was a leading intellectual and a member of the Muslim Brotherhood, a transnational Sunni movement that favors waging jihad in conquest.

Bin Laden issued the first declaration of jihad against the United States in 1996. He also denounced the situations in many places, such as Kashmir, Palestine, Somalia, and Bosnia, and issued several *fatwas* (binding religious edicts) regarding the political situation of those countries, although he does not have the authority to do so as he is not a legal scholar. With these fatwas, al-Qaeda has reinterpreted Islam and Islamic law to justify defensive jihad and the killing of civilians.

The Structure

Osama bin Laden is the head of al-Qaeda; the theoretician is Ayman al-Zawahiri, a physician, author, poet, and former head of the Egyptian Islamic Jihad. It is not possible to give an exact number of al-Qaeda's militants or to gauge the size of the organization, but it is estimated that between 20,000 and 60,000 militants have been trained in camps or fought in Afghanistan. Not all were al-Qaeda members, as it is possible to fight in the name of the group without belonging to it. Some speak of 3,000 members worldwide.

There is a military committee that deals with training, weapons, and strategies; a business committee; a law committee to review Islamic law; a fatwa committee to issue edicts; and a media committee. There is a *shura,* a council that discusses and approves actions; the head of this council is Ayman al-Zawahiri.

The group uses the Internet to raise funds, recruit, inform, and so on. There is also a broad use of video and media, such as al-Jazeera. The group issues regular statements and publications to explain its aims to the world. There is, for example, a February 1998 fatwa written by al-Zawahiri and bin Laden stating that it is the duty of Muslims to kill American citizens and their allies everywhere around the world. Al-Qaeda has many bases around the world where it trains its militants. Its fighters have been seen in Algeria, Chechnya, the Philippines, Indonesia, Somalia, Yemen, Kosovo, and Bosnia.

Because of the structure of al-Qaeda and its globalization—and to escape detection—the group's actions are prepared and carried out by independent military operating cells that do not need authorization from above to act. The call to jihad is general, and there is no need

to be a member of al-Qaeda or to be affiliated with the organization to carry out actions in its name. It helps sympathetic groups and is known to support and foster groups abroad. It encourages and praises terrorist attacks carried out throughout the world. The terrorist actions in Morocco and in Bali were committed with al-Qaeda's blessing.

There is some confusion regarding the structure of the organization: some experts describe it as very structured with a wide reach, while to others it is not cohesive and has failed to expand. Many organizations claim to be linked to al-Qaeda or to act in its name, but their claims cannot be confirmed. No one can confirm whether al-Qaeda operates across continents as a chain of interlocking networks or whether it is a loose-knit organization. Individual groups, or cells, appear to have a high degree of autonomy; they raise their own money, often through crime, and make contact with other groups only when necessary. The organization is now decentralized and relies on many cells spread around the world. That is why many experts believe the organization to be in transition, and the fact that al-Qaeda has lost many leaders to the War on Terrorism reinforces this belief. Many think the fact that al-Qaeda works now through small cells is extremely dangerous, as these units are hard to locate and have an "entrepreneurial spirit" (Cronin 2004). The idea is that the al-Qaeda of today is more of a model or inspiration. Therefore, some experts wonder about its capacity to carry out any other mass-scale terrorist attacks. Others think that al-Qaeda controls these small cells and that the London bombings in July 2005 are proof that it can still strike on a massive scale. In contrast is the failed attempt to bomb a Northwest Airlines flight from Amsterdam to Detroit in December 2009 by a twenty-three-year-old Nigerian man who was linked to al Qaeda. There is as a result much debate about al-Qaeda among experts: some believe that the core structure of al-Qaeda has disappeared as a result of post-9/11 measures and that the organization is now made up only of small, self-radicalized cells, which are dangerous but unable to carry out a substantial attack; others believe that al-Qaeda is as dangerous as ever and is probably reconstituting in Pakistan. Recent events—including military offensives in Waziristan (the tribal region along the Pakistan-Afghan border) in late 2009–early 2010, terrorist attacks in Peshawar in October 2009, and the presence of a Taliban army near Islamabad—demonstrate al-Qaeda's resurgence in the area.

Finances

There was a time when the funding of al-Qaeda came from bin Laden himself with the support of the U.S. and Pakistani secret services. When MAK evolved into al-Qaeda, bin Laden became the main provider. Today al-Qaeda finances its actions through both legal activities (e.g., legitimate businesses, Islamic "charities") and illegal activities (e.g., drug trade, money laundering, illicit sale of diamonds). Funds also come from private donors.

Efforts to control financial transactions have been limited. When al-Qaeda's assets have been frozen or seized, the organization has diversified its activities and found ways of avoiding detection. For example, the movement engages in smuggling or uses *hawalas* (informal money transfers), which are almost impossible to track because no promissory instruments are used.

Actions and Operations

Al-Qaeda has committed or claimed to have committed several terrorist acts. It was associated with the car bomb attack on the World Trade Center in 1993, the destruction of the Khobar Towers in Saudi Arabia in 1993, and the 1995 assassination attempt against Egyptian president Hosni Mubarak (1981–). In 1996, al-Qaeda issued (through bin Laden's voice) threats against the United States and foreign troops stationed in Islamic areas. A fatwa was issued in 1998 to lead a war against the West and the Jews: the World Islamic Front for Jihad against the Jews and the Crusaders. Al-Qaeda also presumably attacked the U.S. embassies in Dar es Salaam, Tanzania, and Nairobi in 1998. The United States responded by attacking an al-Qaeda base in Afghanistan, without harming the organization much. In 2000, al-Qaeda bombed the USS *Cole* off the coast of Yemen. After the attacks on the U.S. homeland in 2001, the group was blamed for subsequent terrorist acts in Madrid (2004), London (2005), Algiers (2007), and elsewhere, in addition to a number of foiled attempts.

Al-Qaeda favors wide-scale terrorist attacks against civilians but has also practiced assassinations, guerrilla warfare, and suicide attacks. It has an interest in biological weapons as well as nuclear.

Conclusion

There have been many governmental attempts to dismantle al-Qaeda before and since 2001; legal, financial, and military steps have been taken in the name of the War on Terrorism. As of 2010, however, the network was still very much alive and its leader still at large.

When, in 2001, Afghanistan was invaded by allied troops, al-Qaeda was disabled for a while, and the network of communications seemed crippled. But al-Qaeda has gone successfully through that phase, from a territorially based, centralized group to a decentralized organization gathering small groups driven by the same ideal. For some al-Qaeda is today an umbrella organization gathering groups connected by the same aims, ideals, and methods. Some analysts have suggested that al-Qaeda is now itself an idea—a sort of model to follow but no longer a structured organization. Other experts believe al-Qaeda has the capacity to regenerate and reorganize.

Most efforts to suppress al-Qaeda have forced

the organization to respond by forming smaller, more autonomous cells that are more difficult to detect. Therefore, the organization today has a limited ability to carry out spectacular actions, but it is also more difficult to detect, especially as the cells tend to act independently.

Anicée Van Engeland

See also: Al-Aqsa Martyrs Brigades; Bin Laden, Osama; Islamic Fundamentalism; Mujahideen; Terrorism.

Further Reading

Benjamin, Daniel, and Steven Simon. *The Age of Sacred Terror: Radical Islam's War Against America.* New York: Random House, 2002.

Blanchard, Christopher M. *CRS Report for Congress: Al Qaeda—Statements and Evolving Ideology.* Washington, DC: Congressional Research Service, Foreign Affairs, Defense, and Trade Division, January 26, 2006, updated 2007. Available: http://www.fas.org/sgp/crs/terror/RL32759.pdf.

Bonney, Richard. *Jihad: From Quran to bin Laden.* New York: Palgrave Macmillan, 2004.

Cronin, Audrey. *CRS Report for Congress: Foreign Terrorist Organizations.* Washington, DC: Congressional Research Service, Foreign Affairs, Defense, and Trade Division, February 6, 2004. Available: http://www.fas.org/irp/crs/RL32223.pdf.

Gunaratna, Rohan. *Inside Al Qaeda: Global Network of Terror.* New York: Columbia University Press, 2002.

Hoffman, Bruce. "The Myth of Grass-Roots Terrorism." *Foreign Affairs* 7:3 (May/June 2008): 133–38.

Ibrahim, Raymond. *The Al Qaeda Reader.* New York: Broadway Books, 2007.

Katzman, Kenneth. *CRS Report for Congress: Al Qaeda—Profile and Threat Assessment.* Washington, DC: Congressional Research Service, Foreign Affairs, Defense, and Trade Division, August 17, 2005. Available: http://www.fas.org/sgp/crs/terror/RL33038.pdf.

Riedel, Bruce. *The Search for Al Qaeda: Its Leadership, Ideology, and Future.* Rev. ed. Washington, DC: Brookings Institution, 2010.

Rollins, John. *Al Qaeda and Affiliates: Historical Perspectives, Global Presence, and Implications for U.S. Policy.* Washington, DC: Congressional Research Service, February 5, 2010. http://www.fas.org/sgp/crs/terror/R41070.pdf.

Sageman, Marc. *Leaderless Jihad: Terror Networks in the Twenty-first Century.* Philadelphia: University of Pennsylvania Press, 2008.

Anti-Abortion Violence

The term *anti-abortion violence* refers to the advocacy of threats or attempted or actual violent attacks against those who provide, receive, or support abortion, with the intention of intimidating, injuring, or killing those targets in order to exact retribution or justice, influence changes to the law, or prevent or end abortions. Such attacks typically involve bombings, arson, assassination through shootings, invasion, vandalism, assault, death threats, kidnapping, or burglary. Anti-abortion violence is most prominent in the United States but has occurred in other countries, including Canada. It is typically committed by what the FBI terms "single-issue terrorists." Most perpetrators are male and religious and have theological justifications for the violence, referred to by some of its perpetrators, advocates, and supporters as "pro-life" violence.

There are a number of organizations associated with anti-abortion violence, such as the American Coalition of Life Activists and the Missionaries to the Preborn. However, violent attacks on abortion providers have typically been committed by lone individuals or "lone wolves," —those on the fringes of the pro-life movement or those belonging to informal groups. The most notable examples of anti-abortion activists who have used violence (e.g., terrorism) include John Salvi, Rev. Paul Hill, Michael Griffin, Rev. Michael Bray, James Kopp, and Eric Rudolph. Those who commit anti-abortion violence are often labeled extremists to differentiate them from the other wings of the anti-abortion or pro-life movement—the mainstream and militant wings. The mainstream wing is made up of religious and political organizations like the National Conference of Catholic Bishops' Committee for Pro-Life Activities and the National Right to Life Committee, which pursue activism and change through legitimate and nonviolent legal and political means such as lobbying and campaigning. The militant wing is made up of organizations such as Operation Rescue, the Pro-Life Action Network, and Lambs of Christ, which employ confrontational direct-action tactics such as blocking clinic entrances and harassing providers and patients.

History of Violence

Anti-abortion violence in the United States began in the aftermath of the *Roe v. Wade* Supreme Court decision, which legalized abortion in 1973. According to the National Abortion Federation, between 1977 and 2009 there have been 8 murders, 17 attempted murders, 41 bombings, 175 arsons, 97 attempted bombings and arsons, 391 cases of invasion, 1,429 cases of vandalism, 2,057 cases of trespassing, 100 butyric acid attacks, 661 anthrax attacks, 184 cases of assault and battery, 416 death threats, 4 kidnappings, 157 cases of burglary, 526 stalking cases, 14,293 cases of hate mail and harassing calls, 345 cases of e-mail or Internet-based harassment, 160 hoax devices or suspicious packages sent to providers, and 643 bomb threats. The first known incident was an arson attack on an Oregon clinic in March 1976 by Joseph C. Stockett, who was convicted and imprisoned for two years. This was followed by four arson attacks in 1977 and three arson attacks and four bombing in 1978, but there were no convictions in any of those cases. On February 15, 1979, in Hempstead, New York, the first legal clinic opened and was subjected to an arson attack by Peter Burkin. Burkin was acquitted of attempted murder and arson and found not guilty, by reason of insanity, of arson and reckless endangerment.

The first attack on an individual took place in 1982, when Don Benny Anderson, Wayne Moore, and Matthew Moore—using the moniker Army of God—kidnapped Dr. Hector Zevellos and his wife in Granite City, Illinois. The victims were released after a week, and Anderson was convicted

on charges of kidnapping, as well as three clinic bombings in Florida and Virginia. This was the first use of the name Army of God, and in the decades that followed, the name frequently appeared on death threats and claims of responsibility, becoming the most prominent anti-abortion terrorist "organization." In its first decade, between 1984 and 1994, the Army of God was associated with bombings of and arson attacks against one hundred clinics. It has been debated whether the Army of God was a formal organization or merely an identification for individual terrorists to use, but experts agree that it was the latter.

Joseph Scheidler's Pro-Life Action Network named 1984 the Year of Fear and Pain; in that year alone there were twenty-five clinic bombings and arson attacks. They included the "Christmas Bombings" of two Pensacola, Florida, clinics on December 25, timed for Christ's birthday and named the Gideon Project after the Old Testament story of Gideon. Those bombings were committed by the Pensacola Four: James and Karen Simmons, Matthew Goldsby, and Kaye Wiggans, who were convicted for the bombings and conspiracy. The same year, Rev. Michael Bray, pastor of the Reformed Lutheran Church in Bowie, Maryland; Thomas Eugene Spinks; and Kenneth William Shields carried out eight bombings, in Virginia, Washington, D.C., Maryland, and Delaware. Bray used the name Army of God in the Virginia attack, and the name was used again that year in another series of bombings, as well as on a death threat against Supreme Court Justice Harry Blackmun, who wrote the *Roe v. Wade* decision. In 1988, John Brockhoeft bombed a clinic in Pensacola, Florida, and in 1990 another in Cincinnati, Ohio. Those bombings, for which he was convicted and imprisoned, made him a hero with the *Brockhoeft Report* newsletter named in his honor (Blanchard 1994, p. 100).

The 1990s represented the most violent period and saw the first assassination of an abortion provider, on March 10, 1993, in Pensacola, when

Rescue America activist Michael Griffin shot and killed Dr. David Gunn. In response to the murder of Gunn and the trial of Griffin, former Presbyterian minister Rev. Paul Hill and thirty-three others, including Michael Bray, signed Hill's "defensive action statement," which declared that the murder of abortion providers was "justifiable homicide" in defense of the unborn. Also in response to Gunn's murder, activist Joseph Scheidler held a summit in Chicago for anti-abortion leaders, which focused on violence and led to the formation of the more militant American Coalition of Life Activists. While most anti-abortion terrorists have been male, in August 1993, Oregon housewife Rachelle "Shelley" Shannon committed a series of arson and acid attacks on clinics. She also wounded Dr. George Tiller of Wichita, Kansas, in a failed assassination attempt. On July 29, 1994, Paul Hill killed Dr. John Britton and his escort-bodyguard James Barrett at the Ladies Center in Pensacola. Hill was convicted and on September 3, 2003, executed for the murders. Bray, released from prison in 1989, served as spokesperson for Hill and Shannon. Also in 1994, defrocked Catholic priest David Trosch, founder of Life Enterprises Unlimited, sent a letter to Congress promising a period of "massive" killing of abortion providers, abortion and women's rights groups, the president, the attorney general, Supreme Court justices, and the manufacturers of intrauterine devices and the morning-after pill. The same year, Missionaries to the Preborn leader Matthew Trewhella called for the formation of militias at the United States Taxpayers Party convention in Wisconsin and began organizing firearms training. In December, John Salvi shot up two Brookline, Massachusetts, clinics, killing two and wounding five.

By the end of the 1990s, anti-abortion terrorists had alienated the more mainstream activists, leading to a shrinking in the ranks of the latter, while the former became more militant and violent. On January 16, 1997, two bombs exploded outside a clinic in Sandy Springs, Georgia, injuring seven people. The attack was later tied to a mail bombing of the New Woman All Woman clinic in Birmingham, Alabama, on January 29, 1998. The bombing injured nurse Emily Lyons and killed guard Robert Sanderson—the first bombing fatality. The Army of God claimed responsibility for both attacks. The suspect Eric Robert Rudolph, affiliated with the Christian Identity movement of the extreme Right, was captured in May 2003. Rudolph, who pled guilty, was convicted and sentenced to life in prison in 2005 for the bombing of the two clinics, the Atlanta Olympics, and an Atlanta lesbian bar. Also in 1998, James "Atomic Dog" Kopp, a devout Catholic, shot and killed Dr. Barnett Slepian in his Buffalo, New York, home. Kopp spent five years on the run and was included on the FBI's Ten Most Wanted list before being brought to trial in 2003. A letter of support for Kopp was posted on the Army of God Web site. His lawyer attempted to turn the trial into a public debate on justifiable homicide, but Kopp pled guilty and received twenty-five years to life. In addition to his murder conviction, in June 2007 he was sentenced to a second life term on federal charges for violating the Federal Freedom of Access to Clinic Entrances Act. He was also a suspect in the sniper shootings of doctors in Vancouver, Winnipeg, and Hamilton, in Canada.

In February 2001, escaped convict Clayton Lee Wagner sent over 500 bogus anthrax letters signed by the Army of God to abortion clinics and posted death threats against forty-two providers on the Internet. He also claimed responsibility for the anthrax envelope sent to congressional offices and media outlets post-9/11. Wagner was arrested in December 2001, convicted, and ultimately sentenced to fifty years in prison on charges of weapons, theft, and escape and, in 2003, fifty-one federal terror charges. On April 25, 2007, Paul Ross Evans attempted to blow up the Austin Women's Health Center in Texas. When he was arrested, the Texas Joint Terrorism Task Force found him in possession of the addresses of other potential targets, including those of a stem cell researcher, a pornography company, and an Austin-based attorney who argued *Roe v. Wade,* the case that continues to have symbolic significance for anti-abortion terrorists.

Religion and Anti-Abortion Violence

The religious affiliations and beliefs of violent anti-abortion activists are primarily Christian, particularly fundamentalist Catholic, Protestant, and Mormon, as well as more extreme theologies such as Christian Deconstructionism, Dominion Theology, Christian Millenarianism, Apocalyptic Catholicism, and Christian

Identity. Reconstructionism is the dominant theology among violent activists, including Michael Bray and Paul Hill. Reconstructionism emerged from Orthodox and Reformed Presbyterianism and rejects the enlightenment separation of church and state, desiring a reconstruction of society in which the Bible is the basis of law and theocracy the form of government. Christian Reconstructionists are postmillennial, believing that in order for Christ to return, it is necessary to make the world a Christian kingdom through social and political activism. The founding text is *Institutes of Biblical Law*, written in 1973 by Rousas John Rushdoony. Its more mainstream strand is referred to as Shaefferism, but violent activists follow the work of Gary North, who believed that the movement needed to prepare for "political and military confrontation." Abortion,

Anti-abortion picketers gather outside of Florida State Prison on September 3, 2003, to protest the execution of former Presbyterian minister Paul Hill, who was convicted of the 1994 murder of abortion provider Dr. John Britton and his bodyguard. Hill expressed no remorse for his crimes and believed he would be rewarded in Heaven for his actions. *(Matt Stroshane/Getty Images)*

which is a capital crime in Reconstruction-ism, provides a central battle front. Dominion Theology is linked to Reconstructionism but exists on the lesser extremes of the spectrum. It holds that Christianity must assert the dominion of God over all things, including society and politics. Christian Millenarianism, which informed the Gideon Project, is, unlike Reconstructionism, premillennial. It holds that only Christ can usher in the new millennium and create a kingdom of God on earth. As such, Christians must take action to prepare for Christ's arrival and judgment. Apocalyptic Catholicism combines elements of Catholicism and Protestantism to justify violence. Leading proponents include James Kopp and David Trosch. One specific strain is related to the miracle of Fatima, which sees abortion as a sign of the apocalypse and stopping abortion as a way of staying God's hand. Christian Identity is a racist, anti-Semitic, and antigovernment theology that emerged from British Israelism; it holds that Jews are the spawn of Satan and America is an Aryan promised land. Christian Identity was popularized by extreme Right groups such as Posse Comitatus, Aryan Nations, and The Order. Eric Rudolph is a noted example of an Identity-based anti-abortion terrorist, and the Phineas Priesthood, a biblically inspired and armed strategy that has its origins in the Identity movement and theology, was employed by Paul Hill. Christian Identity also provides a theological link between the anti-abortion movement and the extreme Right.

Violent anti-abortion activists use a wide variety of sources to justify their actions and communicate and develop strategies, including the Bible, manifestos, periodicals, the Internet, and fiction. The majority of anti-abortion violence is justified through biblical sources, which are used to provide divine authority, motivation, and justification. Primary biblical sources are the stories of Gideon, Herod, and Phineas. In Gideon, from the book of Judges, the protagonist slays those who offered infant sacrifices to Baal, providing a model for anti-abortion violence. Herod, who slaughtered the innocents of Bethlehem in an attempt to kill Christ, provides activists with a biblical model for the demonization of abortion providers. The Phineas story from the book of Numbers in the Old Testament sets the paradigm for a divinely inspired judgment and mission. In the story, the priest Phineas kills an Israelite and his Midianite wife in order to enforce and restore God's law and punish violators.

Movement Material and Sources

A number of manifestos have been written by movement activists. Michael Bray wrote two such documents: *Ethics of Operation Rescue,* a moral call to rescue the unborn, and *A Time to Kill,* an ethical justification of violence. As the second title indicates, Bray found inspiration from the book of Ecclesiastes. Although it has been neither confirmed nor denied, Bray is also thought to be the author of the *Army of God Manual,* which provides instructions on how to manufacture explosives and chemical weapons. It has been printed in several forms; it has also appeared in the anti-abortion newsletter *Media Bypass* in 1999.

In addition to *Media Bypass,* there are a number of periodicals produced by those associated with or implicated in anti-abortion violence, including *Prayer & Action Weekly News,* run by David Leach, which serialized John Brockhoeft's prison diaries. Connected to this was the *Brockhoeft Report,* which was edited by Rachelle Shannon. Another main periodical was *Life Advocate,* coedited by Andrew Burnett, the cofounder of American Coalition of Life Activists, and Paul deParrie. *Life Advocate* publicly advocated violence and supported Paul Hill. As well as writing, Michael Bray also edited *Capitol Area Christian News.* In the December 1992 issue, Bray even printed an article detailing the use and effects of butyric acid, an increasingly popular weapon.

The Internet provided a new forum for anti-abortion activists. The most notorious Web site was Neil Horsley's Nuremberg Files, which lists the names and addresses of those considered pro abortion. In addition to providing activists with the details of potential targets, the names on Horsley's site represent a list of defendants for the Nuremberg-like trials that he proposed. The Web site was shut down in February 1999 on the grounds that it encouraged violence after a red line appeared through Slepian's name the day after his murder. In addition to the Nuremberg Files, the other major Web site is an Army of God site run by Alabama-based Donald Spitz, on which claims of responsibility and statements of support have appeared.

Fiction, particularly that dealing with violence, also plays a significant role in the anti-abortion movement. One novel is *Rescue Platoon*, a futuristic story of a holy war against abortion that was serialized online by David Leach of *Prayer & Action Weekly News*, which also published *ARISE!* Blending fact and fiction, the story includes the execution of a character named Paul Hill (prior to the real Hill's execution) and the mobilization of the Rescue Platoon into service as the Army of God, which attacks clinics and doctors and fights the federal government and National Guard alongside the real Republic of Texas militia. Another novel is *Gideon's Touch*, about a premillennial battle in America, written in 1995 by Ellen Vaughn of *Christianity Today* and former Nixon adviser Charles Colson. *Gideon's Touch* begins with the murder of a female abortion provider and follows its effect on the pro- and anti-abortion forces in the government, as well as the fate of two brothers—Alex Seaton, an anti-abortion terrorist who is killed by federal agents, and his brother Daniel, a nonviolent pro-life minister

who is charged with conspiracy in relation to his brother's terrorist activities. In another nod to real events, the novel uses the Gideon Project's "God's will" defense at Daniel Seaton's trial.

Mapping Mainstream, Militant, and Extreme Anti-Abortion Activism

Although it is necessary to distinguish between mainstream, militant, and extreme or violent anti-abortion activism, the relationship between them is the subject of much discussion and debate. While some mainstream activists, such as Richard Doerflinger, assistant director of the Office of Pro-Life Activities of the National Conference of Catholic Bishops, denounce violence publicly, others, like the conference itself, have blamed clinic bombings on the existence of the clinics. In another example of lines being blurred, Wiley Drake, a California-based Baptist minister, signed the Army of God letter of support for James Kopp and later became vice president of the mainstream Southern Baptist Convention. Many violent activists have had membership in militant organizations such as Operation Rescue (many also signing Paul Hill's declaration) and Rescue America (including Michael Griffin). While some experts implicate the militant wing in violence, many pro-violence activists, such as Michael Bray and the American Coalition for Life Activists, reject their nonviolent tactics. Beyond the movement, the policies and positions of the government in relation to anti-abortion violence have also been called into question. During the Reagan administration, abortion-rights groups accused the administration of downplaying anti-abortion violence when the head of the FBI, William Webster, refused to classify clinic bombings and arson as terrorism. Moreover, Reagan made anti-abortion statements and at the same time refused to condemn bombings. As a result, he was accused of legitimizing the cause and providing tacit approval to violent activists.

While violent anti-abortion activists are considered extremists, it is not because they are necessarily linked to the white supremacists, neo-Nazis, and anti-government patriots of the extreme Right, although there are overlap and relationships. The most notable example is the case of Eric Rudolph, viewed by the Southern Poverty Law Center and Dallas Blanchard, sociologist and expert on anti-abortion violence, as symbolic of the merger of the two movements based on a shared enemies list. This is evident in *Prayer & Action Weekly News*'s call for the formation of militias to resist government attacks on farmers, loggers, miners, fishermen, small businessmen, patriots, and the unborn. Other anti-abortion activists have also embraced the extreme Right. Matthew Trewhella of Missionaries to the Preborn has called for the formation of militias, and Tim Dreste, leader of the American Coalition of Life Activists, is also captain and chaplain for the First Missouri Volunteers militia. Eric Rudolph is not the only extreme Right activist to become involved in anti-abortion activism. *Jubilee,* a Christian Identity publication, declared its support for Paul Hill; Idaho-based Phineas Priests bombed Planned Parenthood offices in Spokane, Washington, in 1996; and Willie Ray Lampley, leader of the Oklahoma Constitutional Militia, was convicted for a conspiracy to bomb abortion clinics, as well as gay bars, the Southern Poverty Law Center; and the Anti-Defamation League the same year. Yet not all on the extreme Right are committed to the cause unconditionally; White Aryan Resistance has called for justice for abortionists except in the case of nonwhite abortions.

Aaron Winter

See also: Christian Identity Movement; Christian Right; Millennialism; Rudolph, Eric Robert; Terrorism.

Further Reading

Blanchard, Dallas A. *The Anti-Abortion Movement and the Rise of the Religious Right: From Polite to Fiery Protest.* New York: Twayne, 1994.

Blanchard, Dallas A., and Terry J. Prewitt. *Religious Violence and Abortion: The Gideon Project.* Gainesville: University of Florida Press, 1993.

Durham, Martin. *The Christian Right, the Far Right and the Boundaries of American Conservatism.* Manchester, UK: Manchester University Press, 2000.

Juergensmeyer, Mar. *Terror in the Mind of God: The Global Rise of Religious Violence.* Berkeley: University of California Press, 2001.

Loucks, Nancy, Sally Smith Holt, and Joanna R. Adler, eds. *Why We Kill: Understanding Violence Across Cultures and Disciplines.* London: Middlesex University Press, 2009.

Mason, Carol. *Killing for Life: The Apocalyptic Narrative of Pro-Life Politics.* Ithaca, NY: Cornell University Press, 2002.

Michael, George. *Confronting Right-Wing Extremism and Terrorism in the USA.* London: Routledge, 2003.

Ross, Jeffrey Ian. *Political Terrorism: An Interdisciplinary Introduction.* New York: Peter Lang, 2006.

Southern Poverty Law Center. "Bombs, Bullets, Bodies: The Decade in Review." *Southern Poverty Law Center Intelligence Report* 97 (Winter 2000): 8–29.

Apocalypticism

Apocalypticism has multiple meanings, but it is commonly thought to refer to the possibility that the world will come to an end in one's lifetime. The Greek word *apokalypsis* translates as "revelation, the unveiling of what was hidden or secret." The book of Revelation, the last book of the New Testament, is a book of apocalyptic prophecies, describing the Second Coming of Christ (also predicted in Matthew 25, Luke 21, and John 16), who will establish a thousand-year kingdom on earth (Revelation 20:1–6), until the Last Judgment.

The author of Revelation, which was most likely written in the first century C.E., identifies himself as John, a Christian exile on the Greek island of Patmos. The book was not immediately accepted in the scriptural canons. Like other similarly popular prophetic writings in the genre of Jewish and Christian revelatory literature (e.g., the nearly coeval Jewish book of Enoch and Apocalypse of Ezra or the apocryphal Apocalypse of Paul and Apocalypse of Peter), the book of Revelation tends to be symbolically and semantically florid and therefore susceptible to multiple controversial interpretations. That is why several early Christian theologians and prominent Eastern Roman bishops like St. Augustine and St. John Chrysostom expressed opposition to or reserved judgment on its inclusion in the New Testament.

Eventually, while other apocalyptic texts were discarded as heretical, the book of Revelation gained wider acceptance in the West, but not in the liturgy of the Eastern Orthodox Church. Martin Luther, an ambitious reformer as well as a skilled theologian, was by no means confident that the doctrinal content of the book was compatible with the orthodoxy of the Christian message: "I can in no way detect that the Holy Spirit produced it," he declared in the preface to various editions of the New Testament, from 1522 to 1527, adding that his spirit "could not accommodate itself to this book," one in which "Christ is neither taught nor known." The vengeful Jesus of Revelation, lashing out against the hedonism and debauchery of a decadent world—which was possibly part of a rhetorical strategy in John's fierce indictment of the Roman Empire and was certainly meant to infuse an eschatological hope in thousands of discouraged Christian believers persecuted by the Roman authorities—seems indeed to have little relation to the peaceful and compassionate Jesus of the Gospels.

Apocalypticism and the War in the Middle East

A literal interpretation of Revelation is today exceedingly popular among millions of American fundamentalists, who believe that they have access to an infallible source of truth. Many of them hold that the signs of the imminent Apocalypse can no longer be ignored and that they can foresee the time of its occurrence through a meticulous reading of Revelation. According to a 2002 Time-CNN poll, only one-third of the U.S. population denied the reliability of the book of Revelation. The *Left Behind* series of novels about the Tribulation before the Second Coming of Jesus has sold 60-odd million copies since the mid-1990s. Other polls show that Apocalypse-inspired Christian Zionism influences the worldview of several million Americans and that as many as 25 million Americans hold that the establishment of the State of Israel has been a God-sanctioned act, resting on the authority of biblical prophecies.

Millions of fundamentalist Christians are strong supporters of the American wars in Iraq and Afghanistan, and many even look forward to an escalation that would involve Israel and Iran. This is because the September 11, 2001, terrorist attacks have invigorated the hopes of End Timers that the clash between Judeo-Christian and Muslim "civilizations" will lead up to the Rapture—the time when the faithful will be swept into heaven, a belief in which stems from a rather arbitrary, fundamentalist interpretation of the scriptures—and, subsequently, to the catastrophic clash of the armies of good and evil on the plains of Armageddon, an unidentified location in the Middle East.

Apocalypticism and Reformation

The rather baffling pervasiveness and persistence of the apocalyptic imagery in American culture attests to the foresight of those founders of the Christian Church who feared that the incendiary tones and content of John's prophecy could be misinterpreted or misused. This trend contrasts rather markedly with the scarcity of apocalyptic motifs in contemporary European culture, where they have been on a downward slide since as early as the Renaissance, with the partial exception of a vibrant, albeit fleeting, revival with national socialism. Now they are embraced by only a disaffected minority. Italian historian Augusto Placanica once remarked that, in Europe, the apocalyptic paradigm survives only in the inmost recesses of the human mind, "in our whispers, in what we say with the most embarrassed discretion: what we dare think, but dare not say" (Placanica 1990).

One is tempted to suggest that contemporary millenarian extremism among Christian fundamentalists in the United States falls along a historical continuum from the first messianic movements of medieval Europe, in the eleventh and twelfth centuries, through the early sixteenth-century Anabaptist revolt in the Westphalian city of Münster, to the seventeenth-century apocalyptic narratives of Reformation Puritans in New England. The Puritans were set on building the "City upon the Hill," namely a model community on the cusp between the Old and the New Age, founded on a covenant with God and on the conviction that the whole of history had been leading up to it. This left an indelible mark on American identity and worldview.

The different evolutions of religious thought and practice in Europe and in the United States may provide a partial answer to the questions of how and why Europe and the United States followed divergent historical paths with respect to millennialism and apocalypticism. Early Calvinists and Puritans maintained that original sin was transmitted by propagation rather than by imitation: the "iniquity of the fathers" would be visited "upon the children unto the third and fourth generation" (Exodus 20:5; Deuteronomy 5:9). The Calvinist interpretation of the doctrine of original sin—the transmissibility of Adam's sin to his descendants—was rigid and inescapable.

In the American colonies, this sometimes translated into determinism and fatalism: Since it was widely believed that God would separate the elect from the damned, regardless of individual merits in this life, certain criminals were thus regarded as born with a constitutional predisposition to break the law, and certain races, such as Native Americans and Africans, as naturally inferior. Puritan ministers also argued that there would be a limited number of the elect, called "visible saints," who contrasted with the depravity of humankind at large. In sum, while Catholics could redeem themselves through good works, contrition, confession, and penance, which would secure forgiveness, absolution, and, ultimately, salvation, Protestants depended on faith alone and could not easily relieve feelings of guilt. They did not believe in the existence of Purgatory, where sinners and miscreants were given a further opportunity to purify their souls. Sins were not simply mistakes that could be corrected but outward manifestations of evil.

Alone before an all-sufficient God and without celestial intermediaries like angels and saints, early Protestants could not easily expiate their sense of guilt. This left them entirely dependent on God and his law, the onus of salvation squarely on their shoulders. The direct relationship with the Creator led many to agonize over the hypocrisy of a course of action designed merely to achieve personal salvation. In the words of Luther, "Even if it were possible, I should not wish to have free choice given to me, or to have anything left in my own hands by which I might strive toward salvation." Furthermore, the considerable influence of the cosmic misanthropy of Luther and Calvin, who were similarly forthright in their portrayal of the mundane human experience as irreversibly wicked and corrupt, meant that Aristotle's and Erasmus's equation of rationality and justice was meaningless, if not itself evil. Calvin went so far as to announce that human nature was "not only destitute and empty of good, but so fertile and fruitful of every evil that it cannot be idle." Not hope for a reward but compliance with divine law would secure salvation. Finally, from a strictly Lutheran standpoint, if the world was spiritually rotten and ruled by the devil, then the most effective way to deal with sin could only be repression: Armageddon would be, as it were, a means to carry out repression on the largest possible scale.

Apocalypticism and American Puritanism

This different theological stance arguably affected the American outlook on social reformism, divine intervention in human affairs, and the larger concerns of social justice. Because they espoused the doctrine of divine election, many Puritan settlers lived in a permanent spiritual crisis, their behavior occasionally verging on the hysterical. They confronted the overwhelming fear of being among the ones who had not been chosen by God at the beginning of Creation—the so-called covenant of grace—and were destined not to heaven but to damnation, no matter how hard they tried to avoid that fate by leading an upright life. Believers were thus compelled to scrutinize the outcome of their initiatives so as to detect signs pointing to their election. The urge to assuage the anxiety about their status convinced many that the clearest indication that they were not doomed to punishment would be the morality and success of the entire community. The belief in collective salvation generated the electrifying feeling that the descendants of the first pilgrims had been chosen en masse to fulfill god's purposes and to inaugurate the kingdom of Christ on earth—"And a King shall reign and prosper, and shall execute judgment and justice in the earth" (Jeremiah 23:5).

Ordinary time evaporated as a result of the emergence of this form of mythic and ritual consciousness built around the belief in an impending turning point in world history and in the ensuing rebirth of human society. Through the injection of a considerable amount of "magic" into a society awaiting its regeneration, selves were transcended in a community of destiny determined to effect epochal changes in the tide of history. They impatiently awaited the coming of a new era, at once within and outside history, and analyzed social issues not in terms of what men actually are but in terms of what they should be and would eventually be if the biblical precepts were duly heeded.

The intransigent moralism of American Puritans—their readiness to use even physical punishment against those who contravened strict and absolute sets of moral rules, their pugnacious legalism and stern inquisitiveness, their self-righteous conviction that they possessed the ultimate truth, their excessive moral perfectionism—generated the constellation of values, habits of thought, norms, and ideals that were the ultimate source of the doctrine of Manifest Destiny, which justified American colonialism. If the United States were the culmination of history, the New Israel where Christ would gather all his forces, then the alleged cosmic mission assigned to the American people by God himself would be to spread across the world its institutions and underlying principles. America would be assigned a central role in the struggle between good and evil, which was in turn part of God's creation. Like that of all other utopias, the sacred, providential American mission was intrinsically antidemocratic and antihumanistic, for it was founded on an ideal configuration of mankind and on the idea of a cosmic fight against evil that could produce hubris and callousness and supported the use of violent means. There was no such thing as human history, only the history of divine Providence. Ironically, this intense sense of responsibility toward the whole universe could be turned against certain categories of people who, because of their rebellion against the Creation, were hardly God's creatures like the others: hence witch hunting, lynching, and the extermination of Native Americans.

The expectation for renewal generally coexisted with a substantial support for existing institutions. The covenant with God that had established the New Israel prescribed that new members would become part of a holy community and would need to keep to the terms agreed upon with God himself, for the very survival of the community depended on that. Wealth and social station were not the product of historical and political circumstances; they were a vocation bestowed upon a person by divine calling.

This form of religious organicism meant that attempts to change the status quo were blasphemous and immoral. This is why the amalgam of a radical revolutionary position with traditionalism that is so typical of apocalypticism does not, by itself, cause turmoil. Apocalyptic believers, because of their reliance on a millennial hope that shores up political quiescence (viz. Revelation 13:10), are more inclined to withdraw from a corrupt society and sometimes attempt mass suicide than to pursue revolutionary action to accelerate the advent of God's kingdom on earth. This was true for the Jonestown community in northwestern Guyana, founded by the Californian sect Peoples Temple under the leadership of Jim Jones; for the Branch Davidians of David Koresh, assaulted and decimated by the FBI in the 1993 siege of their community near Waco, Texas; for the Solar Temple, a secret society based in Switzerland and Quebec; for Heaven's Gate in the western United States; and for the Taiwanese American sect Chen Tao. Alternatively, harsher confrontations with mainstream society may generate paranoid feelings so that opposition is seen as persecutory. Their perpetual antagonism to dominant institutions and lifestyles may then lead them to provoke social conflict in accor-

dance with the nihilistic slogan "The worse, the better." This was the case of the Taborites, who, in fifteenth-century Bohemia, formed an army with the intent of purifying Central Europe; it is also true of the Japanese terrorist sect Aum Shinrikyo, and of neosurvivalists, white supremacists, and adherents of Christian Identity like Timothy McVeigh, who bombed the Alfred P. Murrah Federal Building in Oklahoma City in 1995, killing 168 people.

This millenarian propensity for self-destructive and destructive cruelty is easily explained. The End Times is, by definition, *the* cathartic event, in that it purifies human society and human souls once and for all. But the original Greek noun *kàtharsis* means "purge, selection," and the Greek verb *kathairèo* means "to destroy," indicating that the line between purification and elimination is very thin. Furthermore, the millenarian mélange of Arcadian and utopian sentiments tends to translate into contempt for the present, the hallmark of those people who feel that they are born too early or too late and whose emotional attachments and loyalties have been best described by Nietzsche's Zarathustra: "Higher than love of one's neighbor is love for the remote and for the future" (Nietzsche 1995).

The neutralization of self-determination, which is inherent in apocalyptic thought, also excuses violent behavior. Free will is denied: people are *held by* rather than hold their beliefs, and their self-awareness is "only a flickering in the closed circuits of historical life" (Gadamer 1994). This belief may result in the alienating conviction that humans are helpless spectators of the historical process, whose course cannot be altered by human volition. Active participation in politics to improve things and to transform human consciousness would be pointless, for sinners are locked into their condition and cosmic role, and God controls the unfolding of human history—a cosmic drama consisting of four acts: crisis; divine judgment; the reward of the just and compliant with eternal life; and the retribution of the wayward, forever consigned to hell.

In the early stages of New England's Puritan movement, both the original and the restored purity came from elsewhere, not from free and independent human judgment. Free will was sometimes conceived as not in harmony with the construction of a well-ordered society, which should instead be based on a "free" and voluntary submission to the will of God. Thus, apocalyptic thinking was actually detrimental to social reform because it did not recognize the true value to be gained from personal initiative and from the questionings of received truth. Human plans that were not a response to a divine calling would fall apart, whereas only genuine hope and trust in a divinely predetermined history, together with a great deal of patience, were the key to salvation.

The eschatological character of the apocalyptic spirituality obliged Puritans to grapple with the moral, social, and historical implications of the God-given mission. Social integration and confidence were achieved by propagating the conviction that the inhabitants of New Israel lived at a time when fundamental changes were looming, and ministers could predict when those would occur. What is more, the chosen ones, through their compliance and purity of motives, believed they could become the agents of the unfolding of God's plans and bring forward the Second Coming of the final earthly deliverer, as prophesized by the book of Revelation.

The political and social order was God given and could not be called into question, nor could the authority of Puritan ministers be disputed, since they were divinely appointed messengers and the only recipients of the knowledge of the ultimate truth. Many among their followers, too afraid of sin and damnation to debate the scope of their religious leaders' authority, completely surrendered their independent judgment. The only blessed owners of the future, ministers became moral entrepreneurs and moral crusaders, representatives of social groups who could benefit from the creation of deviance and the exclusion of individuals branded as deviants.

Apocalypticism and Christian Fundamentalism

American anthropologist Mary Douglas has convincingly argued that every culture shapes rituals and symbolic boundaries, which separate what it deems pure ("normal") from what is regarded as polluted ("deviant") (Douglas 2002). American fundamentalism is a case in point. From the start, it exhibited a number of features that would protect the community from the assault of secularization: a fixation with the idea of original purity, the imposition of rigid and arbitrary symbolical and institutional boundaries, the ritualization of everyday life, the demonization of the internal and external other, the inerrancy of sacred texts, a tendency to bend logic to suit the ostensible divine purposes, oppositional sectarianism, the will to absolute power and charismatic leadership. Hard-liners strongly objected to what they believed to be unmistakable indications of moral failure, namely laziness, sloth, waste, poverty, alcoholism, and licentiousness.

Because this apocalyptic logic is characterized by great malleability, doctrinal differences between the North and the South with respect to the understanding and scope of salvation gradually emerged over time. Southerners were more likely to believe that human actions, compared to God's will, were fairly ineffective in terms of personal salvation, and they privileged divine retribution and social vindication, while northerners stressed the importance of individual free will for one's own salvation, as well as for the salvation of everyone else. By and large this discrepancy corresponds to the one described by the German sociologist Ferdinand Tönnies (1855–1936) with the distinction between *Gesellschaft* and *Gemeinschaft,* which roughly translate as "society" and "community." Gesellschaft is the "artificial," heterogeneous, and competitive social milieu of modern urban society, in which ties between individuals are loose and people are held together by personal interest, instrumental rationality, and the social contract. Gemeinschaft is the "natural," organic model of society prevailing in rural areas, which are typified by cultural homogeneity, cohesion, enforced harmony, common objectives, and emotional bonds.

Historically, apocalypticism has served to preserve the attributes of Gemeinschaft (community in modern society). Therefore, it is more likely to affect a comparatively less pluralistic society that values collective good over personal choice and fatalism over human agency, one that divests the actor of choice in order to restore and consolidate spiritual reassurance and the basis of personal and communal identity—that is, a "limited-options culture."

This is what occurred during the first two Great Awakenings, in the 1740s and in the 1820–1840s. This is also the reason literal apocalypticism, or premillennialism—espoused by those who believe that the Second Coming will inaugurate the millennium—which is predicated on the monopoly of truth, irrational fear, inordinate self-righteousness, and in general, a narrow and anxious attitude to life, is poised to dismiss democracy and the rule of law as harmful. The focus is on the period of tribulation preceding the advent of Jesus, on the Rapture of the saints (1 Thessalonians 4:17), and on the threat posed by the Antichrist. In the southeastern states, the transition from Gemeinschaft to Gesellschaft—that is, from a traditional agrarian society to an industrialized society and from an imminent eschatology to

a deferred eschatology—was delayed by about a century. There, the ritualistic, symbolic, and spiritual "collective effervescence" of premillennialism persists to this day, as opposed to the more socially progressive postmillennialism advocated by those who believe that enlightened humankind will inaugurate the millennium and the Second Coming will occur at the end of this inspired age.

This accounts for the fact that the United States is, together with Iran, the only country on the planet with a mass-apocalyptic movement. Most significantly, the rise of the two movements historically coincided, as both the Iranian revolution and the founding of Jerry Falwell's Moral Majority—a conservative Christian organization with strong apocalyptic overtones—took place in 1979, shortly before the election of Ronald Reagan, a self-declared believer in Armageddon.

From the perspective of Christian fundamentalists, there is a clear consistency of purpose in their urgent call for social changes that cannot be procrastinated, their apocalyptic expectations, and the conservative and restorative nature of their movement. Indeed, they all concur to create an all-encompassing vision of life, marking the moral boundaries of the community and reinforcing its collective identity and cohesion. When pursued to its extremes, this logic generates a cultic milieu where everything must be experienced on an all-or-nothing basis. Such a milieu is highly likely to veer toward dystopian developments.

The threat and the promise of the Apocalypse may be of considerable value for those who are incapable or unwilling to adjust to the changed circumstances of a postrural and postindustrial society that is more open, fragmented, heterogeneous, and confusing.

The Apocalypse is therefore a specific social representation that is believed because it is shared, and it is shared because far too many people experience a chronic feeling of discontent, resentment, spiritual hunger, and impending doom. It is one of the possible scenarios of an alternative modernity antagonistic to the diverse, precarious, and unpredictable life typical of liberal democratic societies, one that, all too often, seems outside of one's control and is apt to provoke cognitive anxiety.

Apocalypticists may feel at ease in presuming that increasing levels of personal freedom, the waning influence of the church, and different styles of parental control can be offset by the suppression of temporality: the approaching end of the world completely neutralizes the relevance of human agency and turns back the clock of history to a time prior to the breach of order, to an age of primordial harmony and reassuring moral discipline where each one would find his or her right place in the order of things. In all likelihood, they feel much more comfortable in knowing that their sense of defeat and the mystifying categorical mixture that the globalizing process has brought in its train are only contingent. This shared imaginative (and sedative) vision provides ontological security and soothes their anxieties. This probably also explains why apocalyptic movements, like all social purity movements, generally resurface during times of perceived national crisis.

Apocalypticism as a predictive mechanism need not be accurate: predictions are instrumental to the achievement of social cohesion and spiritual fulfillment in troubled times. Many believe that they are better off knowing that the end is near while clinging to the belief in an ultimate divine justice and interpreting every catastrophe as a welcome sign of the imminent return of Christ. More important, given the temporal proximity of the dramatic resolution of the clash between good and evil, believers find particularly rewarding their role as protagonists of a cosmic drama in which their actions would not be wasted but would instead serve a greater purpose. Millennial expectations truly possess them.

Rather paradoxically, given its goal, the belief in Armageddon thus represents a quest for emotional and psychological satisfaction and for a safe niche—a refuge from the ostensibly greater danger of the moral drift and social degeneration that characterize secularized modernity. It is a vehicle of world-rejecting purification that enables some people to feel that they are more effectively in control of their own destinies.

Stefano Fait

See also: Christian Identity Movement; Christian Right; Christianity; Koresh, David; Millennialism; Weaver, Randy.

Further Reading

Althouse, Peter. "'Left Behind'—Fact or Fiction: Ecumenical Dilemmas of the Millenarian Tensions Within Pentecostalism." *Journal of Pentecostal Theology* 13:2 (2005): 187–207.

Bayer, Oswald. "Freedom? The Anthropological Concepts in Luther and Melanchthon Compared." *Harvard Theological Review* 91:4 (1998): 373–87.

Bock, Kenneth. *Human Nature Mythology.* Chicago: University of Illinois Press, 1994.

Bostick, Curtis V. *The Antichrist and the Lollards.* Leiden: Brill, 1998.

Douglas, Mary. *Purity and Danger: An Analysis of Concepts of Pollution and Taboo.* London: Routledge and Kegan Paul, 2002.

Erikson, Kai Theodore. *Wayward Puritans: A Study in the Sociology of Deviance.* New York: Wiley, 1966.

Gadamer, Hans-Georg. *Truth and Method.* New York: Continuum, 1994.

Gates, David. "Religion: The Pop Prophets." *Newsweek*, May 24, 2006.

Goldfield, David. *Southern Histories: Public, Personal, and Sacred.* Athens: University of Georgia Press, 2003.

Hart, Kylo-Patrick R., and Holba, Annette M., eds. *Media and the Apocalypse.* New York: Peter Lang, 2009.

Morone, James A. *Hellfire Nation: The Politics of Sin in American History.* New Haven, CT: Yale University Press, 2003.

Nietzsche, Friedrich. *Thus Spoke Zarathustra: A Book for All and None.* New York: Modern Library, 1995.

Oliver, W.H. *Prophets and Millennialists.* Auckland: Auckland University Press, 1978.

Tönnies, Ferdinand. *Community and Civil Society.* Cambridge, UK: Cambridge University Press, 2001.

Weber, Eugen. *Apocalypses: Prophecies, Cults, and Millennial Beliefs Through the Ages.* Cambridge, MA: Harvard University Press, 2000.

Wojcik, Daniel. "Embracing Doomsday: Faith, Fatalism, and Apocalyptic Beliefs in the Nuclear Age." *Western Folklore* 55:4 (1996): 297–330.

Aryan Nations

The Aryan Nations is a white supremacist organization that has been designated a "right-wing hate group" by the Federal Bureau of Investigation (FBI). The organization was founded in 1974 by Richard Butler, a Christian Identity preacher who established the Aryan Nations compound in Hayden Lake, Idaho. The white separatist ideas of Aryan Nations call for the creation of a territory solely for members of the white race to live apart from the rest of the United States.

The ideology of the Christian Identity movement helped shaped Aryan Nations; it alleges that members of the white race are the only true descendants of Adam and represent the scattered twelve tribes of Israel. Jews, and other people of color, are descendants of Cain. According to the ideology, the descendants of Cain are inherently evil because Cain is a product of Satan's seduction of Eve.

In addition to advocating white supremacy and separatism, members of Aryan Nations are antigovernment. The government is commonly referred to as the Zionist Occupied Government (ZOG). According to the Aryan Nations Web site, the government is controlled by Jews; thus, only the interests of Jews are reflected in the law. The rights of the Aryan people are not represented by the government. For this reason, members of Aryan Nations do not pledge allegiance to the United States of America and seek to act as an independent nation.

Background

Richard Butler was a World War II veteran working in Southern California as an engineer. He was introduced to the racialist movement and anti-Semitism, inspired by Nazi Germany, at the California Christian Identity Church. The preacher, Wesley Swift, founded the church in the 1940s but changed the name to Church of Jesus Christ-Christian in 1957. Butler worked with Swift for ten years as the director of the Christian Defense League, Swift's Christian Identity organization.

Swift's ideology focused on the separation of the white race from the "mud people" (or people of color) and the Jews. He stated that the Old Testament supported the right of the Aryan people to rule all other races, because they were the only civilized race. In order to save the white race from being ruled by other races, or becoming extinct through assimilation, Swift advocated creating a separate territory in the United States for members of the white race. In the new territory, the mixing of the white race with any other race would not be tolerated. Mixing with other races would constitute a crime punishable by death.

Butler accepted Swift's ideology, and when Swift died in 1971, Butler moved the Church of Jesus Christ-Christian to twenty acres of land in Hayden Lake, Idaho. The area was ideal for the Aryan Nations' goal of creating a racial state because of the rural location and lack of minority residents. Butler hoped to secure the states in the Pacific Northwest, including Idaho, Montana, Wyoming, Washington, and Oregon.

The early activities of the organization revolved around the World Congress of Aryan Nations, an annual summer "festival" held at the compound. The purposes of the event were recruitment and paramilitary training in guerrilla warfare. The popularity of the group increased, and Aryan Nations soon became the headquarters for other right-wing groups. Representatives from a variety of right-wing groups, such as the Ku Klux Klan and Posse Comitatus, attended the annual event. Butler fostered dialogue and support among the various organizations.

In the early years of the organization, Butler implemented a prison outreach program. Along with Robert Miles, a Christian Identity and Ku Klux Klan member, he targeted members of the Aryan Brotherhood who were incarcerated. Members of Aryan Nations would correspond with inmates and distribute Aryan Nations literature in prisons. The prison program continued throughout the 1980s and became a primary goal after some of the members and affiliates of the organization were incarcerated in the 1980s for various terrorist activities.

1980s

In the 1980s, Aryan Nations was trying to establish the identity and goals of the organization. The first annual meeting was held at the compound in 1982. The local residents soon became concerned about the activity of the organization, after some acts of vandalism and harassment of Jewish residents in the county.

Regarding to citizen complaints, Sheriff Larry Broadbent inspected the compound and revealed to local residents some of the group's activities for the first time. In addition to paramilitary training, the compound featured a school in which approximately twenty students were enrolled, a printing operation for the distribution of literature, and about one hundred residents living on the property.

The Kootenai County Task Force on Human Relations formed in 1981 over concerns about the presence of Aryan Nations and the activities at the compound. Its aim was to counter some of the negative publicity northern Idaho was receiving because of the migration of white supremacists to the area and to provide support to any residents who reported harassment because of their race or religion. It continually monitored the group's activity and documented any noteworthy incidents. It contributed to the passage of the Malicious Harassment Law in Idaho in 1983, which made harassment of a person because of race or religion a felony punishable by up to five years in prison.

Bill Wasswuth, a Roman Catholic priest in nearby Coeur d'Alene, became the director of the task force. In 1986, the task force organized a human rights celebration to coincide with the World Congress of Aryan Nations annual event at the compound. After members of The Order, another white supremacy group, were convicted in the mid-1980s on a variety of charges, including racketeering and conspiracy, a new subgroup of Aryan Nations formed, known as the Bruder Schweigen Strike Force II. In 1986, three members of the Strike Force—Robert Pines, Edward Hawley, and David Dorr—were charged with bombing Wasswuth's residence and three other bombings, including one of the federal building in Coeur d'Alene. The publicity surrounding Strike Force activities struck a severe blow to the organization, and members began to move away and form splinter groups.

The Order

In the 1980s, Robert Mathews, a member of Aryan Nations, joined with members of other white supremacy splinter groups to form The Order. The name for the group came from the book by William Pierce called *Turner Diaries,* which features a white revolution by a group called the Order. In the book, the Order is a group of armed militants who plot to overthrow the government. Pierce and Butler were friends, and he was a frequent visitor at the Aryan Nations compound. The book received more publicity after the 1995 bombing of the federal building in Oklahoma City by Timothy

McVeigh and Terry Nichols, who cited it as an influence.

The primary goal of The Order mirrored the novel: overthrow the government and establish an Aryan territory in the Pacific Northwest. The real-life group needed money to purchase weapons, however, and in 1983 launched a crime spree to fund the movement. Members of The Order were responsible for robbing a pornography store in Spokane and a bank in Seattle. They also printed counterfeit money at the Aryan Nations compound; one member, Bruce Pierce, was arrested after trying to pass the counterfeit bills.

In 1984, several members were involved in the robbery of three armored cars (two in Seattle and one in Ukiah, California) and the bombing of a synagogue in Boise, Idaho; no one was injured in any of the incidents. Some of the money was used to buy land for paramilitary training, uniforms, and guns. Members of The Order were also responsible for the murder of one of their own, Walter West, over fears that he would lead authorities to the group. In addition, members of the group shot Alan Berg, the controversial Jewish host of a Denver talk radio program.

The group's demise began when, during the final armored car robbery, Mathews left a pistol behind at the crime scene. The FBI, which had been investigating the crimes by group members, was able to trace the pistol to the organization. Using an informant, the FBI tracked and located Mathews, who was killed during a thirty-six-hour shoot-out with the FBI at his home in Whidbey Island, Washington. The other members of The Order were located and charged with various counts of racketeering, robbery, and murder. Most of the members were convicted and sentenced to long prison terms; David Lane and Gary Yarbrough were convicted of Berg's murder. Thus ended the activities of The Order.

Other Terrorist Activities

In 1984, Aryan Nations members were suspected in a bombing in Boise, Idaho, and a shooting in Denver, according to the FBI's Counterterrorism Division's *Terrorism Report* (1999). Later in 1984, a bombing in Montana by a member of Aryan Nations was thwarted. The following year, an attempted assassination by members of Aryan Nations was prevented in Hayden Lake. Members were also suspected in a 1987 bombing in Missoula, Montana.

1990s

In the 1990s, Aryan Nations experienced an increase in membership, especially among youth. Butler forged alliances with other right-wing groups, such as the neo-Nazi movement, specifically targeting skinhead youth. Along with Tom Metzger, founder of the White Aryan Resistance (WAR), Butler hosted the first Aryan Youth meeting, in 1990. The youth conferences were held around Hitler's birthday and often featured white-power bands. The youth movement reinvigorated the organization, and in 1994, chapters were formed in several states, including Florida, Tennessee, and Michigan.

Although the youth membership increased, struggles within the organization caused splinter groups to form. Some members started their own groups or left the organization entirely, including Charles and Betty Tate, the members responsible for the printing operation and office duties at the Hayden Lake compound. In 1995 Butler's wife died of cancer, prompting him to consider the future of the organization.

Butler remained the leader of the organization until 1998, when ill health caused him to relinquish control of the group to Neuman Britton. Britton served as the leader until his death from natural causes in 2001. The period of turmoil continued for the group when the leadership changed hands and the decision was made to appoint Britton over Louis Beam, considered by many to be Butler's successor.

According to the Southern Poverty Law Center, Louis Beam joined Aryan Nations in the 1980s after serving as a grand dragon in the Texas chapter of the Ku Klux Klan. He was an ambassador for Aryan Nations and during his time with the organization was responsible for establishing a computer network called Aryan Nations Liberty Net. The site contained many useful features, including information about the various chapters, activities of members, and bulletin boards for posting messages.

As one of the most recognized members in the early 1990s, Beam wrote articles advocating a "leaderless resistance," also known as the lone wolf theory, according to which small cells would act without a centralized authority structure and attack targets independently. During the mid-1990s, Beam became increasingly antigovernment in his writing and less popular among members of the movement for his lack of focus on white supremacy ideas. After Britton was appointed to lead the organization, Beam severed ties with Aryan Nations.

Ruby Ridge

In 1992, Aryan Nations received a lot of publicity because of a standoff between United States marshals and Randy Weaver at Ruby Ridge, an incident that eventually ended with Weaver's surrender. Although not an active member of Aryan Nations, Weaver and his wife attended the annual meetings after moving to northern Idaho. During one of those events, Weaver was approached by an undercover agent with the Bureau of Alcohol, Tobacco, and Firearms (BATF), who asked if Weaver could provide sawed-off shotguns for purchase. After meeting with Weaver and identifying themselves, BATF agents offered him a deal on the firearms charges if he agreed to spy on Aryan Nations and report any illegal activities. Weaver refused

and notified the organization that undercover agents were attempting to infiltrate the group.

After Weaver missed his court date due to a typographical error, a warrant was issued for his arrest, and the marshals set up a special operations group to handle it. During a reconnaissance mission on Weaver's compound, a shoot-out took place between Weaver's family and the federal agents. One federal agent was killed, in addition to Weaver's wife and son.

Eventually, Weaver surrendered and went to trial in 1993 on counts of murder, conspiracy, and assault. The jury found him not guilty, in large part due to misconduct by the U.S. marshals, the FBI, and the lead prosecutor in the case. Upon release, Weaver, who had moved his family to Montana, acknowledged that he is a "white separatist," not a "white supremacist," and that his family just wanted to be left alone.

Other Terrorist Activities

A former member and guard of Aryan Nations, Buford Furrow was charged by the FBI for shootings at the Jewish Community Center in Granada Hills, California, in 1999. Furrow injured four children and one employee in the shooting and murdered a Filipino American postal worker, Joseph Ileto, after fleeing the scene. Furrow claimed that he killed the postal worker because he was a member of a minority working for the government.

After the incident, Butler stated publicly that he could not condemn Furrow for his actions, which were that of a "good soldier." Furrow was later convicted and received two life sentences plus 110 years.

Also in 1999, the FBI foiled a plot by Kale Todd Kelly, a member of Aryan Nations, to bomb a federal building and assassinate Morris Dees, chief defense counsel for the Southern Poverty Law Center. Kelly pled guilty to firearms violations and was sentenced to four years in prison on July 30, 1999.

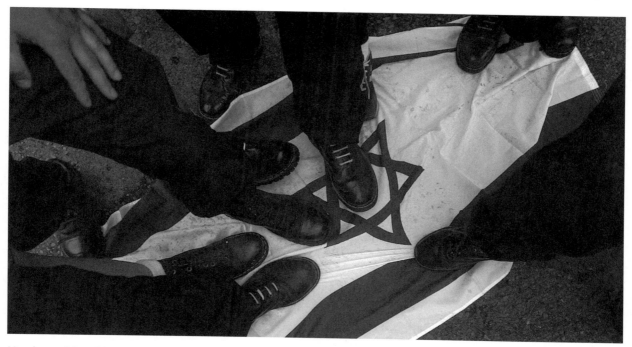

Members of the white-supremacist group Aryan Nations step on an Israeli flag during the 2004 Aryan World Congress Parade in Coeur d'Alene, Idaho. The group bases its claims of supremacy on the Old Testament and advocates separatism from the U.S. government, which they believe is largely controlled by Zionists. *(Jerome Pollos/Getty Images)*

2000s

In 1999, a civil lawsuit was filed against Aryan Nations by Jason and Victoria Keenan, who claimed that they were attacked by Aryan Nation guards. Represented by the Southern Poverty Law Center, the victims alleged that after they stopped their vehicle briefly outside of the compound, the Aryan Nation guards chased and shot at them. The lawsuit stated that the group's leader, Richard Butler, was negligent in the hiring and training of the guards.

In 2000, the jury agreed, and the defendants were awarded $6.3 million in damages. Butler and Aryan Nations were responsible for paying $4.8 million of the settlement. The award effectively bankrupted the organization, and the Hayden Lake compound was auctioned off in bankruptcy court. The Keenans, the major creditors of the organization, purchased the compound in 2001, and the buildings on the property were razed.

After forfeiting the property, Butler moved to a new residence purchased by Carl Story and Vincent Bertollini. The two former computer technology investors from Silicon Valley had moved to Idaho in 1998 and formed a Christian Identity ministry. At the time, they donated a large sum of money to Aryan Nations and worked with Butler to distribute white supremacist propaganda. Butler renamed the organization the Aryan National Alliance, but the bankruptcy and loss of the headquarters damaged the group, and more splinter groups formed.

After Britton's death in 2001, Butler appointed Harold Ray Redfeairn of Ohio the new leader of Aryan Nations. Soon after, however, Redfeairn joined with another member, August Kreis, to form a separate faction. For this infraction, Butler expelled the two members from the organization, although Redfeairn returned to his post a few months later. Redfeairn and Butler died approximately a year apart, in 2003 and 2004, respectively.

During the change in leadership, the group temporarily relocated the Aryan Nations World Headquarters to a rural property in Potter County, Pennsylvania, that August Kreis rented. The Aryan Nations World Congress was held at the new headquarters in 2002. Kreis later relocated the headquarters to Sebring, Florida, after local residents forced the group out.

The group continued to struggle. Kreis formed a competing faction of Aryan Nations with Charles Juba. Juba resigned in 2005, leaving Kreis in charge of the new headquarters of the Aryan Nations, located in Lexington, South Carolina. A different faction, the Church of Jesus Christ-Christian, headquartered in Lincoln, Alabama, claims to be the only group that follows Butler's vision of the Aryan Nations.

During this turbulent period, Aryan Nations continued to receive publicity. In 2003, the FBI arrested and charged a retired Army National Guard intelligence officer, Major Rafael Davila, and his ex-wife, Deborah Cummings, with espionage. The prosecutors accused Davila and Cummings of attempting to transfer classified documents, which included information on chemical and biological weapons, to Aryan Nations. Furthermore, in March 2005, Kreis stated publicly that the Aryan Nations wished to align with al-Qaeda, because of the groups' shared enemies: the Jews and the ZOG.

Tammy Castle

See also: Beam, Louis, Jr.; Butler, Richard Girnt; Christian Identity Movement; Mathews, Robert Jay; Order, The; Posse Comitatus; Terrorism; Weaver, Randy.

Further Reading

Alibrandi, Tom, and Bill Wasswurth. *Hate Is My Neighbor.* Moscow: University of Idaho Press, 2001.

Dobratz, Betty A., and Stephanie L. Shanks-Meile. *The White Separatist Movement in the United States: "White Power, White Pride."* Baltimore: Johns Hopkins University Press, 2000.

Federal Bureau of Investigation, Counterterrorism Division. *Terrorism in the United States.* Washington, DC: Counterterrorism Threat Assessment and Warning Unit, 1999.

Memorial Institute for the Prevention of Terrorism. Available: http://www.mipt.org.

Simi, Pete, and Robert Futrell. *American Swastika: Inside the White Power Movement's Hidden Spaces of Hate.* Lanham, MD: Rowman & Littlefield, 2010.

Swain, Carol M. *The New White Nationalism in America.* New York: Cambridge University Press, 2002.

Walter, Jess. *Ruby Ridge: The Truth & Tragedy of the Randy Weaver Family.* New York: Harper Perennial, 2002.

Walters, Jerome. *One Aryan Nation Under God: Exposing the New Racial Extremists.* Cleveland, OH: Pilgrim Press, 2000.

Zeskind, Leonard. *Blood and Politics: The History of the White Nationalist Movement from the Margins to the Mainstream.* New York: Farrar, Strauss, and Giroux, 2009.

Asia, Central

The region called Central Asia—stretching from the Caspian Sea to western China and from Russia to northern Pakistan—is a good case study of the interaction between competing religions and ways of life. Known for its Silk Road, the centuries-old trade route that connects Europe with China and India, this region has contended not only with its own vast ethnic and cultural differences but also with those of travelers from all parts of the known world. Furthermore, given its vast open spaces and minimal geographical defenses, this region provided an environment for conflict between nomadic peoples and settled populations (who live near a source of water), as well as an opportunity for foreign invasions.

Although the indigenous ethnic groups derive from Iranian, Turkish, and Mongolian peoples, there has also been continual influence from Chinese, Arab, and Russian groups, as well as from the English as they struggled for control of the region against the Russians in the nineteenth and early twentieth centuries. In the later twentieth century, this region received global attention as the location of a drawn-out conflict between a former superpower (the USSR) and resistance fighters (the mujahideen in Afghanistan); it has also harbored Osama Bin Laden, who planned the terrorist attacks of September 11, 2001. Although the Taliban rulers of Afghanistan were overthrown by the United States shortly after the September 11 attacks, they continue to have centers of resistance in Afghanistan and wage a war for control of Pakistan, which has emerged as a nuclear power.

Geographical and Intellectual Boundaries of Central Asia

Central Asia is geographically made up of two parts: a northern region (inner Asia) that consists of steppes and a southern region (outer Asia) composed of desert and mountain terrain. The steppe region (extending from the Ukraine through Central Asian countries like Uzbekistan and Kazakhstan) is well suited for a nomadic, herdsman lifestyle, which also lends itself to political instability and the rise of powerful armies led by charismatic rulers. Some cities that formed around oasis regions were susceptible to being attacked and overrun by the nomadic armies. One of the earliest of such nomadic armies was the Scythians, and others have included the Mongols and the Turks. The southern region is somewhat more favorable to a sedentary or city life, and over the centuries many empires have attempted to rule the area. These include the Greeks, Parthians, Kushans, and Turks. Although names such as "Turk" and "Kushan" are applied to successive groups, it should be kept in mind that each group was composed of numerous smaller ethnic groups with their own view of group identity and authority.

Religious violence in this region is difficult to distinguish from other forms of violence because the religions more closely fit the term "worldview" as a life-encompassing system. The forms of violence in pre-Islamic Central Asia were economically motivated, in that the nomadic groups would raid the city dwellers to secure manufactured goods not available in their homelands. This was supported by two different systems of religious beliefs that justified these two kinds of lifestyle.

Examples of this kind of invasion on a large scale include that of the Huns, led by Attila the Hun (406–453); the Mongols, led by Genghis Khan (1162–1227); and, after conversion to Islam, the Turko-Mongol Timur the Lame (1336–1405), known as Tamerlane in the West. It is difficult to limit any of these as instances of religious violence, but it is also necessary to consider how religion played a role in each. Each of these groups had religious beliefs that included the support of the military leader and his action in conquering others. The case of Timur is especially difficult to categorize, since his use of violence was not limited to attacks on Christians but included other Muslims. He is known as a conqueror who enjoyed slaughter and the razing of cities. Many of the leading Islamic cities of his time, such as Damascus and Baghdad, were conquered and left in a devastated condition that took centuries to recover from. What this illustrates for the study of Central Asia is the complex nature of the violence, which was motivated by a combination of political, economic, and religious concerns. This region was continuously in flux as persons with competing self-identities struggled for control.

From Indo-Iranians to Russians

The steppes of Central Asia have been occupied for thousands of years. The first accounts of the religions of the people there can be found in the Hindu Rig-Veda (ancient Hindu scripture) and the Zoroastrian Avesta (Zoroastrian scripture), in which we are given a description of polytheism (i.e., religious worship of many gods), sun worship, animal sacrifice, and rituals intended to influence the gods. Although this form of polytheism is often accompanied by a belief in the distinctiveness of a specific ethnic group, the need to explain "others," in terms of civilizations in contact and in the market place, required a search for a universal law. One of the first systems that supplied this in the region was Zoroastrianism, a religion based on the Persian worship of the supreme god, Ahura Mazda (associated with the sun), and a pantheon of other gods. Zoroaster, or Zarathustra (c. sixth century B.C.E., although this is debated), sought to purify and reform this religion by emphasizing the worship of Mazda. In this dualistic cosmology (an explanation of origins) there are two eternal (uncreated) beings, Mazda and his twin or counterpart, one responsible for good and the other for evil. This is a move toward greater meaning than polytheism can supply, in that it explains the problem of evil in terms of eternal principles rather than capricious and unpredictable gods. Polytheism's emphasis on rituals and sacrifices is ultimately worthless if the will of the gods is fundamentally changeable.

The other religions that enjoyed influence in this region include Buddhism, Manichaeism, and Nestorian Christianity. The Mahayana form of Buddhism that was most prevalent in Central Asia can easily assimilate polytheism by shifting from gods to bodhisattvas (godlike beings) who aid in the attainment of heaven. However, more consistent understandings of Buddhism that emphasized the impermanence of being were influential in the development of Sufism (a mystical version of Islam). Manichaeism is in many ways a derivative of Zoroastrianism, as it also utilizes the dualistic cosmology of eternal good and evil. Nestorian Christianity is a movement that was rejected by "orthodox" Christians

after much discussion at the council of Ephesus in 431 C.E. Nestorians teach that Christ constitutes two natures and two persons, rather than two natures and one person. Nestorians believed this was necessary to avoid the conclusion that God suffered on the cross, although the orthodox offered alternative solutions to any problems that might pose. Nestorians fled the Mediterranean world and became influential in Persia, where they sent out missionaries along the Silk Road.

In the eighth century C.E. a significant change occurred, as Arab Muslims brought Islam to Central Asia. Since that time, Central Asia has changed from being home to a multitude of religions to being almost uniformly Islamic. Central Asia made Islam its own when the caliphate (centralized government and dynasty) shifted from the Umayyad dynasty in Damascus to the Abbasid dynasty in Baghdad and when groups such as the Turks converted from their tribal religion to Islam. Mirroring what happened on the Arabian Peninsula, Islam encountered polytheism and People of the Book (Jews, Christians, and Zoroastrians). In the case of the polytheists, Islam calls for a pure worship of God and a setting aside of idols as fictions, in contrast to Zoroastrianism, which allows the existence of a pantheon (multiple gods of varying rank and power). Like Nestorian Christianity, Islam rejects the idea of the Eternal Word of God becoming incarnate (taking human bodily form); however, it views Nestorianism as incomplete and in need of the revelation given to Muhammad.

Although there are important variations within Islam, they tend to be about the law and not about theology. Application of the law to the various dimensions of human life was the focus of the Islamic legal scholars, and there are four accepted schools of legal tradition, varying partly due to geographical development in each area. In Central Asia, the Hidaya of Burhan al-

Din al-Marghinani (d. 1197 C.E.) is one of the authoritative sources of legal application to daily life. Islamic law provided a universal context within which laws could be applied to all areas of life and allow for international trade. In many ways, this focus on the law can deemphasize a discussion of the basic beliefs that are presupposed in the law. The assumption seems to be that everyone shares the same beliefs and that what is needed is a knowledge of the law and a will to put it into practice.

The Mongol invasions led by Genghis Khan cannot be overestimated in their impact on Asia and Europe. Although they caused disruption and initiated the spread of the bubonic plague, they also established the means of peaceful trade and sharing of technology. For instance, this new freedom of movement made it possible for Europeans to gain knowledge of gunpowder and the printing press. However, just as the Chinese built the Great Wall to keep out the Mongols, the Mongol invasion motivated the Russians to take measures to guard against a return. This involved expansion eastward from Moscow and the establishment of Russian control throughout Central Asia, a control that did not end until 1989, when the USSR finally disbanded and became the Russian Federation.

Islam and the USSR

The identity of Central Asia had been Islamic for centuries before the Russians appeared and exerted influence. A close study of Central Asia would require noting the many variations of Islam, which are tied to how Islam and preexisting worldviews were interwoven. Yet the Soviet Russians were not concerned about such variations in their persecution of Islam and establishment of the Soviet worldview (1917–1989).

The idea of nation-states organized around a secular and democratic central government was imported to Central Asia by Europeans in the colonial age. As countries such as Afghanistan sought to emerge from English control, they were eager to establish connections with the new communist government in Russia. The Russians supported the idea of alliances that would weaken English influence; however, in the 1920s and 1930s the Soviets sought to limit the influence of Islam in the parts of Central Asia they controlled. Their strategy included the closing of mosques and educational facilities. Local groups could petition to retain a center of worship and a religious leader, but the centers were closely monitored by the state. Although Stalin was unyielding in his persecution of religion, with the advent of World War II, he made concessions to all three theistic traditions. In the 1950s and 1960s the Soviets returned to their program of banning religion. This program included a conversion of mosques into atheist museums and a more sophisticated reliance on sociological study to learn means for undoing religious commitment.

The Soviet persecution of religion in Central Asia isolated this region from the rest of the Islamic world. This led to a unique identity, and also to resistance movements. The "underground" form of Islam that continued to thrive in the context of persecution was called "parallel Islam." This movement was in part due to a general recognition of the failure of Muslim leaders to defend the rights of believers. Especially influential were Sufi leaders, who provided religious education and continued traditional rituals and ceremonies that centered around sacred sites, which filled the vacancy of the forbidden pilgrimage to Mecca.

The final period of Soviet influence included both a fierce guerrilla war in Afghanistan (1979–1989) and Mikhail Gorbachev's attempt to revive moral standards by enlisting both Christian and Muslim religious personnel to help. The USSR's activity in Central Asia reached its peak in 1979, when the Red Army invaded Afghanistan. The resistance fighters, the mujahideen, backed indirectly by the United States, so successfully drained Russian resources that some give them credit for the fall of the USSR. This resistance created a context in which some Muslims sought a return to a "purified" Islamic lifestyle, and the result was the Taliban rule of Afghanistan. The Taliban is a fundamentalist-militant group founded by Islamic theology students in 1994 with the goal of ruling Afghanistan by their interpretation of Islamic law. Like the Soviets, the Taliban was not tolerant of other religions, and one of their actions was to destroy 1,000-year-old Buddhist monuments in 2001.

The Taliban returned to world attention after September 11, 2001, when they took credit for harboring Osama bin Laden (the leader of al-Qaeda and the mastermind of the terrorist attack on the World Trade Center towers). The Taliban were quickly defeated and removed from power by U.S. forces. However, eight years later, they continue to be a presence in Afghanistan and are attempting to control Pakistan through military force.

Although the Soviet era in Central Asia has come to an end, the infrastructure and psychological impact it left continue to have influence. The use of force to require a population to convert to philosophical materialism was predictably unsuccessful. However, this philosophy was itself a response to the fideism (blind belief, or belief without proof) of Orthodox and Western Christianity. Thus, the theme present in the Central Asian history of worldviews held in a fideistic fashion, competing for adherents and punctuated by the use of force to impose a worldview, was continued by the Soviets and is being continued by the Taliban.

Kazakhstan, Turkmenistan, Tajikistan, Uzbekistan, and Kyrgyzstan

The diversity of ethnic groups in Central Asia is partially found in the nation-states that emerged after 1990. In addition to Afghan resistance to the USSR, a handful of other Soviet bloc states in the region demonstrated varying levels of resistance to communism. The largest such state is Kazakhstan, which proclaimed its sovereignty in 1990 but continues to have a communist president suspected of voter tampering. It is in contrast to the communist ideology that Islamic fundamentalists see the need for change and sometimes use violence and terrorism to achieve it. Similarly, Turkmenistan formed a government after 1990 that permitted only Turkmen to participate, and the communist president, Saparmuradi Niyazov, was elected to his office for life. Religious violence in these countries must be contextualized in relation to frustration with the regimes.

Tajikistan, Uzbekistan, and Kyrgyzstan have long-standing ethnic differences but are united by the Fergana Valley and its rich natural resources. The Uzbeks were at the center of Genghis Khan's empire, and the city of Samarkand was Turin's capital. The Sunni Muslims in this region were suppressed by the Soviets, and so after 1991 a commonwealth was formed. However, Russian influence on the government led to dissatisfaction among Uzbeks and an alternative economic union with Kazakhstan and Kyrgyzstan in 1994. The current government of President Islam Karimov has been criticized internationally for human rights violations, and in response to this Islamic fundamentalists have increasingly attempted to overthrow his government. Their goal appears to be the larger unification of the Fergana Valley and the rejection of communist philosophy and government.

Rise of the Taliban and Other Extremist Groups in Central Asia

In 1996, the Taliban imposed its rule on Afghanistan. This group interpreted the Koran through ethnic customs from Central Asia and used force to ensure that the community upheld strict rules about male and female apparel and religious education and restricted the activity of women to the home. Although this kind of group had initially been encouraged by the United States during the Soviet war in Afghanistan, like many other conservative regimes backed by the U.S. to fight the spread of communism, once in power, it limited personal freedom and did not enact a constitutional democracy.

In 1995 a representative of the Islamic Movement of Uzbekistan (IMU), Tohir Yoldosh, appeared in Pakistan. He held a meeting with representatives from groups around the world, including some with officially registered organizations in Germany. He also set up a relationship with the Uighur separatist group, a Muslim fundamentalist society from northwestern China, in 1997. Then in 1999, another meeting was held that brought together the Islamic Movement of East Turkistan and the Islamic Movement of Uzbekistan. At this time, from Kandahar in southeastern Afghanistan, Osama bin Laden promised financial support to these groups, as did the Taliban. A holy war was declared against the Uzbek president and against China. The Chinese government has abolished all such organizations that might be fighting for independence in East Turkistan.

The Taliban sought to aid resistance groups in other former Soviet countries such as Uzbekistan and Kazakhstan. The Jamaat Mojahedin, a terrorist group in Central Asia, was supported by the Taliban in its efforts to spread unrest in Uzbekistan, Kyrgyzstan, Russia, and Kazakhstan. It was not until 2005 that the Kazakhstan government reported having neutralized this group. The group's criminal activities included the trade of illegal drugs and arms, with the goal of earning money to support resistance.

In a 2005 report, a Kazakhstan official said that the biggest threat in the region came from extremist missionaries who promote terrorism as part of their ideology. Some scholars have pointed out that this behavior is a result of resistance to the secular states of modernity and cannot be linked to religious beliefs. However, while it is true that the secular state is the occasion for the promotion of terrorist activity, the goal is a regime such as the Taliban's, where specific religious codes of behavior are enforced through the threat of violence.

Numerous groups operating in the area were identified as promoting terrorist activities. These include Usbat al-Ansar, the Muslim Brotherhood, al-Qaeda, the Islamic Party of East Turkistan, the People's Congress of Kurdistan, and the Islamic Movement of Uzbekistan. Another group, cited as growing in Kazakhstan after 2005, is PureIslam, which is run by Wahhabis. Wahhabism is a fundamentalist form of Islam originating in Saudi Arabia, and its presence in Kazakhstan shows the influence of Islamic groups outside of Central Asia.

Although many of these groups formed around ethnic lines, they find unity in their common cause. In October 2007, Yoldosh (the IMU leader in Pakistan) called members of Islamic groups that use terrorism in the attempt to set up fundamentalist regimes his "brothers." Indeed, having a Muslim president in Uzbekistan is not sufficient, as anyone who does not implement Yoldosh's view of Muslim law is considered an enemy of the faith.

A related issue of religious violence in these regions is the increasing number of suicides by women through the means of self-immolation. Although the exact numbers are unknown, this appears to be an increasing phenomenon in response to frustration with the life assigned to women by groups like the Taliban. Arranged marriages and domestic violence are key causes of these suicides. Indeed, domestic violence is not considered a civil issue; police do not respond to calls because it is a "family matter."

The Taliban's restriction of women to the home and denial of education relegates them to the status of property. Unable to find meaning in this lifestyle, it is unfortunate but not surprising that suicide is contemplated and practiced. The use of self-immolation as the means is an unmistakable manner of communicating the despair that is felt.

Continued Conflict

The continued conflicts in Central Asia raise some basic questions about the region's future. The Soviets implemented a cotton monoculture (growth of cotton to the exclusion of other products, which is harmful for the soil and the long-term economic development of the region) that has had a devastating impact both economically and ecologically. However, the troubles of the region cannot be reduced to socioeconomic problems. The stated purpose of the resistance groups is the imposition of a specific form of Islamic law. Their belief is that this law was directly revealed by God and therefore cannot be questioned. A democratic process is unnecessary for them because it offers choices between different possible laws rather than simply encouraging them to obey what is believed to be the one law from God.

Other groups, including Christian groups, also claim to have special revelations from God. The Islamic Movement of Uzbekistan, as recently as 2007, rejected peacef talks with these other religions, likening them to a drug that kills the pain only for a time. Yoldosh said these groups are involved in a crusade against Islam and must be stopped. The perception is that any form of secular government that encourages the civil protection of minority rights is a conspiracy to silence Islam.

The willingness to use violence to instill one's view of the law is connected to three beliefs: that this is the only law prescribed by God; that violence is an acceptable means to implementing God's law; and that violence will indeed bring about that end. Two problems stand out that seem to raise doubts about the efficacy of this approach. First, the firm commitment to this form of Islamic law is mirrored by the firm commitments of other people to their worldview. The question becomes, How am I to know which view to accept as my view? Simply reiterating that one feels strongly about what one believes is not the same as offering proof of the veracity of those beliefs.

Second, the move from strong commitment to the use of force for implementation relies on a view of humanity that reduces the human to the will. If the human is primarily a will, then that will must be shaped by external force. And yet the variety of beliefs and the rationality of humans persist. Humans will ultimately not be able to will themselves to keep a law that they do not believe is true. Consequently, the first problem reappears: What proof does Yoldosh or any other terrorist leader supply in support of his beliefs? Can a rational dialogue be entered into about the nature of proof and beliefs, God and law, with the aim of coming together to know what is true about these issues? A fuzzy pluralism that ends in a stalemate between numerous worldviews is based on skepticism just as much as the violent assertion of one view; in both cases there is a denial that through the use of reason, humans can reach consensus. Indeed, this kind of solution is rejected by both sides, with governments, such as that of Turkmenistan, "electing" communist presidents for life and terrorists organizations, like the IMU, calling "peace talks" a temporary and failed solution. These partisan and violent politico-religious groups necessarily raise the question, Is there a law under which all humans can live? Although the West appears to be content with secular democracy, under which various groups can have a voice and within which minority religions are protected, this solution is rejected by both the communist governments such as that of Turkmenistan and the IMU.

Central Asia has been a region of intense diversity over the millennia and continues to be a place where these kinds of questions are brought to the forefront through often violent interaction. It is a region that does not allow us to be comfortable with solutions to difference that overlook the need for unity. This is true in both the civil and the religious spheres, especially in a region of the world that rejects a division between these areas of life.

Owen Anderson

See also: Al-Qaeda; Asia, Southeast; Taliban.

Further Reading

DeWeese, Devin A. *Islamization and Native Religion in the Golden Horde.* University Park: Pennsylvania State University Press, 1994.

Foltz, Richard. *Religions of the Silk Road: Premodern Patterns of Globalization.* New York: Palgrave Macmillan, 2010.

Juergensmeyer, Mark. *Global Rebellion: Religious Challenges to the Secular State, from Christian Militias to Al Qaeda.* Berkeley: University of California Press, 2008.

Khalid, Adeeb. *Islam After Communism: Religion and Politics in Central Asia.* Berkeley: University of California Press, 2007.

Thrower, James. *The Religious History of Central Asia from the Earliest Times to the Present Day.* Lewiston, NY: Edwin Mellen Press, 2004.

Williams, John Alden. *Islam.* New York: G. Braziller, 1961.

Asia, Southeast

Southeast Asia is a complex region comprising mainland countries—Cambodia, Laos, Myanmar (Burma), Thailand, and Vietnam—as well as the islands of Brunei, East Timor, Indonesia, Malaysia, the Philippines, and Singapore. Geographically, Southeast Asia lies south of China, east of India, and north of Australia. China's Confucianism has historically been the greatest religious influence in the mainland region,

Mainland Nation	2010 Population
Cambodia	14,494,293
Laos	6,834,345
Myanmar (Burma)	48,137,741
Thailand	65,998,436
Vietnam	88,576,758

Island Nation	2010 Population
Brunei	388,190
East Timor	1,131,612
Indonesia	240,271,522
Malaysia	25,715,819
Philippines	97,976,603
Singapore	4,657,542

followed by Indian Buddhism, and Christianity, which was brought by European colonial powers, most notably the French, Spanish, and Portuguese Catholics. The maritime island nations, on the other hand, are predominately Islamic and Roman Catholic (due to Spanish colonial influence). Today the region maintains a geopolitical bloc known as ASEAN (Association of Southeast Asian Nations). The newest nation in the region, East Timor, is an ASEAN candidate state. The indigenous people are of Austroasiatic, Tai, and Khmer descent but have long been influenced by India and China. As of 2010, according to estimates by the CIA *World Factbook,* the regional population was approaching 600 million.

The aboriginal peoples were primarily animists before contact with Indian and Chinese traders some 2,000 years ago. Hinduism and Buddhism replaced or were integrated into the aboriginal belief systems, especially among those living on the Malay Peninsula. Hinduism was the first official religion in the Khmer Empire in Cambodia, the site of one of the world's most famous Hindu Brahma temples, at Angkor Wat. From the thirteenth to the sixteenth centuries, the Hindu influence spread to the island nations, including Borneo, Sumatra, Bali, and the Philippines. China also had a strong presence in Southeast Asia, bringing Confucianism into the region, in the time before European con-

Country	Religious Composition by Percent
Brunei	Islam (67%); Buddhism (13%); Christianity (10%)
Cambodia	Theravada Buddhism (95%)
East Timor	Roman Catholicism (90%); Islam (5%)
Indonesia	Islam (86%); Christianity (9%); Hinduism (2%)*
Laos	Theravada Buddhism (65%); with Animism (33%)
Malaysia	Islam (60%); Mahayana Buddhism (20%); Christianity (9%)
Myanmar (Burma)	Theravada Buddhism (89%); Islam (4%); Christianity (4%)
Philippines	Roman Catholicism (81%); Islam (5%); Christianity mix (11%)
Singapore	Buddhism (43%); Islam (15%); Taoism (8%); Christianity (15%)
Thailand	Theravada Buddhism (95%); Islam (4.6%)
Vietnam	Mahayana Buddhism (78%); Roman Catholicism (7%); Theravada Buddhism (5%); Cao Dai (2%)

*Hinduism is the predominant religion on the Indonesian island of Bali.

tact. The greatest challenge to Hinduism was the advent of the Islamic influence during the 1400s. The Muslim influence was more passive in Southeast Asia than it was in Arab nations and in South Asia (India, Pakistan, Bangladesh, and Afghanistan) as it was brought there by traders and not imposed through conquest. Beginning in the 1500s, Christianity came to the region with European colonists, including the Portuguese, Spanish, Dutch, French, and British; the American influence came following the Spanish-American War in the late nineteenth century. The *World Factbook* lists the current majority religions in the region.

Generally speaking, contemporary religious violence in the region intensified following World War II, as many of these nations attempted to gain independence from their colonial masters. Hence, political strife has accompanied much of the religious violence during the past sixty-five years. With the world's largest Muslim population residing in this region (some 240 million Sunni adherents), the current twenty-first-century War on Terrorism focuses on the influence of radical Islamic groups, notably the Jemaah Islamiyah (JI) as well as the Moro Islamic Liberation Front (MILF) and Abu Sayyaf. Essentially, Jemaah Islamiyah is a militant Islamic group seeking a pan-Islamic region within Southeast Asia, while the Moro Islamic Liberation Front and Abu Sayyaf are Islamic radical groups in the southern Philippine Islands.

Jemaah Islamiyah

Jemaah Islamiyah is Arabic for "Islamic organization." The group is engaged in an attempt to build a conservative pan-Islamic region consisting of Indonesia, Singapore, Malaysia, Thailand, and the Philippines. The history of the organization dates back to the establishment of Darul Islam and its opposition to Dutch colonialism during and following World War II. The Darul Islam group wanted an Islamic republic following independence from the Dutch in 1948, and its attempt to overthrow the secular government resulted in a civil war that claimed over 27,000 lives. Suppressed by the military dictatorship of Sukarno, the first president of Indonesia (1945–1967), Darul Islam remained underground until the 1970s, when Abu Bakar Bashir joined the organization and used his radio stations to broadcast a call to jihad in Indonesia. Bashir was arrested and imprisoned for his activism, released, and then ordered back to prison in 1985, but he fled to Malaysia. From his Malaysian base, he organized Islamic fighters to fight the anti-Soviet Muslim brigades in Afghanistan. There Darul Islam linked with the Saudi-financed Afghan mujahideen under the leadership of Abdul Rasul Sayyaf—operations that

Members of the terrorist group Jemaah Islamiyah rally in support of their alleged leader, Muslim cleric Abu Bakar Bashir, outside a courthouse in Jakarta, Indonesia, on May 13, 2003. Bashir was convicted on terrorism and treason charges related to the 2002 bombings at a Bali nightclub, but the conviction was later overturned. *(Choo Youn-Kong/AFP/Getty Images)*

were covertly supported by U.S. intelligence agencies. On January 1, 1993, Bashir and Abdullah Sungkar organized Jemaah Islamiyah with veterans of the Afghan mujahideen as their initial members. After President Suharto (1967–1998) retired in 1998, Bashir returned to Indonesia to operate a Muslim seminary (*pesantren*) on the island of Java, as well as to take up the leadership of the Indonesian Mujahideen Council.

Nurjaman Riduan Ismuddin

Nurjaman Riduan Ismuddin ("Hambali") is suspected of being JI's operational chief, especially following Bashir's arrest on terrorism and treason charges. Hambali is associated with the terrorists' operations, including the

October 12, 2002, bombings at a Bali nightclub, which killed 202, and the August 5, 2003, car bombing at the Marriott Hotel in Jakarta, which killed twelve. Hambali was arrested in Thailand following the Marriott attack. Nonetheless, JI continued its attacks on Western targets, including the September 9, 2004, attack on the Australian embassy in Jakarta. Initially, Indonesia was reluctant to join its neighbors and Western nations in labeling JI a foreign terrorist organization, but the attacks in Bali and Jakarta led to its cooperation in the worldwide War on Terrorism. While it is not clear whether JI is an affiliate of Osama bin Laden's al-Qaeda group, JI's terrorist plots, which predate the September 11, 2001, attacks on the United States, include a 1995 plot to bomb eleven U.S. commercial planes flying in Asia. More evidence of its local autonomy is its command structure, which consists of an emir at the top, followed by a governing council (Central Command) with three other councils: religious, disciplinary, and fatwa. Central Command has control of the main brigades (*mantiqis*), which consist of battalions (*wakalah*) and individual cells (*fiah*). There is evidence of a loose confederation of radical Islamic militant groups, including Jemaah Islamiyah, al-Qaeda, the Moro Islamic Liberation Front, Abu Sayyaf, Lashkar Jundullah, and the Kampulan Mujahideen Malaysia, where these groups share training facilities, such as Camp Hudaybiyyah, located in Mindanao in the Philippines.

Cambodia

Cambodia is only now showing signs of political stability following turbulence during the last quarter of the twentieth century. The majority of Cambodians are Khmers, descendants of the Angkor Empire that once dominated much of mainland Southeast Asia. Conflict with its neighbors the Thai and the Vietnamese in the Middle Ages, which resulted in the empire's decline, helps explain the continuing animosities between these parties. The Khmer make up 90 percent of the population of over 14 million. Khmer, the second most widely spoken language in Southeast Asia (second only to Vietnamese), is the official language of Cambodia, where 95 percent of the population are Theravada Buddhist.

Cambodia was once part of French Indochina, a relationship that began in 1863, when the king requested protectorate status from France. It became a part of French Indochina in 1887 and gained independence from France in 1953, following Japanese occupation during World War II.

Cambodia was caught up in the Vietnam War when the United States replaced France as the Western influence in the region, beginning in 1955. When the Vietnam War intensified in 1965, Cambodia was used by the North Vietnamese for portions of its transportation route, known as the Ho Chi Minh Trail. As the United States reduced its presence in Vietnam, the Communist Khmer Rouge intensified its attack on its own people, culminating in the capture of the capital, Phnom Penh. This action resulted in the mass evacuation of all municipal entities in Cambodia and the eventual death of 1.5 million Cambodians through executions, forced slavery, and starvation. The Khmer Rouge also had a brief encounter with the U.S. military during this time. On May 12, 1975, Khmer Rouge gunboats seized the U.S. merchant ship SS *Mayagüez* in international waters in the Gulf of Thailand. After diplomatic efforts failed, the U.S. Air Force undertook a rescue mission that resulted in the death of forty-one U.S. military personnel. Even with this provocation, however, the United States did little to intervene with Pol Pot's Khmer Rouge regime. Ironically, it was the Vietnamese military, the United States's nemesis, that finally rescued Cambodia from Pol Pot's cruel regime with its invasion in 1978. The vast majority of those killed by the Khmer Rouge were Buddhist.

The Vietnamese left Cambodia after a decade of protection from the Khmer Rouge, which still maintained camps in the jungles and along the northern borders with Thailand and Laos. United Nations intervention resulted in the Paris Peace Accords in 1991 and elections in 1993, but continued in-fighting brought down the coalition government in 1997. A second coalition government emerged following national elections in 1998, and the remaining Khmer Rouge militants surrendered in 1999, with many awaiting trial by a UN-sponsored tribunal for crimes against humanity. Elections were held again in 2003 with new elections slated for July 2008. The ruling CPP party won the 2008 elections with 58 percent of the vote, and Hun Sen remained the prime minister. The European Union observers saw the 2008 election process as an improvement over the 2003 elections but still short of international standards.

Cambodia has both a king (King Simamoni), chosen by the Royal Throne Council, and a prime minister. It has a bicameral parliamentary form of government with a national assembly and a senate.

Indonesia and East Timor

Indonesia is the most populous country in Southeast Asia, with nearly 250 million people. It also has the largest Muslim population in the world and is the world's largest archipelagic state. Indonesia was a Dutch colony beginning in the 1600s and remained so until the Japanese occupied it during World War II. Following the war, Indonesia declared its independence, on August 17, 1945, but the Netherlands was reluctant to relinquish its former colony. United Nations intervention resulted in the Netherlands finally recognizing Indonesian independence on December 27, 1949, although Indonesia celebrates the earlier date as Independence Day. The archipelago nation consists of numerous islands (30 provinces) and is multiethnic, the majority Javanese (45 percent) and Muslim (88 percent).

The United States became a major Western influence following Indonesia's independence via U.S. business interests in the oil and rubber industries, notably Standard Oil and Caltex. Leadership over such a diverse population distributed over a wide array of islands required a strong military leader at the beginning of Indonesia's frail democracy. General Sukarno, a popular leader of Indonesia's independence movement since 1927 (who collaborated with the Japanese during their occupation), became the new nation's first president and served from 1945 until he was overthrown in 1967. Discontent with the multiparty parliamentary system erupted in the fall of 1952, when the military attempted to get Sukarno to dissolve parliament. By 1955, three major parties had emerged, with the Communist Party of Indonesia (PKI) being the strongest. In 1957 a failed assassination attempt on Sukarno, with likely U.S. CIA involvement, led to the Gestapu coup of 1965–1967, the assassination of moderate generals, and the eventual extermination of an estimated 500,000 to a million people affiliated with the PKI. The United States under presidents Eisenhower, Kennedy, and Johnson became involved in these events in an effort to curtail the spread of communism in Southeast Asia. General Suharto, the general responsible for crushing the communists in the Gestapu coup, replaced Sukarno as president in 1968. The current chief of state, since October 2004, is President Susilo Bambang Yudhoyono.

East Timor was initially a Portuguese colony, hence the heavy Roman Catholic influence in the province. Portugal retained its colonial status following World War II until East Timor declared its independence on November 28, 1975. The newly independent country was immediately invaded by the Indonesian military and incorporated into Indonesia in July of 1976. Attempts to integrate the Catholics into the Muslim nation led to two decades of conflict and resulted in 100,000 to 250,000 deaths. In 1999, a United Nations–supervised referendum resulted in the vast majority of East Timor voters opting for independence from Indonesia. Between the referendum vote in August and the arrival of a multinational peacekeeping force in September, a military-sponsored reign of terror was conducted, resulting in the destruction of East Timor resources (homes, schools, water supply system, electric grid, irrigation systems), the death of 1,300 Timorese, and the abduction of over 300,000 people, who were forced into West Timor. The violence was quelled by an Australian-led peacekeeping force, and East Timor became internationally recognized as an independent state on May 20, 2002.

Laos

Laos, sandwiched between Thailand and Vietnam, was under the control of Thailand until the late nineteenth century, when the Franco-Siamese Treaty of 1907 established its borders and it was incorporated into French Indochina. Once a monarchy, Laos declared its independence from France in July 1949, and the country became a communist nation in 1975, when the Pathet Lao ("Lao nation") took control. Laos also was involved in the Vietnam conflict, with portions of the country used by the North Vietnamese for its Ho Chi Minh Trail route to South Vietnam. The vast majority of its 6 million people are Theravada Buddhists; tribal Animism is the next most popular religion. The official languages are French and English. Laos's rulers are military generals, and the country is one of the least developed in Southeast Asia, with a poor transportation system and no national rail system. It is part of the lucrative drug trade within the Golden Triangle, which is protected by armed Wa and Chinese smugglers.

Malaysia, Singapore, and Brunei

Malaysia, Singapore, and Brunei were British colonies and protectorates that were occupied by the Japanese during World War II, much like most of Southeast Asia. Malaysia is divided by the South China Sea; the portion on the Malay Peninsula became the Federation of Malaya in 1948, as a British protectorate, and gained independence in 1957. The country Malaysia was formed in 1963 with the consolidation of former British colonies on both the Malay Peninsula and in Borneo. This added Singapore and the eastern Malaysian states of Sabah and Sarawak, excluding Brunei, to the country. Brunei, on the other hand, became a British protectorate in 1888 until its independence in 1984. Singapore left the Malaysia federation in August 1965 and became an independent republic. Today both Brunei and Singapore have the highest standards of living in Southeast Asia. The rest of Malaysia remained a single nation despite its physical division. Half of the population is Malay, followed by those of Chinese heritage (24 percent). The majority of the people are Muslim (60 percent), followed by Buddhists (19 percent) and Christians (9 percent). The nation is run by a constitutional monarchy, and most of the peninsular states have hereditary rulers as well.

Malaysia is experiencing violence among its Muslim population along its borders with Thailand, in the Sabah state in northern Borneo, and from the Moro in the Philippines. Malaysia is also involved in the trafficking of women and children for both the sex trade and involuntary servitude.

Myanmar (Burma)

Burma was part of the British Indian Empire from 1886 until 1937, when it became a self-governing British colony and gained independence from Britain in 1948. The famous 717-mile Burma Road was built by 200,000 Chinese laborers through rough mountain terrain between 1937 and 1938, only to be used by the Japanese when they occupied Burma. Buddhism was introduced into Burma by Indian merchants. Theravada Buddhism was first introduced in what was then southern Burma, and Vajrayana Buddhism was later introduced in northern Burma, along with Hinduism. Burma became unified under King Anawrahta in the eleventh century, when Theravada Buddhism became the national religion. Today, 90 percent of the population of Myanmar is Buddhist. The major ethnic groups are Burmese (68 percent), Shan (9 percent), and Karen (7 percent), with the Shan and Karen being predominately Christian.

Democracy ended in 1962, when General Ne Win overthrew the government, suspended the constitution, and made Burma a socialist state; he ran the country until 1988. The country, renamed Myanmar, has been ruled by the military ever since. The current dictator is Senior General Than Shwe, who has ruled since 1992. When multiparty legislative elections were held in 1990, the National League for Democracy (NLD) won in a landslide, but the military junta refused to turn over power. Instead, the leader of the NLD and presumed prime minister, Aung San Suu Kyi, has been either in jail or under house arrest since then. Civil unrest occurred in August 2007 following the increase in fuel prices, resulting in mass protests led by both prodemocracy groups and Buddhist monks. The ensuing crackdown included raids on Buddhist monasteries. International reaction to the military action resulted in the appointment of Aung Kyi, a moderate, as labor minister; since his appointment, he has initiated dialog with Aung San Suu Kyi. In May 2008, Cyclone Nargis caused considerable damage in Myanmar, especially in the Irrawaddy Delta. Despite the willingness of the United Nations and numerous international aid groups, the ruling military junta refused much of their aid; the aid that was allowed was closely controlled by the military, and what was not saved for the military was sold to survivors.

The government's attack on the Buddhist monks and the raids on their monasteries caused worldwide concern for the safety of those detained. Other religious and ethnic conflict involves the Karen rebels, who operated in and around the Thailand border, and the Indian Nagaland separatists—notably the United Liberation Front of Assam—along the Indian border, who used Myanmar as their sanctuary, as do Burmese Muslim refugees. Human trafficking, including forced or bonded labor and prostitution, is a major problem in Myanmar. Myanmar does not comply with the minimum standards for the elimination of human trafficking and remains the world's second-largest producer of opium and a major source of methamphetamines.

The Philippines

The Philippine Islands, the second most populous nation in Southeast Asia, came under Spanish domination during the sixteenth century, thus creating the largest Roman Catholic population in Southeast Asia. While the Spanish were able to enforce conversion to Catholicism in the northern portion of the Philippines, they never were able to force the conversion of the Muslim population in what was known as Moroland in the southern region, notably the Sulu Archipelago and Mindanao. The Spanish virtually outlawed non-Catholic faiths, forcing Buddhists, Hindus, Muslims,

Animists, and Protestants underground during their colonial reign. The United States had its earliest influence in Southeast Asia in the Philippines as part of the 1898 Treaty of Paris, making the Philippines its first foreign colonial outpost outside the American continent. While encouraging the popular uprising, known as the Katipuneros, that began in 1896, the United States later kept the revolutionaries from gaining power by secretly purchasing the Philippine Islands from Spain in December 1898.

The First Philippine War involved the United States and the Katipuneros, who declared Philippine independence on June 12, 1898. The U.S. suppression of the revolutionary forces for independence continued until 1902. The Second Philippine War was fought in the Muslim South and was not resolved until 1913, when a U.S. civilian became the colonial governor. Deployed U.S. generals who had recently fought in the U.S. West used Indian War tactics for the destruction of entire villages (scorched-earth campaigns), the execution of surrendering prisoners, torture (including waterboarding), and treatment of concentration camps civilians who were thought to be sympathetic with the local revolutionaries. U.S. forces had one of the most disproportionate enemy casualty rates recorded at the time, with fifteen Filipinos killed for every one wounded. The coverage of the atrocities in the world press, along with those associated with the British in the Boer War in South Africa, led to the establishment of the Hague Conventions of 1899 and 1907, which articulated the rules of international and military law and behavior, including the treatment of prisoners and civilians.

Moreover, the famous U.S. generals Arthur MacArthur (U.S. Civil War, Indian Wars), Douglas MacArthur (World War I, World War II, Korean War), Dwight D. Eisenhower (World War II), and John J. Pershing (World

War I) all served in the Philippines during the U.S. colonial era. Arthur MacArthur, Douglas's father, was named military governor of the Philippines in 1900; his son served under him as a second lieutenant and later became the field marshal of the Philippines. Dwight D. Eisenhower, supreme commander of the European theater during World War II, served as Douglas MacArthur's aide when MacArthur was field marshal. John J. Pershing, commanding general of U.S. forces during World War I, served as the last military governor-general of Moro Province (November 1909–December 1913). During the First Philippine War, the U.S. forcefully took over property of the Catholic Church and gave it to U.S. business interests. Nonetheless, Catholicism thrived in the northern Philippines, while Islam survived in the south.

In 1935, the Philippines became a self-governing commonwealth with full independence slated for 1945. World War II and the Japanese occupation delayed independence until July 4, 1946, but the United States continued to play a major role in the Philippines, if only to maintain its two major bases in Luzon: Clark Air Base and Subic Bay Naval Station. The guerrilla forces that fought the Japanese, the Hukbalahap (People's Anti-Japanese Army), participated in the 1946 elections but were thwarted by anticommunist forces and influences, including the United States. This resulted in the Huk Rebellion of 1946–1954 in Luzon and the eventual dictatorship of Ferdinand Marcos, which ended in 1986. Marcos's pro-American stance provided the United States with its most powerful base of operations in Southeast Asia during the Vietnam War. Following Marcos's ousting, American support waned, resulting in the closure of the U.S. bases, the last closing in 1992. Today the Muslim South continues to push for independence, at the same time joining the anti-Western Islamic

jihad with the Moro Islamic Liberation Front and Abu Sayyaf. With the post–September 11, 2001, War on Terrorism, the United States military is again involved in the Philippines, albeit in smaller numbers and in an advisory capacity. The Philippines continues to claim Malaysia's Sabah state in Borneo, but that is a latent issue at this time. Marijuana and hashish continue to flourish in the Philippines, and the country remains a transit nation for heroin and methamphetamine produced within the neighboring Golden Triangle. Today, a small Buddhist population exists among the Chinese and Chinese-Filipino population.

Thailand

Thailand, known as Siam until 1939, has the distinction of being the only country in Southeast Asia that has never been colonized by a Western power. Even during World War II it avoided bloodshed by allying with Japan. Following World War II, it became allied with the United States. Siam became a constitutional monarchy in 1932, the king becoming the chief of staff while the prime minister ran the country along with a bicameral national assembly. Thailand/Siam traces its independence to 1238. It is the fourth most populous nation in Southeast Asia; the vast majority (95 percent) of its 65 million people are Theravada Buddhists, and there is a small Muslim minority. However, the predominantly Muslim southern provinces host separatist activities, including terrorist violence, along the border they share with Malaysia. There are also border disputes with Myanmar (Burma) regarding ethnic rebels and refugees, notably the Karens.

Vietnam

Vietnam, the third most populous nation in Southeast Asia, has a conflicted past extending nearly 5,000 years. During the sixteenth century European powers (Portugal, then France) arrived and replaced the Chinese as colonial powers in what is now Vietnam. France was finally able to consolidate the three sections—Cochin-China in the south, Annam in the central region, and Tonkin in the north—into a unified nation in 1887 and linked the country by road and rail. The French eventually made Vietnam, along with its neighbors Cambodia and Laos, part of French Indochina. The French colonial powers introduced Roman Catholicism into what was a Buddhist region, making it the second-largest Catholic population prior to the communist takeover in 1975.

Prior to World War II, Emperor Bao Dai was the figurehead leader under French colonial rule. He continued in that capacity under Japanese occupation under the Vichy French. Ho Chi Minh and his Viet Minh forces fought both the Japanese and the Vichy French with support from the United States during the war, but that support was withdrawn following the end of World War II, when the United States and Britain supported the return of the French colonial powers. The resistance to continued colonial influence led to the First Indochina War (French War, 1933–1955), which led to the French defeat at the battle of Dien Bien Phu in May 1954, ending the rule of Bao Dai and the French influence in Indochina. The United Nations negotiated temporary north-south divisions in both Vietnam and Korea in 1954, with plans for reunification and general elections slated for 1956. China and the Soviet Union supported the north in both of these nations, while the United States supported the south. With U.S. support, both South Korea and South Vietnam blocked the proposed elections, which would have favored the northern communist powers.

The United States replaced France in Vietnam and played an active military role from 1959 until 1975, when the North Vietnamese Army (NVA) took over the entire country. This was known as the Second Indochina War (American War, 1955–1975). The U.S. initially sponsored Ngo Dinh Diem as president of South Vietnam. The Ngo family was part of the Catholic aristocracy during the French colonial era, with Diem's father serving the emperors Thanh Thai and Bao Dai. Diem's younger brother, Ngo Dinh Nhu, was in charge of the suppressive Can Lao secret police while he and his brother Ngo Dinh Can had virtual control over the ARVN (Army of the Republic of Vietnam) Special Forces. Their autocratic rule and brutal persecution of Buddhist dissidents led to a U.S.-backed military coup, resulting in the assassination of both President Diem and his brother Nhu on November 2, 1963—twenty days prior to the assassination of U.S. president John F. Kennedy. The Tet Offensive of 1968 soured the American public on the war, leading to the eventual pullout of U.S. forces in 1973 and military advisers in 1975, when the NVA took over Saigon. During the Vietnam War, U.S. military forces operated in both Cambodia and Laos, the other French Indochina nations.

Once the United States left, the Vietnamese were embroiled in the Cambodian war from May 1975 until December 1989, when they invaded Cambodia and deposed the Khmer Rouge regime. During that time, Vietnam had an intense battle with China in February and March 1979 when China invaded Vietnam as punishment for its incursion into Cambodia. Vietnam's support for the Cambodian peace agreement in October 1991 led to a lifting of the U.S. trade embargo in February 1994, followed by full diplomatic relations in July 1995. In January 2007 Vietnam became the 150th member of the World Trade Organization (WTO), in which its largest trading partner is currently its former nemesis, the United States.

Most religious conflicts have subsided under communist rule, although today many Vietnamese may be afraid to state their religious affiliation (80 percent do not acknowledge a religious affiliation). Even so, 10 percent are listed as Buddhist and 7 percent as Roman Catholic. Border spats with China, Cambodia, and Laos continue to simmer, including the dispute over the Spratly Islands. Vietnam continues to have a poor record for the treatment of its indigenous mountain tribes, notably the Hmong and Muong.

Larry French

See also: Asia, Central.

Further Reading

Abuza, Z. *Militant Islam in Southeast Asia: Crucible of Terror.* Boulder, CO: Lynne Rienner, 2003.

Blofeld, J. *Mahayana Buddhism in Southeast Asia.* Singapore: Asia Pacific Press, 1971.

Brantl, G., ed. *Catholicism.* New York: George Braziller, 1962.

Jacobs, S. *America's Miracle Man in Vietnam: Ngo Dinh Diem, Religion, Race, and U.S. Intervention in Southeast Asia, 1950–1957.* Durham, NC: Duke University Press, 2004.

———. *Cold War Mandarin: Ngo Dinh Diem and the Origins of America's War in Vietnam, 1950–1963.* Lanham, MD: Rowman and Littlefield, 2006.

Nathan, K.S., and M.H. Kamali. *Islam in Southeast Asia: Political, Social and Strategic Challenges for the 21st Century.* Singapore: Institute of Southeast Asian Studies, 2005.

Porter, D.J. *Managing Politics and Islam in Indonesia.* London: RoutledgeCurzon, 2002.

Rabasa, A.M. *Political Islam in Southeast Asia: Moderates, Radicals and Terrorists.* New York: Oxford University Press, 2003.

Rendu, L. *Hinduism.* New York: George Braziller, 1962.

Ressa, M.A. *Seeds of Terror: An Eyewitness Account of Al-Qaeda's Newest Center of Operations in Southeast Asia.* New York: Free Press, 2003.

Suzuki, B.L. *Mahayana Buddhism: A Brief Outline.* New York: Macmillan, 1969.

Swearer, Donald. *The Buddhist World of Southeast Asia.* Albany: State University of New York, 2010.

Vaughn, B. *CRS Report for Congress: Islam in South and Southeast Asia* (#RS21903). Washington, DC: Congressional Research Service, Foreign Affairs, Defense, and Trade Division, 2005.

Williams, J.A. *Islam.* New York: George Braziller, 1962.

The World Factbook. Langley, VA: Central Intelligence Agency. Available: https://www.cia.gov/library/publications/the-world-factbook/index.html.

Assassins (Hashshashin)

The Assassins were an Ismaili mystic group active in the valley of Alamut, in Iran, from the eleventh to the fourteenth centuries. Ismailis are part of a branch of Shi'a Islam called Ismailism, consisting of the followers of Ismail. The Assassins were part of the Nizari Ismaili branch of Shi'ism, whose founder was al-Hassan ibn-al-Sabbah (1034–1124). Sabbah converted to Ismailism in 1090 and retreated to Alamut, where he created the Assassins community and developed his own religious creed, Nizarism. The Assassins movement was famous for the political assassinations it is said to have carried out. There are debates about whether the Assassins truly existed, but both Sabbah and the group played an important role in the creation, strengthening, and survival of the Nizari branch of Ismailism. The Nizaris are today the strongest of all Ismaili branches.

Etymology

There are several interpretations of the word *assassin*. One says that the word derives from the Persian *hashshashin*, which means "those who use hashish." The martyrs of the group, who committed acts of violence, were called *fedayin* (*feda'i* in the singular form), which derives from *fida*, meaning "sacrifice." The fedayin were said to be addicted to drugs and to commit most of their deeds under the influence. This legend probably derives from Marco Polo, who allegedly visited Alamut and said that Sabbah drugged his men with hashish, especially before they were sent to kill. Marco Polo claims he visited the fortress in 1273; since Alamut fell to the Mongols in 1256, his reports are not reliable. However, he is not the only one to have reported a heavy use of drugs within the community.

For some, then, calling the group Assassins was a way of ill-naming the community.

Others assign the Arabic meaning to the word *assassin*—"the guardians," implying that the community was the "guardian of the secrets." Some contend that the name Assassins simply designated the followers of al-Hassan al-Sabbah: *Hassanisch*. Still others insist that Sabbah called his disciples *assassiyunn*—the ones faithful to the *assas* (a teaching based on the spiritual meaning of the message delivered by the Prophet Muhammed), the Assassins' foundation of faith.

Religious Beliefs

The Ismailis are Shi'a Muslims who seceded from the main branch of Shi'ism when the sixth imam, Jafar, died in 765. They considered Jafar's eldest son, Ismail, to be the next imam, whereas the Twelver Shi'as—followers of the main branch of Shi'ism, which believes in the existence of twelve imams—accepted Jafar's youngest son, Musa-al-Kazim, as the seventh imam. The followers of Ismail are called the Ismailis.

The Assassins were also Nizaris. In 1094, after the death of Caliph al-Mustansir, the eighth Abbasid caliph in Baghdad, the vizier al-Afdal Shahanshah appointed al-Mustali caliph instead of his brother Nizar. The community led by Sabbah in the fortress of Alamut disagreed with the decision, broke their ties with the Fatimid Ismaili regime based in Cairo, and supported Nizar. Thus, followers of this branch of Islam are known as the Nizari Ismailis.

History

Sabbah captured the mountain fortress of Qasir Khan in Alamut in 1090. The reasons for his exile to Alamut are not clear, but many speak of tensions with Vizier Nizam al-Mulk. The fortress was naturally protected, as it was located 6,890 feet (2,100 meters) above the ground, had a very narrow top, and was only accessible by a small and dangerous road. It was called the Eagle's Nest, and Sabbah was named Sheikh al-Jebal, the Prince of the Mountains. This fortress allowed Sabbah and his followers to maintain secrecy and protection. This is why it was so difficult for successive governments to deal with the threat the Assassins soon became. Sabbah was a Persian who claimed descent from a royal lineage, and he asserted his religious legitimacy by initiating many religious reforms within Ismailism through the "new propaganda."

From Alamut, Sabbah and his followers established a community that threatened many political figures through acts of violence. The aim of the sect was to put an end to the Fatimid caliphate in Cairo and the Abbasid caliphate in Baghdad, as well as their overlords, the Seljukids. The community stayed in Qasir Khan until 1256, when the fortress fell to the Mongols of Ulagu.

The struggle against the caliphs of Baghdad and Cairo was led by Sabbah in the name of Imam Nizar (an imam in Shi'a Islam is believed to be appointed by God as his representative on earth). Sabbah and his successors were the imam's representatives. The Nizaris believed that the imam should live in hiding for his protection; this was referred to as *dawr al-satr*, or living in concealment. Nizar actually lived in Alexandria, where he was constantly harassed by Vizier al-Afdal Shahanshah. He was eventually arrested and brought to his brother, Caliph al-Mustali; he died in prison in 1096. From that point, different stories emerge: For some, Nizar had, before his death, designated his son al-Hadi as successor; the son was said to have died in prison as well. It is believed that the grandson of Nizar, al-Muhtadi, later found refuge in the fortress of Alamut. Others say there were no known imams after Nizar and that the period was one of *dawr al-satr*, during which Sabbah and his followers led the community since the imam was concealed and inaccessible. A third version is that al-Hadi became the imam and lived in the fortress of Lamasser. Then his son, Muhtadi, took over the role. For the Nizaris, Hadi and Muhtadi are the twentieth and twenty-first imams, but they remained concealed from the public eye.

The Assassins' creed went beyond religious reforms and political assassinations. They soon expanded and took over the fortresses of Qadmus in 1132 and Maysaf in 1140, both in Syria. Sabbah's aim was to create a network of fortresses throughout Islamic lands. All these fortresses were under constant attacks by caliphs' armies. Sabbah's successor, Kiya Buzurg Ummid, worked on reinforcing this network. There were victories: the Seljuk prince of Aleppo, Ridwan ibn-Tutush, converted to Nizarism.

The Assassins were located mainly in modern-day Iran and Syria. The destruction of their headquarters by the Mongols brought an end to the group, and all the community's records were destroyed. That is why surviving sources from that time are either hostile or indirect. The Assassins recaptured Alamut in 1275 for a while but had to give up, as they had lost all legitimacy. The Mongols captured the fortress of Maysaf in 1260. The final blow was dealt the Syrian Assassins in 1273, when the Mamluk sultan Baybars attacked the last fortresses.

Little is known about the Assassins after 1273. The sect disappeared, but the Nizari philosophy remained. Some followers went to India, where they became the Khojas or Mowlas. Their leader is the Aga Khan, said to be a descendant of Muhammed. Other followers of the cult went to Yemen and founded another community, the Bohras.

Ideology

The Assassins were heretics to the Sunnis because they were Shi'as; they were rejected by the Shi'as because they were Ismailis, and they were perceived as heretics by the Ismailis when they deserted the main branch. As a result,

Muslim scholars have gathered little neutral material about the community. And because all resources and information within the fortresses were destroyed, little is known about its creed. Many scholars believe the Assassins' ideology was a cross between Shi'ism, Sufism, and Sunnism.

Under Sabbah's leadership, the Assassins quickly evolved into a highly organized, secretive, disciplined, and dedicated community of believers. They had elite corps of fedayin, who specialized in political assassinations carried out to overthrow empires and governments. Yet the Assassins were not a purely militant sect of combatants; they were also learned in Islamic sciences.

Sabbah founded a new way of preaching. His creation of the *dawa* (propagation of Islam and invitation to adopt the cause of the *imamat*, a divinely appointed leader) was one of the ideological foundations designed to invigorate his community. It replaced the traditional way of teaching Islamic sciences, which was established during the Fatimid era. This is why the Nizari cult called itself the *al-dawa al-jadida* (the new doctrine). For example, the Assassins insisted on the transcendental nature of God. Indeed, according to them, God was absolute and demanded absolute faith and obedience. This philosophy was perceived as a threat to the rest of the Muslim world, and it was considered heresy to be a member of the Assassins.

The community also developed the doctrine of *ta'lim*, which is often defined as the teaching of the imam. The imam's role was to reveal the esoteric truth: he worked at unveiling the secret meaning of the Koran by explaining its internal dimensions. The Assassins devoted themselves to finding the truth and had a *batin* approach (internal interpretation) to the Koran coupled with a *zahir* approach (external interpretation) to sacred texts. They put an emphasis on spirituality, probably under the influence of Sufism.

The imams and their representatives worked on shaping a spiritual creed for the Assassins. In 1162, Hassan II changed the Nizari religious creed by establishing the Resurrection of Resurrections (Qiyamat al-Qiyamat). He spoke of the hidden meaning (*batin*) of the revelation that had to show the truth (*haqiqat*) and therefore had to discard Islamic law (sharia), symbol of the exoteric, without suppressing it. His successor, Imam Nur al-din Muhammad, continued this spiritual mission until 1210. Imam Jalal al-din Hassan tried to stress the importance of sharia, but his son Ala al-din Muhammad rejected that approach and restructured the doctrine. Ala al-din Muhammad also practiced dissimulation of faith (*taqiyya*), which later became a period of clandestine life to protect the believers.

There were nine degrees of initiation, at the end of which the Assassins' followers received timeless wisdom and hidden powers. The first degree threw new students into a state of doubt: they had to question their knowledge in all fields, and teachers continuously spoke of the hidden truth (*haqiqat*) that had to be sought. At the second level, the student had to discover the inner truth of the Koran given to the imam for guardianship. The third degree was about the nature of the imams and the importance of number seven (as Imam Ismail was believed to be the seventh imam). The fourth degree was about the doctrine of the Seven Prophetic Periods, the assas, the *natiq* (the Ismaili term for the prophet as the promulgator of revelation), and the *samit* (silent imams). At the fifth degree, the student was taught about Islamic sciences and the application of *ta'wil* (elucidation of the inner or esoteric meaning, batin, from the literal wording or apparent meaning of a text, ritual, or religious prescription). The sixth degree criticized the obligations and rites a Muslim should follow, as these were obligations for the "masses." The seventh degree was very important, as it dealt with the teaching of the Assassins' philosophy and their relationship to God. The eighth degree was a development and application of this doctrine with a metaphysical twist. The ninth degree was the completion of the learning process through which the believer became a philosopher.

The imam was God's representative on earth; he had to be a descendant of Nizar. Representing the imam was the head of the cult. Below the main master came the grand priors, who were in charge of a particular district. Then there were three types of chiefs: the main chief (*da'id du'at*), the superior chief (*du'i al kabir*), and the ordinary chief (*du'i*). The propagandists were next. The partly initiated ones were the comrades (*rafiq*), and the uninitiated ones were at the bottom of the ladder—the adherents (*lasiq*) and the fedayin.

The fedayins' training stressed the development of their physical capacities and strength of mind. They were trained not only in military actions but also in masterly disguise, and they learned to speak different languages to carry out their missions. They were isolated from the world, and were devoted and faithful to the master of Alamut, Sabbah, since he was the representative of the only true imam. Reinforcing the internal cohesion was an indoctrination process relying on rites, oaths, and secrecy. The Assassins had a reliable network of information and could act swiftly. An agent could be sent anywhere at any time. He might become a close friend or counselor to a leader either to guide his decisions or to kill him.

Political Killings

The fedayin of the community turned killing into an art. Assassins usually acted alone and used a dagger: the aim of this close-killing act was for the victim to see the eyes of his opponent when death came upon him, so that the victim knew who sent the killer. Eventually, because killing with a dagger was very difficult, the fedayin were trained in the *janna*, a fighting style whose techniques included low kicks. A mere threat could also be issued: a leader might wake up with a dagger lying by his side. The main goal was to demonstrate to the highest rulers that they were only human and could be killed at any time.

The Assassins' victims were primarily important Turkish and Persian political figures. The first assassination took place in 1092 with the killing of the famous Seljuk vizier Nizam al-Mulk by a feda'i disguised as a Sufi. It was the beginning of a series of assassinations, and notorious leaders lived in fear of being attacked. The Fatimid vizier al-Afdal was killed in 1122, and Chagatai, Genghis Khan's second son, was killed in 1242. Some even suspect the Assassins to have carried out their deeds as far away as England, when Prince Edward was wounded by an assassin's poisoned dagger in 1271. The main strategy for spreading terror was to use mechanisms of fear: anyone, anywhere, could be a victim. Hence, the Assassins often slew their victims in public.

Fedayin had no fear of arrest because they were willing to accept martyrdom. They were often tortured, and rather than disclosing the identities of those in their community, they would name their enemies instead so that they would be killed, or they would even name innocent people so as to provide disinformation.

Retaliations

When Sabbah seized the fortress of Alamut in 1090, the vizier Nizam al-Mulk sent troops, in vain. After the first murder committed by an Assassin, the Seljuk sultan Malik Shah sent a force to attack the fortress. The caliph's troops were attacked at night by the fedayin. All other attacks against the Assassins remained fruitless, and the community maintained its supremacy over the fortress. However, despite all their attempts, the Assassins never managed to reach their true goal, which was to supplant the caliph or the sultan. There were also some severe defeats, as one of the Assassins' imams, Ibn Attash, was executed by Muhammad Malik Shah, Malik Shah's son.

The Assassins used the divisions within Islam at the time of the Crusades to put forward their philosophy and creed. They benefited from the conflict between the Fatimid caliphate of Cairo and the Abbasid caliphate of Baghdad.

For many the sect is merely a legend. For others, its actions were exaggerated. Nevertheless, there is proof that the sect existed, and it is probably one of the first groups in history to use political assassinations as a way to spread terror.

Anicée Van Engeland

See also: Islamic Fundamentalism; Middle East; Terrorism.

Further Reading

Burman, Edward. *The Assassins: Holy Killers of Islam.* Wellingborough, UK: Aquarian Press, 1987.

Daftary, Farhad. *The Ismailis: Their History and Doctrines.* Cambridge, UK: Cambridge University Press, 1990.

———. *A Short History of the Ismailis.* Edinburgh, Scotland: Edinburgh University Press, 1998.

Daraul, Arkon. *Secret Societies.* New York: MJF Books, 1999.

Franzius, Enno. *History of the Order of Assassins.* New York: Funk & Wagnalls, 1969.

Hodgson, Marshall. *The Secret Order of Assassins: The Struggle of the Early Nizari Ismailis Against the Islamic World.* Philadelphia: University of Pennsylvania Press, 2005.

Ivanow, Vladimir. "Some Ismaili Strongholds in Persia." *Islamic Culture* 12 (1938): 383–96.

Lewis, Bernard. *The Assassins: A Radical Sect in Islam.* London: Basic Books, 1967.

Lokhandwall, Shamoon T. "The Bohras, a Muslim Community of Gujarat." *Studia Islamica* 3 (1955): 117–35.

Nanji, Azim. *The Nizaril Ismaili Tradition in the Indo-Pakistan Subcontinent.* Delmar, NY: Caravan Books, 1978.

Von Hammer-Purgstall, Joseph. *The History of Assassins,* trans. Oswald Charles Wood. New York: Burt Franklin, 1835, 1968.

Atheism

Atheism comes from the Greek words *a* ("denying") and *theos* ("God"). It signifies any belief system that denies the existence of any supernatural order and argues that the world exists in and through itself. Atheism can be tied to various ideas and philosophical views, such as Marxism, materialism, solipsism (from the Latin *solus*, meaning "only," and *ipse*, meaning "me"), nihilism (denying the existence of values), biologism (whereby human behavior is explained by biological principles), and modernism (relying on science and progress). Philosophically, there are differences between atheism, naturalism (arguing that all there is to be found is in nature), and humanism (based on rationalism, critical thought, and scientific method).

Does Atheism Foster Violence?

Is atheism inherently violent? Is everything permitted when God—to quote the famous Russian writer Fyodor Dostoevsky—no longer exists? Frequently, these questions have been answered in the affirmative. Religious doctrines foster piety (in faith), humbleness (under one's God), modesty (in awareness of the frailty of things), understanding, and patience (awaiting heaven). In religions, peaceful moral dictums (such as the Christian Ten Commandments) are expressed, and numerous religious leaders have advocated the principles of nonviolence. Therefore, in atheism, in the absence of a sense of spiritual community and overarching religious principle, ties between human beings are gradually lost, and violence is bound to escalate.

Stalinism and Nazism: Two Cases of Violent Atheism

One of the easiest ways to link atheism to violence is to bring up the case of Stalinism, the political system that emerged in Russia under the leader Joseph Stalin. Innumerable atrocities were committed against various religious persuasions during Stalin's rule, which, in the eyes of many, seriously tarnished the reputation of atheism. A wide range of Stalinist qualities—among them a distinctly progressive, modernist perspective and a critique against oppressive, conservative forces—would strengthen Stalinism as a distinctly atheist form of political force. Moreover, the plausible view that all communists are atheists has sparked a more challenging view that all atheists are communists.

The case of Nazism, the political system that was prominent in Germany under the leadership of Adolf Hitler, is less clear cut. In fact, Nazism always harbored certain features—such as an idealization of the past, various forms of would-be Christian myths, and a more or less fanatic conservatism—that seem at odds with any progressive atheist conviction. Still, it is uncertain to what extent Nazi adherence to the views of *Gemeinschaft* (an idealized vision of the intimate community of older days) was real or merely tactical. Also, it is often argued that these sentimental emotions were mere cool tactics, as they were thrown aside in 1938 for the benefit of frantic technocratic optimism and the pending war. These ideas have been supported by the argument that atheism and totalitarianism are closely associated. Apart from these speculations, it is worthwhile to examine the National Socialists' opinion about religion. It has been argued that the Nazis saw religion as a potential threat, and rightly so. Furthermore, whereas religious (Christian) sentiments were held by a majority of modest conservatives (i.e., traditionalists, farmers, etc.) in Germany at this time, these Christian beliefs were held only by a minority of radical conservatives and fascists. This would lead to the conclusion that the Nazis, after all, regarded the potential benefits of certain aspects of Christianity, such as myths, elements of ecstasy, and utopian ideas, as weak compared with other aspects: humbleness, forgiveness, and charity.

The Dangers of Reason and Progress

As indicated above, atheists are rationalists. Not only postmodernists have argued forcefully that reason constituted the founding principle upon which the atrocities of the twentieth century were ultimately based. Diligent bureaucrats in the Nazi regime handling "transports by train" illustrate the point where the icy features of reason appear; or, as expressed by the Israeli scholar Jacob Talmon (1980), the moment "when consistency reaches the point of monstrosity." Auschwitz, an extermination camp symbolizing Nazi atrocities, and the Gulag, which operated the vast and inhuman labor camps during Stalin's reign, were not aberrations of reason nor were they merely a plausible consequence of reason. Rather, they constituted an inevitable outcome of a manic belief in discipline, righteousness, and reason (Baumann 1989). As for Nazism, the mass killing of the "racially inferior" was plainly Darwinian—scientific natural selection put in ghastly practice.

Reason and progress are intimately linked to individualism and liberalism and hence to a weakened social sphere. These ideas support the French sociologist Émile Durkheim's classic analysis on suicide—a particular form of violence. In his study, Durkheim suggested that Catholicism, which is characterized by tradition, a sense of community, and general social control, tended to reduce the rates of suicide; whereas Protestantism, in which religious life was carried out by means of a conspicuously worldly, liberal, and "atheist" daily existence, had a boosting effect upon suicide rates (Durkheim 1990). From this perspective, atheism, along with reason and progress, is seen as a virtue we may not be able to afford.

Another way of tying atheism to violence has been exhibited by politicians in recent years. During his presidency, George W. Bush repeatedly stated that Islamist terrorists "were traitors to their own faith, trying, in effect, to hijack Islam itself," for, one might assume, nonreligious, political objectives. This is an attempt to present the basic principles of religion as essentially nonviolent and peaceful, which, at least implicitly, also constitutes a critique against ideas in opposition to religion: science, progress, modernity, and atheism among them. Atheism and politics do not, it is worth adding, have access to this convenient justification. Fascism, for instance, still counts as distinctly political even though it always was very violent.

Thomas Aikenhead and Pierre Charron: Two Atheists Against Violent Religion

Despite the fact that one can indeed argue that atheism—either explicitly or as guilt by association—may foster violence, there are also plenty of reasons atheism may prevent violence. The history of atheism is by and large the story of a struggle against various forms of religious violence: persecutions, bigotry, the stifling of scientific progress, the burning of "witches," and so on. Two early advocates of atheism, Thomas Aikenhead and Pierre Charron, proposed tolerance, skepticism, and recourse to discussion instead of religious dogmatism.

Charron's heretical *De la Sagesse* was published in 1601, and four years later it was put on the Index of Forbidden Books, a list of written material banned by Roman Catholic religious authorities. Aikenhead, a student at the University of Edinburgh, was executed by the Scottish Privy Council for blasphemy in 1697. These two early figures in the history of atheism were both rather cautious in their critiques against religion. Therefore, it is uncertain whether they should be labeled atheists in the modern sense of the word.

Secularism and Religious Pluralism

One hundred years later, during the Enlightenment, atheists started supporting secular ideas about the separation of church and state. In a society based on religious pluralism, mutual respect, and lack of violence between various systems of belief, this political invention was of key importance. This observation leads to another vital aspect in any defense of atheism. Atheism is not a system of elaborate beliefs. In other words, it should not be seen as just any interchangeable "ism" among others, be it Catholicism, Islamism, or New Ageism. Instead, atheism constitutes the very negation of any ambitious doctrine. Atheism is intimately linked to science, and science is not just another dogmatism based on belief, but knowledge based on doubt. Hence, if atheism is allowed to dominate the state, the result will be, not a society dominated by atheism, but a society characterized by religious pluralism.

Social Tranquility and Worldly Religions

Durkheim's analysis on suicide may support the idea that religions tend to prevent violence, whereas violence may be triggered by a more atomistic, atheist existence. In contrast, a core aspect of the theory of the famous German sociologist Max Weber suggests that it is religion that fosters violence and that atheism paves the way for social tranquility. In his famous study on the relation between the Protestant ethic and the spirit of capitalism, Weber argues that Protestantism, characterized by a conspicuously worldly, diligent, and ascetic form of religious life, promoted economic prosperity (Weber 2002). Catholicism, on the other hand, tended to have a somewhat negative impact on economic progress, the reason being that it promoted a more traditional and outer-worldly form of religious life. Any religion that systematically diverts attention from one's sensory experience of the world (e.g., constructing houses, operating businesses, harvesting) to various forms of spiritual behavior (e.g., prayer, fasting, pilgrimage) invariably has a detrimental impact on economic progress. In brief, religion causes economic backwardness and dearth, which was always a principal factor behind political upheaval, revolutions, and wars—all of which are related to violence. It is uncertain to what extent a plausible link between Catholicism and lack of suicide strengthens the connection between atheism and violence. The reason Durkheim saw a link between Protestantism and suicide rates was not chiefly streaks of "atheism" within the Protestant creed, but that it led to individualism, atomism, and loneliness. Atheism, so it seems, can easily be falsely accused of causing social turmoil.

Atheism and the Importance of This Life

At this point, it is important to examine Dostoevsky's famous passage regarding the nonexistence of God. Why, one may ask, would everything be permitted if God does not exist? Evidently, the quotation implies that any lack of divinity would turn us into beasts. Put differently, atheism would erase our entire sense of morality and righteousness. But this is not necessarily the case, and it may actually work the opposite way. Suppose that this brief existence is all there is—there is no God, there is no afterlife. The case of suicide bombers might illustrate this point. Would terrorists be equally willing to give up their life if they believed that they would simply die? Atheism, suggesting a lack of hope of any heaven beyond death, might actually make us not less but more cautious about our worldly existence and consequently less prone to violence.

Furthermore, this atheist "lack of hope" of any ecstatic life beyond death is linked to a fundamental lack of meaning regarding this life. This would lead one to believe that there is no reason, no meaning as to why some are fortunate and others merely struggle to survive. Nothing was "meant to be." It could have been the other way around. In other words, atheist humility involves a recognition of the tremendous contribution of blind chance to the fates of human beings, and it is such a recognition that leads us to acknowledge an obligation to assist the less fortunate ones among us. A sense of meaninglessness and perhaps even absurdity makes life humane and meaningful. If human beings believe that their situation is not the product of some higher meaning, a sense of community with other individuals will intensify, which, in turn, leads to understanding, tolerance, less inequality, and consequently, reduced violence in society. The religious quest for "meaning," on the other hand, often prides itself for being spiritual and cultivated—for graciously seeking to elevate human beings above the bare bones of physical existence. In a sense, this is reasonable. Human beings need to understand, and find meaning. Still, religious meaning suggests that there is a reason for some being prosperous while others starve. This is the downside of meaning in the religious sense. It is simply a highly dubious idea to argue (on a principal level) that anyone ought to suffer and die. In short, from this perspective, the religious quest for meaning is self-righteous, egotistic, narrow-minded, and cynical. These conclusions are strangely incompatible with love and understanding, altruism, and related official religious rhetoric. Religious meaning offers an excellent breeding ground for political violence, whereas social harmony requires an atheist sense of meaninglessness.

Stalinism, Nazism, and a Questionable Allegation

As mentioned, Stalinism is perhaps the best argument for anyone inclined to associate atheism with violence. As noted above, religious people suffered during Stalin's reign. However, the relationship between Stalinism and atheism is questionable. One must ask if Stalin ever justified his killings by explicitly appealing to atheistic ideas. Attacking conservative, religiously inspired forces is not necessarily a result of a belief in scientific atheism. Indeed, Stalinism and atheism are both products of modernity—that is, the belief in science and progress. Still, it is a fundamental error to link Stalin's left-wing extremism—his dogmatism, irrationalism, and pseudo-progressive technological disaster—with the denial of the existence of God, characterized by sober skepticism and scientific method. Conclusively, while all communists may be atheists, all atheists are not communists. Stalin's rule was political, not atheist.

Turning from Stalinism to Nazism, atheism is no longer explicitly in focus. As was seen above, arguments about a plausible link between atheism and violence had the character of guilt by association; the Nazis generally saw religion as a potential threat. Hence, Nazism harbored atheist ideas. Therefore, the attempts to counter these allegations against atheism are also associative by nature. First, one of the pillars of atheism—reason—must be examined. In case reason opens the gates of violence, atheism must also be dismissed. However, this interpretation is often seen as exaggerated. For instance, Nazi "evolutionism" rested not on Darwinism but on a misunderstanding of his ideas. Charles Darwin never "wanted" the strong ones to survive. As a scientist, he was merely an observer. Admittedly, the atrocities committed at Auschwitz would have been impossible without modern science, but this is not an argument against science in its entirety.

To blame science is to mythologize; it is to personify science and furnish it with a malicious will of its own. In fact, Nazism has been described as the very negation of reason and of atheism along with it. What, for instance, was the "reason" behind the mass killing of millions of Jews? Their private fortunes do not add up to the price of the extermination camps, not to mention the loss of workforce. The main thrust behind Nazism was never bland rationalism, but forceful irrationalism; never historical evidence, but myths of passion; never truth, but powerful fiction; never passive intellectualism, but cheerful anti-intellectualism; never insipid thoughts, but violent emotions; never content, but shows and exhibitions; never essentially politics, but aesthetics and action. Furthermore, attempts have been made to associate the atrocities of Nazism with religion and, in so doing, to suggest that religion is inherently violent and atheism at heart peaceful. It has even been argued that the Holocaust has its roots in biblical traditions that advocate genocide (Avalos 2005).

The More Atheism, the Less Violence?

The relation between violence and religion must also be noted. Initially, it is plain to atheists at least; they claim that Christianity has killed more people historically than atheism ever has. The link between atheism and violence, however, appears weaker when the thought-provoking but essentially mistaken attacks against rationalism (and atheism) made by postmodernists and related critics are subtracted. A forceful, albeit indirect link between religion and violence has been suggested. This idea also suggests that atheism, in being diametrically opposed to religion, forcefully contributes to a nonviolent society. Advocates of atheism often argue that religion has historically prevented scientific, economic, and social progress. Were it not for religious persecution of science, humankind might have landed on the moon hundreds of years ago. For centuries, the Christian Church did not allow the dissection of dead human bodies, calling it "a dese-

cration of the temple of the Holy Ghost." Only in the late eighteenth century was Protestantism partly forced to retreat to the confines of the private domain by the rhetoric of materialistic atheists such as Baron D'Holbach and Jacques-André Naigeon, only to be followed a few decades later by a no less forceful attack by Karl Marx, who declared that religion is the opium of the people. Other religions, such as Islam, were never confronted with the ordeal of modernity and the principles of doubt, which some say explain the social, political, and economic backwardness of those religions. The power of religion creates scarcity, and scarcity causes violence; hence, the weaker the influence of religion and the stronger the impact of atheist ideas, the more affluent the society and the fewer reasons for violent social upheaval.

Göran Adamson

See also: Christianity.

Further Reading

Avalos, Hector. *Fighting Words: The Origins of Religious Violence.* New York: Prometheus Books, 2005.
Bauman, Zygmunt. *Modernity and the Holocaust.* Cambridge, UK: Polity Press, 1989.
Darwin, Charles. *The Origin of the Species by Means of Natural Selection.* London: Penguin, 2003.
Durkheim, Émile. *Suicide: A Study in Sociology.* London: Free Press, 1990.
Griffin, Roger. *The Nature of Fascism.* London: Routledge, 1991.
Kors, Alan Charles. "The Atheism of D'Holbach and Naigeon." In *Atheism from the Reformation to the Enlightenment,* ed. Michael Hunter and David Wootton, pp. 273–300. Oxford: Clarendon Press, 1992.
Mills, David. *Atheist Universe: Why God Didn't Have a Thing to Do with It.* Bloomington, IN: Xlibris, 2006.
Norman, Richard. *On Humanism.* London: Routledge, 2004.
Russell, Bertrand. *Why I Am Not a Christian and Other Essays on Religion and Related Subjects.* London: Simon and Schuster, 1957.
Talmon, Jacob Leib. *The Myth of the Nation and the Vision of Revolution: The Origins of Ideological Polarisation in the Twentieth Century.* Berkeley: University of California Press, 1980.

Weber, Max. *The Protestant Ethic and the Spirit of Capitalism.* Oxford: Blackwell, 2002.

Wielenberg, Erik J. *Value and Virtue in a Godless Universe.* Cambridge, UK: Cambridge University Press, 2005.

Aum Shinrikyo

In the spring of 1995, Japan, the reportedly safest country in the world, was shocked by a terrorist attack against Tokyo's subway, which killed 12 and injured approximately 5,000 people. The perpetrators of this attack were Japanese students who were mesmerized by a mix of beliefs: Christian and Buddhist millennialism (the belief that a Golden Age is about to dawn), Vajrayana tantric techniques, Taoist belief in cycles of cosmic recurrence, and Hindu notions of destruction and rebirth, with bits of Nostradamus thrown in. Many found it hard to believe that the highest ranks of Aum Shinrikyo, the organization that carried out the attack, comprised several relatively young scientists and doctors who, far from simply going along with their guru's instructions, actually pressed for the adoption of extreme measures toward the "final solution" for all Japanese plights—the obliteration of government agencies. The weapon of choice was sarin gas, a cheap and simple chemical developed in Nazi Germany in 1938 and used by Saddam Hussein in the war against Iran.

Shoko Asahara

The man behind all this, Shoko Asahara, was the embodiment of the "banality of evil," an expression used by political philosopher Hannah Arendt in a letter to the philosopher and historian Gershom Scholem. Arendt argues that "evil is never radical . . . it is only extreme . . . it possesses neither depth nor any demonic dimension. . . . It spreads like a fungus on the surface. . . . Thought tries to reach some depth, to go to the roots, and the moment it concerns itself with evil, it is frustrated because there is nothing. That is its banality. Only the Good has depth and can be radical" (Arendt 1964).

Born as Chizuo Matsumoto in Kyushu in 1955, Asahara suffered from impaired vision due to congenital glaucoma and was sent to a school for the blind. There he bullied his blind schoolmates and sought to create a milieu that he could wholly control. He confided to his closest friends his plan to become the Japanese prime minister. Then he would set up his own "robot kingdom."

Asahara had originally aspired to become a doctor. When he failed the entrance exams at Tokyo University, he resigned himself to earning his living as an acupuncturist and a healer. He soon became aware that he could not cure his patients through either the Western or the Chinese medical tradition and gradually turned into an obsessively religious person. When his business failed, he made a trip to India in 1986, determined to attain enlightenment. Later, he claimed he had gained a considerable level of sanctity and command of his magical powers. He changed his name to Shoko Asahara and founded a new religion, christening his sect Aum Shinri-kyō, which is derived from the words Aum ("powers for destruction and creation in the universe") and Shinrikyō ("teaching of the supreme truth"). Approximately 40,000 Japanese and Russians flocked to him to learn his synthesis of Buddhism, Taoism, Hinduism, and biblical scriptures. Like Joseph Goebbels, who in his semiautobiographical novel, *Michael* (1929), submitted that "it is almost immaterial what we believe in, so long as we believe in something," Asahara selectively assembled all that could appeal to young educated Japanese of the 1990s and to himself.

In the course of time, his teaching changed, shifting toward a more radicalized sectarianism.

Asahara warned his disciples of an imminent Armageddon and prophesied that Pluto's entry into Sagittarius in January 1995 would have catastrophic consequences. The Kobe earthquake of January 17, 1995, strengthened the resolve of his followers. He then inaugurated a segregated community on the slopes of Mt. Fuji, where his ascendancy over his followers increased inexorably. Aum Shinrikyo initially sought to develop forms of therapeutic treatment aimed at the spiritual salvation of psychologically and physically sick individuals. Over time, however, as Asahara realized that nobody outside the sect took him seriously, Mahayana Buddhism—aimed not only at personal salvation but at the salvation of the whole of humankind—together with messianic and millennial expectations, took the upper hand.

The utopian plan to use medicine and science to redeem the world and create a harmonious and peaceful society was falling apart, and the sect's leaders grew restless and slightly paranoid. If the Japanese were indifferent to Asahara's enlightened leadership, he would make them take notice. As is often the case with utopias, Aum's goal of achieving total liberation and perfection called for the subjugation and purposeful deception of individuals, who were regarded as essentially incompetent and selfish. When ordinary citizens, by ignoring his call for action, showed that they were not sufficiently prone to self-deception, Asahara and his entourage lost their residual faith in humankind. Like a Nazi ideologue, Asahara claimed that while killing animals was wrong because they are innocent by definition, human beings, who commit crimes intentionally, should not be spared when they stand in the way of the greater good.

Acolytes of the Charismatic Leader

In keeping with this misanthropic tenet, the acolytes of the charismatic leader developed sophisticated techniques for mass killing and stored weapons and high technology designed to support their plan to annihilate the Japanese government. On June 27, 1994, they carried out the first bioterrorist attack in history in Matsumoto, causing a death toll of seven and injuring hundreds of people. On March 20, 1995, they carried out their most infamous action: the assault of Tokyo's subway network. The terrorists used the tips of their umbrellas to puncture several bags filled with sarin gas. The number of victims was comparatively low because passengers on the train opened the windows and dispersed the gas. On both occasions, more careful planning and execution would have caused a more dire result.

The Psychology of Terrorism

Following the 1995 terrorist attack, the celebrated Japanese novelist Haruki Murakami interviewed some of the followers of Aum Shinrikyo and revealed traits of their personalities that warrant a closer examination. When he was an adolescent, Hiroyuki Kano, an Aum member who was not involved in the attack, was driven by the urge to attain superior knowledge, but he was unable to achieve his goal. He spent hours pondering over the most vexing existential questions without reading through a single book because he did not like to read: "When I read something I just see what's wrong with the book." Although he was primarily interested in finding a mathematical demonstration of the soundness of Buddhist philosophy, he conceded that he never got into depth with any study of Buddhism, as the books he read "didn't seem very direct in their approach. I couldn't discover the remedy I was searching for." When he met the Aum instructors, he was delighted to see that all his questions were answered: "We were told: 'Do this and this will happen.' No matter what question we had, we got an answer straight away. I was completely immersed in it."

Japanese Defense Agency personnel in biohazard gear clean the platform of a Tokyo subway station after the March 20, 1995, terrorist attack by members of the Aum Shinrikyo sect. Japanese students released sarin nerve gas in the metro system during rush hour, killing twelve and injuring thousands. *(Japanese Defence Agency/Getty Images)*

Another member, Akio Namimura, pointed out that Fumihiro Jōyū, the sect's spokesperson, "could answer any question clearly," and Mitsuharu Inaba recalled that he was really impressed by what Jōyū said: "It was so clearly stated—the way he used metaphors, for instance. . . . After the sermon he took questions, and his answers were extremely precise, each one perfectly tailored to the person who asked it." Members felt their lives were greatly improved, as they were freed from the burden of their responsibilities. For Harumi Iwakura, the way Aum did things made life easier: "They'd give the order and you just did what they said. No need to think for yourself, or worry about every little detail, just do what you're told" (Murakami 2001).

These young people were manifestly unprepared to take responsibility for their own actions or to grasp the gravity of what they were doing. They candidly pointed out the simplicity of the choices they made, and their eagerness to completely surrender their critical faculties, without spending too much time considering the morality of their actions, was evident. Those who joined the sect did so in order to withdraw from reality, shut out their fears and misgivings, as they were already estranged from real life. They wanted someone else to cope with the problems of their lives. For them, relinquishing critical thought, systematized ideas, and ethical concerns in exchange for protection and support was a matter of course.

As a result of their moral obliquity, these cultists thought little or nothing of their victims. A hermetically sealed milieu, dominated by reductionism, narcissism, and self-centeredness, disabled their moral faculties. Their absolute moral certainty prevented them from becoming aware of the depravity of their behavior. The scope of their endeavor was so absolute that they were drawn into a parallel, suspended reality in which their previous nagging duties and concerns could be ignored, and all norms and conventions were turned upside down; hence their disinclination to accept that they should feel guilty about what they had done. Social order and conventional morality were perverted to such an extent that the boundary between right and wrong completely dissolved, while adepts' self-denial came very close to self-imposed mind control.

The cultists' atrophied morality, which was in stark contrast to their fervid imaginations, was further exacerbated by a deterministic view of the effects of karmic influence on one's personal life. They were persuaded that the negative consequences of past misdeeds could only be counteracted by escaping from the bonds of karma through meditation (*karuma kara no dasshutsu*) or overturning deleterious social institutions and conventions that had caused what they saw as widespread spiritual degeneration. By living in a sick and corrupted society, people accumulated a large amount of bad karma that, like a genetic burden, would affect them for the rest of their lives and possibly beyond. Therefore, Aum preached positive spiritual cleansing through ascetic practices at the same time that it called for the annihilation and subsequent regeneration of Japanese society.

But too few Japanese were eager to follow this path of spiritual cleansing through meditation. According to Asahara's understanding of tantric Buddhism, these millions of skeptics were unworthy of life. They deserved a "compassionate" death, which would ultimately accelerate their cosmic journey of reincarnation. Additionally, to take the life of people who represented an obstacle for those engaged in the reduction of bad karma in the world was actually a meritorious act. Thus, Aum Shinrikyo was not amoral or ethically indifferent: rather, it embraced an inverted ethical system that

was both "primitive" and "modern." Asahara's philosophy tapped into the deepest, ungovernable recesses of the human mind, but it also affirmed its determination to demonstrate that humankind, not God, is in charge of the future and that happiness and spiritual fulfillment can be achieved in this life and in this world.

A Japanese Distinctiveness?

The most important question is where this predisposition to self-deception came from. In other words, what are the distinctive features of modernity in general or Japanese culture and society in particular that make some persons less prepared to face such a challenge. It seems undeniable that magic has not been banished from contemporary society, for it clearly satisfies a social and psychological need. While on the one hand science destroys traditional mythologies, it also paves the way for all sorts of postmodern mythologies inspired by a blend of science and religion, which results in the persistent and widespread belief in astrology even among the educated public and the proliferation of subcultures and countercultures that merge science and magic in order to ease people's existential angst. What is remarkable about Aum Shinrikyo is how successful the sect was in making science a sacred enterprise. Sacred and profane mingled, while fascination for state-of-the-art technology and science was employed to awe potential followers.

Asahara gave instruction to his aides to screen the top Japanese universities and lure brilliant researchers into joining the sect. This task did not prove exceedingly difficult. In Japan, traditional religions are giving way to occultism and mysticism. In 1993, there were 231,019 sects registered in Japan, with 200 million members. This means that thousands of Japanese joined more than one religious organization, indifferent to possible theoretical and ethical inconsistencies. Some of these sects profess a millenarian faith in an incipient new world order, reflecting in so many ways the rather bleak and apocalyptic view of society conveyed by Japanese science fiction and anime. That the new religions' millenarianism has much to do with the apocalyptic visions of Japanese *manga* is further indicated by the fact that Asahara was himself the author of a manga tellingly entitled *Metsubō no hi* (The Doom's Day). Furthermore, the enormous popularity of Nostradamus's prophecies in Japan led many to believe that the *saikimatsu* (the end of the century) would coincide with the *jidaimatsu* (the end of time). Some, like the Aum cultists, went a step further and became obsessed with the possibility of actively bringing about the Armageddon.

Asahara's plan was also inspired by Isaac Asimov's *Foundation* series, whose key character, Hari Seldon, is a mathematical prodigy and the discoverer of a new discipline—psychohistory—that enables its practitioners to predict the future. When the Empire's leadership fails to heed his warning of an impending catastrophe, he summons the best thinkers of the Empire and founds a sect that will preserve wisdom and knowledge. Following the predicted disaster, the sect's acolytes find themselves ruling the universe; as no one else has a sufficient command of science and technology to challenge their authority, they are looked upon as wizards.

Asahara believed he was a postmodern hero, like Kaneda, the protagonist of *Akira,* a milestone of the Japanese techno-apocalyptic genre that first appeared in *Young Magazine* in December 1982. Kaneda struggles in a postnuclear Neo-Tokyo that has been completely destroyed by a nuclear experiment and then rebuilt. He is a member of a gang of bikers, *bōsōzoku,* literally "violent running tribe" (from *bo,* "violent"; *so,* "to run"; and *zoku,* "tribe"). *Bōsōzoku* defy police authority, use Chinese characters for their gang names, and wear uniforms of kamikaze pilots—all symbols usually associated with extreme right-wing political movements and *yakuza* (a major Japanese organized crime group) members. Although Kaneda is poorly schooled and ignorant, he is also *kōha* (a gallant, tough guy) and displays *makoto* (purity of motives), which makes him a qualified candidate for the leadership of the new, uncorrupted society that will rise from the ashes of the old society. It is possible that Asahara identified with Kaneda and thought himself a messianic leader on a mission to rid Japan of its "impurities."

It is also plausible to assume that the declining role of Shintoism and Buddhism may have produced a moral void for thousands of young Japanese and that while new religions enjoy the clear advantage of not having to prove any consistency of behavior or doctrine, they may not always be able to provide the desired spiritual anchor in troubled times. Under extreme circumstances, this loss of firm religious and ethical landmarks is apt to provoke a fluctuation between the idolatry of humankind and the nihilism of the "humans pollute the earth" kind.

Aum Shinrikyo could be fairly described as a progressive, millennialist response to the prolonged stagnation of the Japanese economy and the suffocating traditionalism of Japanese society. Initially drawn to Asahara's philosophy as a result of a feeling of emptiness, boredom, isolation, and possibly hopelessness, thousands of cultists increasingly saw themselves as the instruments of a superhuman agent whose decisions could change the course of history and usher in a millennial kingdom.

Like Hong Houxiu, the leader of the disastrous Taiping Rebellion in mid-nineteenth-century China, who believed he was the younger brother of Jesus Christ, Asahara proclaimed himself "today's Christ" and "the Savior of This Century" and promised collective salvation after the ultimate battle between good and evil. This doctrinal shift caused a momentous transition from a progressive and tolerant gradualist attitude to social reform and spiritual cleansing to an apocalyptic and violent revolutionary fervor. Aum adepts had been chosen to fulfill a providential purpose and felt enormously empowered. The eschatological dimension of the movement, which was bound to create an alternative society and an alternative modernity—the beginning of a new era of peace and prosperity—conferred a sacred status on those who were entirely committed to the cause and gave a transcendental significance to their murderous actions. Their calling, as "metaphysical agents of reform," would in turn fill the spiritual void that haunted them.

The fact that this movement could flourish so vigorously in a peaceful and generally affluent society like Japan's raises a number of thought-provoking issues. Because of economic stagnation, these disgruntled and alienated young Japanese men and women were the first generation since the end of World War II who could expect to have a worse standard of living than their predecessors. Tired of vicarious emotional experiences, they were probably going through a severe identity crisis and viewed middle-class, overbureaucratized corporate life and materialistic, rampantly consumerist society as dehumanizing and intolerable. They despised a public structure that enforced a conservative, authoritarian, unchangeable, and corrupt system. At the same time, docile and virtuous, hopelessly mediocre, desperately bored, perfectly trained in the art of self-denial, these level-headed young citizens had never experienced material deprivation. Too lethargic to feel compelled to become politically active, they were nonetheless eager to resanctify the world.

Like a demigod, Asahara offered them collective empowerment and a false sense of individuality. Then he molded them into an army of drone-like radical revolutionaries fighting against the same society that had shaped them. Estrangement, disenchantment, discontent, powerlessness, the urge to find a way to liberate their emotions, and a paradoxically nihilistic search for meaning caused them to become enemies of their own peers. They ended up thinking that "life-affirming" violence was a solution to their resentment and emasculation. Creation would follow destruction, and the terrorist assault on Kasumigaseki and Nagatacho, home to the Japanese government, was part of a plan meant to wipe out the ruling elite to make room for the dropout elite, hungry for status and motivation.

Ultimately, Aum Shinrikyo should serve as a cautionary tale: There is a limit to the amount of pressure and constraints that a democratic society can place on its citizens. When that limit is reached, society will pay the consequences.

Stefano Fait

See also: New Religious Movements.

Further Reading

Arendt, Hannah. "Letter to Gershom Scholem." *Encounter* (January 1964): 51–56. Cited in *Hannah Arendt: For Love of the World*, by Elisabeth Young-Bruehl. New Haven, CT: Yale University Press, 1982.

Dostoevsky, Fyodor M. *The Brothers Karamazov.* London: Heinemann, 1912.

Lifton, Robert J. *Destroying the World to Save It: Aum Shinrikyo, Apocalyptic Violence, and the New Global Terrorism.* New York: Henry Holt, 1999.

Murakami, Haruki. *Underground: The Tokyo Gas Attack and the Japanese Psyche.* London: Harvill Panther, 2001.

Reader, Ian. *Religious Violence in Contemporary Japan: The Case of Aum Shinrikyō.* Honolulu: University of Hawaii Press, 2000.

Standish, Isolde. "Akira, Postmodernism and Resistance." In *The Worlds of Japanese Popular Culture: Gender, Shifting Boundaries and Global Cultures,* ed. D.P. Martinez, pp. 56–74. Cambridge, UK: Cambridge University Press, 1998.

Bahá'í Faith

The Bahá'í Faith is the youngest of the world's major religions. Founded by Bahá'u'lláh in 1844, the Bahá'í Faith teaches that religious truth is not absolute but relative, that divine revelation is progressive, and that all the great prophets have revealed the same truth in progressively unfolding ways. Shoghi Effendi, guardian of the Bahá'í Faith from 1921 to his death in 1957, professed that the aims and purposes of the divine messengers, or manifestations of God, are "one and the same, that their teachings are but facets of one truth, that their functions are complementary, that they differ only in the nonessential aspects of their doctrines, and that their missions represent successive stages in the spiritual evolution of human society."

Bahá'u'lláh proclaimed to the world that the evolutionary stages of human society, namely infancy and childhood, are past, that the "convulsions associated with the present stage of its adolescence are slowly and painfully preparing it to attain the stage of {adulthood}, and are heralding the approach of that Age of Ages when swords will be beaten into plowshares . . . and the peace of the planet definitely and permanently ensured." Bahá'u'lláh did not claim finality for his own revelation but rather stipulated that divine guidance will continue throughout the ages when humanity's plight is such that God sends another prophet or messenger with teachings to guide it to its next stage of spiritual, material, and social development. The message he brought to the world is unity, and his teachings, laws, and ordinances all revolve around this central point. He proclaimed the unity of God and of his divine messengers, as well as the unity of humanity.

Mirza Husayn 'Ali Nuri, surnamed Bahá'u'lláh ("the glory of God"), was a native of Mazandaran, a northern province that borders the Caspian Sea in present-day Iran. He was born in 1817 in Tehran, but because his family was from the village of Nur ("light"), his name reflects the homeland of his family. In his twenties he was an outspoken supporter of Siyyid Ali Muhammad Shirazi, the "Báb," who in the midst of the great anticipation of the 1840s proclaimed himself to be the return of the twelfth imam (the Qaim, or Mahdi) of Shi'a Islam. It was through this support for the Báb that Bahá'u'lláh eventually was imprisoned, subsequently exiled, and handed over to the Ottoman Empire. After spending a decade in Baghdad, he was exiled to Constantinople and Adrianople and finally to the prison city of 'Akká in Palestine, where he died in 1892.

Today the Bahá'í Faith is a dynamic worldwide religious movement of great scope. It is the second most widespread religion, next to Christianity, and has attracted followers from diverse religious and ethnic backgrounds, a fact that supports the Bahá'í Faith's claims to universality.

Bábism and the Bahá'í Faith

In its short history, the Bahá'í Faith has undergone a considerable transformation. The faith has its origins in the earlier Bábí movement. In 1844, Siyyid Ali Muhammad Shirazi (1819–1850), surnamed the Báb ("the Gate"), claimed to fulfill the messianic expectations of Shi'a Islam. The Báb established a movement that soon spread throughout the land of Persia. The movement was vehemently opposed by both clergy and government and through bloody confrontation. Up to 20,000 Bábís were killed, ending with the Báb's own execution on July 9, 1850, in spectacular fashion.

The Báb's execution has been recorded in a number of sources, including a French journal, *Journal Asiatique.* No sooner had the *farrash-bashi* (the chief attendant) secured the necessary documents than the Báb was delivered into the hands of Sam Khan, a military regiment commander, who was ordered to carry out the execution orders. At about noon on that summer day, the Báb was tied to a wall along with one of his young disciples in a public square in Tabriz, where tens of thousands had gathered to witness the spectacle. The regiment of 750 soldiers fired their muskets at the Báb, filling the air with a cloud of smoke. As described by Shoghi Effendi, when the smoke cleared "an astounded multitude were looking upon a scene which their eyes could scarcely believe." The young disciple was left standing alone and unscathed, and the Báb was nowhere to be found. After a frantic search, the guards found the Báb in his cell completing the dictation of a letter to his secretary. He informed the guards that they were now permitted to complete their assigned mission. The regiment that had originally gathered refused to carry out the order, and their own commander Sam Khan, stunned by the force of this event, ordered his men to leave the barracks immediately.

Aqa Jan Khan-i-Khamsih, colonel of the bodyguard—also known by the names Khamsih and Nasiri—volunteered to carry out the execution. This time the bodies of the Báb and his disciple were shot into pieces, blending them into one mass of bone and flesh. "Had you believed in Me, O Wayward generation," said the Báb as he stood before the firing squad, "every one of you would have followed the example of this youth, who stood in rank above most of you, and willingly would have sacrificed himself in My path. The day will come when you will have recognized Me; that day I shall have ceased to be with you."

Perhaps the renowned and distinguished Orientalist professor E.G. Browne best captured for posterity the life and character of the Báb. Professor Browne wrote, "Who can fail to be attracted by the gentle spirit of Mirza Ali-Muhammad (the Báb)? His sorrowful and persecuted life; his purity of conduct, and youth; his courage and uncomplaining patience under misfortune; his complete self-negation; the dim ideal of a better state of things which can be discerned through the obscure and mystic utterances of the Bayan; but most of all his tragic death, all serve to enlist our sympathies on behalf of the young Prophet of Shiraz. The irresistible charm which won him such devotion during his life still lives on, and still continues to influence the minds of the Persian" (Browne 1989).

The Báb's short ministry (1844–1850) witnessed the most violent period of Bahá'í history. During his ministry the Bábís were given permission by the Báb himself to defend their community, thus leading to such upheavals as those in Mazandaran, Nayriz, and Zanjan—the first being the most famous due to its length and heroism. It was Bahá'u'lláh, though, who made fundamental changes to the way his followers understood themselves and their role as nonviolent members of the larger community. In his most holy book, the *Kitáb-i-Aqdas,* Bahá'u'lláh states, "Ye have been forbidden in the Book of God to engage in contention and conflict, to strike another, or to commit similar acts whereby hearts and souls may be saddened. . . . Wish not for others what ye wish not for yourselves; fear God and be not of the prideful. Ye are all created out of water, and unto dust shall ye return." In another passage of that same book he states, "Let none contend with another and let no soul slay another; this verily, is that which was forbidden you in a Book that hath lain concealed within the Tabernacle of glory. What! Would ye kill him whom God hath quickened, whom He hath endowed with spirit through a breath from Him? Grievous then would be your trespass before His throne! Fear God, and lift not the hand of injustice and oppression to destroy what He hath Himself raised up; nay, walk ye in the way of God, the True One."

Thus, in the Bahá'í Faith, violence on the part of the believers is forbidden. This however, did not curb the violence toward this newborn faith. The persecutions that the Bahá'ís as a religious minority have endured in the country of its inception and under other governments are well documented. Numerous resolutions from the highest international bodies, including the United Nations, have brought the persecutions of this community to the attention of the international community. Over the past 150 years the Bahá'í community in Iran, the largest religious minority of the country, has experienced ebbs and flows in the level of violence perpetrated against it. The most recent persecutions have occurred since the Iranian revolution of 1979. The members of the National Spiritual Assembly of the Bahá'ís of Iran, the elected body that represented the Bahá'í community of Iran, were killed along with their replacements in the early years of the revolution. The examples of violence perpetrated against the Bahá'ís of Iran are too numerous to list, but its victims have included men, women, and youth and continue to the present day.

Bahá'í Teachings on Violence

The foundation of the teachings of the Bahá'í Faith is unity and the oneness of humanity. All races, ethnicities, nationalities, religions, and genders are created by God, and all people are citizens of one world. Two fundamental principles of the Bahá'í Faith are justice and the equality of men and women. As Bahá'u'lláh, quoted by the Bahá'í International Community, has stated, "The friends of God must be adorned with the ornament of justice, equity, kindness and love." The Bahá'í writings state, "When all mankind shall receive the same opportunity of education and the equality of men and women be realized, the foundations of war will be utterly destroyed. Without equality this will be impossible because all differences and distinction are conducive to discord and strife. Equality between men and women is conducive to the abolition of warfare for the reason that women will never be willing to sanction it." In its statement titled "The Promise of World Peace" (1985), the Universal House of Justice, the supreme governing body of the Bahá'í Faith stated, "Racism, a baneful evil, is a major barrier to peace. The inordinate disparity between rich and poor keeps the world in a state of instability, virtually on the brink of war."

Violence and peace can be considered to exist on opposite ends of the spectrum. Spiritual development within the individual is vital in promoting nonviolence within the community. "In essence, peace stems from an inner state supported by a spiritual or moral attitude, and it is chiefly in evoking this attitude that the possibility of enduring solutions can be found" (Universal House of Justice 1985). In a talk given in Paris in 1911 'Abdu'l-Bahá captured the essence of the Bahá'í teachings on peace and nonviolence:

> There is nothing so heart-breaking and terrible as an outburst of human savagery! I charge you all that each one of you concentrate all the thoughts of your heart on love and unity. When a thought of war comes, oppose it by a stronger thought of peace. A thought of hatred must be destroyed by a more powerful thought of love. Thoughts of war bring destruction to all harmony, well-being, restfulness and content. Thoughts of love are constructive of brotherhood, peace, friendship, and happiness. . . . Do not think the peace of the world an ideal impossible to attain! Nothing is impossible to the Divine Benevolence of God. If you desire with all your heart, friendship with every race

on earth, your thought, spiritual and positive, will spread; it will become the desire of others, growing stronger and stronger, until it reaches the minds of all men. Do not despair! Work steadily. Sincerity and love will conquer hate. . . . Take courage! God never forsakes His children who strive and work and pray! Let your hearts be filled with the strenuous desire that tranquility and harmony may encircle all this warring world. So will success crown your efforts, and with the universal brotherhood will come the Kingdom of God in peace and goodwill.

In understanding the vital importance of moral and character development, the Bahá'í community has developed many educational tools to contribute to this process. One example of these tools is the courses and accompanying literature developed by the Ruhi Foundation in Colombia, the first course of which is entitled Reflections on the Life of the Spirit. This course gives the participants a chance to better understand the Bahá'í writings, the importance of prayer, and the subject of life and death, through applying the concepts to their own lives, and gives them a chance to reflect and grow spiritually. The Bahá'ís have also developed training materials to be used for character-development classes for children and junior youth. These classes, offered by the Bahá'í community worldwide, are open to all. Bahá'ís believe that developing good character is more important than book learning, although to have both is "light upon light." Children who develop good character will be a benefit to society, but if they are not trained and their spiritual character refined, they will more likely reflect the animalistic nature inherent in us all.

Bahá'ís believe that consultation within the community is critical to avoiding conflict and contention. With the process of consultation, each individual involved has a right to voice his or her opinion. Once the individual has stated his or her view, the point that has been made is no longer owned by the individual who voiced

it. It is, rather, offered with the purpose of discovering what is best, and further consultation should be made to reveal this truth and not to attack the individual who offered the suggestion. An atmosphere of love, fellowship, and detachment is necessary during consultation. It is after differing views are heard that a better understanding of the subject is brought forth and agreement can be reached.

Bahá'í Remedies to Violence

Many have come to understand that the underlying cause of violence and transgression in the world is ignorance. In the Bahá'í Faith, there is a strong emphasis on education. To promote nonviolence, it is understood that society needs to enforce peaceful means and strategies and to bring about an understanding of unity, healing, and reconciliation in children from a young age.

Education begins within the home with the parents or guardians, who are examples to their children from day one. If they are unable to promote a life without violence, it will be hard for the children to avoid it in some form. According to the Bahá'í view, families should be built upon the foundation of respect and love, not on domination or the struggle for power. All family members have rights that must be respected. As experience has shown, a lack of respect for the rights of family members within a household can result in domestic violence and abuse between family members.

The environment that a child grows up in has a great effect on his or her life. Education within schools would benefit from incorporating all aspects of nonviolence. Parents and teachers should regard their students as "mines rich with gems of inestimable value." It is only through education that all potentialities and capabilities inherent in a child will be released. Schools are miniature societies in which students from diverse backgrounds interact with each other. It is within this environment that students learn about the diversity in the world and grow to respect and love others. Thus, within the family and school prejudice finds no place, and young people are taught to understand the core principle of the oneness of humanity. Children must be taught such virtues as peacefulness, justice, truthfulness, tolerance, courage, and love to help prevent violence in society.

The Bahá'í Faith teaches the importance of universal education; however, according to Bahá'u'lláh, "If it is not possible . . . for a family to educate all the children, preference is to be accorded to daughters since, through educated mothers, the benefits of knowledge can be most effectively and rapidly diffused throughout society."

When men and women are given the same opportunities of education and when women are viewed as having equal status with men, wars will be abolished, as women will not give up their sons to die on the battlefield. There is a natural instinct for a mother to protect her young, as seen in the animal world. The Bahá'í writings state, "When women participate fully and equally in the affairs of the world, when they enter confidently and capably the great arena of laws and politics, war will cease; for woman will be the obstacle and hindrance to it."

Bahá'ís believe that God has always given humanity divine teachers to guide the world. It is up to the individual, however, to internalize those teachings and to manifest them in his or her daily life. Human society is now entering the stage of maturity, and people of the world must work together for peace and universal brotherhood.

The Bahá'í Faith, the most recent of all the great universal faiths, teaches that humanity is fundamentally spiritual, and violence of any kind runs counter to the benefit of both the individual and the collective. Violence will find no place in an ever-advancing society and will in fact be replaced by love and unity. The transition from a world that is burdened with violence to one that is blessed with justice, cooperation, love, and unity is what the Bahá'í community worldwide is diligently working toward.

Kirk Johnson and Ana Cornwell

See also: Middle East.

Further Reading

'Abdu'l-Bahá. *Paris Talks: Addresses Given by Abdu'l-Bahá in Paris in 1911–1912.* London: Bahá'í Publishing Trust, 1995.

———. *The Promulgation of Universal Peace: Talks Delivered by Abdu'l-Bahá During His Visit to the United States and Canada in 1912.* Wilmette, IL: Bahá'í Publishing Trust, 1982.

———. *Selections from the Writings of Abdu'l-Bahá.* Haifa, Israel: Bahá'í World Centre, 1978.

Amanat, Abbas. *Resurrection and Renewal: The Making of the Babi Movement in Iran, 1844–1850.* Ithaca, NY: Cornell University Press, 1989.

Bahá'í International Community. *Ending Violence Against Women.* New York: Bahá'í International Community, 1995.

Bahá'u'lláh. *The Compilation of Compilations Prepared by the Universal House of Justice 1963–1990, Volume II.* Victoria: Australian Print Group, 1991.

———. *Gleanings from the Writings of Bahá'u'lláh.* Wilmette, IL: Bahá'í Publishing Trust, 1952.

———. *The Hidden Words,* trans. Shoghi Effendi. Wilmette, IL: Bahá'í Publishing Trust, 2002.

Balyuzi, H.M. *Edward Granville Browne and the Baha'i Faith.* Oxford: George Ronald, 1970.

Browne, E.G. "The Bábís of Persia." *Journal of the R.A.S.* (1989): 933.

Bushrui, Suheil. *The Style of the Kitab-i-Aqdas: Aspects of the Sublime.* Bethesda: University Press of Maryland, 1995.

Collins, William P. "Apocalypse and Millennium: Catastrophe, Progress, and the Lesser Peace." *Journal of Bahá'í Studies* 12 (2002): 1–30.

Farhoumand-Sims, Cheshmak A., and Charles Lerche. "Perspectives on Peace-building: An Overview and Some Insights from the Baha'i Writings." In *Healing the Body Politic,* ed. Charles Lerche, pp. 1–46. Oxford: George Ronald, 2004.

Gervais, Marie. "The Baha'i Curriculum for Peace Education." *Journal of Peace Education* 1 (January 2004): 205–24.

Lerche, Charles. "Human Nature and the Problem of Peace." In *Emergence: Dimensions of a New World Order*, ed. Charles Lerche, pp. 131–44. London: Bahá'í Publishing Trust, 1991.

Momen, Moojan. "The Babi and Baha'i Community of Iran: A Case of 'Suspended Genocide'?" *Journal of Genocide Research* 7:2 (June 2005): 221–41.

———. *The Babi and Baha'i Faiths, 1844–1944: Some Contemporary Western Accounts.* Oxford: George Ronald, 1982.

———. "Millennialism and Violence: The Attempted Assassination of Nasir al-Din Shah of Iran by the Babis in 1852." *Nova Religio: The Journal of Alternative and Emergent Religions* 12:1 (2008): 57–82.

———. *Understanding Religion.* Oxford: Oneworld, 2009.

Shoghi Effendi. *The Dawn-Breakers: Nabil's Narrative of the Early Days of the Baha'i Revelation.* Wilmette, IL: Bahá'í Publishing Trust, 1932.

Smith, Peter. *The Babi and Baha'i Religions: From Messianic Shi'ism to a World Religion.* Cambridge, UK: George Ronald, 1987.

———. *An Introduction to the Baha'i Faith.* Cambridge, UK: Cambridge University Press, 2008.

Smith, Peter, and Moojan Momen. "Babi Martyrs." In *Encyclopaedia Iranica* (online). Available: http://www.iranica.com/.

Universal House of Justice. *Peace Statement.* Haifa, Israel: Bahá'í World Center, 1985.

Walbridge, John. "The Babi Uprising in Zanjan." *Iranian Studies* 29 (1996): 339–62.

Zabihi-Moghaddam, Siyamak. "The Babi-State Conflict at Shaykh Tabasi." *Iranian Studies* 35 (2002): 87–112.

Beam, Louis, Jr. (1946–)

Louis Ray Beam Jr., a former Klansman and member of Aryan Nations whose aliases have included Turner Ashby, Nathan Bedford Forrest, Ken Harrison, Robert Johnson, Travis Wilkerson, "Calvary [*sic*] General," and "Lonestar," was a racist, anti-Semitic, and anticommunist white separatist with a history of advocating violence. If there is any individual who represented and influenced the transition from the civil-rights-era Ku Klux Klan of the 1950s and 1960s to the post-civil-rights-era extreme Right of the 1970s to the 1990s, it

was Beam. The most common analysis of this transition is that the majority of the Klan and wider extreme Right underwent a process of radicalization in the 1970s and 1980s, rejecting hegemonic state-supportive ideologies and electoral activism in favor of antigovernment ideologies, paramilitarization, and political violence. Nothing articulates this transformation as well as Beam's own moniker and call to arms, which stated, "Where ballots fail, bullets will prevail." More directly, Beam's influence can be seen in several significant developments: the paramilitarization of the Klan in the 1970s; antigovernment patriotism over state-supportive patriotism; the popularization of Christian Identity—a racial-national religion and theology based on British Israelism, which holds that the Aryan race is God's chosen people and the true Israelites—over the traditional Protestant Christianity of the Klan; the advocacy of white separatism over white supremacy and white nationalism in the 1980s; the development of the Leaderless Resistance combat strategy; and the emergence of the militia movement in the 1990s. While primarily a strategist, Beam's influence on Christian Identity and white separatism within the wider movement came through his relationship with Richard Butler's Aryan Nations and Church of Jesus Christ-Christian.

History and Background

Louis Beam Jr. was born on August 20, 1946, in Lufkin, Texas. At the age of twenty, at the height of the Vietnam War, Beam joined the army, where he served for eighteen months as a machine gunner. He returned home a staunch anticommunist, angry at both antiwar protestors and the American government, which he blamed for his alleged exposure to Agent Orange and his post-traumatic stress disorder. He began his career as a political activist in the Ku Klux Klan during the civil rights era, soon after his return from Vietnam. He first joined the Klan in 1968, as part of the Texas chapter of the Alabama-based United Klans of America. Between 1974 and 1976, he decided to go to university and study history, but he failed to complete the degree. Beam left the United Klans in 1976 to join David Duke's Knights of the Ku Klux Klan and was appointed the "Grand Dragon," or leader, of the Texas Knights.

At the time of Beam's ascent under the leadership of Duke, the Klan and the wider extreme Right were undergoing a major transformation. As the battle to preserve white supremacy looked like it had been lost in the face of the Civil Rights Act, more radical elements within the John Birch Society and the Klan had been forming paramilitary units, rejecting the state-supportive ideologies and strategies of their predecessors and advocating political violence in an attempt to resist, incite revolution against, and overthrow the government. Examples of such violent paramilitary groups included the Minutemen, formed in the early1960s by former John Birch Society member Robert DePugh; the California Rangers and Christian Defense League, set up by fellow Klansmen and Christian Identity adherents Wesley Swift, Richard Girnt Butler, and William Potter Gale; and the Identity-based constitutionalist organization Posse Comitatus, established in 1969 by a former member of the fascist Silver Shirts, Henry Beach, and led by Gale from 1971.

At the end of the 1970s, the Knights of the Ku Klux Klan were at a crossroads in terms of both their ideological and strategic direction. By the late-1970s, David Duke, the grand dragon of the Louisiana Knights, developed a mainstream strategy by which the Klan would reject violence and explicit racism in favor of democratic electoral activism, such as running for elected office, as Duke did on numerous occasions (including twice for the presidency).

This created a split within the Klan in which the majority of klantons, including Duke's, established supplemental armed paramilitary units, much like the Minutemen and others had done in the 1960s. These included the Invisible Empire, established by Bill Wilkinson, who replaced Duke in the Louisiana Knights; the White Patriot Party, established by former Green Beret and American Nazi Party member Glenn Miller of the North Carolina Knights; the Texas Emergency Reserve, established by Beam of the Texas Knights; and White Aryan Resistance (WAR), established by John and Tom Metzger of the California Knights.

Beam, who was widely seen as one of the architects of this new development, and his Texas Emergency Reserve first emerged on the scene in 1981, when he set up a paramilitary training camp and attacked Vietnamese shrimp fishermen on Galveston Bay, Texas. These developments mobilized the Southern Poverty Law Center and led to the establishment of Klan Watch, which monitored this new paramilitarized and radicalized extreme Right. Soon after, the Southern Poverty Law Center filed a lawsuit against Beam and forced him to close down his training camp. By this time Beam, a Christian Identity adherent, had already joined his fellow Klansman Robert Miles in Richard Butler's Aryan Nations, which was established in the mid 1970s and would come to dominate the extreme Right in the 1980s and 1990s in terms of influence and profile. Beam was appointed Aryan Nations' national ambassador and played a role as strategist.

Writings, Strategy, and Influence

Beam's influence was based primarily on his writings, many of which were published and republished through Aryan Nation's Teutonic Unity Press and almost all of which advocated violence. In fact, Beam was critical of other leaders who failed to recognize the link between violence and the potential success of the movement. The first and most significant of his works was his manifesto "Understanding the Struggle, or Why We Have to Kill the Bastards," which was also published in his book *Essays of a Klansman.* The second publication was his *Seditious Conspiracy,* a booklet included in issue 58 of *Calling Our Nation,* published in 1987 in response to his indictment for seditious conspiracy. Beam's third publication and his most significant strategic initiative was "Leaderless Resistance," an essay published in issue 12 of the *Seditionist* in February 1992. In addition to these publications, Beam is also noted for creating the first white supremacist computer bulletin board network.

"Understanding the Struggle, or Why We Have to Kill the Bastards" detailed Beam's analysis of the movement's conflicts with the state and Jews and, most notoriously, included an assassination hit list. The list outlined categories of potential enemy targets, from government officials to racial and ethnic minorities, and represented a clear move toward explicit political violence. Each target was designated a point value corresponding to the victim's position and significance, ranging down from one point for the assassination of those in the category of "Control Center" to 1/1,000th of a point for those classed as "Recipient." This point system provided members with incentives, as, the higher the level of the target who was assassinated, the higher the status the assassin would be able to attain within the movement. According to Beam, the highest status one could attain in the movement was "Aryan Warrior," while the lowest was "Cannon Fodder."

In April 1987, a federal grand jury in Arkansas brought charges against Beam, Butler, Miles, and their associates for the crime of seditious conspiracy dating from the 1983 Aryan World Congress, which spawned The Order. The charges included conspiracy to overthrow the government; to assassinate an FBI agent and a federal judge; to bomb federal buildings, utility pipelines, and electrical transmission lines; and to poison water supplies and sabotage railroads—as well as robbery, transportation of stolen money, and counterfeiting. Upon his indictment Beam escaped to Mexico, thus becoming a fugitive and earning a place on the FBI's most wanted list. He was eventually recaptured and put on trial with his codefendants. All were acquitted when the trial ended a year later, in April 1988.

It was in this context that Beam published *Seditious Conspiracy.* This document was a direct response to his indictment and a statement on his status and philosophy as a political dissident, if not a revolutionary. Most notably, the booklet included a copy of Beam's official wanted poster and his thoughts on the American government, power and freedom, freedom of religion, the "system," and political strategy, as well as a general call for sedition against the federal government and for white secession from the United States, corresponding to Miles's and Butler's Northwest Imperative. According to Beam, "Political, economic, religious, and ethnic conditions in the United States have reached the point where patriots are faced with a choice of rebellion or departure. That this is indisputably the case, and further, that the sun has forever set on the American Republic of our Forefathers, resulting in the necessity of such choice being made, is clear upon a collateral deduction that departure . . . is a sound method of re-establishing a new constitutional republic."

As the new decade emerged and conflict between the government and the movement increased, so did Beam's profile. It was also at this time that Beam solidified his relationship to Aryan Nations and the Northwest Imperative by relocating from his Texas base to Idaho. In February 1992, he published his essay "Leaderless Resistance," in which he called for a paradigm shift in paramilitary combat strategy, from traditional hierarchical forms to that of numerous autonomous cells that would function like a guerrilla army in the movement's resistance against the state. For Beam, "Leaderless Resistance" represented a rejection of traditional top-down leadership structures. He viewed such structures as dangerous because of the history of infiltration by progovernment forces.

The dangers that Beam identifies with the traditional organizational structure were of particular concern for the movement, as was demonstrated to Beam and others when the FBI recruited The Order's Tom Martinez as an informant against them. According to Beam, Leaderless Resistance is based on a "Phantom Cell" structure, where each cell operates independently and without any central control over, communication with, or knowledge of the others, thus preventing the possibility of the infiltration or capture of one cell potentially affecting other cells.

The conflict between the movement and the government increased later that year. Between the 20th and 31st of August 1992, the Ruby Ridge, Idaho, home of Aryan Nations associate and Identity adherent Randy Weaver became the site of an eleven-day standoff with the FBI and BATF, following an attempt to arrest him for failing to appear in court on weapons charges. The siege resulted in the deaths of Weaver's wife and son, which mobilized the entire antigovernment extreme Right and led directly to the Rocky Mountain Rendezvous at Estes Park, Colorado, on October 23, 1992. This event, which Richard Butler, Robert Miles, and Beam all attended, was organized by Christian Identity minister Pete Peters in order to plan a response to the Ruby Ridge incident. It was at this event that Beam's Leaderless Resistance strategy was unveiled publicly. The Rocky Mountain Rendezvous and Leaderless Resistance have frequently been cited as major influences on the development and growth of the militia movement, which became increasingly promi-

Louis Beam Jr., Aryan Nations member and advocate of the antigovernment Leaderless Resistance movement, is escorted out of a March 18, 1993, news briefing in Waco, Texas, following the siege of the Branch Davidian complex by the FBI and ATF. Beam was arrested for refusing to leave the premises after confrontations with the FBI. *(Associated Press)*

nent over the next few years leading up to the Oklahoma bombing in 1995.

Diminished Influence and Decline

In the year following the Estes Park event, Beam reemerged at the FBI and ATF standoff with the Branch Davidians in Waco, Texas. The standoff mobilized the antigovernment movement in much the same manner as Ruby Ridge had done and gave Beam a new outlet for his writings and strategies. Under the auspices of his role as a reporter for the Christian Identity paper, *Jubilee*, he attended the daily press briefings and got into confrontations with the FBI, eventually getting arrested. As the decade progressed, he made occasional appearances at major events such as militia and Christian Identity conferences in 1994 and

1996, and continued posting messages on the Internet. By the end of the decade, he was married for the fifth time, had two sons, and made frequent trips to Costa Rica to visit a fugitive friend. He was also engaged in a custody dispute with his fourth ex-wife and had been accused by her of child molestation and cited as a bad ideological influence. The case revealed that Beam was living on government benefits, awarded to him because of his post-traumatic stress disorder.

Aaron Winter

See also: Aryan Nations; Butler, Richard Girnt; Christian Identity Movement; Ku Klux Klan; Mathews, Robert Jay; Order, The; Weaver, Randy.

Further Reading

Barkun, Michael. *Religion and the Racist Right: The Origins of the Christian Identity Movement.* Chapel Hill: University of North Carolina Press, 1997.

Beam, Louis, Jr. "Leaderless Resistance." In *Encyclopedia of White Power: A Sourcebook on the Radical Right,* ed. Jeffrey Kaplan, pp. 504–11. New York: Altamira Press, 2000.

———. "Seditious Conspiracy." *Calling Our Nation* 58 (1987): 8–21.

———. *Understanding the Struggle, or Why We Have to Kill the Bastards.* Hayden Lake, ID: Aryan Nations–Teutonic Unity, n.d.

Berlet, Chip, and Matthew N. Lyons. *Right-Wing Populism in America: Too Close for Comfort.* New York: Guilford Press, 2000.

Dobratz, Betty A., and Stephanie L. Shanks-Meile. *The White Separatist Movement in the United States: "White Power, White Pride!"* Baltimore: Johns Hopkins University Press, 2000.

Ridgeway, James. *Blood in the Face: The Ku Klux Klan, Aryan Nations, Nazi Skinheads, and the Rise of the New White Culture.* New York: Thunder's Mouth Press, 1990.

Southern Poverty Law Center. "Bombs, Bullets, Bodies: The Decade in Review." *SPLC Intelligence Report* 97 (Winter 2000): 8–29. Available: http://www.splcenter.org.

———. "The Firebrand." *SPLC Intelligence Report* (Summer 2002). Available: http://www.splcenter.org.

"13 White Supremacists Acquitted of All Charges." *Seattle Times,* April 7, 1988, p. A1.

Bin Laden, Osama (1957–)

Osama bin Laden is an Islamic extremist and founder of the al-Qaeda network. He was born on March 10, 1957, in Riyadh, Saudi Arabia, to one of the kingdom's wealthiest families. He is the son of a Yemeni immigrant father and a Syrian mother. His billionaire father, Sheikh Muhammad bin Laden, was an uneducated, self-made businessman who founded the Jeddah-based Saudi bin Laden Group in 1950. The multibillion-dollar global construction company and equity management conglomerate was created with the support of a personal friend, King Abdul Aziz (Ibn Sa'ud), the first monarch of Saudi Arabia. The private connections between the Saudi royal family and the bin Laden family enabled the latter to amass a fortune via exclusive government contracts throughout the 1950s.

Bin Laden's parents divorced while he was still a child. His mother remarried, and he grew up with the new couple and their four children. Although he was raised as a committed Sunni Muslim, he went to a mostly secular Jeddah school, the prestigious Al-Thager Model School, from 1968 to 1976. Bin Laden was enrolled in after-school Islamic study programs, where he was introduced to the fundamentalist political philosophy of the Muslim Brotherhood, an influential Sunni Islamist movement seeking to reestablish an Islamic caliphate. Sayyid Qutb, one of the foremost thinkers of the Egyptian Muslim Brotherhood, had a significant influence on bin Laden. Qutb's teachings, notably his writings on martyrdom, also played an essential role in the development of the Islamist movement throughout the 1970s.

Rise

Bin Laden first married at age seventeen. He attended King Abdul Aziz University in Jeddah and began working in the family construction business. It is unclear whether he ever earned a degree. While at the university, he was exposed to two prominent Muslim Brotherhood members: Muhammad Qutb, brother of Sayyid Qutb, and Abdullah Azzam, a Palestinian Islamic scholar who educated him in Islamic law. Bin Laden was also mentored by Musa al-Qarni, a Saudi *mufti* who viewed all Christians and Jews as enemies of Islam. Qutb and Azzam further promoted a worldwide jihad against non-Muslims. Azzam was particularly vocal about the necessity of jihad against the Soviets, who invaded Afghanistan in 1979.

According to the CIA unclassified factsheet on bin Laden, he left Saudi Arabia in 1979 in order to fight Soviet Union forces in Afghanistan. Within a few years, he and Azzam cofounded Maktab al-Khidamat (MAK, or Services Office) in Pashawar, a major city in the Pakistani North-West Frontier Province. The purpose of MAK was to help bring in fighters and provide funds to the Afghan resistance movement. The organization quickly established recruitment centers around the globe (including in Egypt, Saudi Arabia, Pakistan, and the United States) to enlist, give refuge to, and transport thousands of international recruits from over fifty countries to fight in the Soviet-Afghan War. MAK established paramilitary training camps in Afghanistan and Pakistan. Throughout the 1980s, the Afghan mujahideen (Muslim fighters) resorted to asymmetric warfare tactics to fight relentlessly against Soviet military forces. They received substantial funding, as well as training and weapons, from the United States (via the CIA), Saudi Arabia, Pakistan, China, Iran, and some European countries—all likely to benefit from a Soviet defeat in Afghanistan and its negative impact on Soviet expansionism. Bin Laden also used his family connections to import construction equipment in order to build roads, tunnels, hospitals, and storage facilities throughout Afghanistan.

In the late 1980s, while Azzam remained focused on supporting Muslim resistance in military campaigns against non-Muslims, bin Laden decided to spread his call to jihad around the globe. In 1988, he founded an organization called al-Qaeda ("The Base") in order to create an international alliance of militant Sunni Islamist groups. The organization included an intelligence component, a military committee, a political committee, and a committee in charge of media affairs and propaganda. In 1989, the Soviets completely withdrew from Afghanistan, and the United States abandoned the mujahideen. When Azzam was assassinated in a car bombing outside a mosque in western Peshawar on November 24, 1989, MAK was dissolved and its extremist faction joined al-Qaeda's ranks.

The leader of the Egyptian Palestinian Jihad, Ayman al-Zawahiri, suggested that bin Laden create an umbrella organization to take control of Afghanistan and spread the new Islamic empire. Bin Laden secured substantial funding for al-Qaeda's expansion through the Pakistani ISI (Directorate for Inter-Services Intelligence), which managed to use the massive funds obtained from the United States and Saudi Arabia during the Soviet-Afghan War. In addition, bin Laden effectively turned al-Qaeda into a sheltering organization in charge of supply and resource management, intelligence gathering, and logistical support for a variety of semiautonomous militant Islamic groups around the globe.

Meanwhile, bin Laden returned to Saudi Arabia to work for the family company. In 1991, his sustained antigovernment activities within the kingdom and in Yemen led the Saudi government to banish him (they also revoked his citizenship in 1994). Bin Laden moved to Sudan and continued to recruit mujahideen from various countries to join al-Qaeda. Pressured by the United States and threats of United Nations sanctions, following the 1995 attempted assassination of Egypt's president Hosni Mubarak, Sudan expelled bin Laden in May 1996. He quickly found refuge in Afghanistan, where he was welcomed by Abdul Rasul Sayyaf, a leader of the Afghan Northern Alliance, and other prominent Afghan figures. He grew closer to Mullah Mohammed Omar and other leading members of the new Taliban regime, a puritanical Sunni and Pashtun movement that remained in power until 2001. Bin Laden promptly provided financial and paramilitary support to the Taliban government, and, in 1997, he moved to its stronghold in Kandahar.

Beliefs and Goals

In bin Laden's own words, the goal of al-Qaeda is to "unite all Muslims and establish a government which follows the rule of the Caliphs." Since he considers that the caliphate can be established only by force, the main mission of al-Qaeda consists of overthrowing corrupt Muslim governments, ridding their countries of any and all Western influence, and ultimately, obtaining worldwide political supremacy of the Muslim *ummah* (nation). Dedicated to the global development of the jihadist movement, bin Laden has outlined al-Qaeda's four major objectives as (1) the purification of Islam, (2) the establishment of an Islamic caliphate, (3) the annihilation of the infidels (nonbelievers), and (4) the destruction of Israel. Thus, bin Laden has declared that al-Qaeda's enemies are the United States, the West, Israel, and any Muslims who disagree with jihadist theology. It has been argued that bin Laden's ideological rhetoric denotes a pragmatic form of messianism, as his focus on and commitment to seemingly limited nationalistic ideals and political goals can in fact be interpreted as powerful instruments within a much more expansive anti-Western ideology and a staunch, morally rigid interpretation of Islamic reform.

In February 1998, bin Laden announced the creation of the World Islamic Front for Jihad Against the Jews and Crusaders. The international alliance included Egyptian Islamic Jihad and three other groups representing the jihad movement in Egypt, Pakistan, and Bangladesh. Al-Zawahiri later officially merged his Egyptian Islamic Jihad organization into al-Qaeda. On February 23, 1998, bin Laden and al-Zawahiri released a joint *fatwa* (a legal, binding ruling regarding Islamic law) under the banner of the World Islamic Front. The comprehensive statement enjoins Muslims to kill Americans and their allies, both civilians and military personnel, across the globe. Bin Laden, who has referred to the position of the United States against Muslims in Palestine as "despicable and disgraceful," has explained the fatwa as essentially requiring the indiscriminate killing of "all those who participate in, or help the Jewish occupiers in killing Muslims." The much-publicized document was used by the 9/11 Commission to informally link bin Laden to the September 11, 2001, attacks on U.S. soil.

Most Wanted

On August 7, 1998, just a few months after the issuance of the World Islamic Front fatwa, two bombings were perpetrated against U.S. embassies, in Nairobi, Kenya, and Dar es Salaam, Tanzania. They killed 224 people. Bin Laden was directly linked to the bombings, and as a result, assets potentially linked to him were frozen. President Bill Clinton signed an executive order authorizing his capture or assassination. On November 4, 1998, a federal grand jury indicted bin Laden, and the U.S. Department of State offered a $5 million reward for information leading to his arrest or conviction. Bin Laden has since been one of the FBI's Ten Most Wanted Fugitives and is also listed as its Most Wanted Terrorist. He is officially wanted for murder of U.S. nationals outside the United States, conspiracy to murder U.S. nationals outside the United States, and attack on a federal facility resulting in death. The Department of State is offering a reward of up to $25 million via the Rewards for Justice Program for information leading directly to bin Laden's apprehension or conviction (an additional $2 million reward is being offered through a program created by the Airline Pilots Association and the Air Transport Association).

Bin Laden is also "a suspect in other terrorist attacks throughout the world," including the October 2000 suicide bombing against the USS *Cole* in Yemen and the September 11, 2001, attacks against the World Trade Center and the Pentagon. Bin Laden and al-Qaeda were immediately named as prime suspects by U.S. authorities. However, to this day, there is no direct evidence linking bin Laden to the September 2001 attacks, and he has not been indicted for them. Bin Laden officially denied any involvement in the attacks in an interview published in a Pakistani newspaper on September 28, 2001, in which he declared: "I am not involved in the 11 September attacks in the United States. As a Muslim, I try my best to avoid telling a lie. I had no knowledge of these attacks, nor do I consider the killing of innocent women, children and other humans as an appreciable act. Islam strictly forbids causing harm to innocent women, children and other people. Such a practice is forbidden even in the course of a battle." In November 2001, a videotape supposedly discovered by U.S. forces in Afghanistan included a conversation in which bin Laden admitted knowing about the attacks beforehand; although the tape was released to the media and broadcast extensively the following month, it has yet to be authenticated. Another videotaped statement surfaced at the same time, in which bin Laden praised the acts of terrorism against the United States, as he had done on multiple occasions with past attacks against U.S. interests, but no claim of responsibility was ever officially recorded. In March 2007, Khalid Sheikh Mohammed, a suspected terrorist who had been detained by U.S. authorities since March 2003, allegedly confessed that he had been the mastermind of the September 2001 attacks (among other high-profile incidents), claiming, "I was responsible for the 9/11 operation, from A to Z." The veracity of his statements has yet to be confirmed, and they have been challenged by many U.S. and foreign government officials, as well as various human rights groups.

Bin Laden has eluded capture for several years now, in spite of a massive U.S.-led manhunt in and beyond Afghanistan. In January 2002, Pakistani president Pervez Musharraf said that bin Laden had "probably" died in late 2001 as a result of his long-standing kidney disease and inability to receive proper treatment. In July 2002, Dale Watson, the head of the FBI's counterterrorism unit, declared also that bin Laden was probably dead but offered no hard evidence to corroborate his claim. In October 2002, Afghan president Hamid Karzai concurred with the idea that bin Laden was probably dead, unlike Taliban leader Mullah Omar. In late September 2006, the DGSE (Directorate-General for External Security, the French secret service) claimed to have reliable evidence that bin Laden had died of complications of typhoid fever in Pakistan. On August 23, 2006. French and U.S. officials soon disavowed the DGSE report, however, which was widely reported in the American media as a hoax.

Reports of bin Laden's demise were definitively refuted by the resumption of videotaped messages in September 2007 to mark the sixth anniversary of the September 11 attacks. All in all, from 2001 to mid-2010, bin Laden and second-in-command Ayman al-Zawahiri broadcast more than sixty audio and video messages to the world, claiming credit for various attacks and threatening others.

Already by 2005, meanwhile, Western intelligence sources indicated that at least two-thirds of bin Laden's original top associates had been killed, captured, or scattered. Moreover, it was reported, he no longer had the financial resources to support al-Qaeda terrorist activities. Although the majority of the world's Muslims do not share his militant views, Osama bin Laden—said to be hiding somewhere in the mountainous border region of Pakistan or Afghanistan—has remained a hero in jihadist circles and the most sought-after figure by the U.S. military.

Cécile Van de Voorde

See also: Al-Qaeda; Islamic Fundamentalism; Middle East; Mujahideen; Taliban; Terrorism.

Further Reading

Anti-Defamation League. *Osama Bin Laden: Profile.* New York: Anti-Defamation League, 2007. Available: http://www.adl.org/terrorism_america/bin_L.asp.

Bergen, Peter. *The Osama Bin Laden I Know: An Oral History of Al-Qaeda's Leader.* New York: Free Press, 2006.

Blanchard, Christopher M. *Al Qaeda: Statements and Evolving Ideology.* Washington, DC: Congressional Research Service, 2007.

Gutman, Roy. *How We Missed the Story: Osama bin Laden, the Taliban, and the Hijacking of Afghanistan.* Washington, DC: United States Institute of Peace, 2008.

Hellmich, Christina. "Al-Qaeda: Terrorists, Hypocrites, Fundamentalists? The View from Within." *Third World Quarterly* 26:1 (2005): 39–54.

"Interview: Osama Bin Laden." *Frontline.* Arlington, VA: PBS, 1998. Available: http://www.pbs.org/wgbh/pages/frontline/shows/binladen/who/interview.html.

Olsson, Peter A. *The Cult of Osama: Psychoanalyzing Bin Laden and His Magnetism for Muslim Youths.* Westport, CT: Praeger Security International, 2008.

Sasson, Jean, Omar bin Laden, and Najwa bin Laden. *Growing up bin Laden: Osama's Wife and Son Take Us Inside Their Secret World.* New York: St. Martin's Press, 2009.

Snyder. Robert S. "Hating America: Bin Laden as a Civilizational Revolutionary." *The Review of Politics* 65:4 (2003): 325–49.

"Special Report: War Against Terror—Osama bin Laden." CNN (online), 2007. Available: http://www.cnn.com/SPECIALS/2001/trade.center/binladen.section.html.

White, Jonathan R. *Terrorism and Homeland Security: An Introduction.* 5th ed. Belmont, CA: Wadsworth, 2006.

Bloody Sunday

Bloody Sunday is one of the worst examples of government violence against Catholics in Northern Ireland. It refers to Sunday, January 30, 1972, when the First Paratroop Regiment of the British army opened fire on a civilian anti-internment march in Derry, Northern Ireland, killing or injuring a total of twenty-eight members of the Nationalist community. It resulted in the recruitment of many persons into the Irish Republican Army (IRA) and is held to be one of the reasons behind an escalation of the armed struggle by the Republican forces.

Background

Northern Ireland is made up of the Protestant majority population and the Catholic minority population. Historically the Catholics have been treated as second-class citizens and suffered discrimination in housing, employment, and the right to vote. The Catholic minority is made up of Nationalists (constitutionalists) and Republicans (formerly proponents of physical force) who want to reunite with Ireland; the Protestant majority is made up of Unionists (constitutionalists) and Loyalists (formerly proponents of physical force) who wish to remain part of Great Britain. While the two communities are divided along denominational lines, the nearly thirty-year conflict referred to in Ireland as the Troubles has less to do with religion than with the fact that Northern Ireland was created as a separate political entity to ensure Protestant rule in the six counties that had Protestant majorities.

The late 1960s saw the rise of the civil rights

movement in Northern Ireland. Discrimination in employment and housing and gerrymandered electoral borders were particularly acute in Derry, the second-largest city in Northern Ireland, making it a hotbed of discontent. Derry is a divided city, with the Catholic (Nationalist, Republican) population living in enclaves known as the Creggan Estate and the Bogside on one side of the River Foyle and the Protestant (Unionist, Loyalist) population inhabiting the Waterside district on the opposing bank.

It was a sign of the times when the Derry Civil Rights Association was created in the late 1960s, and it flourished as Nationalists from the Bogside began to demand changes to the status quo. The repressive use of force by the security forces in Derry paved the way for heightened tension among the Nationalist population. On October 5, 1968, a civil rights march took place that was brutally repressed by the Royal Ulster Constabulary (RUC, the 95 percent Protestant police force). Police with batons charged the crowd, and a Nationalist politician was hit in the head. The event was captured on television. This episode prompted the first of many riots in Derry. The following summer saw the Battle of the Bogside, a three-day episode of violence that stretched the resources of the RUC to such a point that Stormont leaders requested the British government to send in the army as reinforcement. "No-go Areas" were created in the Bogside, where a mural declared, "You are now entering Free Derry," meaning the area was out of bounds to the security forces.

In August 1971 internment—the imprisonment of people without charges or a trial—was instituted, resulting in the incarceration of an overwhelming number of Nationalists. The purpose of this measure was to take the leaders of the IRA off the street. In reality, most who were swept up in the raids were not associated with the guerrilla force. This policy had the dubious benefit of bringing together all the

Nationalists, as everyone had family, friends, or neighbors who were behind bars. It mobilized the community, and soon they were protesting internment in the streets.

The anti-internment march of Sunday, January 30, 1972, which was organized by the Northern Ireland Civil Rights Association (NICRA), had been banned by the authorities but went ahead anyway. According to various reports, somewhere between 10,000 and 25,000 people marched. The route of the march had been blocked by an army barrier at William Street, preventing the protesters from attaining Guildhall Square, where they were to converge to hear speeches from Nationalist MPs (members of Parliament) and civil rights leaders. In order to avoid a direct confrontation with the army, the march was diverted up

A British paratrooper assaults a Catholic protestor during a civil rights march on January 30, 1972, in Derry, Northern Ireland. The Bloody Sunday conflict resulted in the deaths of fourteen Catholic Nationalists and was a major catalyst for recruitment into the IRA and the escalation of its armed struggle against Northern Irish Protestant Loyalists. *(Thopson/ AFP/Getty Images)*

Rossville Street toward "Free Derry Corner." In the confusion created by the change of route, some continued toward the Bogside, while some young men stayed around William Street, where the army had erected the barricade. The young men began their ritual of throwing stones at the army, a regular feature in Derry. It was then that the paratroopers opened fire on the crowd. Within ten minutes, fourteen victims lay dead and another fourteen injured. Following the carnage, the army asserted that they had been fired upon first, but none of the dead or injured had been found carrying weapons.

Reaction was fierce. Violence escalated in the six counties of the North. In Dublin, two days later, the British embassy was burned down. Bernadette Devlin, the youngest member of the Westminster Parliament, in a heated exchange with Home Secretary Reginald Maudling over the Bloody Sunday events, walked across the floor of the House of Commons and slapped him in the face. Dublin called a national day of mourning when the victims were buried. The Irish government also recalled the Irish ambassador to London. In the weeks following the massacre the Provisional IRA escalated its campaign of violence and killed fifty-six soldiers. Ten weeks following Bloody Sunday, Stormont was suspended by the British, and the affairs of Northern Ireland were thereafter run directly from London, until the New Assembly was created in response to the Belfast Agreement of 1998, otherwise known as the Good Friday Agreement.

The Widgery Tribunal

The magnitude of the atrocity on Bloody Sunday necessitated that the British government institute an inquiry, and within forty-eight hours, the Widgery Tribunal had been set up, under the chairmanship of Lord Chief Justice Widgery, in order to establish the facts surroundings the shooting of civilians by the army. Its objectivity was questioned by the Nationalist community. First, the chairman was a former member of the British Armed Forces. Moreover, many key eyewitnesses were not called to testify in the hearings, and Widgery decreed that 700 eyewitness statements had arrived too late and did not take them into account. The wounded were not asked for any statements. Widgery quickly moved to restrict the investigation to "the period beginning with the moment when the march first became involved in violence and ending with the deaths and the conclusion of the affair." It eventually emerged that, in a meeting between then Prime Minister Edward Heath and Lord Widgery, a discussion had ensued on the manner in which the inquiry was to take place in order to favor the army. The Widgery Report was produced ten weeks after the events and consisted of a mere thirty-six pages. It exonerated the army from any wrongdoing. The report stated that no weapons had been found on any of the victims and no traces of gelignite (a substance used in making explosives) were discovered on the victims' clothing.

The complete exoneration of the armed forces by the Widgery Report left the Nationalist population of the North embittered and further committed to the struggle to rid the North of the British presence. John Hume, of the Social Democratic and Labour Party, asserted after the ordeal, "Many people down here [the Bogside] feel now that it is a united Ireland or nothing." An inquest into the deaths was carried out in August 1973. The coroner, Major Hubert O'Neill, stated that "the Army [had] run amok that day and shot without thinking what they were doing. They were shooting innocent people. These people may have been taking part in a march that was banned but that does not justify the troops coming in and firing live rounds indiscriminately. I would say without hesitation that it was sheer, unadulterated murder. It was murder."

Remembering Bloody Sunday

A commemoration of Bloody Sunday has taken place every year since, on the anniversary of the event. A monument to the victims was unveiled in January 1974. The Bloody Sunday Initiative (BSI) was created in 1987 in order to push for a new inquiry. Among other things, in 1992, it commissioned a book entitled *Bloody Sunday in Derry: What Really Happened* to denounce the Widgery Report. The same year, which marked the twentieth anniversary, it collaborated on a Channel 4 television documentary exposing the problems with Widgery and created a broader support group, the Bloody Sunday Justice Campaign (BSJC), to step up the campaign to secure a second inquiry. Another group, the Pat Finucane Centre (PFC)—named after a solicitor who was gunned down by the Loyalist paramilitary group the Ulster Defence Association (UDA) in collusion with the British Security Services in 1989—was involved in dealing with the broader human rights issues. In 1996 a large bag full of statements was discovered— statements that had been ignored by the Widgery Tribunal. This propelled campaigners to push harder for a new inquiry. The following year the Bloody Sunday Trust was established to provide a "Derry-based history and educational project . . . to commemorate the events of Bloody Sunday and to preserve the memory of those murdered that day."

The Saville Enquiry

In 1997, the Irish government gave the British government a critique of the Widgery Report and suggested that in the context of the peace process, a new independent inquiry would be in order. The Saville Enquiry was called in January 1998, a few weeks before the signing of the Belfast/Good Friday Agreement. Lord Saville, the chairman, was flanked by an Australian and a Canadian judge. The mandate of the inquiry was broader than that of Widgery and called for the examination of any new evidence. The inquiry began March 27, 2000, and ended on November 23, 2004. A total of 912 witnesses were heard, including soldiers, IRA members, civilians, journalists, and politicians. The results were finally made public on June 15, 2010, laying blame for the deaths and injuries of Bloody Sunday on British forces. According to the report, paratroopers had "lost control" and fired the first shots on unarmed civilians. British Prime Minister David Cameron, addressing the House of Commons, apologized on behalf of the government for what "should never, ever have happened."

Commemoration: A New Museum

The opening of the Museum of Free Derry: The National Civil Rights Archive in 2007 coincided with the thirty-fifth anniversary commemoration of Bloody Sunday. Though established by the Bloody Sunday Trust, it has exhibits that cover the entire period of the civil rights era in Derry. In its first phase, it focuses on, among other things, the Battle of the Bogside, internment and Free Derry, and Bloody Sunday. Situated in Glenfada Park, in the heart of Free Derry, the museum displays 25,000 items pertaining to the civil rights history of the area. One of the museum's objectives is to provide "a means of education and information on an era that had, and continues to have, major local, national and international significance."

Claire Delisle

See also: Adams, Gerry; Northern Ireland; Paisley, Ian; Roman Catholicism; Sands, Bobby.

Further Reading

Bloody Sunday Trust. Available: www.bloodysundaytrust.org.

Coogan, T.P. *The Troubles: Ireland's Ordeal and the Search for Peace.* New York: Palgrave, 2002.

McCann, Eamonn, ed. *The Bloody Sunday Enquiry: The Families Speak Out.* London: Pluto Press, 2006.

———. *War and an Irish Town.* Boulder, CO: Pluto Press, 1993.

McCann, Eamonn, with Maureen Shiels and Bridie Hannigan. *Bloody Sunday in Derry: What Really Happened.* Dingle, Ireland: Brandon, 1992.

Museum of Free Derry: The National Civil Rights Archive. Available: www.museumoffreederry.org.

Rolston, Bill. *Unfinished Business: State Killings and the Quest for Truth.* Belfast: Beyond the Pale, 2000.

Walsh, Dermot P.J. *Bloody Sunday and the Rule of Law in Northern Ireland.* London: Macmillan, 2000.

Buddhism

During twenty-five centuries of history, Buddhism has encountered and has merged with various and diverse cultures, religions, and philosophical traditions. It has been involved in political conflicts, it has been persecuted, and it has confronted various kinds of historical contingencies. As a consequence, Buddhist schools present a number of different and sometimes contrasting perspectives, attitudes, and texts on violence.

Orthodox View on Violence

From an orthodox point of view, a Buddhist should avoid all forms of violence. The most ancient texts are very clear on this, and the historical Buddha Siddhartha Gautama is said to have condemned all kinds of violence on many occasions. The refusal of violence is necessary so that one does not accumulate bad deeds and is able to walk the path of Buddha, the ultimate goal being the extinction of desire and ignorance, which is called nirvana. The refusal of violence is rooted in the conception of karma—the idea that actions cumulate and are the cause of one's own destiny. This notion of life, governed by laws of cause and effect, implies the rebirth in a higher or lower form of life after one's death.

The concept of abstention from violence appears to be very important among the first Buddhist groups, which were mainly monastic communities (Sanskrit: *sangha*), and this is still a central principle in most of the contemporary Buddhist schools. The complete absence of animal sacrifices (a common custom among pre-Buddhist Indian religions) in Buddhist rituals is also ascribable to the emphasis put by Siddhartha on abstaining from violence, a theme that is repeated and elaborated throughout the body of the most ancient records on the teachings of Siddhārtha: the Pali Canon, traditionally known as the Tipitaka ("three baskets").

The Pali Canon is the central body of texts of the Theravada branch of Buddhism and the earliest comprehensive source on Buddhism. The canon is also incorporated—sometimes in reduced forms or variants—in the body of texts of virtually all of the existent Buddhist schools, although it is sometimes reputed to be of lesser value than other books by non-Theravada schools. Today Theravada Buddhism is the main religion in Sri Lanka, Cambodia, Laos, Myanmar, and Thailand and is present in many other countries. According to tradition, the Pali Canon is the result of the first Buddhist council, which was held shortly after the death of Siddhartha, during which disciples and relatives of the Buddha recited his teachings and sermons. Transmitted orally, it was transcribed, together with commentaries and later additions, during the first century B.C.E. In the canon, the heart of Siddhartha's teachings is resumed in four points, known as the Four Noble Truths: (1) All is suffering. (2) The origin of suffering is craving. (3) The ending of craving is the way to end suffering. (4) The way to end craving is the Eightfold Path.

The Eightfold Path—the way to the extinction of suffering—is implemented through the actuation of eight precepts: right view, right intention, right speech, right action, right livelihood, right effort, right mindfulness, right concentration. In the Pali Canon, almost all of these eight guiding principles are explicitly related to the avoiding of all forms of violence. Right intention (or right thought), for example, includes the commitment to *ahimsa,* a Sanskrit term usually translated as "nonviolence" or "noninjury." Ahimsa indicates the disposition of not harming or damaging any living being and the abstention from the use of all kinds of violence. Right action, right livelihood, and right effort also entail the implementation of this principle, together with a number of other notions, such as compassion, harmlessness, unattached benevolence, goodwill, and loving-kindness toward everyone; self-discipline; and the extinction of desires, pride, and hatred.

Hatred, blame, and violence are considered the major obstacles for the abolition of ignorance, the ending of suffering through the Eightfold Path, and the attainment of nirvana. This is a major theme thoroughly developed in the course of the entire Pali Canon: Siddhartha exhorted his followers to train themselves not to provoke or cause hatred inside or outside themselves, to be compassionate and patient, to abstain from acts that construct a negative karma, to implement ahimsa, and to put into practice the ideal of a spiritual practitioner who has understood the illusive nature of this world and is reaching the tranquility of mind that derives from it. This state lets a person endure all kinds of trials without hatred or violence arising, even if treated with cruelty or violence, like "a flattened metal pot that doesn't resound."

The first part of the Pali Canon, called *Vinayapitaka,* or "basket of discipline," comprises the monastic rules for the monks and nuns and remains in spirit fundamentally the same for most of the historical and contemporary Buddhist schools. One of the four misdeeds that causes expulsion from the monastic order is murder or incitation to murder: "Whatsoever Bhikkhu ["a male monk"] shall knowingly deprive of life a human being, or shall seek out an assassin against a human being, or shall utter the praises of death, or incite another to self-destruction, saying, 'Ho! my friend! what good do you get from this sinful, wretched life? death is better to thee than life!'—if, so thinking, and with such an aim, he, by various argument, utter the praises of death or incite another to self-destruction . . . he is no longer in communion." Among the lesser offenses, many point to a respect of life in all of its forms: for example, it is forbidden to damage living plants, to pour or use water containing living beings, to deprive an animal of life, and to wander in the woods during the rainy season, which causes killing of the newborn grass and plants. Moreover, interpersonal conflicts are to be carefully avoided, and a monk is supposed to refrain from actions like stealing (another of the four misconducts that lead to expulsion from the sangha), provoking quarrels or discord, lying, and generating hatred or resentments. Rules for nuns are basically the same.

In the second part of the Pali Canon, called *Sutrapitaka,* or *Suttapitaka* (pali)—a very extensive writing composed of anecdotes, dialogues, discourses, verses, and fables of the Buddha's former births (*Jatakas*)—the theme of (abstention from) violence is discursively developed and abundantly treated. The words and stories of the Buddha always condemn violence to any kind of beings. In the *Dhammapada,* one of the many subsections of the *Sutrapitaka,* it is said that hatred produces hatred and that hatred ceases by love alone; that a monk has to stay in a village, like a bee in a flower, without injuring it; that a Buddhist shall not occupy himself or herself with other people's misdeeds but with his or her own; that the real conquest is the one against the self, worth more than the victory in innumerable battles; that a person who offends a harmless one is like a fool throwing dust against the wind;

how to be tolerant with the intolerants; how a right man does not further his purposes with violence; how a Buddhist endures abuses as an elephant supports the arrows during a battle; how the sage man injures nobody; and that anger of the body, of the tongue, and of the mind has to be controlled and abandoned. The command "Do not kill nor cause slaughter" and the ones against anger, hatred, pride, and envy are repeated many times. In another section of the *Sutrapitaka*, called *Sabbasava Sutta*, the Buddha exhorts his followers to tolerate the touch of flies and mosquitoes, reptiles, unwelcome words, and bodily feelings even when they are life threatening, while in the book called *Kakacupama Sutta,* he addresses his followers by saying, "If anyone were to give you a blow with the hand, or hit you with a clod of earth, or with a stick, or with a sword, even then you should abandon those urges and thoughts which are worldly. There . . . you should train yourself thus: 'Neither shall my mind be affected by this, nor shall I give vent to evil words; but I shall remain full of concern and pity, with a mind of love, and I shall not give in to hatred.' . . . Monks, even if bandits were to carve you up savagely, limb by limb, with a two-handled saw, he among you who let his heart get angered . . . would not be doing my bidding."

Mahayana Buddhism

Around the first century C.E., new interpretations and philosophies appeared, while Buddhism expanded its horizons and popularity. Great emphasis began to be put on formerly secondary concepts, and a body of new *sutras* and notions developed. A new branch of Buddhism calling itself Mahayana ("the great vehicle") emerged in opposition to the existing Theravada schools, which the founders of Mahayana viewed as conservative and narrow minded and referred to, pejoratively, as the Hinayana ("lesser vehicle"). Today schools be-

longing to the Mahayana branch are found in most of Central Asia and the Far East. The major teachings followed in China, Japan, Korea, and Vietnam, as well as the Vajrayana schools prevalent in Tibet, Mongolia, Nepal, and Bhutan, belong to the Mahayana branch. A fundamental difference between the two branches was the birth of a universalistic perspective among the Mahayana originators—the idea that everybody can attain nirvana, not only the monks; hence the name Great Vehicle. Whatever the differing perspectives of the two branches, the fundamental views on violence, hatred, and compassion expressed in the Pali Canon are present and shared in most of the Mahayana sutras. In the *Sutra of the Five Greatest Gifts,* for example, the historical Buddha explains how nonviolence is the "greatest gift."

Among the differences between the two traditions are the dietary obligations. As a logical consequence of the precepts against taking life and an implementation of the principles of ahimsa, harmlessness and compassion toward all sentient beings, vegetarianism is adopted, today, by many monastic orders. Siddhartha was not vegetarian, and he is said to have died of food poisoning after eating pork. In the oldest rules (*vinaya*) for monks and in the versions used by Theravada communities, there is no prohibition on eating meat, although it is stated that monks should not consume meat or fish if they know or suspect that the animal has been killed for them.

With the birth of universities and monasteries, where food for the monks was produced and prepared—especially in China, where the practice of requesting alms was not very popular and monasteries owned land—a problem arose: it was, in fact, unacceptable for monks to have animals killed for their nutrition. Vegetarianism was then adopted and seen as a logical consequence of the spirit of the teachings. Mahayana writings were produced, expressing this new view. The Mahayana *Brahma Net Sutra,* a text composed in China in the fifth century, forbids the consumption of meat and fish by monks, explaining this prohibition with the necessities of being compassionate, of not producing fear in other living being, and of refraining from putting obstacles on their path to nirvana. Another text, the *Lankāvatāra Sūtra,* explains that Mahayana followers should forget the precepts on food in the ancient texts and understand and practice the higher custom of vegetarianism. The discordance between this teaching and traditions attributed to Buddha is explained using a conventional Mahayana theme, which presents new views as the disclosure of a higher truth taught by Buddha but not passed on in the past because people were not ready to understand. The perspective on vegetarianism as being a way to implement ahimsa and compassion spread in many nations, including China, Korea, and Japan, where it is practiced by virtually all the monastic communities, although rarely by the common people. No country with a relevant Buddhist population is predominantly vegetarian.

Buddhism, War, and Geopolitics

Even though the major fundamental texts clearly prescribe a profound refusal of violence and the need of commitment toward ahimsa, the history of Buddhist Asia is filled with wars waged by Buddhist nations and massacres ordered by Buddhist rulers. Very few times, if any, has Buddhist thought had a stronger influence than geopolitical matters, and the belonging of kings or nations to the community of followers of Siddhartha's teachings has not proven to prevent war.

In Buddhist historiography, four ancient kings are traditionally regarded as followers of the teachings of Siddhartha and champions in protecting or promulgating the Buddhist truth, or *dharma.* They were also great warriors and

skilled military commanders. In Buddhist historiography the conversion to Buddhism of these personalities coincided with their abandonment of violence, although historical evidence does not always confirm this perspective. Buddhism was more likely used as an ideological tool for the pacific coexistence of different peoples. A first major impulse to the expansion of Buddhism was given by King Aśoka (r. 273–232 B.C.E.). He patronized the construction of many Buddhist structures and sent missions and embassies to promulgate the Buddhist philosophy to the main known nations of his time. Buddhist historiography depicts him as a ruler who stopped his war campaigns and his violent attitudes after the conversion, promulgating then a pro-Buddhist policy and ahimsa inside his domains, going as far as forbidding unnecessary animal slaughter and promoting vegetarianism. Many contemporary Buddhist scholars hold the view that "after he embraced the teachings of the Buddha, he transformed his polity from one of military conquest to one of Dharmavijaya—victory by righteousness and truth" (Seneviratna 1994). It is probably true that at one point, traditionally seen as the bloodshed of the Kalinga War (c.261), he converted to Buddhism and focused on the internal building of his vast empire. However, it is unlikely that he abandoned the punitive aspects of the civil law or the military defense of the empire. Moreover, many scholars have pointed out that the implementation of ahimsa was essentially a political effort to introduce an ideology of pacific coexistence in a multicultural and multireligious empire. The pattern of violence-before-conversion is visible in the Buddhist historiography of the other three dharma champions and most probably disguises a more complex rapport between Buddhism, political-military violence, state ideology, and ruling elites.

The second of the Buddhist-championing kings is the Bactrian Menander I (r. c.150–110 B.C.E.), who was always escorted by 500 Greek-speaking soldiers. According to a Buddhist source, the *Milinda Pañha* ("Debate of Milinda"), after creating a kingdom in northern India through military conquests, he converted to Buddhism. The *Milinda Pañha* tells how he adopted Buddhism after receiving a number of answers to his questions on Buddhism from the monk Nàgasena. He then had residences constructed for the monk and for his numerous followers and eventually left the throne for the life of a Buddhist monk himself.

The third king famous for his military successes and praised for his attitude toward Buddhism was the head of the Kushan Empire, Kanishka (r. 127–151 C.E.), who, according to the Buddhist tradition, summoned the fourth great Buddhist council.

The fourth king to be regarded as a major supporter of the teachings of Siddhartha, Harshavardhana (r. 606–647), also fits the pattern of a skilled general who put together an extended empire and supported many Buddhist institutions, favoring the building of religious and civil constructions alike. He strongly supported the University of Nalanda, for which he pragmatically built a great defensive wall.

Similar cases of zealous Buddhists who are also skilled warriors are recurrent in Buddhist countries. The adoption of Theravada Buddhism as the national religion in modern-day Thailand, for example, is traditionally attributed to King Ramkhamhaeng (r. 1279–1317), ruler of the Sukhothai kingdom, who participated in his father's war campaign before starting his own campaigns of expansion as a king, earning the epithet of "Bold." Likewise, the fervent Buddhist king of the Khmer Empire Jayavarman VII (r. 1181–c.1220), who is renowned for his compassionate construction of hospitals and relay houses along the roads and especially for the rebuilding of the city of Angkor and many of its religious structures; who led a number of Khmer armies in victorious battles against external and internal

enemies alike; and who was also responsible for the sacking of the capital of the Champa kingdom. The lack of sufficient historical records makes difficult a proper reconstruction of the philosophical strategies used to justify war and violence from a Buddhist perspective during the reigns of the dharma champions and warrior kings, although it seems probable that some of the Buddhist views on ahimsa and compassion were considered to be high moral teachings and useful instruments of power.

In other cases, disagreements on religious issues have been used to justify wars between Buddhist nations, masking other interests and objectives. King Anawrahta (r. 1044–1077), for example, who formed what is celebrated today as the first Burmese unified kingdom and worked actively to convert the population of his kingdom from a Mahayana tantric school called *Ari* to Theravada Buddhism, commanded a successful military campaign in 1057 against the neighboring kingdom of Thaton, on the pretext of a refusal by its king, Manuba, to lend him and his people a copy of the *Tipitaka*. Anawrahta besieged the capital and destroyed it after its surrender, bringing home as captives the 30,000 survivors, including King Manuba.

A similar strategy of masking geopolitical disagreements with religious matters can be seen in the centuries-long struggle over the government of Tibet between indigenous and Chinese authorities. In 1705, the reason for the intervention of an army in Tibet, led by the Mongol prince Lhabzang, was the allegedly disreputable and shameful life that the sixth Dalai Lama, Tsangyang Gyatso, was conducting. Arrested, he died on the road to the Chinese capital. The attempt by Lhabzang to install his own son as the new Dalai Lama led to a military intervention in Tibet of a western Mongolian army. Such events became the pretext for a military intervention ordered by the Chinese emperor Kang Xi in 1718, which resulted with the enthroning of a new Dalai Lama. Since that time, the dispute over who has the right to appoint the religious-political authorities of Tibet has surfaced whenever the Chinese government and the Tibetan authorities struggle for control of the region escalates. Today the exiled government of Tibet, headed by the Dalai Lama, and the Chinese government are again disagreeing over the proper divination method (i.e., who should be the diviner) used to recognize the reincarnation of the next lamas.

Maitreyan Violent Upsurges

A number of theories have been advanced to justify exceptions to Siddhartha's admonitions against violence. One of these is the claim that defense of the faith itself overrides all other Buddhist precepts. In other words, when dharma is threatened, it may be necessary to fight the forces of evil with violence. Kill them, it is said, and Buddha will both recognize the true faithful and grant them recompense. Among the most widespread examples of this kind of justification are found in millenarian movements in the name of Maitreya.

Maitreya is the Sanskrit version of a term found in the Pali Canon by which Siddhartha indicated the Buddha who would come after him. A common belief is that when the teachings of Siddhartha have become completely corrupted or have disappeared from earth, Maitreya will come preaching the truth. His iconography is among the most common in the Buddhist world and can be found in all the regions where traces of Buddhism are visible. Sometimes, during periods of serious large-scale social difficulties or mass suffering, when the world has appeared to be completely corrupted, hopeless, and evil, the cult of Maitreya has become the polarizer for the hopes and needs of renewal. Claims of the advent of Maitreya or its near arrival have often been used by political or religious leaders to justify the seizing of power or to furnish an ideology to

violently promote political changes. The belief in the advent of Maitreya has provided a strong symbol and an ideological background for millenarian, utopian, and egalitarian movements. Especially in China, Korea, and Japan, such movements have co-opted the revolutionary or rebellious forces that spring from poverty and social inequality and promised the advent of a new era.

Between the fifth and the sixth centuries, historians have counted from seven to ten rebellions led by monks in China, probably a mixture of millenarian-social revolts fueled by the cult of Maitreya and widespread poverty. One of the best recorded of these rebellions is the Mahayana Rebellion, which took place in 515. It was led by a Buddhist monk called Faqing, financially and politically supported by a local aristocrat called Li Guibo, who was given the titles of bodhisattva ("enlightenment being") and commander of the demons-overcoming army. The motto of the insurgents was "A new Buddha has come: eradicate the demons of the former world." Violence was actively used to accelerate the advent of the new era, which would start with a new world of social justice and religious enlightenment. The Mahayana rebels are depicted by official historiography as merciless and bloodthirsty, especially aggressive against the existing Buddhist clergy and structures, and are considered demons: those who killed over a certain number of enemies were proclaimed bodhisattvas. The rebels were finally outnumbered by the imperial army, and the uprising was crushed in a bloodbath.

Insurgencies with a similar Maitreyan ideology appeared in other parts of China during the seventh century. In 613, two persons—Song Zixian and the monk Xiang Haiming—in different parts of the country claimed to be Maitreya and tried to organize a rebellion. The authorities were informed of the plot of the former before it was put into action, and thousands were executed. The latter led his uprising sustained by local aristocracy and peasants, and his army grew to impressive size before being defeated by governmental forces. Besides other lesser events of Chinese history, one major surge of violence in the name of Maitreya happened in 1047, when the army officer Wang Ze claimed the end of the age of Siddhartha and the advent of the age of Maitreya. Crushed after some initial successes, the upsurge led to a governmental ban of Maitreya sects and to the slaughter of a large number of believers.

The mixing of Maitreya beliefs with Manichean and Taoist notions is the religious basis of the White Lotus religious-political groups. Particularly relevant are the Red Turban Rebellion (1351), a major contribution to the end of the Yuan dynasty, and upsurges during the 1700s, including the rebellion of the Dacheng sect (1746), whose female leader predicted the close advent of Maitreya; the upheaval in Fujian (1748); the insurrection of the Ch'ing-shui sect (1774); and the revolt in Taiwan (1787). The longest White Lotus revolt endured for almost ten years, from 1796 to 1805. Elements of Maitreyan cults were present in many groups of bandits and rebels, as well as in the egalitarian, millenarian, and utopian movements that were active during the second half of the nineteenth century.

In Korea, the warlord and former monk Kungye declared himself the reincarnation of Maitreya in 918 and established an ephemeral kingdom in which he ruled despotically until his life was ended in a revolt by his own people. The most famous case of a Korean Maitreyan movement is the Tonghak revolt of 1894–1895, which followed a series of numerous similar smaller uprisings. In Japan, especially during the end of the Edo period (1600–1868) and at the beginning of the Meiji era (1868–1912), movements of revolt or of millenarian religious frenzy, often included claims of the arrival of Maitreya but had a less violent attitude compared with the continental ones.

Buddhism and Persecution

From the alleged persecutions of the first king of the Sunga Empire, Pusyamitra (r. c.185–150 B.C.E.), to the contemporary policies in North Korea and Tibet, the history of violence against Buddhism is long and widespread. Much more rarely, Buddhists have initiated violent discrimination against the followers of other religions. In Chinese historiography, it is common to talk about the "destruction of the dharma by three Wu emperors" to indicate that three emperors who were major persecutors of Buddhists all had the character for "Wu" in their names. They were Emperor Taiwu (r. 424–451), who, between 446 and 451, set off a campaign that associated monks and rebels, killing a high number of monks and destroying many monasteries; Emperor Wu Di (r. 561–578); and Emperor Wuzong (r. 841–847), who in 845 ordered that all Buddhist constructions and organizations be destroyed, starting the largest persecution against Buddhism in ancient Chinese history. During the years of implementation of Wuzong's edict, some sources says that up to 4,600 temples and 40,000 hermitages were destroyed and 260,500 monks and nuns forced back to secular life. This period marks the beginning of the decline of Chinese Buddhism. The arrival to power of Mao Tse-tung marked another period of hardship and persecution of Buddhism, a period that is not yet over, although the worst persecutions occurred during the years of the Cultural Revolution.

In Korea, the adoption of neo-Confucianism by the Joseon dynasty (1392–1910) and the preceding involvement of monks in politics caused a long, negative attitude toward Buddhism: with alternating force, and especially during the first centuries of the Joseon age, prohibitions, persecutions, and restrictions were inflicted on Buddhist clergy and followers. Temples were destroyed, prohibitions were issued against the building of new temples near towns, and for many years monks were forbidden to enter the capital. After the division of the peninsula into two independent states in the 1950s, Buddhism has been strongly persecuted in North Korea.

Besides other numerous cases of violent policies against Buddhism, such as those in the Khotan kingdom by King Yuchi Gui around 740 C.E., the greatest strikes have been inflicted during the Arab, Turkish, and Mongol conquests and the consequent expansion of Islam into Central Asia, India, and Southeast Asia, which in the span of few centuries has wiped out Buddhism from Iran, Afghanistan, and India and almost completely from modern-day Indonesia. Especially after the eleventh century, Buddhists became the targets of looting and raids, such as those of the warrior chief Mahmud of Ghazni (971–1030), who was renowned for his mercilessness. Many relevant universities and monasteries were destroyed, texts burned or lost, and monks slaughtered. The Mongol expansion brought more violence and destruction. It is probable that the support of Buddhism in the Ilkhanate kingdom (roughly corresponding to modern-day Iran), which started when the first Khan, Arghun, made Buddhism the state religion (1258), embodied a certain degree of discrimination against the Muslim population. With the conversion of Ghazan Khan to Islam a few years later, persecutory policies against the Buddhist communities were activated.

In recent history, Buddhists have been persecuted, among other places, in the USSR; in Vietnam during the war and after it; and in Cambodia when the Khmer Rouge controlled the country, when virtually all the monks were slaughtered, died of hardship, or were imprisoned in forced labor camps.

Buddhist Justification of Violence

Probably more than any other historical factor, these persecutions of Buddhists, which have often included mass death and the possible extinction of the dharma, have posed the dilemma of how to defend oneself, one's people, and Buddhism itself without using violence. The argument of self-defense has two contrasting views and many variants in between. On one side, there is the orthodox condemnation of violence (and especially of killing) even in self-defense: if the law is real, it cannot disappear and will reappear without need of violence. On the opposite side, there is the justification of violence and military action for self-defense or for social, ideological, and religious projections: the defense of society and of the dharma. In that context, arguments sometimes follow the logic of a "war for peace"—that is, the merits of defending the law and other living beings are higher than the demerits acquired with a violent act, and therefore the combination of the bad deed of violence with the positive counterpart of compassion and defense of the dharma gives a final result of a positive karma.

In contemporary Sri Lanka's civil war, the majority of the population, which is overall Buddhist and ethnically Sinhalese, is facing the insurgence for independence of the Tamil Hindu minority. The majority of Buddhists, including many monks, back up the military actions of the government army to end the minority insurgence. Numerous views are produced on this issue. Some pragmatically divide the Buddhist from the national duty, eventually underlining the necessity of violence despite its regretful karmic consequences. Some idealize violence as a righteous action, advocating that it can be employed for higher purposes under the condition that it is used ethically and in the minimum possible quantity. Some look for legitimacy in passages of the Pali Canon, and especially in a body of indigenous Buddhist texts, later than the canon, such as the Mahavamsa, which tells the story of three alleged visits of Siddhartha to Sri Lanka and of the military victories of ancestral Sri Lankan Buddhist warrior kings. The most extreme view, which has been described as Buddhist fundamentalism, argues that there is an ethico-religious identification between the Sinhala people and Buddhism in Sri Lanka—seen as the island of dharma (*dhammadwipa*)—which three times received the visit of the historical Buddha and which is adorned with his relics. In this nationalistic-religious context, the violent defense of such a holy unity is seen as rightful.

Similar reasoning to provide a Buddhist justification for conflict is found in many other violent scenarios involving Buddhist communities. That idea that protecting the dharma is a higher deed than keeping with the (selfish) interest for self-salvation and nirvana is among the most common forms of rationalization and justification of conflicts. A variant of such an interpretation is the notion that compassion toward all beings and their salvation is greater than the search for self-enlightenment. A further interpretation justifies murder as killing out of compassion, when a being (and especially a demon) is evidently tormented and afflicted, to procure its liberation, releasing it in the hope of a better rebirth. This kind of justification is used, for example, to explain the murder, in 842, by a Buddhist monk dressed as a dancer during a feast, of the last Tibetan emperor and persecutor of Buddhism, King Lang Darma (r. 838–842), an act still represented in ritual dances, when a monk stabs an image that represents the demon forces.

Buddhism and Martial Arts

Buddhism has had a strong influence on the development of many martial arts. The funda-mental principle behind the practice is usually that the practitioner does not have to commit violence if he is the object of an attack but can defend himself within the limits of minimum damage to the attacker and eventually bring him to reason. The legend of the introduction of fighting self-defense techniques in China by the Indian monk Bodhidharma (fourth or fifth century c.e.) represents the archetypical explanation of the existence of martial arts among Buddhist (monastic) communities. The tradition says that Bodhidharma learned these defensive techniques by himself (through meditation) as a way of training and for protection against brigands and wild animals and passed them on to his disciples.

Martial arts were developed and practiced by monks for different reasons: for their qualities as a strong form of self-discipline and self-training, because they reconciled the dharma with the necessities of daily life in unfriendly environments, and for their potential employment in political struggles. Monks have eventually become some of the best warriors, and monasteries have housed and brought to battle fearful armies of warrior monks, renowned for their discipline, skills, and disregard of death.

In Japan, violent clashes between warrior monks (Japanese: *sōhei*) belonging to rival monasteries and schools have been reported since the tenth century, and all the major temple complexes located close to the cities of Nara and Kyoto were involved for many years in violent feuds over political power, hiring mercenaries and organizing troops of warrior monks. In 1121 and 1141, for example, bands of monks from the Enryaku-ji set fire to and destroyed the rival temple complex of the Mii-dera. The former monastery, some four centuries later, at the height of its power, had a complex of 3,000 structures and a small but powerful army of sōhei. Troops of warrior monks from different temples and monasteries were employed during the wars of Genpei (1180–1185), fighting beside the armies of their political referents. The sōhei troops reappear at the end of the fifteenth century, and the century of civil war that followed saw their large-scale involvement.

Another type of warrior monk, which appeared in Japan at the end of the 1400s, is the so-called *ikkō-ikki*: of peasant origin, they were devoted to the Pure Land school. The pacification of Japan at the end of the sixteenth century, under three subsequent warlords, put an end, with great waste of lives, to the existence of the sōhei armies. For example, in 1571, Oda Nobunaga (1534–1582) attacked the Enryaku-ji and the Mii-dera and, after a fierce battle, razed the buildings and killed most of the monks. When the successor of Nobunaga, Hideyoshi, invaded Korea, Korean Buddhist monks and monasteries actively participated in the fight against the invading army, forming some of the fiercest insurgent militias.

Zen and Violence

Bodhidharma is also the legendary founder of the Buddhist school of Chan, better known by its Japanese name: Zen. Although Zen teachings do not foster violence in itself, some aspects of this doctrine have proved to be a good basis for the construction of violence-accepting Buddhist perspectives, which found their most famous example in the Japanese samurai ethics. Zen stresses, among other principles, spontaneity and nonattachment and has been described as tending to be antinomian and amoral, since it maintains that the ultimate truth transcends standard moral categories. Some Zen texts claim that killing does not implicate responsibility if the one who commits it does so in a completely spontaneous and detached way. In that case, violence would fall in the same category as a natural disaster. Zen was adopted as the favorite school of the ruling warrior class after its introduction in Japan in the twelfth

to thirteenth centuries. As the warrior cast was exposed to Zen, spontaneity and detachment were developed into an ethic of fighting in which killing came to be considered as irrelevant, or even favorable, to enlightenment if conducted with a completely detached attitude, with no desire or hatred.

Such views were recycled and adapted with the rise of Japanese militarism during the twentieth century. A discourse between the clergy, the political elite, and military leaders readapted Zen teachings, using the most suitable parts, to portray an idealized spirit of the samurai for propaganda purposes. The majority of Japanese Zen masters actively supported or tried to justify Japanese militarism during World War II via a number of views, often making a distinction between a conventional (i.e., political-ideological) truth and an ultimate truth (Buddhist teachings), which could coexist. The politicians used a distorted version of Zen to promote the idea of pan-Asian Buddhism and the internal implementation of a doctrine of sacrifice. The military leaders used Zen as a useful ideology of detachment toward suffering, death, and fate and modeled army training on the example of monastic orders.

Asceticism and Suicide as Forms of Self-Violence

Buddhism views on self-violence in the form of both asceticism and suicide are various. Siddhartha himself abandoned the most extreme asceticism and taught what he defined as "the middle path." However, asceticism has been widely practiced among Buddhists and can lead to remarkable cases of self-violence. Self-violence in different forms is also common during rituals: self-mutilation consisting of burning or cutting off one's own fingers, for example, was practiced among Chinese monks for many centuries until recently. The practice of burning parts of the body during ordination ceremonies to show determination has also been reported. Japanese Zen masters have used violent acts, such as slapping their students, as a teaching method. Moreover, in many situations the ultimate self-sacrifice takes place as a way of resolving conflict without harming another. This may be understood as the highest form of mysticism, walking the path of truth through renouncement of the most precious, and last, possession of an arhat (a Buddhist who has attained enlightenment): his or her own life. During the Vietnam War, thirty-seven monks and one lay woman performed such a sacrifice, the first being Thích Quảng Đức, who self-immolated himself by first soaking his body with gasoline and then setting himself on fire. He burned to death in a public space while remaining perfectly still, seated in the lotus position, as a way to protest the war that was destroying his country and inflicting suffering on his people and the persecution of Buddhism by a corrupt regime. Religious suicide by means of fire, as well as by other means, has been frequently reported in Chinese, Korean, and Japanese traditions and is often justified as an action of extreme selflessness or as a present to Buddha.

Different passages of some canonical texts suggest that suicide can be accepted if for a higher cause. In the Lotus Sutra, for example, one of the most influential texts in Chinese, Korean, Vietnamese, and Japanese Buddhism, it is stated that the bodhisattva medicine king (Mahāsattva Sarvasattvapriyadarsana), after making many offerings to Buddha, thought:

> I have employed my supernatural powers to make this offering . . . it is not as good as making an offering of my own body. Thereupon he swallowed various perfumes, sandalwood . . . and he also drank the fragrant oil of champaka and other kinds of flowers. . . . Anointing his body with fragrant oil, he appeared before the Buddha Sun Moon Pure Bright Virtue, wrapped his body in heavenly jewelled robes,

poured fragrant oil over his head and, calling on his transcendental powers, set fire to his body. The glow shone forth, illuminating words equal in number to the sands of eighty million Ganges. The Buddhas in these worlds simultaneously spoke out in praise, saying: "Excellent, excellent, good man, this is real diligence. This is what is called a true Dharma offering. . . . Though one may use flowers, incense . . . he can never match this! . . . This is called the foremost donation of all. Among all donations, this is the most highly prized."

Another tradition of self-violence and suicide is that of self-mummification, which was particularly popular in Japan but also occurred in China and India, where it probably originated. Monks who felt ready and willing would be buried alive in a hole with some ventilation, and they would die of dehydration while meditating. After some years the body is dug out: if it has not decayed and has self-mummified, it is honored, cleaned, adorned, and put on display for worship. The common belief is that the mummies (Japanese: *mīra*) are in deep meditation and that they will wake up with the advent of Maitreya.

Paolo Barbaro

See also: Asia, Central; Asia, Southeast; Jainism; Shintoism.

Further Reading

Chodron, Thubten. *Buddhism for Beginners.* Ithaca, NY: Snow Lion, 2001.

Deegalle, Mahinda, ed. *Buddhism, Conflict and Violence in Modern Sri Lanka.* London and New York: Routledge, 2006.

Hagen, Steve. *Buddhism Plain and Simple.* New York: Broadway, 1998.

Houbon, Jan E.M., and Karel R. Van Kooij, eds. *Violence, Non-Violence and the Rationalization of Violence in South Asian Cultural History.* Boston: Brill, 1999.

Jerryson, Michael, and Mark Juergensmeyer. *Buddhist Warfare.* Oxford and New York: Oxford University Press, 2010.

Rhys Davids, T.W., and Hermann Oldenberg, trans. *Vinaya.* Oxford: Clarendon Press, 1881.

Seneviratna, Anuradha, ed. *King Aśoka and Buddhism: Historical and Literary Studies.* Kandy, Sri Lanka: Buddhist Publication Society, 1994.

Turnbull, Stephen. *Japanese Warrior Monks A.D. 949–1603.* Oxford: Osprey, 2003.

Victoria, Brian Daizen. *Zen at War.* Lanham, MD: Rowman and Littlefield, 2006.

Watson, Burton, trans. *The Lotus Sutra.* Delhi: Sri Satguru, 1999.

Zimmermann, Michael, ed., with Chiew Hui Ho and Philip Pierce. *Buddhism and Violence.* Wiesbaden, Germany: Reichert Verlag, 2006.

Butler, Richard Girnt (1918–2004)

If there was one relatively stable presence on the extreme Right throughout the post–World War II period and dominant in the post–civil rights era, it was Christian Identity preacher and Aryan Nations founder Richard Girnt Butler. Among Butler's contributions were the popularization and dominance of the Christian Identity organization, which, with its explicit racist and nationalist theology, replaced the more traditional Protestant Christianity of the Ku Klux Klan as the dominant religious affiliation among the racist extreme Right. He also influenced the popularization of white separatism as an ideology, political platform, and objective through his Northwest Imperative, which replaced the more traditional white supremacy and nationalism of the Klan and wider extreme Right. He attempted to unify the diverse sectors of the extreme Right—ideologically, politically, and practically—through his annual Aryan World Congress. He was tied to almost all major acts of violence during the era, from the murder of Alan Berg by members of The Order to the Oklahoma City bombing.

History and Background

Butler was born on February 23, 1918, in Bennett, Colorado. He studied aeronautical engineering and science at college in Los Angeles after his family moved there during the Depression. He was sent by his employer, Consolidated Vultee Aircraft Company, to Bangalore, India, to fix airplanes for the Royal Indian Air Force. It is thought that the foundation of his racial ideas came from his experience in India, where he learned about the caste system. He returned to the United States in 1941, married Betty Litch, and joined the Army Air Corps following the attack on Pearl Harbor. Butler never saw action and became skeptical of the war effort. During that period, he became increasingly anti-Semitic and anticommunist and joined the California Committee to Combat Communism. It was at this point that he met William Potter Gale, who introduced him to Christian Identity, and Wesley Swift, a former Klansman and pastor of the Anglo-Saxon Christian Congregation (ASCC) in Lancaster, California, which Butler joined.

In the late 1960s, racial desegregation occurred, and the Voting Rights Act and the Civil Rights Act were passed. Just as the battle to preserve and maintain white supremacy seemed to be lost, a number of John Birch Society and Klan members—particularly those who were also followers of Swift and Christian Identity—formed smaller, more radical groups that advocated violent resistance, if not the revolutionary overthrow of the federal government. Among these groups were Butler and Gale's California Rangers and Swift's Christian Defense League, which Butler ran as national director from 1962 to 1965.

In 1969, Henry Beach, the former leader of the fascist organization the Silver Shirts, formed Posse Comitatus, an Identity-based, constitutionalist, antigovernment organization, which was joined by Gale and Butler. Swift died in 1970, and the following year Gale emerged from his shadow to take over for Beach as leader of Posse Comitatus, which he then moved to Cali-

Butler, Aryan Nations, and the Movement

In 1977, Butler purchased a large piece of land at Hayden Lake in Coeur d'Alene, Idaho, where he reestablished Swift's ASCC as the Church of Jesus Christ-Christian (CJCC) and founded its political wing, Aryan Nations. In doing that, he was attempting to reestablish the link between the religious and political activist wings of Christian Identity and dominate both. The CJCC provided him with a pulpit to preach from and the opportunity to establish his authority as the modern voice of Identity and successor to Swift, as well as provide Identity adherents within Aryan Nations and the wider extreme Right with a religious organizational affiliation. Aryan Nations was an explicitly political organization that represented Butler's political program and objectives: to establish a national mass movement, like the Klan before it, that could extend beyond the limits of Posse Comitatus with its fragmented regional makeup, historically regressive constitutionalist ideology, and protest-based strategies. Upon its inception, Butler recruited and appointed numerous high-profile Identity adherents who had been members of the ASCC, Klan, John Birch Society, and Posse Comitatus, including Robert Miles and Louis Beam Jr., as its national ambassadors.

Richard Girnt Butler speaks from the pulpit of his Church of Jesus Christ-Christian on the Aryan Nations compound in Hayden Lake, Idaho, on September 9, 2000. Despite a civil suit against Butler and his organization, which resulted in a $6.3 million judgment and the seizure of the compound, Butler vowed that his white separatist organization would continue to thrive. *(Barbara Minton/Associated Press)*

fornia and used as a platform for both Christian Identity and himself. At that point, Butler was the coinventor of a repair system for tires that made him quite wealthy, allowing him to retire at the age of fifty-five and devote himself to the cause. By 1974–1975, he was leading his own Posse in Kootenai, Idaho, but his period in the Posse was marked by conflict. By 1976, his Posse was rebelling due to his leadership style. Moreover, that same year he had a falling out with Gale over the legacy of Swift and the rights to the ASCC, and as a result, Butler left the Posse to establish himself beyond the shadow, leadership, and organizational umbrellas of others.

From his Hayden Lake compound, Butler attempted to establish the organization as a mass movement with himself as its intellectual leader. During that time he produced and distributed three publications: *Calling Our Nation, Aryan Nations Newsletter,* and the prison newsletter *The Way.* In addition to those platforms for his writing, he wrote and published two manifestos: *The Aryan Warrior* and *The Aryan Warrior's Stand.* Those booklets, published between 1978 and 1983, laid out Butler's beliefs, worldview, and political program. As well as the foundations, goals, and prayers of Aryan Nations, they included sections on everything from population, property, and finance to women, law, and international relations. A third and more specific political document was Aryan Nations' "Platform for the Aryan National State," in which Butler laid out his objectives for his white separatist movement and proposed a white homeland.

Butler's objectives were twofold: the unification of the white race and the establishment of a white homeland. The strategies for these also represent his most important contributions to the post–civil rights era extreme Right. The first was his own annual Aryan World Congress, and the second was Robert Miles's white separatist strategy, the Northwest Imperative, which Butler made into the centerpiece of the Aryan Nations' program. The plan was to establish an independent Aryan nation or homeland in the Pacific Northwest—specifically Idaho, Washington State, Oregon, Wyoming, and Montana—with full sovereignty from the United States.

Nowhere is Butler's contribution and significance more evident than in the creation of the annual Aryan World Congress. First established in 1979 as a small gathering in Kansas, the Aryan World Congress was held annually starting in 1982 at the Aryan Nations' Hayden Lake compound. These congresses were conceived as a means of unifying the disparate strands of the wider extreme Right; developing a social forum and network; and most important, enabling the development of a coherent strategy. The first official Aryan World Congress included, among others, members of various former Klan organizations and paramilitary units, neo-Nazi skinheads, and different Identity groups and churches. The program for these congresses included, among other activities, strategy sessions, general networking, educational seminars, speeches, and religious worship, as well as camping and family picnics. The notoriety of these congresses and their concrete influence on the movement began the second year they were held. The Aryan World Congress of 1983 is perhaps the most infamous and significant, as it was attended by Robert Mathews—already an Aryan Nations member—and Bruce Carroll Pierce and led directly to the formation of The Order. The 1986 congress was also significant, as it was attended by Randy Weaver, who would later become a central figure in the movement through the FBI siege at his Ruby Ridge home in 1992.

In April 1987, a federal grand jury in Arkansas brought seditious conspiracy charges against Butler, Miles, Beam, and ten others. The charges, dating to the 1983 Aryan World Congress that had hatched The Order, included conspiracy to overthrow the federal government; assassinate an FBI agent and a federal judge; bomb federal buildings, utility pipelines, and electrical transmission lines; poison water supplies; and sabotage railroads, as well as robbery, transportation of stolen money, and counterfeiting. However, in April 1988, the accused were acquitted of all charges. In the year following his trial, Butler attempted to broaden the appeal of his movement and recruit a younger membership by launching his first Aryan Youth Conference, which was followed in 1994 by the Aryan Youth Music Festival. Perhaps the most significant and influential of all the gatherings of the era was not an Aryan World Congress but the Rocky Mountain Rendezvous, held on October 23, 1992, in Estes Park, Colorado, in response to the events at Ruby Ridge. The Rocky Mountain Rendezvous was organized by Christian Identity minister Pete Peters and attended by Butler, Miles, and Beam, whose Leaderless Resistance was introduced as a strategy for combating the federal government and its agents. This event and strategy influenced the development of the militia movement, which came to increasing prominence in the mid-1990s.

Although Butler's projects were overshadowed by the militia movement in the wake of Estes Park, they did reenter the spotlight with the 1995 bombing of the Alfred P. Murrah Federal Building in Oklahoma City. That event returned attention to the broadly defined antigovernment movement and domestic terrorism in the United States, implicating Butler, Aryan Nations, and The Order. In spite of that short-lived return to the media and government attention, Butler would see his fortunes dwindle as the millennium approached. Soon after the bombing, several power struggles occurred within Aryan Nations. Butler's leadership had been in question since soon after Estes Park, as he was aging, the movement was coming under increased scrutiny by the authorities, and new ideologies and movements were emerging and competing for dominance. In 1997, he survived the first of two challenges and appointed Identity minister Neuman Britton as his successor, thus ensuring that his interests and legacy would be protected following his retirement or death.

Decline, Death, and the End of an Era

In spite of this, Butler's control and the stability of Aryan Nations were tested again soon after. In 1998, Aryan Nations security guards assaulted members of the Keenan family, private citizens who had become lost while driving and stopped their car outside the Hayden Lake compound. In response to the assault, the Southern Poverty Law Center launched a civil suit against Butler, the security guards, and the organization on behalf of the family. In September 2000, the jury found them all guilty and awarded $6.3 million in damages to the Keenans. This resulted in the sale of the Hayden Lake compound in 2001, forcing Butler to declare bankruptcy and move to a donated house nearby. Shortly after that, his appointed successor, Neuman Britton, died. Butler then appointed Harold Ray Redfeairn as his succes-

sor and August Kreis as his minister of propaganda. The two men had other plans, however, including the relocation of Aryan Nations to their base in Ulysses, Pennsylvania, which Butler rejected. In January 2002, Redfeairn and Kreis announced that they had removed Butler from the organization, and Butler responded by claiming to have removed them. As a result, Redfeairn and Kries joined with Posse Comitatus and Aryan Nations member James Wickstrom to set up a competing organization, which they named Aryan Nations–Posse Comitatus. Although Butler attempted to regain control and authority, by this point his health was fading and the entire movement had been overshadowed by the terrorist attacks of September 11, 2001, its own internal conflicts, and waning momentum. On September 8, 2004, Butler died of heart failure.

Aaron Winter

See also: Aryan Nations; Beam, Louis, Jr.; Christian Identity Movement; Mathews, Robert Jay; Order, The; Posse Comitatus; Weaver, Randy.

Further Reading

Aho, James A. *The Politics of Righteousness: Idaho Christian Patriotism.* Seattle: University of Washington Press, 1995.

Barkun, Michael. *Religion and the Racist Right: The Origins of the Christian Identity Movement.* Chapel Hill: University of North Carolina Press, 1997.

Berlet, Chip, and Matthew N. Lyons. *Right-Wing Populism in America: Too Close for Comfort.* New York: Guilford Press, 2000.

Butler, Richard. *The Aryan Warrior.* Hayden Lake, ID: Aryan Nations–Teutonic Unity, n.d.

———. *The Aryan Warrior's Stand.* Hayden Lake, ID: Aryan Nations–Teutonic Unity, n.d.

Cox, Michael, and Martin Durham. "The Politics of Anger: The Extreme Right in the United States." In *The Politics of the Extreme Right: From the Margins to the Mainstream,* ed. Paul Hainsworth, pp. 287–311. London: Pinter, 2000.

Diamond, Sara. *Roads to Dominion: Right-Wing Movements and Political Power in the United States.* New York: Guilford Press, 1995.

Dobratz, Betty A., and Stephanie L. Shanks-Meile. *The White Separatist Movement in the United States: "White Power, White Pride!"* Baltimore: Johns Hopkins University Press, 2000.

Flynn, Kevin, and Gary Gerhardt. *The Silent Brotherhood: The Chilling Inside Story of America's Violent, Anti-Government Militia Movement.* New York: Signet, 1990.

Ridgeway, James. "Aryans Without a Nation." *SPLC Intelligence Report,* no. 100 (Winter 2000): 30–34.

———. "Bombs, Bullets, Bodies: The Decade in Review." *SPLC Intelligence Report,* no. 97 (Winter 2000): 8–29.

Simi, Pete, and Robert Futrell. *American Swastika: Inside the White Power Movement's Hidden Spaces of Hate.* Lanham, MD: Rowman & Littlefield, 2010.

Southern Poverty Law Center. "Aryans, Interrupted." *SPLC Intelligence Report* (Summer 2002). Available: http://www.splcenter.org/intel/intelreport/article.jsp?aid=88.

———. "The Last Outpost." *SPLC Intelligence Report* (Spring 2001). Available: http://www.splcenter.org/intel/intelreport/article.jsp?aid=234.

Zeskind, Leonard. *Blood and Politics: The History of the White Nationalist Movement from the Margins to the Mainstream.* New York: Farrar, Strauss, and Giroux, 2009.

Chinese Folk Religion

Popular religions or folk religions, sometimes referred to as community traditions, are distinguished from the world's major religious traditions by their lack of organization; scripture; and systematic doctrine, beliefs, and practices. Popular or folk religions typically focus on local or regional issues of concern and local or regional religious figures, gods, or spirits, though globalization is changing the local face of folk religion. The relationship between folk religions and the leading organized religions in a culture is complex in that both groups borrow freely from each other. The practices of a folk religion are often drawn from very ancient, even prehistoric tribal customs. Folk and organized religions share a dynamic historical development such that it can be difficult, if not impossible, to determine whether a belief or practice began in the folk or the organized religion. Because early anthropologists and historians who studied religion in China encountered a good deal of confusion about what constituted Daoism, Confucianism, and Buddhism in China, scholars have referred to Chinese folk or popular religions to classify those beliefs and practices that are not strictly part of the organized religions. Folk religions also exist in other cultures. Though often associated with the common people, elements of folk religion are practiced by people from all classes and social strata.

Defining Folk Religions

Speaking from the perspective of organized religion, scholars note that for the past two thousand years, Chinese religious culture has pivoted around the three major traditions of Confucianism, Daoism, and Buddhism. Based on the teachings of Confucius (551–479 B.C.E.), Confucianism became a state religion in the Early Han dynasty (206 B.C.E.–8 C.E.), and it was the state religion for most of the subsequent dynasties. For the most part, it was practiced by the emperor and imperial family in the form of elaborate court rituals. Confucianism is grounded in basic family values, such as respect for parents, elders, and relatives, which makes it appealing to people from any social status. Based on the teachings of Laozi (Lao Tzu, sixth or fourth century B.C.E.), the Daoist religion was usually practiced by scholars who did not pass the civil service exam or who had fallen out of favor with the ruling class. Daoism became the state religion in the Tang dynasty (618–907 C.E.), and it was also supported by a number of smaller dynasties such as the Northern or Later Wei dynasty (386–535 C.E.). Because Daoism offered an alternative to Confucianism, it was popular among those people who wanted an alternative way of life from the one imposed by the Confucian state.

Buddhism was founded in ancient India, in the sixth century B.C.E., and had entered China by the first century C.E. Buddhism received some imperial sponsorship, especially under the Mongol Yuan (1271–1368) and the Manchu Qing (1644–1912) dynasties. Because Buddhism is a foreign religion and its teachings ultimately propose that people must remove themselves from worldly attachments, including government service, it never achieved the long-lasting imperial patronage that Confucianism and even Daoism experienced. The fourth leg of Chinese religious culture is the folk religions. The dynamic, syncretizing, and synthesizing aspects of Chinese culture in general add to the complexity of the relationship between the organized religions and the folk religions, in that all of the traditions borrow from and influence each other.

Chinese Folk Religions

Chinese folk religions are difficult to describe because of their great diversity and their lack of organization and identifiable hierarchy of religious leaders, doctrine, scriptures, and practices. Chinese popular religions are defined in contrast to the major traditions. In addition to Confucianism, Daoism, and Buddhism, other world religions entered China. Aspects of Hinduism fused with Buddhism and spread into China. Judaism, Christianity, Islam, Manicheanism, and other traditions traveled along the trade routes to China. Islam began to enter China during the Tang dynasty, and its practice in China both influenced and was in turn influenced by Chinese folk religions. By the nineteenth century, when Christian missionaries were becoming active in China, Chinese folk religion borrowed from Christianity and in turn influenced the development of Christianity in China. By the twentieth century every major world religion had been in China, and many of them are still actively practiced, which further complicates the matter of attempting to identify Chinese folk religions.

One characteristic shared by many of the various forms of popular religion worldwide is use of the religion to obtain a practical physical or spiritual result by using some form of magical or supernatural power—often associated with numerology, astrology, or a complex religious calendar. Practitioners usually employ the use of a shaman, medium, magician, or one or more of various minor, local ancestor or nature spirits. Because of the desire to achieve physical or spiritual results, folk religions are often associated with political and peasant rebellions. Popular religions require the expenditure or sacrifice of large amounts of raw materials (animals, gold, silver, precious gems, agricultural produce, and so on) or wealth to pay for the services rendered by the shaman, medium, or spirits.

There is historical information about some of the ancient Chinese folk religions because Confucian and Daoist writers criticized them. The Daoists were especially keen to criticize the folk practices because those practices were and still are very similar to the practices of religious Daoism. One of the major differences between Chinese folk religion and religious Daoism is the issue of legitimate authority. Ordained Daoist priests (*daoshi*) are given a register or list of gods and spirits (*lu*) whom they are authorized to summon and command. Daoist rituals are performed for specific deities and thearchs. Although Daoists make use of alcohol, animal-blood sacrifices are prohibited. Historically and to this day Chinese folk religions, borrowing from Confucian ritual and ancient custom, perform animal-blood rites.

Daoist scriptures and texts vehemently criticize and attack the popular cults. R.A. Stein (1979) delineated a number of characteristics of popular religious practices, such as the costly expenditure of wealth and materials; the use of unauthorized prayers, talismans, songs, and dances; the employment of blood sacrifices; the employment of mediums, shamans, or sorcerers and sorceresses; the use of faith healing and exorcisms; the use of rites of atonement to cure illness; and offerings of sacrifices to a pantheon of uncodified local spirits. Stein distinguished the characteristics of the folk religions and the major traditions as differences in degree rather than in kind. Practices of Chinese folk religions persist to this day. For example, in Taiwan, when the Black Head (*heitou*), ordained Daoist priests, so called because of their black skullcaps, perform esoteric rituals inside a closed temple, the so-called Red Head (*hongtou*) "priests" display ritualized theatrical performances for the villagers in the temple courtyard. The Red Head priests are practitioners of folk religion. The villagers also slaughter thousands of pigs for the ritual festival and host expensive banquets after the rites.

Another distinguishing trait of Chinese folk religions is that they have been the impetus for as well as involved in the majority of political and peasant revolts throughout Chinese history. They fought on two fronts. First, they engaged in spiritual battle against the ghosts and demons that were believed to cause sickness, bad luck, ruined harvests, destructive weather, pestilence, flood, famine, and death. Second, they waged war against the state in the form of armed rebellions. Generally speaking, violence is a basic fact of life in the Chinese culture. According to the Yinyang philosophy, which became part of both Daoism and Confucianism, violence is the outcome of excessive yang energy. In Confucianism, civilization rests upon both literary culture (*wen*) and martial culture (*wu*). Confucian texts developed the concept of the Mandate of Heaven (*tianming*) to justify political authority and the overthrow of a dynasty. Added to this complex tapestry of inevitable, aggressive yang violence and state- or religiously sanctioned violence is the romantic ideal of the noble warrior hero, which was supported by popular legends and historical reports of skilled warriors who defended or liberated defenseless and weak peasants.

The warrior heroes appear to have been influenced by the teachings of Master Mo (fl. 479–438 B.C.E.), who advocated equal justice and benevolence for each and every person regardless of social rank or interpersonal relationships. These warrior hero figures were iconoclasts with a strong sense of social justice and fair play who, like Master Mo, defended the underdog and were not afraid to oppose the aristocrats and government officials. Popular religious movements often become engaged in violent rebellions when ethics, social justice, and the warrior spirit are combined with astrological and numerological thinking tied to the ebb and flow of yin and yang, the Mandate of Heaven, and the expectation that the dynasty is in decline.

History of Chinese Peasant Revolts in the Han Dynasty

The history of Chinese dynastic overthrow and peasant revolts is long and complex. The legendary Yellow Emperor (third century B.C.E.) suppressed the tribal rebel Chi You. The ancient histories recount how the Xia and Shang dynasties were deposed. One of the Confucian classics, the *Spring and Autumn Annals,* a historical record of the State of Lu, contains early references to peasant revolts. Legend and history worked together to maintain a peasant ideology for rebellion. When a dynasty was in decline, a tribe or state would appeal to the Mandate of Heaven and other religious concepts to justify the overthrow of that dynasty and its own claim to rule.

Folk religions often play a role in political rebellions. An early historical example that set a model for later revolts involving folk religion is the Yellow Turban Rebellion in 184 C.E. against the Later Han dynasty (25–220 C.E.). Zhang Jue (d. 184) led the Yellow Turban rebels, using a religious text known as *The Classic of Supreme Peace (Taiping jing)* and faith healing techniques. Based on the text, their teachings were also known as the Way of Supreme Peace. Astrology and numerology were also involved. The year 184 was a *jiazi* year, that is, the first year in a sixty-year cycle, equivalent to the beginning of a century in Western thinking, marking a time for change and new beginnings. The Yellow Turbans expected the Yellow Heaven to arise, and the "red" Han dynasty was expected to crumble. A century of floods and famines increased the people's need for relief and their belief that the Han had lost the Mandate of Heaven. The Way of Supreme Peace taught that moral virtue was in decline but was necessary to establish a righteous state to secure peace and order in the country. The Yellow Turbans also employed amulets and talismans for personal protection in battle.

Many of these themes recur in subsequent rebellions inspired by folk religions. Because the Celestial Masters, a sect of the early Daoist religion, rejected Zhang Jue and the Yellow Turbans, they were relegated to the ranks of a folk religion. When the Yellow Turbans were taking shape in eastern China, the Celestial Masters were organizing in western China. Zhang Daoling (fl. 180 C.E.), the first Celestial Master, and his son, the second Master, established the Way of the Celestial Masters, also known as the Five Baskets of Rice sect (so called after their tithing practices). The Celestial Masters did not marshal a violent revolt, however, but merely established an interregnum state and eventually relinquished control to General Cao Cao in 215, when he began to establish the Wei dynasty (220–264 C.E.).

The third Celestial Master, Zhang Lu (fl. 190–220), who surrendered to Cao Cao, never officially declared himself emperor. He and his mother practiced religious folk rituals (*guidao*). The orthodox (*zhengyi*) teachings of Daoist religion were closely associated with folk religion, but at the same time Daoist leaders tried to distance themselves from folk religion. The social, political, and economic unrest of the second century poured into the third century, and religious Daoism and folk religion continued to inspire revolt. The period known as the Six Dynasties (220–581) was marked by political unrest, peasant movements, and ethnic violence when the Han Chinese and various ethnic groups (the Toba, Ruan-Ruan, and Tujue) vied for political power. In 277, Chen Rui rebelled against the Western Jin dynasty (265–317) in

Sichuan. Chen Rui was a follower of the Celestial Master sect and even declared himself to be a Celestial Master who practiced folk religion. In 301, Li Te initiated a revolt against the Western Jin. After Li's death in battle in 303, his son, Li Xiong, continued the revolt and named himself king of Chengdu City in 304. The ethnic Li family established what came to be known as the Cheng Han dynasty. With the assistance of the Daoist priest Fan Chang-sheng, Li Xiong held the throne for thirty years. The Li and Fan families were members of the Celestial Masters sect, and they were also members of the Miao-Man tribal ethnic group, who practiced shamanism and other elements of folk religion.

Peasant Revolts After the Han

After the fall of the Han dynasty, Li Ah and Li Kuan migrated with their families from Sichuan in the west to eastern China, bringing the Li lineage's version of the Celestial Masters teachings with them. One or more Daoists named Li Tuo also migrated to the East. Li Tuo and his disciple Li Hong plotted a rebellion, but they were killed by General Wang Dun's commander, Li Heng, between 323 and 324. The messianic notion of a coming "savior-king" had begun to develop during the Han dynasty, which served the Celestial Masters and the folk religions well. The Celestial Masters drew on Han apocryphal writings to promote the prophecy that Lord Lao would rule the empire and Li Hong would be his chief minister.

Over the generations the prophecy became garbled or was intentionally revised, and Li Hong was understood to be an avatar of Lord Lao, such that the name Li Hong became associated with the anticipation of the messianic movement. From 250 to 450 C.E., numerous rebellions throughout China were led by people named or called Li Hong. Because these movements advocated land reform and grain distribution and challenged the aristocratic rule and Confucian family values, they are severely criticized in the official dynastic histories written by Confucian scholars. At the same time, Mahayana Buddhism had taken root among both the common people and the aristocrats. The Buddhists taught that the coming of the Maitreya Buddha would usher in a new world order of peace and material well-being. As the aristocrats, small landlords, and peasant farmers lost their land or suffered plagues, famines, and floods, popular uprisings were rampant. The folk religions and religious Daoism had focused people's attention on personal protection from ghosts, demons, and death. With the Mahayana Buddhist teaching of the universal liberation of all sentient creatures, Daoism and the folk religions responded by becoming less concerned with individual protection and more concerned with social justice and universal liberation from suffering. The political turmoil, warfare, plagues, floods, famines, and other forms of social and economic discord also helped foster greater concern for social justice and fueled the peasant revolts.

Sun En Revolt

In 399, after the rebel Sun Tai was executed, his nephew, Sun En (d. 402), led a religious and political rebellion in eastern China. Sun En promised the disaffected peasants he led that they and their families would be granted physical immortality and a place of residence in Penglai, the blessed islands of the immortals. Although the Sun family had been members of the Celestial Masters sect for generations, elements of their rebellion are drawn from folk religion as well, and Sun En was in part opposing the power of the Wang family, which also adhered to the way of the Celestial Masters. Sun En was criticized for participating in rebellion by the leading reformer Kou

Qianzhi (365–448). Kou Qianzhi claimed to receive revelations from Lord Lao, instructing him to reform the practices of the Celestial Masters. Kou sought to strengthen the role of moral virtue in Daoism. He wanted to stop the payment of five bushels of rice tithing and to eliminate the sexual arts from the religion. He especially criticized those who claimed to be Daoists and who led, participated in, or were associated in any way with political rebellions. Kou's attempt to reform the Celestial Masters sect did not succeed, and the sect's authority began to wane. Shortly thereafter, two other Daoist sects developed the Upper Clarity and Spiritualized Treasure, gaining acceptance among the aristocrats and setting the stage for imperial patronage in the Tang dynasty. As the social identity of religious Daoism took shape, Daoist religious leaders and believers tried to distance themselves from violence, but aspects of their teachings were constantly being co-opted by the practitioners of the folk religions to justify rebellion.

Tang Dynasty Revolts

During the turbulent unrest of the Six Dynasties period (220–581), there was a prevalent expectation that an avatar of Lord Lao, Li Hong or even someone else would bring peace and order to the empire. The avatar belief became a defining aspect of the Han Chinese attempt to establish a dynasty and usher in political stability. After the brief but stabilizing Sui dynasty (581–618), the founders of the Tang dynasty (618–907) traced their lineage through the Li family back to Master Lao, an early avatar of Lord Lao. The Tang supported religious Daoism. Two daughters of Emperor Rui Zong (r. 684–690 and 710–713) were ordained as Daoist nuns in 711. The subsequent reign of Emperor Xuan Zong (713–756) marked the golden age of the Tang. As trade, commerce, and China's population grew, tax revenues declined, and the dynasty began to weaken. Late in life the emperor fell in love with his consort Yang Gufei, who was one of his son's ladies-in-waiting. The consort adopted a general of Turkic origin, An Lushan, as her legal son and possibly as her lover. In 755, An Lushan came into conflict with Yang's brother, who controlled the central government, and he initiated a rebellion. In 757 An Lushan was killed by his own son, An Qingxu, who was himself killed by another Turkic general, Shi Siming, who continued the revolt until he was executed in 763. It is estimated that close to 40 million people died because of the rebellion and natural disasters at that time. The Tang dynasty was not able to regain stability, and China again fell into a brief period of political fragmentation, known as the Five Dynasties, from 907 to 960.

The dynastic cycle continued to repeat itself. The Song dynasty (960–1279) began with a golden age of peace and security, but the latter years of the dynasty saw peasant revolts, and there was continuous ethnic political pressure from the kingdoms and tribes of Central and northeastern Asia. As the pressure mounted from the tribal people to the north, the Song capital moved south to Nanjing in 1126. When the Mongols took control of China and established the Yuan dynasty (1279–1368), even Han Chinese aristocrats were interested in marshaling rebellion against the foreign rulers.

Yuan and Ming Dynasty Revolts

Because the Mongol Empire spanned all of Asia, the Mongol generals brought Nestorian Christianity, Islam, Manicheanism, and Tibetan Buddhism, along with their own shamanistic religion, into China. The Mongols were great warriors, but they were not effective rulers. Strife within the ruling Mongol families, along with a series of famines and floods, left the countryside open for peasant

revolts. By the 1340s rebellions occurred in almost every province. Some of the rebels claimed that their ancestors were Song emperors. Many rebel leaders were peasants who drew on folk religions, Buddhism, and Daoism to inspire their revolts. The well-known White Lotus secret society had begun in the early part of the twelfth century as an offshoot of Tiantai Buddhism. Using the messianic expectation of the coming Maitreya Buddha, various groups used the name of the White Lotus society to lead revolts in the Yuan, Ming, and Qing dynasties. An impoverished orphan peasant, Zhu Yuanzhang (1328–1398), joined a band of rebels in 1352. He may have been a member of a White Lotus society, and there is speculation that he had Manichean connections as well. By 1356, Zhu and his band had taken Nanjing, absorbing or defeating other rebel groups. They captured Peking in 1368, declaring Zhu to be the emperor of the Ming dynasty (1368–1644). Zhu warned that eunuchs must not be allowed to work in the government, but by the end of the fifteenth century, eunuchs were actively engaged in the administration. By the fall of the Ming, eunuchs contributed to the government corruption and along with the natural disasters, political intrigue, and peasant revolts aided in its collapse. The Ming was both founded and concluded in peasant revolt. Zhang Xianzhong and Li Zicheng led peasant revolts against the Ming that assisted in the Manchu conquest.

Qing Dynasty Revolts

After capturing Peking in 1644, the Manchu established the Qing dynasty (1644–1912) and suppressed the remnants of the peasant rebellions against the Ming. They improved upon Mongol rule by assigning a Manchu official alongside every Han Chinese official, a practice that maintained loyalty among the people and efficient operations in government management. Despite their more affective administration, the Manchu were a foreign, or non–Han Chinese, people and so the Han Chinese resented their rule and opposed them. The Qing dynasty suffered a share of natural disasters and government corruption that fostered peasant revolts. Qing rebellions show a marked difference from previous revolts in that a growing number of them, especially in the nineteenth century, were politically, not religiously, motivated. Although many of the peasant rebellions were politically motivated in an attempt to oust the foreign Manchu rulers, elements of folk religion maintained a role in these revolts because the rebels continued to employ the physical and spiritual trappings of the folk religions in the form of amulets, talismans, and martial arts practices believed to make the practitioner invincible.

Wang Lun Revolt

The first major religious rebellion during the Qing dynasty began in 1774 in Shandong (Shantung) Province and was led by Wang Lun. Wang Lun was a charismatic leader, who was skilled in both the healing and the martial arts. He was associated with a White Lotus society. The millenarian expectations of a new world order continued to promote hope among the peasants and the aristocrats who suffered under Manchu rule. Wang Lun turned his success at proselytizing into a call for revolt, promising his followers salvation and guiding them in esoteric arts of magical protection in battle. Various White Lotus groups continued to spawn revolts in the north. In 1813, Li Wencheng led the Eight Trigrams Rebellion, an offshoot of a White Lotus group. This rebellion may have been the last millenarian movement that was based on native Chinese folk beliefs; subsequent religious rebellions were Christian or Muslim inspired.

Taiping Rebellion

From 1851 to 1868, the Heavenly Kingdom of Great Peace (Taiping Tianguo) Rebellion wreaked havoc over most of southern China, especially around Nanjing, which the rebels held from 1853 to 1864. The Taiping leader, Hong Xiuquan, came from a poor farming family in the Hakka district in Guangdong. After failing the highest level of the civil service exam several times, he suffered a physical and emotional collapse. When he recovered, he converted to Christianity. Shortly thereafter he began to describe himself as the younger brother of Jesus Christ and the new messiah. Hong had read only a few Christian tracts; he did not have a deep knowledge of the New Testament or Christian theology. He criticized Daoism and Buddhism for being the work of the devil. In his early sermons he employed some Confucian expressions and values, which he later avoided to further distinguish the unique Christian character of his revolt. In fact, the Taiping Rebellion was a peasant-led folk religion revolt with a few Christian elements and expressions that appealed to the disenfranchised peasants just as Daoist and Buddhist concepts had.

The Taiping Rebellion was able to hold Nanjing and persist for so long for a number of reasons. Internally, the movement appealed to various ethnic minorities in the South, and the early use of a type of cooperative leadership gave each group a strong sense of ownership in the newly founded rebel kingdom. Externally, the Qing had been severely weakened by the Opium Wars (1839–1842, 1858–1860) and by natural disasters—especially the repeated flooding of the Yellow River in 1853, when the mouth of the river moved 500 miles from southern to northern Shandong Province. Moreover, the Qing encountered many small uprisings and three major rebellions during this time.

Prompted by the massive floods of 1853, Zhang Luoxing led the Nian Rebellion from 1853 to 1868. He had connections with a White Lotus society. He earned a living as a salt smuggler, which gave him many clandestine connections. Unlike the Taiping, the Nian were not centralized, and they behaved more like traditional peasant groups in their spontaneous activity and looting of government *yamen* granaries and storehouses. Low-ranking officials and military officers were members of the Nian, which greatly assisted their strategy. The Nian Rebellion had its folk religion and Buddhist elements in seeking economic relief, but it was also a political movement that opposed the foreign Manchu rule and sought to reestablish the Ming mandate.

Muslim Rebellions

Muslims had been migrating and trading in and out of China since the Tang dynasty. The Uyghur minority group, living mostly in the west and northwest, constitutes the majority of China's Muslims. Radical militant Islamic teachings had reached China by the eighteenth century, and a few minor Muslim-led uprisings were attempted in the late eighteenth and early nineteenth centuries. Du Wenxiu (1823–1873) led a religiously motivated separatist movement against the Qing in Yunnan Province from 1856 to 1873, called the Panthay Rebellion. He captured the city of Dali in 1856 and declared himself the sultan of the Kingdom of the Pacified South. In the northwest the Hui, or Muslim, Rebellion erupted in 1863 and ended in 1873. It also had a religious and ethnic base and sought to establish an independent Muslim state. From 1854–1872 the Miao minority in Guizhou Province marshaled a rebellion. Even though these revolts were led by ethnic groups, they relied heavily on the Han Chinese peasantry for support and soldiers. In southern China the Triads led many politically motivated rebellions.

The political rebellions still appealed to the trappings of folk religion. The rebels believed that they had esoteric spiritual powers; they preached equality and treated men and women, poor and rich, alike. There were 115 major rebellions in China from 1860 to 1895; between 1885 and 1895 at least one revolt occurred in every province. The well-known Boxer Rebellion (1898–1901) was politically motivated. Initially, the Boxers were opposed to the Manchu, but the movement quickly turned against the European and Japanese imperialists who were carving up China's resources. The early members of the Boxer movement, strongly influenced by folk religion, believed that their amulets, talismans, and special martial arts practices would make them invulnerable to traditional and modern weapons. They also supported women rebel forces known as the Red and Blue Lanterns. When the Qing dynasty buckled in 1912 with the Xinhai Rebellion, the dynastic system itself collapsed.

Folk Religion Under Communism

In the early Republican period, provincial warlords and rebel groups challenged the newly established government. Chinese peasant groups, such as the Red Eyebrows, a folk Daoist group, were employed by the Communist Party. After consolidating power at the end of World War II, the Communists began to discourage all religious practices, in keeping with Marxist teachings. By the time of the Cultural Revolution (1966–1976), religion was outlawed. Confucian, Daoist, Buddhist, and local folk religion temples were closed, but Muslim mosques were not. The folk religions were used to operating as secret societies, and they continued to do so. In 1982 the newly revised Chinese constitution reclaimed freedom of religion with government controls, and the Buddhist, Daoist, and local temples reopened. The Falun Dafa, or Falungong, movement became a public group in 1992. The Falun Dafa is a popular organization that employs moral teachings from Buddhism; includes Daoist-style *qigong,* calisthenics, and breathing exercises; and teaches self-cultivation, health, social harmony, and peace. However, the organization is not recognized as a legitimate religion, and so its followers are persecuted and prosecuted.

Given the long history of peasant revolts spawned by, influenced by, or otherwise associated with folk religions in China, it is little wonder that the People's Republic of China places strong controls on religion in an effort to prevent the formation of secret societies or cults, which might pose a threat to the government or the social order. Even with such government attempts to control them, people continue to practice folk religions in China.

James D. Sellmann

See also: Buddhism; Confucianism; Daoism/Taoism.

Further Reading

Atwil, David G. *The Chinese Sultanate: Islam, Ethnicity and the Panthay Rebellion in Southwest China, 1856–1873.* Palo Alto, CA: Stanford University Press, 2005.

Chesneaux, Jean. *Peasant Revolts in China 1840–1949.* New York: W.W. Norton, 1973.

Dean, Kenneth. *Taoist Ritual and Popular Cults of Southeast China.* Princeton, NJ: Princeton University Press, 1993.

Michael, Franz. *The Taiping Rebellion.* Seattle: University of Washington Press, 1996.

Naquin, Susan. *Millenarian Rebellion in China: The Eight Trigrams Uprising of 1813.* New Haven, CT: Yale University Press, 1976.

———. *Shantung Rebellion: The Wang Lun Uprising of 1774.* New Haven, CT: Yale University Press, 1981.

Stein, Rolf A. "Religious Taoism and Popular Religion from the Second to Seventh Centuries" In *Facets of Taoism: Essays in Chinese Religion,* ed. Holmes Welch and Anna Seidel, pp. 53–81. New Haven, CT: Yale University Press, 1979.

Yu, David C., trans. *History of Chinese Daoism,* vol. 1. Lanham, MD: University Press of America, 2000.

Christian Crusades

The Christian Crusades were a series of wars initiated mostly by the Holy Roman Empire and fought primarily by Europeans to regain control of Jerusalem and the Holy Land from the Muslims. The events spanned from 1095 through the thirteenth century. There were nine major waves of crusaders in Euorpe who left everything behind to fight for Christian control of their holy city. Impassioned monks, peasants, nobles, and kings alike sacrificed everything, enduring famine, disease, and bloody warfare in a distant foreign land, in order to further the Christian cause, although ultimately the Crusades resulted in minimal Christian control of the area.

First Crusade (1095–1099)

In the medieval city of Clermont, France, at the Council of Clermont in November 1095, Pope Urban II and several bishops and abbots from Europe discussed a plea for help from Alexius Comnenus, the Byzantine emperor. Turks were invading the Eastern Roman Empire, which posed a serious threat to Christians in the area. On November 27, after several weeks of deliberation, Pope Urban called for peasants and nobles alike to take arms against the "savage heathens" who had stolen the sacred Christian city of Jerusalem. Pope Urban preached tales of godless warriors, ravaging and defiling Christ's sacred churches and altars and carrying off or murdering Jerusalem's inhabitants.

Convincing the people to go to war to save Jerusalem from "infidels" was no easy task; thus, Pope Urban promised the crowds "complete remissions for their sins" and "heavenly rewards." For those who were not easily swayed by religious promises, he also offered the crusaders possession of newly conquered lands in return for their victories and a chance not only to spread Christianity but to increase their personal wealth and power. The crowd's furor was ignited, and they began to chant, *"Dieu li volt! Dieu li volt!"* ("God wills it"). They sewed red crosses to their clothing and on banners to signify their Christian allegiance and etched crosses into their swords and armor. Pope Urban spent the next several months traveling around France preaching and calling others to join the cause and take up the cross. He attempted to ignite passions while preaching to the masses by declaring that they would be better off dying in battle than tolerating the abuses in the Holy Land.

In early April 1096 the first crusaders, or pilgrims, as they referred to themselves, set out for Constantinople (present-day Istanbul, Turkey) in the first of nine major waves of people to journey east. There were up to 100,000 people, all led by Peter the Hermit, an impassioned monk who had spent the previous months preaching and gathering followers even before Pope Urban's speech at Clermont. This group later became known as the Pauper's Crusade—a band of mostly untrained peasants who had no more than an axe at most to fight with. Nearly one-third of these pilgrims were women and children, and most had no military training. Although there were a number of knights accompanying these pilgrims, many were peasants escaping the impoverished living conditions of Western Europe; their hope that the crusade would give them a reprieve from famine and disease was not realized. Peter departed several months before August 15, the date of departure set by Pope Urban; thus, his band of followers were short of food almost immediately and were forced to pillage local villages for food and supplies along the way. They eventually arrived in Constantinople in 1097.

A second wave of crusaders left Europe in August that same year. However, the majority of these pilgrims were of noble birth; that is, more skilled and educated fighters from West-ern Europe's elite society. Historians estimate that one-fifth of France's knights (approximately 7,000 knights total) embarked on this journey. These crusaders were not only more experienced and prepared for the journey than the first wave of fighters, they were also better supplied. They were led by four nobles: Robert of Flanders, Raymond of Toulouse, Godfrey of Bouillon, and Bohemund of Taranto.

The armies of these four nobles converged on Constantinople between August 1096 and April 1097. Throughout the first half of 1097, Peter the Hermit and his followers from the first wave of crusaders met up with the second wave of crusaders. Almost 100,000 crusaders encamped around the walls of Constantinople. The crusaders, along with an army from the Eastern Roman Empire stationed in Constantinople, marched to Nicaea, just on the other side of the Bosporus Strait, and laid siege against the Turks. The Turks could not stand against the powerful Frankish army and surrendered in two months. After returning from Nicaea to the Byzantine Empire, the crusaders marched on to Dorylaeum, an ancient city in Anatolia, where the most violent battle of the crusades ensued.

At Dorylaeum, after the crusaders recovered from the initial shock of massive foreign forces raining down arrows from all sides, they realized their armor could withstand the arrows. They won another significant victory and marched toward Antioch (present-day Antakya, Turkey), conquering every village and returning them to the Byzantine Empire. Antioch proved to be another significant victory in their march to reach Jerusalem; however, that victory was not easy. After the crusaders surrounded the city in an attempt to cut the Turks off from food and supplies, it took eight months before they captured the city. After finally conquering Antioch, the noble leaders fought over who should control the city. Bohemund had led the initial raid on the city and therefore believed Antioch should be his. His refusal to turn Antioch back over to Alexius Comnenus's control resulted in the Western and Eastern Roman Empires permanently severing their alliance. Despite the quarreling, Raymond of Toulouse continued the journey and led the crusaders to Jerusalem, their final destination.

Jerusalem was well prepared for the attack. The Fatimids of Egypt had recently captured Jerusalem, and the city was heavily fortified and well supplied. Nonetheless, in as little as two months, the crusaders stormed the city, killing Muslims and Jews, men, women, and children. The First Crusade had finally come to an end, three years after it began. Pope Urban died before news of the victory at Jerusalem reached Clermont. Godfrey of Bouillon was chosen by the papacy to be defender of the Holy Sepulcher—king of Jerusalem; thus, the first Christian ruler from the Roman Empire took his throne in the newly created Kingdom of Jerusalem.

Second Crusade (1147–1149)

Pope Eugene III called for the Second Crusade because of deteriorating conditions in the newly founded Christian states. The end of the First Crusade resulted in the formation of four Christian territories: the County of Edessa, the Princedom of Antioch, the County of Tripoli, and the Kingdom of Jerusalem. The County of Edessa, the weakest of the four, was the first to fall to Muslim control, leading Pope Eugenius to call for a Second Crusade. King Louis VII of France, along with Conrad III, the German emperor, led the Second Crusade in 1147 to assist the remaining Christian citizens. The armies reached Jerusalem in 1148, despite famine and hardships, and planned an attack on Damascus. Why the crusaders chose Damascus to attack is not known, since it was the only Muslim ally the Christian crusaders had. The leaders of the Second Crusade made a

second fatal mistake: they chose not to attack on Sunday because it was considered a sin to fight on the Lord's Day. By Monday, Muslim reinforcements had reached Damascus and far outnumbered the Christian crusaders. The crusaders were defeated and humiliated.

After the Second Crusade the conditions in the East deteriorated further, as the newly conquered and created Christian territories in the East were left vulnerable. By 1183 they had become surrounded by a unified Muslim nation ruled by Saladin, sultan of Egypt and Syria, who would eventually launch his own "holy war" against this Christian kingdom. In 1187, Jerusalem surrendered to Saladin's forces, and the Christian crusaders lost control of their sacred holy city.

Third Crusade (1187–1192)

Europe was devastated and shocked that Jerusalem had fallen to Muslim control in 1187. As a result, Pope Gregory VIII proclaimed the need for a third crusade in 1187. The three most powerful kings of Europe—King Richard I of England, Emperor Frederick Barbarossa of Germany, and King Philip Augustus of France—answered his call and launched the Third Crusade, which became known as the Kings' Crusade. The Kings' Crusade began in 1189, when Frederick departed with the first crusaders, approximately 100,000 men, under his leadership; however, he drowned while crossing the Saleph River—a river in modern-day Turkey—after which most of his followers returned to Germany. Richard and Philip set out with their armies in 1190 from Marseille, France, headed toward Sicily, Italy. Richard's sister, Joan, had been married to William II of Sicily; however, he died in 1189, and his successor, Tancred, had Joan imprisoned. When Richard took Messina, the capital city of Sicily, he released Joan from prison.

Philip left Sicily on March 30, 1191, and

Richard followed soon after. Shortly after Richard set sail, a violent storm struck his fleet, and several of his ships were grounded on the island of Cyprus. Isaac Ducas Comnenus of Cyprus seized Richard's cargo. He and Richard agreed on a peace treaty, but Isaac broke the treaty, prompting Richard to conquer the island. Philip's and Richard's armies finally met in Acre, located in modern-day northern Israel. One month after Richard's army met Philip's army in Acre, the city fell to Christian hands, in July 1191. Richard and Saladin reached a peace treaty, but when Saladin refused to uphold his part of the deal, Richard slaughtered 2,700 Muslim prisoners; Saladin responded by slaughtering his share of Christian prisoners.

After the victory at Acre, Philip returned home, leaving Richard to lead the crusaders. Richard then marched to the city of Jaffa, an ancient city on the Mediterranean Sea, in present-day Tel Aviv, Israel. It was there that Saladin attacked his army on September 11, 1191. Saladin and Richard reached a peace agreement on September 2, 1192, which resulted in a five-year truce and safe passage for all Christians to Jerusalem, leaving Jerusalem in the hands of the Muslims. Richard left the Holy Land to return home that same year but died before reaching England.

Fourth Crusade (1202–1204)

Pope Innocent III launched the Fourth Crusade in 1201. He was an ambitious pope who dreamed of a unified church governing the world; thus, the Fourth Crusade set out once again to conquer Jerusalem. The majority of the crusaders were from France but had gathered in Italy to set sail from Venice, led by Boniface of Montferrat (in Italy). The crusaders sailed for the port city of Zara, a city on the Adriatic Sea in Croatia, and conquered it; however, their next move shocked the pope. The crusaders decided to march to Constantinople against the pope's wishes. They sacked Constantinople, raping and murdering the inhabitants, defiling the temples, and looting the churches of their holy relics. This had consequences that lasted for centuries; the rift between the Catholic Church and the Eastern Orthodox Church has persisted even into modern times. The capture of Constantinople marked the end of the Fourth Crusade.

Fifth Crusade (1217–1221)

The Fifth Crusade, also launched by Pope Innocent III, in 1217, was led by Duke Leopold of Austria and King Andrew of Hungary. The goal was the conquest of Jerusalem via Egypt; however, Pope Innocent died shortly before the crusaders embarked. They sailed to Damietta, a port city near the Nile River in present-day Egypt, and in 1218 successfully captured the port. In 1219 reinforcements arrived, along with a Spanish cardinal named Pelagius. Pelagius quickly took control of the expedition. Now that they had successfully captured the port, they turned their focus toward launching a new attack on the city of Damietta. The siege of Damietta took place in June 1218.

The Egyptian sultan al-Kamil negotiated with Pelagius, much to the crusaders' advantage. He promised not only to return the city of Jerusalem to the Christians but also to rebuild the city walls. However, Pelagius stubbornly refused. After conquering Damietta, the crusaders marched south for Cairo, hoping to reach and conquer Alexandria because it was an important trading route in the Mediterranean. However, the sultan destroyed the flood barriers and drowned most of the crusader army. Pelagius managed to escape in a boat, which held most of the army's food and supplies. Thus, the Fifth Crusade ended with the remaining crusaders wandering aimlessly back to Acre, having accomplished nothing.

Sixth Crusade (1228–1229)

Seven years after the end of the Fifth Crusade, Frederick II, emperor of the Holy Roman Empire, pursued another crusade to recapture Jerusalem. The Sixth Crusade began in 1228. Frederick was entitled to the kingship of the Kingdom of Jerusalem through his marriage to Isabelle de Brienne in 1225. Frederick's wife was the daughter of the Jerusalem rulers John of Brienne and Maria of Montferrat.

Prior to Frederick's crusading campaign, Gregory IX became pope and excommunicated Frederick. Gregory's justification for excommunication was the numerous delays of the crusade, which was a violation of the crusader vow. Despite his excommunication, Frederick proceeded with his crusade and traveled to Acre in 1228.

After gaining support from the people of Acre, who supported papal authority, Frederick's crusade was once again delayed by the sultan of Egypt, al-Kamil. After his victory during the Fifth Crusade, al-Kamil and his brother al-Nasir divided the territory of Syria. Unsatisfied with his brother, however, al-Kamil established a ten-year truce with Frederick on February 18, 1229, creating an allied force against al-Nasir and returning Jerusalem to Christian hands. Although papal authority opposed the truce, Frederick proceeded with it and appointed himself as king. In May 1229, Frederick left for home, and the following year his truce with al-Kamil expired. The Egyptians began attacking Jerusalem and were successful, regaining control of the city by 1244.

Seventh Crusade (1248–1254)

In 1248, the Seventh Crusade began, under the leadership of Louis IX of France. Near the end of the Sixth Crusade, the overthrow of power in Jerusalem by the Egyptian Mamluks did not prompt the need for Pope Innocent IV (r. 1243–1254) and Holy Roman Emperor Frederick II to initiate another crusade to the Holy Land to reclaim power in Jerusalem. King Henry III of England was also unable to pursue a crusade to Jerusalem because his military was struggling against the French nobleman Simon de Montfort. The only kingdom strong enough to mount a crusade to the Holy Land during this time was France. In 1245, Louis IX indicated his desire to lead a crusade to regain power in Jerusalem. Assisted by his brothers, Alphonse and Charles I of Anjou, Louis began a campaign to get funding for the crusade. By 1248, his crusade was prepared to set sail with nearly 20,000 men.

After sailing to Cyprus to gain support from other forces during the winter, Louis denied a request for military assistance to support the Latin Empire against the Byzantine Empire of Nicaea. During this time, in 1248, he also refused to assist others requesting his help, including William II Villehardouin, the Principality of Antioch, and the Knights Templar, against the Muslim forces who overthrew the Syrian city of Sidon.

Louis reached Damietta in Egypt in 1249. Initially, the strategy of beginning the crusade in Egypt was to use it as a primary base from which to conduct assaults against Jerusalem while pillaging the wealth and foods of Damietta. While stationed in Damietta, Louis and his men were able to fortify the city and prepare for future attacks against the Muslim army in pursuit of regaining control of Jerusalem.

On June 6, 1249, Louis and his crusading army easily conquered Damietta, forcing opposing Muslim forces to flee along the Nile. However, Louis and his men were forced to reside in Damietta for nearly six months due to the unexpected flooding of the Nile. During this time, Louis established an archbishopric in Damietta, but he failed to acknowledge the agreement set during the Fifth Crusade that ceded control of Damietta to the Kingdom of Jerusalem.

After the flood waters receded, Louis marched forward to Cairo. During his march Louis's men were attacked by the Mamluks' general, Baibars, and were defeated. In spite of their defeat, Louis proceeded onward to the Egyptian camp at al-Mansourah, located east of Damietta in the Nile River delta, where the Knights Templar had recently been defeated, resulting in the loss of their military leader, Robert of Artois. Instead of returning to Damietta to regroup and reestablish his army, Louis focused on overtaking al-Mansourah.

The hardships and defeat at al-Mansourah forced Louis back to Damietta. Upon his return, he was apprehended by the Muslim army and became ill after contracting dysentery. He was restored to health by a Muslim physician and held for a ransom of 400,000 livres and the return of Damietta to Muslim power. After fulfilling the ransom, Louis returned to Acre to rebuild other crusader cities.

During the period when Louis was reestablishing his army and other crusader cities, Cairo experienced a revolt from the Mamluks, which resulted in Turanshah becoming sultan of Cairo and thereby succeeding the sultan as-Salih. Although an alliance was established between Louis and the Mamluks, Louis began negotiations with the Mongols in an attempt to gain their alliance against the Muslims. Meanwhile, the Muslim forces were simultaneously engaging in negotiations with the Mongols for assistance in fighting the Christian opposition in their lands. The Mongol ruler, Mongke Khan, insisted that Louis submit to him because he was superior and would not subject himself to the proposal of converting to Christianity. Although Louis did not submit to the authority of Khan, Khan's Mongol army proceeded to attack the Mamluk and Muslim armies.

By 1254, the funding for Louis's crusade was depleted, and he returned home to France. Although his crusade to the Holy Land was considered a failure, the people of France honored Louis as a saint.

Eighth Crusade (1270)

In 1260, Baibars became sultan of the Mamluks by assassinating Qutuz, who had reigned as sultan for less than one year. The growing number of Baibars's military conquests, over the Middle Eastern cities of Nazareth, Haifa, Toron, and Arsuf, influenced Louis IX to lead another crusade in 1267, which led to the beginning of the Eighth Crusade, in 1270. Although there was a lack of support and funding for another crusade, Louis knew that something must be done to protect the progress of the crusading states into the Holy Land. The primary objective of the attack was to pick up where his previous crusade had ended in Egypt. The first attack was planned against the city of Tunis, which is located in the northern part of Africa near the Mediterranean Sea. It was believed that Tunis could provide a centralized base for carrying out future attacks in Egypt.

In July 1270, Louis arrived in Africa and began his second crusade to the Holy Land. Soon after, however, the majority of his men became sick from drinking the water. Coming to aid Louis in his crusade was his brother, Charles of Anjou. Unfortunately for Charles, Louis died on August 25, 1270, one day after his brother's arrival. Because Louis's son was too young to lead such a campaign, Charles took charge of the army. Creating an alliance with Prince Edward of England, Charles proceeded to attack the city of Tunis. By October 30, 1270, with much of the army sick from various diseases, the siege of Tunis came to an end and a peace agreement was settled between Charles and Baibars, leaving Prince Edward and his men to march on to Acre to assist in protecting the city from overthrow by the Mamluks. The agreement between the Baibars and Charles was a success; missionaries and Christian teachers were allowed in the city to share the Gospel and convert Muslims to Christianity.

Ninth Crusade (1271–1272)

The Ninth Crusade is considered to be the final major crusade into the Holy Land from the Christian European kingdoms. Due to the progression of the Mamluk kingdom, crusade cities feared the power of the Mamluks and the possibility of losing their cities along the coast of the Mediterranean Sea. The growing force of the Mamluks under the power of Qutuz, sultan of Egypt, led them to victory over the Palestine Mongol army in 1260 at the city of Ain Jalut. As a result, Christian cities feared they would not be able to match the power of the Mamluks. Qutuz was later assassinated by his general, Baibars, after suppressing the Mongols. Baibars continued to expand his territory by attacking the Christians and crusade cities. The European kingdoms were unable to provide supporting forces to the Middle East before Baibars conquered the cities of Arsuf, Athlith, Haifa, Safad, Jaffa, Ashkalon, and Caesarea.

Prince Edward's arrival in Tunis was too late for him to assist Charles of Anjou, and so he proceeded on toward the Holy Land to support Bohemund VI, Count of Tripoli, against the Mamluk forces probing the major Christian city of Tripoli, located in the northern region of Lebanon. Baibars conquered Tripoli in 1271, enslaving and killing tens of thousands of Christians who populated the city. Prince Edward and Charles of Anjou worked together in an attempt to prevent the fall of Acre to the Mamluks. Charles launched attacks from the island of Cyprus, south of Turkey, while Edward attacked inland from Acre. Charles and Edward were able to slow down the army of Baibars

by attacking from both land and sea. Baibars focused primarily on establishing a fleet to attack Cyprus and ceased his attacks. The army of Cyprus was too strong for Baibars, and the Mamluks were forced to retreat from battle.

Shortly after the retreat of Baibars and his army at Cyprus, Prince Edward initiated peace within the Christian kingdoms. The call for peace was an attempt to unite the Christians as one force against the growing power of the Mamluks and other Muslim kingdoms. After mediating peace among the Christian groups, Edward negotiated a truce with Baibars for eleven years. Baibars attempted to end the truce within the first year with an assassination attempt on Edward. While Edward was preparing for retaliation against the Mamluks for the assassination attempt, King Henry III died, and Edward was summoned back to England to take the throne as king. Edward and Baibars signed a treaty in 1272, permitting Edward's return to England and Baibars's return to Cairo. The truce between the Christian kingdoms did not last long after the departure of Edward. Charles of Anjou capitalized on the disputes between other Christian kingdoms such as the Ghibelline-ruled Genoa, Knights Templar, and Venetians to help him achieve control of the several remaining kingdoms.

In 1281, Pope Martin IV supported Charles of Anjou's claims against the Byzantine Empire ruled by Michael VIII, founder of the Palaeologan dynasty, to divert attention from the Mamluks. Charles was not successful in defeating the Byzantine Empire. Throughout the next nine years, the Mamluks increased their demands, which breached the truce between empires. In response to unsatisfied demands, the Egyptian sultan Qalawun prepared an attack on Tripoli in 1289. During the battle, both the Christians of Tripoli and the Mamluks lost a great number of men, including Qalawun's eldest son. Qalawun's army regained strength over the next two years before launching an attack against Acre.

In 1291, Qalawun justified an attack against Acre when Christians from Acre killed several Muslims out of retaliation. After the Christians failed to respond to the demand for monetary reparation, Qalawun declared a jihad against Acre. During that battle, Qalawun was killed, and Khalil became the Mamluks' sultan. After Acre was conquered, approximately 60,000 citizens were killed or enslaved by the order of Khalil. Baibars's dream of reclaiming the Holy Land under Muslim power was achieved through the final battle at Acre, which represented the crusaders' last stand for a Christian kingdom within the Holy Land.

Conclusion

The crusading wars created disparity and distance between religious believers while expanding the Christian civilization of Europe. The Crusades began with Pope Urban II declaring a holy war against Muslims who claimed control of Jerusalem. The establishment of one church under one God was preached, and Muslim believers were referred to as heathens and opposers of the doctrine of the Christian God. Recruitment for the battle to regain control of Jerusalem was accomplished not only by the promise of gaining wealth and land but also for the remission of sins. Through the centuries of war between Christian and Muslim believers, the Crusades were successful at preventing the spread of Islam and the Muslim population into Europe; however, Christians failed to gain Muslim territory and control over the Holy Land.

Kilby Raptopoulos and Nicholas D. ten Bensel

See also: Christianity; Pope Urban II.

Further Reading

Billings, Malcolm. *The Crusades: Five Centuries of Holy Wars.* New York: Sterling, 1996.

Boase, Thomas. *Kingdoms and Strongholds of the Crusaders.* Indianapolis: Bobbs-Merrill, 1971.

Gabrieli, Francesco. *Arab Historians of the Crusades.* Berkeley: University of California Press, 1969.

Housley, Norman. *The Later Crusades.* Oxford: Oxford University Press, 1992.

Jones, Terry, and Alan Ereira. *Crusades.* New York: Facts on File, 1995.

Riley-Smith, Jonathan. *The Crusades: A History.* New Haven, CT: Yale University Press, 2005.

Tout, Thomas. *The Empire and the Papacy.* Westport, CT: Greenwood Press, 1980.

Christian Identity Movement

Christian Identity is a white supremacist religion, primarily practiced in the United States, that grounds its ideology in a racist reading of the Christian Bible, resulting in the use of violence against non-Whites and perceived enemies of the group. Identity ideology and important texts provide a rationale for violence. Christian Identity was closely aligned to the U.S. militia movement in the 1990s, and exceptional violence was produced by that relationship. Additionally, Christian Identity has insinuated itself into portions of the violent arm of anti-abortion protests from the latter part of the twentieth century to the present.

Christian Identity Ideology and Significant Texts

According to Christian Identity adherents (and based on an earlier version of Christian Identity known as British-Israelism), Aryans represent the lost tribes of Israel who settled initially in England. These Aryans saw themselves as God's chosen people, made in God's image. Thus, they believed that God is white. Christian Identity adherents believe that those Aryans eventually immigrated to the United States.

Supporters of Christian Identity view Jews and other non-Aryans as their enemy. Many members believe that Satan's seduction of Eve in the Garden of Eden was a literal seduction,

A Michigan militiaman oversees the training of fellow survivalists at a paramilitary camp in northern Michigan on December 11, 1994. The militia movement, an offshoot of the Christian Identity Movement, is an antigovernment group committed to gun ownership as a means of protecting their individual freedoms from government control. *(Michael Samojeden/AFP/Getty Images)*

not merely persuasion. Therefore, this "mating" between Eve and Satan is said to have produced the Jewish race—a natural and mortal enemy of the Aryans. Since Aryans are the chosen children of God, Christian Identity embeds its hatred of Jews in a historic and mythical struggle between good and evil.

This struggle is played out in several conspiratorial narratives. Members of the movement see the government of the United States as an evil force that has been secretly captured by Jews. This Zionist Occupied Government (ZOG), as they call it, is believed to be secretly helping the State of Israel, using the power of the United States to impose the will of Jews on the world. According to the group, Israel's ultimate goal is world domination and the extermination of all Aryans. Christian Identity followers also believe that Jews control the international media and news organizations in the United States. Among other things,

this media control allows Jews to hide Israel's atrocities and to represent Jews positively to citizens of the United States. Adherents also believe that the Hollywood industry is part of this conspiracy: films or television shows that portray a positive romantic relationship between a mixed-race couple is taken as evidence that the Jewish-controlled media is attempting to encourage racial intermixing that will eventually breed Aryans out of existence. In addition, they view people enjoying such movies as a group that is hypnotized and distracted from the presence of the ZOG. The abortion-clinic bomber and Christian Identity member Eric Rudolph would, according to his sister, fast-forward through movies to the credits and count the number of Jewish names affiliated with the making of the movie. Such actions became a form of self-persuasion that confirmed his racist worldview.

Many Christian Identity followers believe

that God cannot return to earth until the enemies of God are destroyed; that is, one who wants the return of God must literally kill the evil that exists here now. Thus, followers subscribe to an ideology that constructs them as the children of God with a natural enemy that worships Satan and possesses a genocidal hatred of the white race. Therefore, they must kill their enemies, and their reward will be the coming of God to earth.

A hate group within the Christian Identity movement is an association known as the Phineas Priesthood. This is not a membership organization with structured gatherings or a membership process—it is more an honorary society in which one "claims" membership. The Phineas Priesthood is taken from the Israelite Phineas in the Old Testament's book of Numbers. According to Christian Identity interpretation, many Jews had been consorting with people of other faiths and ethnicities to the great offense of God. God therefore told Moses to slay the Israelites who mingled with the "others." In Numbers 25: 6–13, we see what may be the first recorded hate-motivated murder at the hand of Phineas:

> And, behold, one of the children of Israel came and brought unto his brethren a Midianitish woman in the sight of Moses, and in the sight of the congregation of the children of Israel, who were weeping before the door of the tabernacle of the congregation. And when Phineas . . . saw it, he rose up from among the congregation and took a Javelin in his hand; And, he went after the man of Israel into the tent, and thrust both of them through, the man of Israel, and the woman through the belly. So the plague was stayed from the children of Israel. . . . And the Lord spake unto Moses, saying, Phineas . . . hath turned my wrath away from the children of Israel, while he was zealous for my sake among them, that I consumed not the children of Israel in my jealousy. . . . Behold, I give unto him my covenant of peace: And he shall have it, and his seed after him, even the covenant of an everlasting priesthood; because he was zealous for his God, and made an atonement for the children of Israel.

Christian Identity adherents can claim membership in the Phineas Priesthood by committing violent acts, including murder, against an enemy of the Aryan people, typically an interracial couple. It is believed that a host of murders have been committed over the years by individuals earning membership in the Phineas Priesthood. The sign of the Phineas Priesthood is a capital P with a straight line horizontally bisecting the P, possibly representing Phineas's javelin.

A prominent leader of the Christian Identity Church was the late Richard Butler, leader of the neo-Nazi group the Aryan Nations and reverend of the Church of Jesus Christ-Christian. Butler was also known for his connection to the Silent Brotherhood, more widely known as The Order. Several members of the Aryan Nations formed The Order and carried out armed robberies of armored bank vehicles to finance a racial holy war. Butler's connection to The Order is one prominent example of his violent influence on criminals in the hate movement. It is believed that for decades Butler's followers have engaged in criminal acts that range from assassination to armed robberies, counterfeiting, and racial assaults. Christian Identity ideology is also epitomized in the leadership of Pete Peters, reverend of the LaPorte Church of Christ (Peters, like Butler, ministered to The Order in his church). Both Butler and Peters preached that the ZOG of the United States had become the enemy of white people and was using minorities and "perverted" gay men and lesbians to threaten the white population. Butler and Peters preached that white people should cut as many ties to this corrupt government as possible, withdraw from anyone who is not of their kind, and stockpile weapons in preparation for the coming war with ZOG.

Christian Identity Violence

Christian Identity's ideologically driven violence has various manifestations. One is found in the militia movement. The militia movement is an element of the hate movement that has its ideology based on a suspicion of the federal government and a commitment to gun ownership in order to protect its members from a government that has increasingly strayed from the intentions of the Founding Fathers. More broadly, some strands of the militia movement shares many of the anti-Semitic and racist beliefs of the Christian Identity movement. From the militia movement's perspective, the federal government is orchestrated by Jewish political and financial interests. Members also believe that the only legitimate form of government is local. The values of racist militia groups have a long history in American life that is appealing to southern segregationists and to those in the American West who believe that the federal government is out to destroy their way of life through land management regulation. All militia groups base their worldview on the protection of an individual's "right" to own, store, and trade guns in sufficient quantities so that individual citizens may protect themselves from the ZOG.

With supporters in key geographical pockets across the United States, the modern militia movement became prominent through highly publicized activities in Ruby Ridge, Idaho; Waco, Texas; and Oklahoma City. In 1990 Randy Weaver, a member of Aryan Nations, was approached by the FBI and threatened with arrest for selling an undercover agent an illegally altered shotgun. The FBI offered to drop the gun charges if Weaver would be willing to spy on members of Aryan Nations (the group's headquarters was near Weaver's cabin). He refused and hid with his family in his home in Ruby Ridge. A bungled arrest attempt by FBI agents turned the home into a battleground between the Weaver family and what appeared to be an elite team of jack-booted federal agents.

The eventual arrest of Weaver came at the expense of an eleven-day standoff that resulted in the death of Weaver's wife and son. The string of foolish decisions by administrative agents and FBI snipers made the general public sympathetic to the Weaver family's ordeal. This impression would eventually be a factor in Weaver's successful $3 million civil suit against the FBI. The Ruby Ridge incident made Weaver into a living hero of the militia-patriot movement, an ordinary man attempting to pursue his own happiness apart from the interference of an intrusive federal government. Christian Identity and the patriot movement recognized one another as natural allies, and their ideas cross-pollinated in a way that made the 1990s a very dangerous time in the history of hate groups.

David Koresh and his Branch Davidians offered many in the militia movement another opportunity to see the face of America's "shadow" government. The Branch Davidians were a millennialist group that believed they were living in the "end of times"—that period of time before Christ's return to earth following the Battle of Armageddon. The Bureau of Alcohol, Tobacco and Firearms (BATF) knew that Koresh was stockpiling illegal weapons and attempted to execute a search warrant at the compound on February 28, 1993. Branch Davidian members were tipped off about the raid and were able to prepare for it. A gun battle erupted when BATF agents approached the compound, in which several people were killed. A fifty-one-day Federal Bureau of Investigation (FBI) siege of the compound ensued, with the final assault occurring on April 19, 1993. On that day the FBI moved in with tanks and at some point a fire broke out that resulted in the deaths of some seventy-five people. Though it is in dispute whether the fire was accidental or deliberately set by Branch Davidian members, the siege tactics used by the FBI were viewed by many as extreme. The confrontation became a symbolic event for the militia movement, with its leaders arguing that if this could happen to the Davidians, it could happen in any American church. Following the Waco siege, the militia movement experienced its greatest growth. By 1995, militia groups were active in thirty-six states.

The Waco incident was a catalyst for the 1995 Oklahoma City bombing, which was the most significant terrorist act prior to the attacks of September 11, 2001—though the September 11 attacks were so horrifying to Americans that they actually prompted a decline in the militia movement (Crothers 2003). A man named Timothy McVeigh visited the site of the FBI-Davidian standoff and observed the FBI's assault on the Davidian complex on April 19, 1993. McVeigh, a lifelong gun enthusiast, had joined the army in 1988, aspiring to earn an appointment to a Special Forces unit. His racism grew in the army, where he began to read increasing amounts of racist literature, including *The Turner Diaries,* a text that he encouraged other soldiers to read.

After leaving the army in 1992, McVeigh eventually moved in with Terry Nichols and Michael Fortier, two former soldiers with similar racist views. Under those living conditions, McVeigh was cocooned in an environment that focused on racialist and militia interpretations of current events, including the FBI assault on the Davidian compound in 1993. Steeped in racist militia ideology, McVeigh, Nichols, and Fortier planned and executed the bombing of the Alfred P. Murrah Federal Building in Oklahoma City on April 19, 1995—two years to the day after the Waco incident and national Militia Day. Following the guidelines provided in *The Turner Diaries,* McVeigh fashioned a rental truck into a mobile bomb with multiple barrels containing diesel fuel and ammonium nitrate fertilizer and parked it in front of the Murrah Building. At 9:02 A.M. the bomb exploded, taking the lives of 168 men, women, and children—people that McVeigh viewed as co-conspirators in ZOG's attempt to ravage the rights and lives of "ordinary Americans."

The Oklahoma City bombing was the explosion that would ultimately extinguish the militia movement. It is not certain that McVeigh was a Christian Identity adherent, but he was unquestionably familiar with the ideology of that racist church. It is known, however, that Terry Nichols and his brother James were connected to the church. James Nichols pledged both of their lives to the Christian Identity church and the struggle against ZOG through the oath of "Aryan warriorhood." As reported by the Southern Poverty Law Center in 2002,

> On Day Two of the gathering of Christian Identity adherents, after listening to a series of calls to exterminate the Jews, Nichols walked up to a makeshift altar in the back of the furniture store and dropped cents into a basket—two helpings of the Old Testament "soldier's ransom" of cents, paid to ensure God's protection. Nichols spoke his name out loud, then told the rapt Aryans that he had come on behalf of his brother, too.

Following the ceremony the first person to shake James Nichols's hand was James Wickstrom, former leader of Posse Comitatus—one of the first militia groups, dating back to the 1970s—and an Christian Identity church pastor.

Christian Identity and Anti-Abortion Violence

The ideas of the Christian Identity movement also pollinated the violent potential of another group sympathetic with its ideology: anti-abortion protestors. Most violent and nonviolent anti-abortion protestors do not belong to the hate movement; however, many do. Women are celebrated in the hate movement for their ability to bear white children who will eventually become warriors in the war against ZOG. Consequently, doctors who give abortions to white women and the white women who have abortions are seen as a genocidal threat to the white race. The perceived impending race war and the fact that minorities are seen as "out producing" the white race add to the exigency of the situation.

In 1995, three Christian Identity adherents

—Verne Jay Merrell, Charles Barbee, and Robert Berry—robbed a local bank and bombed the Spokane, Washington, offices of Planned Parenthood and the *Spokesman-Review* newspaper. All three identified themselves as Phineas Priests. A host of violent anti-abortion protestors who were influenced by Christian Identity and militia ideology have been arrested for their illegal activities, including the Rev. W.N. Otwell, who participated in armed standoffs with federal agents in 1996 and 1997 in Texas; Willie Ray Lamply, who served time in prison for plotting to blow up abortion clinics, gay bars, Anti-Defamation League offices, and the Southern Poverty Law Center; Tim Dreste, leader of several raids on abortion clinics, who, after physician and abortion provider Dr. David Gunn was shot and killed, carried signs that read "Dr. . . . Are you feeling under the Gunn?"; and Paul Hill, who killed Dr. John Britton and his escort after receiving information about Britton's schedule and home address from anti-abortion protestors.

In 2003 James Kopp pleaded guilty to the second-degree murder of Dr. Barnett Slepian. In 1998, Kopp shot Slepian through his kitchen window, in front of his wife and children; he claimed that he meant to wound but not kill Slepian. Kopp was also suspected in four other shootings of abortion doctors in New York and Canada.

Perhaps one of the most "heroic" figures among the anti-abortion protestors is Eric Robert Rudolph, who was raised by his parents in the Christian Identity church of Dan Gayman, in Schell City, Missouri. Later, in North Carolina, Rudolph had ties to the late Nord Davis Jr., a Christian Identity leader whose compound was close to the Rudolph home.

On May 31, 2003, Rudolph was arrested and charged with four terrorist bombings between 1996 and 1998. His last bombing was particularly notorious: he detonated a nail bomb in an abortion clinic by remote control. His broad range of targets made Rudolph the perfect operant of the hate movement, as he attacked all of its despised enemies: an abortion clinic with abortion doctors and white women killing white babies; a gay bar containing "pedophiles," "perverts," and people betraying their race by engaging in sexual behaviors that would not produce white children; and the 1996 Olympic games, which celebrated globalism and multiculturalism. August Kreis and James Wickstrom, both longtime leaders of the violently racist and anti-Semitic Posse Comitatus and Christian Identity adherents, praised Rudolph on their Web site as "a true warrior of YHVH [God]."

Conclusion

The Christian Identity movement has over the years proven to be an exceptionally violent and dangerous racist religion. While more recently emergent race-based religions weave violence into their culture more effectively than Christian Identity has, Christian Identity has maintained its violent approach over a longer period of time. The power of Christian Identity is the religious framework that provides ideological substance to the believer's hatred. The sophistication of Christian Identity is evident in the ease with which its beliefs were commingled with the beliefs and needs of other social movements. When actions by the federal government facilitated the emergence of a more organized and coherent militia movement, Christian Identity was there to give a religious fervor to militia beliefs. When the violent extremes of the anti-abortion movement emerged during the 1990s, Christian Identity capitalized on the momentum of the movement to make itself more visible.

Michael S. Waltman

See also: Aryan Nations; Beam, Louis, Jr.; Butler, Richard Girnt; Creativity Movement and Church of the Creator; Mathews, Robert Jay; Order, The; Posse Comitatus; Rudolph, Eric; Terrorism.

Further Reading

"Anti-Abortion Violence: Five Years Later." *Southern Poverty Law Center Intelligence Report* (Summer 2003). Available: http://www.splcenter.org/intel/intelreport/article.jsp?aid=62.

Barkun, Michael. *Religion and the Racist Right: The Origins of the Christian Identity Movement.* Chapel Hill: University of North Carolina Press, 1996.

"Bulter and His Aryan Nations: A Life of Hate, and the Future in the Balance." *Southern Poverty Law Center Intelligence Report* (Summer 1998). Available: http://www.splcenter.org/intel/intelreport/article.jsp?aid=415.

Clarkson, Frederick. "Anti-Abortion Extremists: 'Patriots' and Racists Converge." *Southern Poverty Law Center Intelligence Report* (Summer 1998). Available: http://www.splcenter.org/intel/intelreport/article.jsp?pid=698.

Crothers, Lane. *Rage on the Right: The American Militia Movement from Ruby Ridge to Homeland Security.* Lanham, MD: Rowman and Littlefield, 2003.

"Extremism in America: Christian Identity." ADL/Anti-Defamation League (online). Available: http://www.adl.org/learn/ext_us/Christian_Identity.asp?LEARN_Cat=Extremism&LEARN_SubCat=Extremism_in_America&xpicked=4&item=Christian_ID.

Guttentag, W., and V. DiPersio (writers and directors). "Hate.com: Extremists on the Internet." Television series episode. In *America Undercover,* produced by J. Anderson. New York: Home Box Office, 2003.

Kaplan, Jeffrey. *Encyclopedia of White Power: A Sourcebook on the Radical Racist Right.* Walnut Creek, CA: AltaMira Press, 2000.

Levitas, Daniel. *The Terrorist Next Door: The Militia Movement and the Radical Right.* New York: St. Martin's, 2002.

Perry, Barbara. *In the Name of Hate: Understanding Hate Crimes.* New York: Routledge, 2001.

Potok, Mark. "Eric Rudolph, at Last." *Southern Poverty Law Center Intelligence Report* (Summer 2003). Available: http://www.splcenter.org/intel/intelreport/article.jsp?aid=46.

Quarles, Chester, L. *Christian Identity: The Aryan American Bloodline Religion.* Jefferson, NC: McFarland, 2004.

Roberts, Charles H. *Race over Grace: The Racialist Religion of the Christian Identity Movement.* Lincoln, NE: iUniverse, 2003.

Scofield Study Bible. New York: Oxford University Press, 2003.

"A Soldier's Ransom." *Southern Poverty Law Center Intelligence Report* (Winter 2002). Available: http://www.splcenter.org/intel/intelreport/article.jsp?aid=71.

Christian Right

The Christian Right, also referred to as the Religious Right, consists of various right-wing social movements that advocate a return of so-called Christian values to the public sphere. Individuals in the movement accept and use both labels to define themselves. The Christian Right emerged in the late 1970s and is generally considered to be part of a wider right-wing resurgence known as the New Right. Christians who are not affiliated with the Christian Right often object to the movement's name, arguing that there is nothing Christian about right-wing policies. Secular opponents (on the left and the right) argue that the movement is "hateful," "radical," and "extremist" because its leaders want to establish a theocratic government in the United States. It has also been argued, however, that such terms should only be applied to branches of the Right that operate outside of the democratic process.

The "Old" Right

To understand the rise of the New Right generally and the Christian Right more specifically, it is useful to compare it with what scholars refer to as the "Old Right." After the Great Depression began, the power and influence of the political Right in the United States began to wane. Its decline was apparent in both economic and cultural spheres. In the economic realm, the election of Franklin Delano Roosevelt to the presidency in 1932 and the subsequent implementation of the New Deal cemented a left-leaning economic orientation in the United States. Laissez-faire economic policy gave way to Keynesianism, an approach that supported government intervention to prevent economic downturns. The approach, named after its founder, John Maynard Keynes, also advocated government action to distribute wealth more evenly among the population. By the end of World War II, efforts to undermine traditional cultural hierarchies were also percolating, with grassroots activism emerging around feminist and civil rights causes. In the wake of such changes, the political Right was a largely fragmented and ineffective opposition, both in and out of government.

The Old Right's marginal status was solidified by leaders who publicly embraced racist and anti-Semitic beliefs. During the 1920s and 1930s, for example, the fundamentalist preacher Robert Shuler was renowned for sprinkling his sermons with invectives against Catholics, Jews, and African Americans. Likewise, the Mothers Movement against U.S. involvement in World War II embraced fascism, and members often started their meetings with Nazi salutes. As the twentieth century progressed, more and more Americans voiced concern over blatant displays of racial and religious bigotry in culture, religion, and politics.

By the 1960s, most commentators believed the right wing to be in decline. Scholars depicted the political right wing as an aberration from an American political consensus built on liberal pluralism, democracy, and modernity. These scholars, known collectively as the Consensus School, argued that right-wing activism was a reflection of status anxiety. Before World War II, the privileged in American society often obtained their power through wealth and property, and they maintained it along familial lines through inheritance. The postwar economic boom upset this alignment of class and power. While not unseating old families, per se, the new economy created new avenues for obtaining power. An expanding government bureaucracy after World War II provided a wealth of new, middle-class jobs, while governmental education subsidies for returning GIs opened up opportunities for rural, poor, and working-class men to advance up the social ladder.

The shake-up that ensued cut across class lines, but Consensus scholars identified two categories of people whose relative position on the country's socioeconomic ladder was called into question: the older privileged classes and upwardly mobile immigrant groups of European origin. Old-money families, while not losing money in the postwar boom, grew anxious because their business interests were growing at slower rates than those of the new entrepreneurial class. Likewise, second- and third-generation immigrant families, having finally "become" Americans, voiced concern over new immigrants joining their ranks and diluting their social gains.

Because status anxiety was associated with good economic times, Consensus scholars argued that status politics were "irrational." This irrationality, they contended, often translated into extremism. Whereas the goals of economic conflict (i.e., redistribution of income) are clear and can be controlled by the government, there is no clear-cut solution to status anxiety. Thus, it follows that political movements that have successfully appealed to status anxiety and resentments have been irrational in character and have scapegoated those who symbolize the status threat (Lipset 1963). Many scholars have thus described members of the New Right as discontented, radical, and pathologically paranoid.

The New Right

Despite the conventional wisdom of the period, the 1960s proved to be a period of renewal for those on the political Right. Revitalization occurred on two fronts—within the Republican Party and in evangelical quarters. During the 1960s and most of the 1970s, growth on those two fronts was largely disconnected. However, during the 1980s leaders from the respective quarters formalized their connections, a union

Republican presidential candidate Ronald Reagan (right) speaks to evangelical leader and Moral Majority founder Jerry Falwell (center) at a Lynchburg, Virginia, campaign appearance for religious broadcasters, October 3, 1980. Falwell successfully lobbied evangelicals to back Reagan, establishing a connection between the Christian Right and the Republican Party that continues to the present day. *(Charles Harrity/Associated Press)*

that has been described as a "state-movement alliance" (Diamond 1995). The Republican Party became the institutional home for the new alliance, and it was soon supported by a plethora of civil society groups, including right-wing publishing houses, think tanks, advocacy groups, and volunteer corps.

On the political front, many scholars cite Barry Goldwater's 1964 presidential campaign as a harbinger of the right-wing resurgence to come. In 1964, the Arizona native won the Republican nomination in an insurgent campaign aimed at toppling the party's eastern establishment, which kept tight control over the party's platform and finances. Although Goldwater's run for president was a failure—he won in only six of fifty states—his campaign spawned a new breed of activists. The campaign was a truly

grassroots affair—fostered at kitchen klatches organized by suburban housewives, at golf games attended by employees of the burgeoning defense industry, and in the local halls of the California Republican Assembly. Although Goldwater lost the election, the networks created through his campaign did not wither away. Rather, Goldwater activists turned their attention to the 1966 California gubernatorial race into which a young Goldwater supporter, Ronald Reagan, had thrown his hat. Reagan would win that election and go on to capture the White House in 1980 with the help of those activists.

The 1960s were also an active time for mobilization among evangelical Christians. After the infamous Scopes Monkey trial in 1925, most evangelicals had turned away from politics. The trial involved a Tennessee high school teacher named John Scopes, who was fined for breaking a state statute prohibiting teaching evolution in science classes. The trial garnered national publicity because of the renown of the two lawyers who argued the case's opposing sides. Clarence Darrow, a founding member of the American Civil Liberties Union and a well-known defense attorney, represented Scopes, while William Jennings Bryant, a former presidential candidate and well-known populist, argued the case for the state of Tennessee. Although Scopes's fine was upheld, evangelical suspicion of evolution was lampooned in the national media as backward and ignorant. In response, evangelical leaders instructed parishioners to avoid "worldly" matters such as politics and concentrate on the afterlife. When evangelicals voted, they tended to vote Democratic, but they were not a recognizable or reliable voting bloc. When they did vote, they usually cast ballots on the basis of their class interests, as rural producers and industrial workers. To the extent that they were targeted by politicians, it was on these lines as well.

By the late 1950s and early 1960s, however, evangelical leaders had begun to develop organizational capacity in much the same way that Goldwater's activists in Southern California had done. In the late 1950s, for example, evangelical broadcasters formed a trade association to lobby for changes to Federal Communications Commission (FCC) regulations that would benefit evangelical fundraising. Evangelicals also renewed their focus on domestic evangelism. Self-imposed exile gave way to activism as pastors instructed parishioners to "witness" to their friends and neighbors about God's promise of salvation. Even the young were brought into the process; pastors often tasked their youth groups with reaching "secular" children in local schools and playgrounds. The effect was to inculcate a sense of activism among young evangelicals that would set them apart from their more insular parents.

For most of the 1960s and 1970s, growth on Republican and evangelical fronts was disconnected. By the end of the 1970s, however, the possibility of a "state-movement" alliance was increasingly attractive to leaders on both fronts. A meeting organized by Robert Billings in 1979 was crucial to formalizing an alliance between the two groups. Billings, who was then the head of the National Christian Action Council, arranged for televangelist Jerry Falwell to meet Republican super-operatives Paul Weyrich and Howard Phillips. At the meeting, Phillips and Weyrich proposed that the two groups make common cause around the then budding Reagan presidential candidacy. They suggested that evangelicals (who were still largely apolitical or Democratic) should back Reagan because of his opposition to abortion. They told Falwell that a "moral majority" could help Reagan win the election. Within the year, Falwell had formed a group with the name Moral Majority, and he used it to lobby evangelicals behind Reagan's candidacy. Falwell's television show, broadcast across the country, gave him a national audience of evangelicals, and his insider status gave his message a resonance that one delivered by an outsider could never have had. It was a big step for a man who had railed against the activism of black churches during the civil rights era. Many scholars regard his lobbying efforts as crucial to Reagan's victory, and evangelicals are now considered the base of the Republican Party by Democrats and Republicans alike.

Explanations and Assessments of the Rise of the Christian Right

There is no dominant explanation for the rise of the Christian Right. Explanations vary by academic discipline and theoretical orientation. Historians tend to view Christian activism as a constant, if episodic, feature of the American political landscape. For example, it has been argued that the modern Religious Right is the fourth wave of conservative Christian activity during the twentieth century. Sociologists, on the other hand, analyze the rise of the Christian Right using a social-movement perspective, in which the rise of the Christian Right can be explained as the result of resource mobilization by Christian activists. Cultural studies theories situate the movement as part of a wider backlash against 1960s social movements that questioned white male hegemony in the social sphere. Political economists see the rise of the Christian Right as a response to a crisis in capitalism and the colonization of the evangelical lifeworld.

Scholars also offer divergent interpretations of the movement's overall effect on American political culture. Some argue that the Christian Right has failed to meet most of its goals and that its impact on American society has been negligible, as evidenced by the fact that it has not produced a more Christian America or prevented the secularization of its own constituency. In fact, it has been observed that the civil rights and feminist movements have had a much more transformative effect on society than has the Christian Right. Alternatively, it has also been argued that the New Right (which includes the Christian Right) has had a far greater impact on U.S. political culture than the counterculture movements of the 1960s. The New Right has, for example, successfully dismantled a large part of the welfare state, from regulatory capacity to social guarantees, making it at least as influential as the New Deal it sought to overturn.

There is also disagreement on how to describe the movement's goals. Some observers define the movement as traditional and antimodern, arguing that the Christian Right rejects the key values of modernity: egalitarianism and democracy. The movement's support of policies that protect social hierarchies of race, gender, and religion are examples of this antimodernist stance. Other commentators reject the "antimodernist" and "traditional" labels as not useful in analysis of the rise of the New Right, arguing that the early leaders of the movement were indeed quite modern while also embracing a fundamentalist and apocalyptic religious worldview.

Key Issues

The Christian Right has mobilized its constituents around a variety of issues since the 1980s. These issues may be grouped broadly into two categories: social and economic. For most of its history, social issues have dominated the movement's platform, although some scholars argue that economic issues are accounting for a greater share of the movement's agenda.

Social Issues

Individuals and groups on the Christian Right often describe their social agenda as antisecularist. They believe that a patriarchal social system built around the nuclear family is biblically ordained, and that so-called secular humanists are trying to undermine it. While secular humanism is broadly defined to include anyone who embraces a secular rather than spiritual worldview, most activists define secular humanists more narrowly, by reference to groups it believes pose the greatest threat to patriarchy and the nuclear family. In Christian Right discourse, feminists, gays, and lesbians are most often singled out as key offenders.

Opposition to abortion was one of the first issues around which Christian Right activists mobilized their nascent constituency. And it remains a central part of the movement's agenda today. Christians believe that abortion is murder. They also believe that abortion undermines the nuclear family by giving women decision-making power that belongs to men. Although Christian evangelicals have failed to meet their ultimate goal—the repeal of the *Roe v. Wade* (1973) ruling that defines a woman's access to abortion as constitutional—most abortion-rights groups concede that Christian Right activists have succeeded in limiting access to abortions through state and local legislative initiatives. It has been argued that the central place of abortion on the Christian Right's agenda is more symbolic than it is ideological, with the fetus serving as the epitome of all that is pure and untainted. Fundamentalists identify with the fetus and see it in their own image; thus, in saving the fetus, they see themselves as guardians of moral purity in an immoral world (Balmer 1994).

Another social issue activists on the Christian Right have rallied around is opposition to gay rights. Most people on the Christian Right believe that homosexuality is both unnatural and sinful. They believe that homosexuality is a choice rather than a biologically based orientation. Groups on the Christian Right also oppose efforts by gays and lesbians to secure legal rights (freedom from discrimination in housing and employment, marriage and adoption rights, etc.) on the grounds that the U.S. government should not sanction or support a sinful lifestyle. While many evangelicals oppose gay rights on moral grounds, they also situate their opposition to gay and lesbian rights in wider geopolitical discourse. Christian Right leaders argue that God bestowed wealth and power on the United States because of the country's attachment to a godly social order and that he will take them away should American leaders stray from that order. Shortly after the attacks on September 11, 2001, for example, Jerry Falwell implied that God had allowed the attacks to occur because the U.S. government had appeased the American Civil Liberties Union, feminists, and gays and lesbians.

While opposition to abortion and gay rights are the key pillars of the Christian Right's social agenda, its activists have focused on a number of other issues since its inception. During the 1980s, for example, many Christian Right activists called on school districts to include daily prayers as a part of the school day. Christian Right activists have also rallied school boards to include the theory of Creationism (also known as Intelligent Design) in public school science classes. While these issues are not directly relevant to Christian familial norms, they provide a means for establishing biblical teachings as those of the state.

Economic Issues

While economic populism figured prominently in Old Right discourses, it plays a marginal role on the New Right generally and the Christian Right more specifically. The declining interest in populist themes was precipitated in large part by the socioeconomic position of the movement's new activists, who were largely middle class or upwardly mobile. Many of Goldwater's early supporters, for example, worked in the burgeoning defense industry in Orange County, California, where wages were above the national mean. Likewise, evangelical activists in the 1970s were often suburbanites, at least one generation removed from an agrarian background. This demographic change is also reflected in contemporary evangelical churches, where the modesty and economy of form in rural churches have given way to the grandeur and spectacle of suburban megachurches. Televangelist Robert Schuller's Crystal Cathedral in Orange County, for example, has 10,000 glass windows and a 3,000-seat auditorium.

While social and economic conservatism are not natural bedfellows, their "union" in the 1980s was facilitated by a number of common assumptions about the world, including distrust of bureaucracy, suspicion of "forced" equality, and an explicitly economic understanding of freedom. The state-movement alliance that created the New Right has led Christians to become reliably Republican voters. However, its members have not engaged in activism around economic issues to the same degree they have around cultural ones. Instead, most defend the economic status quo. The movement rejects arguments that explain social inequality as a matter of structural bias, arguing that spiritual salvation and a strong work ethic are the key determinants to material success (or lack thereof). They embrace consumerism in their personal lives and often justify and reconcile it with biblical principles. Evangelical preachers, for example, encourage constituents to "Christianize" their consumerism by opening and shopping at Christian businesses. Evangelical universities further cultivate the message by promising prospective parents to teach their children how to achieve the Christian good life.

While the Christian Right economic agenda emphasizes upward mobility, its middle-class constituents are increasingly vulnerable to downsizing, outsourcing, and increased economic risk. In response, some leaders on the New Right have broken with the free trade policies of the Republican Party. For example, the Eagle Forum, an organization on the Christian Right, publicly opposes American participation in free trade agreements and the Bretton Woods system of monetary management on the grounds that it diminishes both the American middle class and American sovereignty.

What the Future Holds

When most scholars discuss the future of the Christian Right, they note a fundamental tension in the state-movement alliance that created it. While economic and social conservatives are both suspicious of government, their distrust stems from different concerns. Economic conservatives, many of whom are libertarian, believe in small government as a matter of principle. They argue that human systems

(markets, the family) have internal mechanisms for taking care of problems; government intervention in them leads only to greater problems. By contrast, social conservatives do not distrust government so much as they distrust contemporary government. Evangelicals believe that American government has abandoned the biblical principles on which the nation was founded by permitting and encouraging ungodly behavior, including but not limited to abortion, premarital sex, and divorce. Many social conservatives would have no problem with a big government so long as it enforced the principles they hold dear.

The movement's economic and social conservatives disagree on a number of issues. Many economic conservatives are, for example, strident opponents of the U.S. Patriot Act, while evangelicals tend to support it. Likewise, while economic conservatives are free trade boosters, many evangelicals question whether free trade is good for the middle class. Within the Republican Party, tensions between the two camps are also evident. Many economic conservatives believe government has no place legislating so-called moral issues such as abortion and gay marriage, while evangelicals are ardent supporters of legislation banning gay marriage and barring domestic-partner benefits.

Almost since the Christian Right emerged, commentators have predicted its imminent collapse, arguing that the alliance that undergirds it is too unstable to sustain. Most scholars, however, believe that quick collapse is less likely than a gradual decline, as Christian conservatives trickle out of the Republican Party because of its failure to outlaw abortion and pass key elements of the evangelical legislative agenda. Regardless of its future, the Christian Right has been a remarkably robust movement. If and when it subsides, it will have left an indelible stamp on the American political landscape.

Carolyn Gallaher

See also: Anti-Abortion Violence; Christianity; Creativity Movement and Church of the Creator.

Further Reading

Balmer, Randall. "American Fundamentalism: The Ideal of Femininity." In *Fundamentalism and Gender,* ed. J. Hawley, pp. 47–62. Oxford: Oxford University Press, 1994.

Berlet, Chip, and Jean Hardisty. "An Overview of the U.S. Political Right: Drifting Right and Going Wrong." *NCJW Journal* (Winter 2002): 9–11.

Berlet, Chip, and Matthew N. Lyons. *Right-Wing Populism in America: Too Close for Comfort.* New York: Guilford Press, 2000.

Brennan, Mary. *Turning Right in the Sixties: The Conservative Capture of the GOP.* Chapel Hill: University of North Carolina Press, 1995.

Bruce, Steve. *The Rise and Fall of the New Christian Right: Conservative Protestant Politics in America 1978–1988.* Oxford: Oxford University Press, 1988.

Cobb, John, ed. *Progressive Christians Speak: A Different Voice on Faith and Politics.* Louisville, KY: Westminster John Knox Press, 2003.

Diamond, Sara. *Roads to Dominion: Right-Wing Movements and Political Power in the United States.* New York: Guilford Press, 1995.

Fields, Echo. "Understanding Activist Fundamentalism: Capitalist Crisis and the Colonization of the Lifeworld." *Sociological Analysis* 52 (1994): 175–90.

Gallaher, Carolyn. "Identity Politics and the Religious Right: Hiding Hate in the Landscape." *Antipode* 29:3 (1997): 256–77.

———. "The Religious Right Reacts to Globalization." In *Gods, Guns, and Globalization: Religious Radicalism and International Political Economy,* ed. M. Tetreault and R. Denemark, pp. 31–56. Boulder, CO: Lynne Rienner, 2004.

Galst, Liz. "Pious Moralism: Theocratic Goals Backed by Misrepresentation and Lies." In *Eyes Right! Challenging the Right Wing Backlash,* ed. C. Berlet, pp. 50–58. Boston: South End Press, 1995.

Jeansonne, Glen. *Women of the Far Right: The Mothers' Movement and World War II.* Chicago: University of Chicago Press, 1996.

Lipset, Seymour Martin. "The Sources of the Radical Right." In *The Radical Right: The New American Right,* ed. D. Bell, pp. 259–312. New York: Anchor Books, 1963.

McGirr, Lisa. *Suburban Warriors: The Origins of the New American Right.* Princeton, NJ: Princeton University Press, 2001.

Niebuhr, Gustav. "After the Attacks: Finding Fault." *New York Times,* September 14, 2001.

Shields, Jon A. *The Democratic Virtues of the Christian Right.* Princeton, NJ: Princeton University Press, 2009.

Wilcox, Clyde. *Onward Christian Soldiers: The Religious Right in American Politics.* Boulder, CO: Westview, 2000.

Christianity

History shows that violence among Christians occurs rarely, relative to the millions of acts and thousands of years of Christian history. In keeping with the tenets of pacifism and non-violence inherent in the teachings of Jesus and the birth of the Christian church in the first century C.E., the great majority of Christians were not involved in perpetuating violence either among themselves or against others in both U.S. and world history. What produces violence are a myriad of factors other than religious views, including historical circumstances, socioeconomic conditions, and political goals, policies, and ideologies. Nevertheless, violence can be found both in acts perpetrated against Christians and in Christian acts made "in the name of God" in several notable events, including the Crusades and the Holy Inquisition; the Protestant Reformation; Christian exploitation of and violence against Native American Indians; slavery and abolition in the transatlantic world; Nazi violence and genocide during World War II; and fringe acts of violence, such as attacks on U.S. abortion clinics. The motivations for and circumstances of these diverse events reveal a web of complex factors that have created and/or contributed to occasions for violence.

Defining Violence

The relationship between Christianity and violence is best demonstrated by the way various Christian institutions, communities, and individuals have played a role in large-scale violence. In some cases, the examples may point to potential violence rather than actual perpetrated events, but in the context of this entry violence is be defined as any intentional plan to promote violent acts against other humans or communities and to cause large-scale harm.

Focusing on large-scale events, there are at least three ways that Christianity has played a role in violence: (1) Christians, through their beliefs, have often supported and/or tolerated violence that is committed for purposes other than strictly religious objectives; (2) Christians have justified their actions by their beliefs, arguing that violence is the way to safeguard the religious community and tradition; and (3) Christians have seen violence as a way of eliminating undesirable people. These three types of involvement often merge, making strict distinctions problematic.

The Crusades and the Inquisition

Early Christianity, beginning with the teachings of Jesus and the birth of the early Christian church in the first century C.E., was generally pacifist in nature. This approach changed with the imperialization of Christianity beginning in the fourth century C.E. as Christians and the ascendancy of Christian leaders to power in Rome. During this time, views of justified use of violence, particularly the violence imposed by the ruling power, were developed in the late fourth and early fifth centuries C.E. in the Western Empire, primarily by the church leaders Ambrose and Augustine. With the threat of the invasion of the Visigoths, Augustine developed the notion of just war, which has played a role in Christian views of violence and power to this day.

The early Christian thinkers who devised such views had clear limits in mind—that war was waged only as a defense of the faith and only as a last resort. On the other hand,

with the demise of the Roman Empire in the West, the churches were left as the principle power throughout Medieval Europe. Given this reality, defense of the faith was mixed with the need to maintain political power, and this mixture was part of both the various Crusades and the extended period of the Inquisition. This idea was also influenced by the belief in an exclusive rule of the Christian God, which leaves all others outside of "the truth," and the notion of sovereignty, which leaves God's demands outside of the law and accountability to it.

The Crusades began with a Papal call in the twelfth century C.E. and included a number of different efforts to mount forces from Christian Europe to retake the holy land from so-called Muslim infidels. This set of events

An engraving from the mid-eighteenth century depicts the turmoil and violence of the Spanish Inquisition. Established in 1478 by the Catholic monarchs Ferdinand II and Isabella I, the Tribunal of the Holy Office of the Inquisition was a church court instituted to preserve orthodoxy by identifying and prosecuting heretics. Those who were found guilty and refused to recant were burned at the stake. Torture was often used to extract confessions. (Fotosearch/Stringer/Getty Images)

arose because of the development and perceived threat of Islamic power that extended Islamic rule over lands from India to the Middle East to northern Africa and into part of Europe. The idea of Crusades to capture the Holy Land tied this political threat to the sovereignty of the churches and Christianity in Europe.

The actual conflict with the Muslim leaders in the Middle East was much less dramatic than the quest suggested, and the results were apparently a failure if measured by the initial religious purposes. However, casting these Crusades as religious events designed to protect the faith fit the mold of a just war and provided a framework for the justification of broader violence. The perpetration of violence in the name of Christianity was typically found in Europe along the route as the Crusaders found their way to the Holy Land. Because they were seen as outside of God's protection and fair game for violence in defense of the faith, as many as between 1 million and 2 million Jews and Muslims caught in the path of Crusaders were killed and had their villages plundered.

Spurred by a perceived threat to the Christian faith, the Inquisition of 1231 was charged with eliminating heretics and infidels from Christian Europe through torture, life imprisonment, and burning at the stake. It is possible that the Inquisition represented a justification for violence that could actually produce violent acts by random individuals (for example, the attacks on Jews during the severe threat of the plague may be linked with the institutional activity to see Jews as a threat to the faithful within Europe). But the Inquisition was a just war conducted principally by the Institutional church and its authority. The church viewed violence as a measure either to punish the guilty or to persuade the accused to repent.

By 1570 the Inquisition had established independent tribunals in various Latin American countries, including Peru and Mexico, for the purpose of suppressing and eliminating non-Christians. Blessed by the Pope and generally of Dominican and Franciscan orders, Inquisitors spread as far as Goa, India, in the late sixteenth and early seventeenth centuries.

Conquest and Colonization

Christian explorers, conquistadors, and missionaries have traditionally used both nonviolent and violent methods to subdue native populations. For example, Christopher Columbus's voyage to the Caribbean in 1492. The native population of the island of Hispaniola (Santo Domingo and Haiti) dropped by one-third due to extermination at the hands of Christian missionaries whose goal was the Christianize "heathens" in the name of Jesus Christ. The exhaustion of gold deposits and slave labor in the Caribbean led to European occupation and exploitation of Puerto Rico, Jamaica, and Cuba in the first two decades of the 1500s. Conquest of native populations included rape, murder, and enslavement, forced conversion to Christianity, settlement of the land, and exploitation of labor and natural resources. In the Far East, Portuguese missionaries decimated and destroyed pagodas, forced scholars to burn and hide their religious manuscripts, and raided and forcibly converted local populations, including women and children.

In America, Christians were involved in colonial development in the 1600s and 1700s and supported efforts to subdue native populations for the sake of political and economic gain. Christians also supported the forced conversion, relocation, and decimation of native populations in the Americas, including the Cherokee, Chickasaw, Choctaw, Muscogee-Creek, and Seminole in the early 1800s, and gave justification for these efforts through religious arguments, such as the need to convert barbaric and heathen population to Christ at all costs. At the same time, Christians in Australia and Latin America were subduing indigenous populations.

Slavery and the Abolitionist Movement

Still, the most obvious examples of the way Christians have supported violence or accepted it are the cases of slavery in the United States and the Nazi genocide during World War II. In both cases, the overall objectives of these historical events and/or processes were primarily not religious, but the churches and individual Christians used arguments that were based on Christian beliefs, which contributed to and justified both slavery and genocide.

The institution of slavery in the United States enabled the agrarian society and economy to flourish, which helped the United States to emerge as an economic power. As demonstrated in the *Narrative of the Life of Frederick Douglass* (1845), the autobiography of one of the most prolific African American intellectuals of the nineteenth century, slavery survived, in part, because of the support of the churches and the church leaders who owned slaves and sold them to raise funds to spread the Gospel. Clearly, those leaders were able to persuade a general population of the justice of slavery because they could depend on a notion, built on the Bible and other Christian texts, that the slaves were not fully deserving of humane treatment and that God had intended the white man to be master over the African slaves. In fact, Douglass argued that some of the most abusive slave owners were leaders in local churches.

Not all Christians accepted these ideas, as Protestants, Methodists, and Baptists in New England denounced slavery and Methodists, for example, voted to expel members who bought and sold slaves. A handful of individuals were prepared to lead a resistance to the institution of slavery, including evangelists such as Charles

G. Finney, Theodore Dwight Weld, and Lyman Beecher. Some of them were also willing to use violence as a means of both liberating the slaves and destroying those who perpetuated slavery. John Brown, a key abolitionist in the mid-nineteenth century, acted when the New England abolitionists that Douglass came to admire were unwilling to join his revolution to fight slavery with guns and raids. For Brown, such a view of the use of violence was based on the notion of God's justice, which now turned the tables and aimed God's wrath at the slave owners.

Nazi Genocide

Before and during the Holocaust, the Catholic, Calvinist, and Lutheran Christian denominations in Germany and Hungary espoused hateful anti-Judaism and anti-Semitism statements and propaganda that portrayed the Jews as a people who had betrayed God would forever be held responsible for the crucifixion of Jesus.

In Germany, some Christian leaders and churches not only supported the Nazi cause but used religious arguments and symbols to form Christian Nazi propaganda. The Nazification of the German churches included some of the most noted theologians of the period, including Ludwig Mueller, who led a so-called German Christian movement within the Protestant church. The Nazi plan of genocide was built on an ideology that advocated absolute political power and domination as well as the elimination of those who were considered unfit to live. Historians and religious scholars have noted that such an ideology could have been accepted so fully by Christian leaders and by the masses had it not been for the history of Christian animosity toward the Jewish people.

Despite support among Catholics in particular, the Nazis persecuted Jesuits and members of Catholic organizations such as the social-service organization Catholic Action. In 1933, Martin

Niemöller and a small group of Protestant clergy formed the Pastors' Emergency League to resist Nazi domination of the church. The next year they founded the Confessing Church, which represented a minority of all Protestant pastors in Germany, in order to expose the hatred of the pro-Nazi German Christian movement. Only a small percentage of individual German theologians, such as Dietrich Bonhoeffe, denounced Hitler's regime; the majority of the Protestant church leadership supported or did not publicly speak out against Nazi actions against the Jews.

Later Conflicts

Twentieth-century conflicts that are connected to the notion of just war include conflicts in Northern Ireland between Roman Catholic Nationalists and Protestant Unionists, and the Serbian violence in Kosovo against Albanians during the 1998 Kosovo War. From the late 1960s through 1998, during the ethno-religious-political conflict known as The Troubles, Unionists fought to have Northern Ireland remain part of the United Kingdom as the Nationalists fought for the area to be politically reunited with the rest of Ireland. The Troubles was based on fundamentally religious and political differences and purposes and mimicked elements of the religious wars of the post-Reformation period, during which two sides of Christians used a just-war approach to defend their use of violence against other Christians. The violence in Kosovo, in which predominantly Muslim ethnic Albanians were persecuted, raped, murdered, and driven from their homes by Serbs, was perpetuated by followers of the Serbian Orthodox Church. During the war, Serb forces destroyed numerous Islamic facilities, including Islamic libraries and archives. After the war, Albanians reacted by destroying Orthodox churches. The Troubles, in particular, mimics elements of the religious wars of the post-Reformation period, during which two sides of Christians used a just-war approach to defend their use of violence against other Christians.

Another form of violence can be seen in the actions of members of Christian Identity and Christian Patriot groups, which rely upon a literal interpretation of Scripture to justify acts of terrorism, or those, such as Saving Babies and the Army of God, that use violence to oppose abortions, abortion facilities, and facility personnel. Individuals, such as the North Carolina Lutheran pastor Michael Bray—who spent between 1985 and 1989 in federal prison in connection with the destruction of several abortion facilities—have stated that their violence is justified. For Bray, attacking abortion clinics is justified because he believes abortion is an immoral, sinful, and evil action. Similarly, in 2010, Pastor Terry Jones, a fundamental Christian pastor in Gainesville, Florida, ignited a media frenzy—and aroused the anger of Muslims worldwide—when he announced plans to burn the Koran on September 11, the ninth anniversary of the terrorist attacks on the World Trade Center and Pentagon; Jones was finally persuaded not to carry out the burning

Martyrdom and the Apocalyptic

Christians have sometimes, even if not regularly, been the victims and not the perpetrators of violence. The Greek word *martyr*, which translates to "witness," provides a base for the early Christian idea of martyrdom. In the face of attack, precisely because of the beliefs of early Christians, a number became "witnesses" who would die for their beliefs. Early Christians were persecuted by both Jews and the Roman Empire for their faith, and this continued from the first to fourth centuries until the Roman emperor Constantine legalized Christianity.

This idea of martyrdom did not fade away after the early period, since minority Christian groups have, at times, been subjected to the threat of death for their beliefs. Indeed, under the charge of heresy individual Christian denominations experienced persecution at the hands of other Christians during the sixteenth-century Protestant Reformation, a Christian reform movement initiated in 1517 by the German monk Martin Luther. However, Christians saw their fate differently from those who may not have shared their view of an imminent salvation. Thus, the idea of martyrdom was fused with a notion of the apocalyptic—death was embraced with the hope of the end and God's kingdom near at hand.

Christians continued to be persecuted for their faith. According to groups such as Human Rights Watch and Washington Watch, many Islam-dominated nations practice a militant doctrine of persecution against non-Muslims, including Christians, which includes violent acts of torture, starvation, enslavement, and murder. According to some estimates, more than 250 million Christians around the world, primarily in Burma, China, Egypt, Ethiopia, Greece, Saudi Arabia, Sudan, Turkey, and Vietnam, suffer for their faith in Jesus Christ. Increasing persecution is also experienced by Christians in Cuba, Laos, and North Korea.

The fusion of martyrdom, apocalypticism, and imitation of Jesus is a pattern that has developed and become a powerful image in U.S. Christian circles, feeding contemporary fringe groups who see themselves as a minority with the hope of embracing violence and death as the only way to safeguard their beliefs. The development of various identity groups in America may be an extreme element of a form of Christian fundamentalism, which has taken on the vestiges of white supremacy that has been especially powerful in the Midwestern and southern portions of the United States. The groups are small and see themselves as often under attack by the pluralistic world that is both non-Christian and non-white. The attacks are often seen as an affront to the dominance of both Christian beliefs and Euro-American groups. Such a view of attack can lead to an apocalyptic vision, which understands the current events as a preamble to some great final battle. Given this view, violence can be justified as a way of joining the forces of God in ensuring the intended end of the conflict. Such acts of violence become acceptable in the context of such a worldview even though the perpetration of violence does not match the majority view of those who faced certain death as martyrs in the early days of Christianity.

The Violent Thread in History

The aforementioned events share common elements, because those who have carried out acts of violence and those who have explicitly or implicitly accepted such acts have demonstrated that Christianity allows for violence and even justifies such violence in certain circumstances. Although not the norm, and while violence continues to aimed at Christians in Islam-dominant countries, they provide a corrective to the view of Christianity as solely promoting a vision of peace and peace making. The stark contrast between these two visions depends on a fragile barrier that can come down easily given the pattern of justifying violence by Christians and in the name of Christianity.

James F. Moore

See also: Christian Identity; Crucifixion; Crusades; Joan of Arc; Puritanism; Roman Catholicism.

Further Reading

Agamben, Giorgio. *Homo Sacer.* Palo Alto, CA: Stanford University Press, 1995.

———. *State of Exception.* Chicago: University of Chicago Press, 2005.

Aichele, George, and Tina Pippin, eds. *Violence, Utopia and the Kingdom of God.* New York: Routledge, 1998.

Bauer, Yehuda. *Re-thinking the Holocaust.* New Haven, CT: Yale University Press, 2002.

Botwinick, Rita. *A History of the Holocaust.* New York: Pearson Prentice Hall, 2004.

Douglass, Frederick. *Narrative of the Life of Frederick Douglass, an American Slave, Written By Himself.* New York: W.W. Norton, 1997.

Fluehr-Lobban, Carolyn. *Race and Racism.* Lanham, MD: AltaMira Press, 2006.

Huber, Wolfgang. *The Unrelenting Assault on Human Dignity.* Minneapolis, MN: Fortress Press, 1996.

Juergensmeyer, Mark. *Terror in the Mind of God.* Berkeley: University of California Press, 2000.

Malinowski, Bronislaw. *Magic, Science and Religion.* Prospect Heights, IL: Waveland Press, 1992.

McTiernan, Oliver. *Violence in God's Name.* Maryknoll, NY: Orbis Books, 2003.

Moore, James F. *Toward a Dialogical Community.* Lanham, MD: University Press of America, 2004.

Selengut, Charles. *Sacred Fury: Understanding Religious Violence.* Lanham, MD: AltaMira Press, 2003.

Stern, Jessica. *Terror in the Name of God.* New York: HarperCollins, 2003.

Waller, James. *Becoming Evil.* New York: Oxford University Press, 2005.

Church Bombings

During the period of gradual racial desegregation of the American South (1954–1965), militant opponents of desegregation often relied upon violence to quell the demand for increasing civil rights for African Americans. One form of this violence was the bombing of occupied African American establishments, including churches. Church bombings garnered attention from both supporters of the civil rights movement and media outlets during the 1950s and 1960s, due largely to the terrorizing of innocent individuals and the devastation aimed at peaceable assemblies. The most notorious church bombing resulted in the death of four young girls in 1963 at a Birmingham, Alabama, church. Civil rights leader Martin Luther King Jr. delivered a now-famous eulogy for the girls a few days later in Birmingham, calling for courage in the face of such danger. With decreased frequency, church bombings have continued into the twenty-first century, though often with different motives than the bombings of the civil rights era.

Southern Context

Bombings in the American South were most frequent in areas of high racial tension during the middle decades of the twentieth century. Meant to intimidate and hinder the rising prominence and political influence of African Americans, bombings often targeted black homes and businesses. Generally, members of the Ku Klux Klan (KKK)—a white supremacist organization founded shortly after the Civil War by disaffected supporters of the Confederacy—or other like-minded persons carried out the bombings. The KKK's secrecy, infiltration of and in some cases complicity with local government, and subsequent cover-ups frequently prevented prosecution or conviction for such crimes.

While bombings and other forms of violence aimed at intimidating African Americans occurred prior to the midpoint of the century, the Supreme Court's decision in *Brown v. Board of Education* (1954) intensified the animosity toward southern blacks. This landmark case decided that separate institutions for blacks and whites were inherently unequal, thus rendering racial segregation unconstitutional. The prescribed way of life heretofore encouraged by many southern whites was now in jeopardy. As civil rights leaders attempted to integrate schools and other institutions, violence continued to increase. Some African American neighborhoods were terrorized during the late 1950s, usually by planting dynamite near the foundation of a building or hurling firebombs through windows. Recalling the tumult in Birmingham, witnesses and victims have described bombings as a common occurrence during this period.

Further exacerbating racial tensions in the Deep South after 1960 was the targeting by civil rights activists of areas in which segregation was deeply entrenched. In 1961, black and white civil rights supporters boarded desegregated buses in the North and traveled to the South. These "Freedom Rides" brought about violent opposition, including the firebombing of buses in Alabama. Additionally, Martin Luther King Jr., who had led organized protests in Albany, Georgia, had explicitly focused his efforts on Birmingham for its segregation and brutal opposition to civil rights proponents. Indicating further achievement of the civil rights cause was the federal order to integrate the University of Alabama in June of 1963. Resisting this order, Alabama's governor, George Wallace, stood in front of an entrance to the campus and refused to allow racial integration of the university. President John F. Kennedy then federalized the Alabama National Guard and later that night issued his strongest support to date for the civil rights movement by indicating that a civil rights bill would soon be introduced to Congress. By this point, the practical manifestations of southern white supremacy had all but eroded.

Sixteenth Street Baptist Church Bombing

In opposition to the cause of civil rights, white segregationists bombed numerous homes, businesses, and churches; the most egregious and glaring example of this intimidation tactic was the September 1963 bombing of a Birmingham church, in which four children died and twenty people were wounded. During the civil rights movement's 1962–1963 concentration on Birmingham as the site of great oppression, organized marches and demonstra-

Police, emergency workers, and citizens gather around the Sixteenth Street Baptist Church in Birmingham, Alabama, which was bombed by white segregationists on September 15, 1963. Many African American homes, businesses, and churches in the American South were targeted by those opposed to the civil rights movement of the 1950s and 1960s. *(Associated Press)*

tions typically began at a conveniently located black church. The Sixteenth Street Baptist Church was located near downtown Birmingham and near a hotel where visitors and leaders stayed. A nearby park allowing for larger gatherings and the support of the church's leadership made the church the ideal headquarters for protest, a voter registration campaign, and meetings of civil rights leaders such as Martin Luther King Jr. and Fred Shuttlesworth.

The city of Birmingham had a complex history, which fostered divisiveness in general and racial discord in particular. Social stratification among whites had been an issue in Birmingham since its founding by wealthy northerners shortly after the Civil War, in 1871. This contentiousness spilled over into the race relations of the deeply segregated city, especially as blacks increasingly moved into the heart of the city from the rural areas. The history of violence and racism, furthered by a large KKK constituency and gradually more vocal calls for African American rights, made Birmingham a proverbial tinderbox. Both civil rights leaders and staunch segregationists seemed to recognize the importance of this city for their respective causes. Neither side was prepared to acquiesce to the demands of the other.

On the morning of September 15, 1963, while Sunday school classes were concluding at the Sixteenth Street Baptist Church, a bomb exploded. Four little girls, ages eleven through fourteen, were killed. By that night, chaos had erupted in Birmingham. Blacks and whites alike staged riots, lootings, and fires. Three days later, Martin Luther King Jr. eulogized the girls at a nearby Birmingham church. While comforting the families with references to Horatio's eulogy of Hamlet, King also explained that the deaths of these martyred girls called racist whites, cowering blacks, and ambivalent politicians to act for justice. Not until 1977 was one man, Robert Chambliss, found guilty for the murder of one of the girls.

Failed Attempts

The racist destruction of black churches did not end with the passing of civil rights legislation, nor were African American religious sites the only targets of bombings, as the example of the 1958 bombing of an Atlanta Jewish temple demonstrates. In the last few decades, numerous black churches in America have been destroyed, most often by arson. The violence perpetrated in this context raises the question of motivation. The motive in the numerous church bombings is not the annihilation of African Americans but an attempt to convince African Americans to remain second-tier members of society. It is evident that this strategy failed miserably, as it only strengthened the resolve of the civil rights movement and convinced many moderates of the atrocities committed in areas of stringent segregation. The topic of church bombings in the mid-twentieth-century South reveals the perplexity of religious violence as a means of coercion. Ironically, the intimidation intended in the destruction of religious sites often reveals that the aggressor holds a rationally indefensible position that relies on an appeal to fear.

Brandon M. Crowe

See also: King, Martin Luther, Jr.; Ku Klux Klan.

Further Reading

Kirk, John A. *Martin Luther King Jr.* Harlow, UK: Pearson, 2005.

Lee, Spike, director. *4 Little Girls.* HBO documentary film, 1998.

McWhorter, Diane. *Carry Me Home: Birmingham, Alabama: The Climactic Battle of the Civil Rights Revolution.* New York: Simon and Schuster, 2001.

Sikora, Frank. *Until Justice Rolls Down: The Birmingham Church Bombing Case.* Tuscaloosa: University of Alabama Press, 2005.

Smith, Petric J. *Long Time Coming: An Insider's Story of the Birmingham Church Bombing That Rocked the World.* Birmingham, AL: Crane Hill, 1994.

Circumcision (Female)

Female circumcision is a highly controversial practice whereby external genitalia are typically altered for religious rather than medical reasons. Alternative terms include "female genital mutilation" (FGM), which is used by many activists and some Western governments, while "female genital cutting" is preferred by most social scientists.

Female circumcision is practiced by many Muslim and Christian groups in approximately thirty African countries and by some Muslim groups in the Arabian Peninsula, as well as in Malaysia, India, and Indonesia. One Jewish group, the Beta Israel of Ethiopia, also called Falasha Jews, is known to have their girls undergo circumcision. This group, however, was transferred to Israel in the 1980s and 1990s by the Israeli state, and it is believed that the migrants abandoned this tradition in Israel. The estimated number of circumcised women in the world is between 100 million and 140 million, and according to a World Health Organization report in 2000, two million girls are at risk of being circumcised each year. In many groups, female circumcision is seen as a religious duty. It is a much debated issue, however, whether female circumcision is required by religion, and if so, what sort of procedure should be followed. Neither the Koran nor the Bible mentions female circumcision, and the majority of Muslims and Christians in the world do not practice it. Nevertheless, traditions of female circumcision existed in Africa before the region was Christianized and Islamized, the earliest evidence being a mention of the practice in an Egyptian papyrus from 163 B.C.E. When other world religions reached Africa, imported religious norms became intertwined with local concepts regarding female circumcision.

For centuries, Christian missionaries in Africa have waged campaigns to combat female circumcision. Muslim scholars, in particular, have a long history of opposing female circumcision, the first evidence dating back to the eighth century. Later examples include successful anticircumcision efforts in Sudan in the middle of the nineteenth century. One of the Koranic passages used in campaigns is "Let there be no alteration in Allah's creation" (30:30). There is, however, a gap between scholarly and grassroot-level discussions. In many groups there are people without access to the religious sources. To many of them, female circumcision can be comprehended as an authentic way to exercise their religious faith and as having significant meaning as a sign of devotion. In Somalia, "to be circumcised" is

among ordinary people metaphorically interchangeable with "to become Muslim" (Gallo and Viviani 1988). In some Christian groups in Ethiopia, a baby girl cannot be baptized unless she is ritually "clean," after circumcision. In folklore there are often strong connections between female circumcision and religion, and tales about biblical or koranic characters may be used as justifications for the practice.

A Wide Range of Practices

What is categorized as female circumcision encompasses a wide range of practices that have little in common besides the genitals of a girl or woman being manipulated or altered. The term refers to the symbolic pricking of the clitoris of a five-year-old girl in Indonesia as well as to the clitoridectomy (removal of the clitoral hood with or without excision of part of the clitoris) of a woman giving birth in West Africa. It includes the more extensive form of female circumcision, called *infibulation*—which means the inner labia, part of the outer labia, and sometimes also part of the clitoris, are cut away before the vagina is almost entirely closed with stitches—performed primarily in East Africa on girls aged four to ten. The term also refers to practices in which teenage girls volunteer to go through an operation on their clitoris as a way to show female courage and strength and to mark their status as adult women, as among the Gikuyu in Kenya.

Violence as Physical Coercion of Young Girls

There is a considerable amount of variation with respect to types of female circumcision, and that makes it difficult to generalize about the element of violence. In some contexts it is obvious that violence in the sense of physical coercion is used against the girls being circumcised. Where infibulation is done in traditional ways, as in rural parts of Sudan or

Somalia, physical coercion is needed to keep the girl in place during the procedure—since the operation causes immense pain, the girl will instinctively try to move her body away from the cutting. In urban settings, where the same procedure is carried out by health care professionals with access to analgesics, the situation is often described as less violent. There is still immense pain during the healing process, but the procedure itself is carried out with less immediate pain and involves perhaps no coercion at all.

In the West, the most violent versions of female circumcision are often referred to in the mass media. In news stories about female circumcision, the most horrifying versions are repeatedly printed, while less dramatic descriptions get less attention. In its typical form, the anecdote of female circumcision captures only the worst-case scenarios. This is a genre that dates back some time, here exemplified by a medical article from the 1930s:

> The naked girl is laid across a bed, being securely held by the arms and ankles, while the midwife, with a deft sweep of the razor, removes the anterior two-thirds of one of the labia, together with the clitoris. The unfortunate girl's shrieks are drowned by loud shouts of "That's nothing to make a fuss about!"—and the midwife proceeds to remove the other labium in the same way. There is always a sadistic smile of delight upon the face of the operator, and the whole business is thoroughly enjoyed by the privileged spectators (Worseley 1938).

Such stories fit well with a more comprehensive scheme of the "enlightened world" versus the "dark continent," where African parents choosing circumcision for their daughters are depicted as ignorant, cruel, and in acute need of Western enlightenment.

Other versions of instances of infibulation procedures are offered by fieldworkers in Africa—stories in which the mothers' and other female relatives' concern and consideration are emphasized. The following description is from a field study in Sudan:

> Loving relatives, some of whom have traveled great distances in her honor, are with the girl constantly, supporting her, focusing her attention away from the anticipated ordeal, and in the direction of the acceptance, love, empathy, and good will that is radiating toward her from all sides. . . . She is surrounded by loved and loving faces that weep for her pain and offer sympathy and encouragement. Whether the child is able to perceive this at the time is a moot point, but I have been in anterooms while circumcisions were taking place, and have seen the personal torment women were undergoing, the frantic weeping and wailing that took place as shrieks of terror and pain issued from the other room (Lightfoot-Klein 1989).

A majority of the girls who are infibulated are old enough to understand what is happening. Many are very willing to undergo the procedure in order to conform to societal expectations and look forward to being categorized as "circumcised" like practically all older girls and women around them. Others may resist and try to escape the procedure.

Violence as an Act of Revenge?

Some writers claim that among women who themselves have been exposed to circumcision, there is a compulsion to reiterate against their own daughters what they themselves have suffered. During the trials in France in the 1990s, when circumcisers and parents were prosecuted and sentenced, the prosecutor claimed that "the mothers take some sort of revenge for their own suffering by inflicting the same thing on their daughters, saying to themselves, 'Well, I had to go through this; why should my daughter be spared?'" This point of view has also been voiced by scholars who comment on the fact that women themselves practice and often defend this tradition.

There are no studies that support this assumption, however, and it seems more reasonable that mothers base their decisions on what they think their daughters will experience and hope that the procedure will be as painless as possible. This explanatory model does not account for women who are not themselves circumcised but have chosen to embrace the tradition by having their daughters circumcised. Mothers and other female relatives opt for female circumcision when it is seen as the best strategy to optimize a girl's future opportunities.

Female Circumcision on Infants

Is there reason to see violence in practices involving newborn or very young infants, who cannot protest or resist and will have no memory of the act when they grow up?

International campaigns against FGM have argued that any procedure performed on a female child's genitals is a violation of bodily integrity and hence a form of symbolic violence. Amnesty International asserted, in its 2007 statement on FGM and reproductive rights that "human rights are universal and violence against women is never acceptable, regardless of the justification offered. Amnesty International has recognized FGM as a violation of women's rights to bodily integrity, sexual autonomy, and the right to enjoy the highest attainable standard of health." In this view, female circumcision on infant girls is an act of violence, even when such procedures do not involve any physical coercion.

The procedures of "nicking" the clitoral hood of a newborn Ethiopian baby girl and the circumcision of an American baby boy may be comparable from a medical perspective. Accepting male circumcision in the West, while banning and combating milder forms of female circumcision in Africa is, then, purely ideological. It reflects a prohibition against any contact with female genitals, constituting such contact as abuse.

Optional Female Circumcision Among Teenagers

Cases of teenage girls who go through the procedure by their own choice are not often discussed in public debates, since they seem to confuse the image of female circumcision as a procedure that by definition involves a defenseless victim. An American sociologist of Kenyan origin conveys the story of her own circumcision at the age of sixteen in these words: "It may seem ironic, given the tales of 'flight from torture' told in the media, but my parents refused to allow me to be circumcised, as it was against Catholic teachings. I had to threaten to run away from home and drop out of school before my parents relented and allowed me to be circumcised" (Njambi 2004).

Njambi went to a trained nurse, who cut through her clitoris hood. After having entered into the social category of "circumcised," she was met with increased respect by peers and adults. She was able to join more serious conversations on topics such as menstruation, pregnancy, and sexual fantasies; and she was no longer expected to cover her ears when grown-ups made sexual jokes. Yet few activists would condone such an act, since there is a general agreement that all forms of female circumcision must be condemned.

Radical Feminist Views: Female Circumcision as Male Violence

When the issue of female circumcision in Africa was introduced to the public in the West in the late 1970s, it was framed within a radical feminist explanatory model. The key actor was American activist researcher Fran Hosken, who coined and propagated the phrase "female genital mutilation." In her view, the violence inherent in these practices underscores male brutality toward women and girls. Hosken argued that FGM is a training ground for male violence and that it enables men to assert absolute dominance over women throughout Africa. She uses the case of Somalia as an example, claiming that "the practice of infibulation as family custom teaches male children that the most extreme forms of torture and brutality against women and girls is their absolute right and what is expected from real men" (Hosken 1994).

In reality, it is well known that in general women are the agents and often the most fervent advocates of female circumcision. In modern times, when practices of female circumcision have been introduced in new local settings in Africa, women are the initiators and strongest defenders. For instance, a 2001 study by Swedish anthropologist Liselott Dellenborg reports from the Jola in southwestern Senegal, where clitoridectomy was introduced by women at the beginning of the twentieth century, that many men have joined the Senegalese government's campaign against female circumcision, arguing that it is neither a Muslim nor a Jola custom and that it ruins women's health. Women, on the other hand, fight their fathers, brothers, and husbands for their right to be initiated and circumcised.

Yet the radical feminist view is still very influential when it comes to public understanding of female circumcision. Men are seen as the real perpetrators behind all practices involving cutting of female genitals, irrespective of women's agency. The men's alleged motives are the need to control daughters and, more generally, to curb women's sexuality.

Lately, the radical feminist stance has been criticized for several reasons, not least by feminist scholars of African origin, among them for its treachery to basic feminist values (by muting African women's own voices when the views expressed are not in accord with Western feminist views) and for its inherent neocolonialist attitude. They question the image of circumcised African women as, in the words of the Sudanese feminist anthropologist Rogaia M. Abusharaf (2001), "downtrodden, forlorn, helpless casualties of male dominance," a depiction globally established through the Western public debate on female genital mutilation.

More generally, the radical feminist view has been criticized for its inability to explain why female circumcision is not a universal practice, while patriarchy is said to be, or to explain the different kinds of painful and also mutilating genital rituals that are inflicted on boys around the world. Some authors have pointed out that female circumcision, especially when optional, can work as a trial of womanhood, a ritual to display female courage and ability to endure pain. In many non-Western societies young girls—just like young boys—are expected to go through painful and demanding ceremonies to establish their adult status and meet with local gender-specific requirements. It is a very Western idea that young girls per definition are victims as soon as there is pain and hardship involved.

Contested Issues

More recently, African and Western scholars have begun to discuss Western genital procedures in relation to female circumcision, comparing motives and justifications. Circumcision of infant boys is generally accepted in Western countries and performed in hospitals and clinics, while Western governments take an active part in international campaigns to eradicate all forms of female circumcision. Some argue that Westerners' tendency to condemn female while condoning male circumcision has to do with medical and commonsense cultural constructions of the human body and assumptions about the nature of male and female sexuality. It has also been argued that this is a result of the fact that the Western world accepts the religious foundation of the practice of male circumcision (i.e., Judaism), while female circumcision is established outside the Judeo-Christian cultural sphere.

Further, female circumcision has been discussed in relation to Western phenomena such as surgeries for aesthetic or sexual reasons, so-called designer vaginas, which may include clitoriplasty, and also the general acceptance of piercing of the female genitals by teenagers in many Western countries.

In recent years, the founder of the Intersex Society of North America, Cheryl Chase (2005), has argued that intersexed children—1 out of 2,000 babies born with ambiguous genitals—should have the right to protection from reconstructive genital surgery during childhood. Most of these operations (most commonly, removal of penile or clitoral tissue to "make" a girl) are done for social and cultural reasons, not medical ones. Hence, she argues, this phenomenon qualifies to be included in campaigns against genital mutilation. So far activist organizations working against female circumcision have not responded favorably to this claim.

Conclusion

Depending on how an individual chooses to define the concept of violence and also on what type of female circumcision one chooses to focus on, a variety of conclusions about the relation between these concepts can be reached. Religion is not always an issue in contexts where female circumcision is practiced. However, in those settings where the practice is seen as a religious imperative, one might argue that violence is at times inflicted in the name of religion.

Sara Johnsdotter

See also: Africa, Sub-Saharan; Christianity; Circumscision (Male); Islam.

Further Reading

Abusharaf, R. "Virtuous Cuts: Female Genital Circumcision in an African Ontology." *Differences: A Journal of Feminist Cultural Studies* 12:1 (2001): 112–40.

Amnesty International USA. "Stop Violence Against Women: Reproductive Rights." Available: http://www.amnestyusa.org/women/reproductiverights.html.

Bell, K. "Genital Cutting and Western Discourses on Sexuality." *Medical Anthropology Quarterly* 19:2 (2005): 125–48.

Chase, C. "'Cultural Practice' or 'Reconstructive Surgery'? U.S. Genital Cutting, the Intersex Movement, and Medical Double Standards." In *Genital Cutting and Transnational Sisterhood,* ed. James M. Stanlie and Claire C. Robertson, pp. 126–51. Chicago: University of Illinois Press, 2005.

Gallo, P.G., and F. Viviani. "Female Circumcision in Somalia." *The Mankind Quarterly* 9:1–2 (1988): 165–80.

Gruenbaum, Ellen. *The Female Circumcision Controversy: An Anthropological Perspective.* Philadelphia: University of Pennsylvania Press, 2001.

Hosken, F.P. "Editorial: Male Violence Against Women—a Growing Global Cancer." *Women's International Network News* 20:3 (1994): 1–2.

———. *The Hosken Report: Genital and Sexual Mutilation of Females.* Lexington, MA: Women's International Network News, 1993.

Lightfoot-Klein, H. *Prisoners of Ritual: An Odyssey into Female Genital Circumcision in Africa.* New York: Haworth Press, 1989.

Miller, A. *Breaking Down the Wall of Silence,* trans. Simon Worrall. London: Virago Press, 1997.

Njambi, W.N. "Dualisms and Female Bodies in Representations of African Female Circumcision: A Feminist Critique." *Feminist Theory* 5:3 (2004): 281–303.

Obiora, L.A. "The Little Foxes That Spoil the Vine: Revising the Feminist Critique of Female Circumcision." *Canadian Journal of Women and Law* 9:1 (1997): 46–73.

Shweder, R.A. "'What About Female Genital Mutilation?' And Why Understanding Culture Matters in the First Place." In *Engaging Cultural Differences: The Multicultural Challenge in Liberal Democracies,* ed. Richard Shweder, Martha Minow, and Hazel Rose Markus, pp. 216–51. New York: Russell Sage Foundation, 2002.

Skaine, Rosemarie. *Female Genital Mutilation: Legal, Cultural and Medical Issues.* Jefferson, NC: McFarland, 2005.

Winter, B. "Women, the Law and Cultural Relativism in France: The Case of Excision." *Signs: Journal of Women in Culture and Society* 19:4 (1994): 939–74.

World Health Organization. "Fact Sheet: Female Genital Mutilation." Available: http://www.who.int/mediacentre/factsheets/fs241/en/index.html.

Worseley, A. "Infibulation and Female Circumcision: A Study of a Little-Known Custom." *Journal of Obstetrics and Gynecology* 45 (1938): 686–91.

Circumcision (Male)

Circumcision is a long-standing practice and tradition that has been promoted and stipulated under Judaic and Islamic law and customs and involves a variety of distinct surgical procedures applied to human genitals. Historical records indicate that it was practiced in ancient times, suggesting that not only Muslims and Jews, but also older societies relied on the procedure as a medical precaution and means of cleanliness. Today not only Muslims and Jews, but also people from other faiths and ethnic backgrounds perform the procedure. For instance, it is reported that the majority of South Koreans, Americans, and Filipinos, as well as some African Christians, practice circumcision.

Although both boys and girls are subject to circumcision, this entry focuses on the practice as applied to males. Only boys at their minor ages—and adult converts to the respective faith—are required to be circumcised under Islam and Judaism. It should be noted, however, that though not as controversial as female circumcision, the practice of male circumcision is also attacked by similar circles on the grounds that it is a form of violence and breaches the rights of minors who are not competent to make a sound decision in regard to their bodies. Interestingly, the list of critics includes not only human rights activists and medical experts but also what could be called insider critics—that is to say, Muslims and Jews who strongly oppose the practice, be it male or female circumcision. Despite the criticisms and medical research that considers circumcision as a harmful procedure, it is still widely practiced among practicing Jews and Muslims. Regardless of their piety and the degree of their commitment to their respective religion, families of these faiths attach a great importance to their sons' being circumcised.

While there is a great resemblance between the two faiths in terms of the practice of circumcision, certain differences exist. Above all, circumcision of boys is not a strict obligation under Islam. That is, lack of circumcision does not entail some sort of divine damnation. Conversely, circumcision is considered a sign of being a faithful believer under Judaism. Second, while boys may stay uncircumcised until puberty under Islam, Judaism requires circumcision upon birth.

The issue of whether the practice of circumcision could be considered harmful violence inflicted upon the human body is very controversial given its wide acceptability among Muslims and Jews. Even though there are groups from those two faiths that strongly oppose the practice, most fellow believers consider it a sign of commitment to their religion. Furthermore, the growing interest in circumcision by Christians and others makes the discussion even more complicated.

Circumcision Under Islam

Despite no single verse in the Koran requiring circumcision, it is considered a sign of being Muslim. In other words, Muslims do not necessarily have to be circumcised, but circumcision is one of the distinctions that can confirm Muslim identity. Even legally, if there is no other sign that tells anything about the identification of an unknown man, circumcision may be considered a sufficient connection to Islam. This implies that the practice of circumcision is highly regarded among Muslims even though it is not mandatory.

Circumcision was already practiced among the Arabs even before the birth of Islam. Arabs put a special emphasis on the circumcision of both boys and girls. Islam also embraced the practice, though with some minor revisions. The Prophet Muhammad cited circumcision as part of *fitra,* the original healthy constitution of the nature of humans as created by God. In reference to this *Hadith* (saying of the Prophet), some Islamic scholars resolved that circumcision is obligatory in the case of men, and *Sunnah* (recommended under the Prophet's sayings and actions) in the case of women.

Those who view circumcision as a duty that every Muslim has to observe refer to another *Hadith*, where the Prophet said that the prophet Abraham circumcised himself when he was eighty years old, as proof of this assertion. Muslims believe that Abraham was the first person who was circumcised and that this tradition was subsequently passed on through the following generations. Some Islamic scholars concluded that circumcision is an obligation for every Muslim male under Islam. The fundamental justification of those scholars is relevant to *taharah* (cleanliness), a condition that has to be met by Muslims before most prayers. They believe that without proper circumcision, male believers cannot be clean as defined by the Koran and the Hadith, and therefore their prayers are destined to be void. It is asserted that even the major prayers such as *hajj* (the Islamic pilgrimage to Mecca) and *salat* (the prayer performed five times a day) will not be valid if they are performed by an uncircumcised male. Regardless of Islamic law, usually local customs and traditions have a determinative role in the practice of circumcision.

Religious Basis for Male Circumcision

Islamic law mainly recognizes four sources for religious rulings that will be issued by Islamic scholars. These are the Koran (the holy book of Islam), the Sunnah of Muhammad (the Prophet's sayings and actions that interpret and clarify divine orders), *icma'* (consensus by scholars over the same conclusion), and *qiyas* (legal reasoning based on the Koran and Sunnah). A discussion surrounding circumcision is not found in the Koran, whereas the other

three documents clearly state that it is a tradition and ritual that should be performed and observed by Muslims. There are reliable Hadith that refer to the salience and prominence of the practice. In one of them, the Prophet Muhammad cited *khitan* (circumcision) as one of the five practices considered part of fitra. Likewise, he stressed that circumcision was one of the four regular practices performed by the prophets. On the basis of this Hadith, some scholars assert that a number of prophets were born circumcised, including the Prophet Muhammad himself. However, some scholars challenge the assertion, noting that he was circumcised by his grandfather seven days after he was born.

Muhammad's emphasis on circumcision was so strong that he reminded the newly converted of the practice even if they were very old. In reference to this Hadith, some scholars concluded that old people have to be circumcised even if it jeopardizes their lives. However, it should be noted that this is the view of the minority of scholars; the majority holds that the said Hadith cannot be interpreted this way.

The scholars who adopt the strict interpretation are of the opinion that the Prophet's sayings also imply that those who have been converted to Islam are required to undergo a circumcision. They resolve that otherwise the prayers of the uncircumcised convert would not be accepted by God and he would not be able to perform the hajj. In short, these scholars believe that without circumcision, the faith of the converted would not be complete and solid. But because the Hadith those scholars refer to is not *sahih* (a very reliable one), most others do not consider it a basis for legal ruling.

It should also be noted that this strict view is objectionable in many respects. Above all, in theory, no condition is sought other than open and willing acknowledgment of conversion to Islam for somebody who wishes to become a

Muslim. Circumcision is not cited either as a precondition or as a requirement after conversion. Furthermore, historical records indicate no incident in which an inquiry was made to ascertain whether the converted had undergone circumcision.

Even though most scholars do not consider circumcision an obligation for Muslims, it is regarded as a sign of Islam. To this end, it is comparable to *azan*—the Islamic call to prayer five times a day. In other words, while both azan and circumcision fall into the category of sunnah, they are accepted as major signs of Islam. Scholars contend that recital of azan in a certain place indicates that the population of that residential area is predominantly Muslim. Likewise, if nothing is known about somebody found dead who is circumcised, he is treated as a Muslim; his funeral is organized in compliance with Islamic precepts, and he is buried in accordance with Islamic traditions and rituals.

Another important reason for the strong emphasis on circumcision by Islamic scholars is its correlation with taharah, the primary precondition for the initiation of most prayers under Islam. Without proper cleaning, as stipulated and defined by Islam, believers cannot perform major prayers, including salat. Scholars uphold that noncircumcision prevents the complete cleanliness strictly sought before prayer.

Timing and Procedure of Circumcision

Scholars and religious leaders overwhelmingly agree that boys should be circumcised before puberty. But this does not mean that elders cannot undergo the procedure. However, it should be emphasized that the same scholars hold quite different views on the exact timing. While some refer to the very first days of the newborn as the appropriate time, others insist that the procedure should be postponed until the boy knows himself well. A small number of scholars go even further, stressing that males must not be circumcised until after puberty. They even assert that circumcision before puberty violates Islamic rules and constitutes a sinful action.

This suggests that the issue of circumcision age is a controversial one. Absence of clear and straight religious evidence is the main reason for the disagreement. Even though Muhammad reportedly stressed that the newborn should be circumcised within seven days after birth and followed that tradition in the circumcision of his grandchildren Hassan and Husayn, some reliable interpreters of the Hadith say that the Prophet referred to a preference rather than a requirement. The scholars who believe that circumcision should not be done until the boy gets closer to puberty rely on a Hadith reported by Ibn-i Abbas, a reliable companion of the Prophet Muhammad who reportedly noted that male circumcision should be delayed until the boy understands what manhood means and what his genital organ is for. Based on this report, a large group of Islamic scholars concluded that it is best to wait until the boy matures enough to understand the whole procedure but not later than puberty. To this end, some from this group of scholars hold that circumcision may be done at age six or seven, and others that it can be done around ten.

Despite the huge disparity among the views held by different scholars with regard to the timing of male circumcision, the mainstream view holds that there are mainly two timing specifications: one is the age when the circumcision is required, and the other is the age when it is best. Age of puberty is considered the upper limit for the timing of circumcision; in other words, boys have to be circumcised before that age. On the other hand, anytime before puberty but well after birth is considered the best timing for circumcision.

In addition to the differences in scholarly views and approaches, the timing of circumcision significantly varies in different societies and customs. Turks and Central and South Asian Muslims circumcise boys between the ages of six and eleven; in Pakistan, Muslims may be circumcised at any age from the newborn period to adulthood; in Iran, the procedure is performed at the age of five or six if the child is born at home and within two days after birth for newborns delivered at the hospital.

With regard to how male circumcision should be done, Islam does not prescribe a certain procedure to be followed during the operation; rather, it specifies certain limitations that the circumciser should fully observe. Basically, the procedure involves cutting the foreskin from the penis. However, there is disagreement as to whether the entire foreskin should be removed in order for the procedure to be deemed valid. While some assert that at least half of the skin has to be cut off, moderates assert that less than half will suffice for completion of the ritual. Those who do not hold that removal of half of the skin is enough for the proper performance of circumcision require another procedure so that the other half is removed.

In all cases, what matters most is to ensure that the boy is not hurt. For this reason, Islam puts a special emphasis on the safety of the procedure. Moderate cutting is always preferable, and the circumciser should be skilled in his job. It could be said that this is the only requirement, as most scholars believe that the circumciser has to be able and competent only and does not necessarily have to be Muslim if he is good at what he does.

Circumcision Under Judaism

Circumcision occupies a central place in Judaic faith. As opposed to Islam, Judaism considers circumcision an obligatory procedure for all male Jews, who will not become true believers unless they undergo the specified procedure. It is also generally held that the other monotheist religions borrowed the practice from Judaism; therefore, it is fair to say that the Islamic practice of circumcision is essentially based on the legacy of Judaism. This observation is further backed by the weak emphasis on female circumcision in Islam, considering that Judaism normally views circumcision as a procedure exclusive to males. It seems that Islam softens the rules on circumcision as conveyed by the Jews by introducing flexibility in terms of its timing and procedure and also recognizes the role of local traditions by allowing, yet remaining indifferent to, female circumcision.

Religious Basis in Judaism

Male circumcision is a strict requirement under Judaism. There are two particular sources that impose it as an obligation. The Hebrew Bible describes circumcision as part of the covenant between God and Abraham in the book of Genesis (17:1–14). It appears that Islam and Judaism agree that it was Abraham who performed circumcision first. The book of Genesis says, "The selfsame day was Abraham circumcised and Ismael his son. And all the men of his house, as well they that were born in his house, as the bought servants and strangers were circumcised with him" (26–27). This agreement also reinforces the assertion that the Islamic view on circumcision was overwhelmingly influenced by the earlier Judaic approach.

In Leviticus, the Lord speaks to Moses and tells him to call the children of Israel to comply with this ruling: "If a woman has conceived, and borne a male child, then she shall be unclean seven days; as in the days of her customary impurity she shall be unclean. And on the eighth day the flesh of his foreskin shall be circumcised. She shall then continue in the blood of *her* purification thirty-three days. She shall not touch any hallowed thing, nor come into the sanctuary until the days of her purification are fulfilled" (Leviticus 12:1–4).

In the Genesis quotation circumcision is the clear sign of the covenant between God and Abraham. For this reason, it is called *brit milah* (Covenant of Circumcision). The Leviticus quotation addresses circumcision in terms of the cleanliness of the child and the mother. In many sacred texts of Judaism, a comparison is made between the circumcised and the uncircumcised. According to the Old Testament, the uncircumcised are not pure and clean. The sanction provided in the Judaic scripts for noncompliance is severe, since noncompliance would mean a breach of the covenant between God and Abraham. Those who do not comply are denied attendance at religious ceremonies. This sanction is explained in Exodus: "And when a stranger shall sojourn with thee, and will keep the Passover to the Lord, let all his males be circumcised, and then let him come near and keep it; and he shall be as one that is born in the land: for no uncircumcised person shall eat thereof" (12:48).

The Jewish Bible also prohibits uncircumcised males from entering houses of worship (Ezekiel 44:9). However, the state of noncircumcision does not entail expulsion from the Jewish faith. In other words, a Jew who became entitled to possession of this identity by birth will remain so even if he is not circumcised. In such a case, the liability remains with the father until the son's puberty (Yoreh De'ah 246:1). Nevertheless, the boy will have to face the penalties provided for noncompliance with the Covenant of Circumcision if he does not have himself circumcised when he becomes an adult.

Procedure and Timing of Male Circumcision in Judaic Tradition

Circumcision has been performed by the Jews for millennia, a fact that proves their commitment and attachment to the ritual. They did not cease performing circumcision even during the Nazi reign under which they were persecuted. However, despite no change in their level of commitment, the procedure did not remain the same; the current procedure is slightly different from the original. While the rite of *milah* originally involved cutting off only the tip of the foreskin, today the usual practice consists of complete removal of the foreskin. The operation is justified by the assumption that the foreskin is a blemish and perfection sought in the sacred Judaic texts can be attained only by its removal.

The timing of the operation is very important under Judaic precepts. The Jews mostly have their boys circumcised on the eighth day after birth, with the exception of the Falasha Jews of Ethiopia, who perform the procedure on the seventh day. The fellow believers are urged to observe the rule on timing. Postponing the performance of the operation to allow attendance by family members is not permissible under Judaic precepts. However, if the boy was born prematurely or with some serious medical condition, circumcision is postponed to a more proper time. Furthermore, a boy is not circumcised if three of his older brothers died of complications in connection with the procedure. Likewise, a man who converts to Judaism is not circumcised if he was already circumcised before conversion (even if the procedure was not performed in accordance with the Judaic rituals) or if he has a serious medical condition that potentially jeopardizes his life in case of circumcision. In such a case, a small drop of blood is symbolically extracted to honor the conversion.

The entire procedure involves very precise and detailed steps that should be strictly followed for a proper completion of the rite. Above all, although it is the father who is responsible for having his son circumcised, because not all fathers are competent or knowledgeable enough to perform the procedure in compliance with

Judaic traditions, a *mohel*—a cleric who studied the sacred scripts and rules of brit milah and the medical aspects of circumcision—is invited to circumcise the boy.

Before the milah, the mohel recites the relevant parts from Judaic sacred texts on the wisdom of the ritual circumcision. The mohel's role during the operation is exclusive; he performs *metzitzah b'peh*, or *mezizah*, a rite that refers to using suction to remove blood from the circumcised area. The mohel sucks out the blood to clean the wound and spits it. While most Jews have abandoned this particular practice, mezizah is still common to more Orthodox sects of the religion.

However, while mezizah is still widely practiced, a good segment of the Jewish community has sought alternatives to avoid the spread of diseases caused by mouth-genital contact. The most popular alternative is use of a glass tube between the circumcised area and the mohel's mouth. This alternative is endorsed by most rabbinical authorities as fulfilling the requirements of mezizah.

Spilling of blood is another requirement for considering brit milah complete. Therefore, the methods used in the ritual circumcision differ from those used in the medical procedure, which is mostly performed after the necessary precautions are taken to prevent excessive blood spill. For a proper performance of circumcision under Judaic rules, only certain types of knives can be used during the operation to ensure that blood is spilled.

How Violent Is Circumcision?

The issue of whether the practice of circumcision constitutes a violation to the human body has attracted a great deal of attention. While some activist groups oppose the procedure on the grounds that it is violent, proponents stress that it is a safe procedure whose benefits exceed any possible harm.

Piety or strong attachment to the faith is not the only reason for the wide observance. Medical studies mostly confirm that circumcision helps reduce risks of certain diseases. For that reason, even the World Health Organization recommends the practice, provided that it is performed properly and consistent with medical rules and standards.

It appears that the procedures provided in the religious texts of Islam and Judaism on circumcision have evolved to meet contemporary standards. As a consequence, the violent character of the practice has been diluted with time. Currently, circumcision is performed under safe conditions that do not threaten the life or bodily integrity of the subject. Religious authorities mostly tend to cooperate with the medical profession and make room for slight alterations in the practice that do not affect the gist of the ritual procedure.

This does not necessarily mean that circumcision is not a violent procedure. There are a number of reported incidents that involve deaths and serious harm in connection with the procedure. However, what should be underlined is that both faiths adopt a lenient approach and disallow use of excessive violence during the circumcision operation. They do not abandon the rituals, but they require compliance with medical standards.

Probably mostly for that reason, the influential opposition to circumcision usually refers to violation of the circumcised boy's right to an intact body rather than to the use of excessive violence during the operation. The activists who oppose circumcision base their action on the assertion that circumcision is a human rights violation simply because such a dramatic and irreversible modification of the body must require the consent of the adult and that the procedure should be avoided until one becomes an adult who can make his own decisions.

An opposition that draws attention to the rights of minors seems convincing and plausible considering that the harm caused by circumcision is not confirmed through medical research. In other words, reliance on a discourse making reference to medical studies will fall short to advance the cause anticircumcision activists promote. However, it seems almost impossible to promulgate laws to prevent circumcision until the boy turns into an adult, particularly in Islamic countries. Nevertheless, the activists' efforts to raise public awareness for recognition of the right to an intact body have so far at least been partially promising and influential.

Cenap Çakmak

See also: Circumcision (Female); Islam; Judaism.

Further Reading

Al-Sabbagh, Muhammad Lutfi. *Islamic Ruling on Male and Female Circumcision.* Alexandria, Egypt: World Health Organization, 1996.

Bigelow, Jim, ed. *The Joy of Uncircumcising!* Aptos, CA: Hourglass, 1994.

Boyd, Billy Ray. *Circumcision: What It Does.* San Francisco: Taterhill Press, 1990.

Brigman, William E. "Circumcision as Child Abuse: The Legal and Constitutional Issues." *Journal of Family Law* 23:3 (1984–1985): 337–57.

Dekkers, Wim, Cor Hoffer, and Jean-Pierre Wils. "Bodily Integrity and Male and Female Circumcision." *Medicine Health Care and Philosophy* 8:2 (2005): 179–91.

Denniston, George C., Frederick Mansfield Hodges, and Marilyn Faye Milos, eds. *Male and Female Circumcision: Medical, Legal, and Ethical Considerations in Pediatric Practice.* New York: Kluwer Academic Press, 1999.

Gairdner, Douglas. "The Fate of the Foreskin: A Study of Circumcision." *British Medical Journal* 2 (1949): 1433–37.

Glass, J.M. "Religious Circumcision: A Jewish View." *BJU International* 83:1 (1999): 17–21.

Goldman, Ronald. *Questioning Circumcision: A Jewish Perspective.* Boston: Vanguard, 1998.

Gollaher, David A. *Circumcision: A History of the World's Most Controversial Surgery.* New York: Basic Books, 2000.

Goodman, J. "Jewish Circumcision: An Alternative Perspective." *BJU International* 83:1 (1999): 22–27.

Leitch, I.O.W. "Circumcision: A Continuing Enigma." *Australian Pediatric Journal* 6 (1960): 59–65.

Paige, Karen Eriksen. "The Ritual of Circumcision." *Human Nature* (1978): 40–48.

Remondino, P.C. *History of Circumcision from the Earliest Times to the Present.* Whitefish, MT: Kessinger, 2003.

Rizvi, S.A.H., S.A.A. Naqvi, M. Hussain, and A.S. Hasan. "Religious Circumcision: A Muslim View." *BJU International* 83:1 (1999): 13–16.

Sahlieh, A.A. "To Mutilate in the Name of Jehovah or Allah." *Medicine and Law* 13:7–8 (1994): 575–622.

Smith, Jacqueline. "Male Circumcision and the Rights of the Child." In *To Baehr in Our Minds: Essays in Human Rights from the Heart of the Netherlands,* ed. Mielle Bulterman, Aart Hendriks, and Jacqueline Smith, pp. 465–98. Utrecht: Netherlands Institute of Human Rights, 1998.

Zoske, Joseph. "Male Circumcision: A Gender Perspective." *Journal of Men's Studies* 6:2 (1998): 189–208.

Civil Disobedience

In democratic societies citizens observe law as essential to the proper functioning of the state, but they may choose not to obey laws carte blanche because some laws and systems necessitate objection when they are of contested legality. When a law or policy causes undue suffering or does not serve the common good, people claim the right to dissent; they may also reject a law viewed as symbolic of or involved with some other law or general policy being contested. Conscientious objection to a law or action of the state is an act of civil dissent, viewed as an alternative recourse in resolving issues of conflicted legality in a free society. Civil dissent or disorder, known popularly as civil disobedience, has come to represent actions taken by an agents against a law deemed illegal, unjust, immoral, irreligious, unconstitutional, or ideologically objectionable. Whether performed by an individual or a group, civil disobedience (hereafter CD) involves public, premeditated noncompliance with a government-established law or policy, which the actor understands to be of disputed legality. CD is carried on to a limited public end or with a specific objective. Political, social, economic, and religious concerns are the most common originations of CD.

CD is a common practice worldwide; even people who do not readily define it in legal terms know what it means, hear of it, or participate in it. Yet actions of CD can be complex and a source of controversy. Generally, "civil" connotes the responsible and intelligent interaction of citizens with the state and with each other. Civil disorder, a synonym for CD, may involve both violent and nonviolent action. Over the last two centuries, a wide range of civil unrest has occurred in many countries, often very violent, some of which may not be classified as CD. Deciding whether an act of disobedience is civil and justified is often the prerogative of the state. An act of disobedience may be civil and conscientious but still be contested as inappropriate and untimely by persons in authority or by other citizens. Martin Luther King Jr.'s "Letter from Birmingham Jail," to clergy he called "white moderates" critical of his action, argues that no time or place may be considered appropriate for an act of CD in a recalcitrant and oppressive society. U.S. civil rights leaders had explored peaceful avenues for redeeming the unacceptable social condition of African Americans only to be told no or to wait.

Sometimes the state calls into question the moral, religious, or ideological veracity and motive of an act of CD. This was done in cases of conscientious objection to the U.S. military draft during World War II. In 1940, eight Union Theological Seminary students (the Union Eight) refused to recognize the conscripting authority of the United States in its first peacetime draft, but they did not choose the legal exemption available to conscientious objectors on religious grounds. Instead, they chose defiance resulting in federal imprisonment;

their intent was to start a national movement in libertarianism and radical passivism against American militarism.

Some consider CD to be justified and distinguishable from uncivil actions, anarchy, and revolution if it meets specific criteria: the act is peaceful and eschews violence; other viable methods of correcting the problem are not available to objectors; objectors prepare for the consequences of their actions; a major moral issue is clearly at stake; debate and agitation precede the CD; and if the action is unavoidable, "there must be some rhyme and reason in the time, place, and target selected" (Hook 1971). It is doubtful whether all of these conditions are possible in every case of CD. Though CD often eschews violence, the idea that it "must be nonviolent is a fallacy on law and order" since it is "the deliberate violation of law for a vital social purpose," whether the law is unconstitutional or not (Zinn 1971). This was the case in 1776, when conscientious objectors in the colonies rose up in a bloody revolt against the British policy of taxation without representation. The outbreak of the Civil War of the 1860s was fueled by secessionists against the Union for its opposition to the expansion of slavery in frontier states.

Civil Disobedience and the State

The debate on law, government, and CD has involved John Locke, Thomas Jefferson, William Paley, and many others, but its contemporary discussion owes much to American writer Henry David Thoreau (1817–1862). The free-thinking New Englander articulated the modern definition of CD in his actions and use of its principles. Thoreau spent much of his life contesting the legality of slavery, the Mexican War, and what he called abusive state and federal powers. He defended passionately the right of a people to reject oppressive and unjust laws of the state. In his essay "Resistance to Civil Government" (1849)—reissued as "On the Duty of Civil Disobedience" (1971)—Thoreau urged citizens to conscientiously object to a government that, if it had to choose, would rather "keep all just men in prison" before it gave up war and the evil system of slavery. Thoreau said, "Government is best which governs least," or "which governs not at all." Citizens should be independent human beings first and subjects of the state only afterward; they should not cultivate a respect for law that makes it so sacred and infallible it cannot be contested. Thoreau claimed that "law never made men a whit more just; and, by means of their respect for it, even the well disposed are daily made the agents of injustice" and that under an unjust law of a government, people think "they ought to wait until they have persuaded the majority to alter" the law. About a hundred years later, those words would be brought to life again by Mahatma Gandhi in India and Martin Luther King Jr. in Montgomery, Alabama.

In his objection to the overreaching authority of government and in defiance of his state law, Thoreau did not pay taxes on moral grounds, an act for which he was convicted and sent to prison. He wrote, "If a thousand men were not to pay their tax-bills this year that would not be a violent and bloody measure, as it would be to pay them, and enable the state to commit violence and shed innocent blood. This is, in fact, the definition of a peaceable revolution." Paying taxes to a misguided government only contributes to its ability to commit violence against its slaves, he said. Thoreau urged CD as "a peaceable revolution, if any such is possible," but he left open the possibility of a violent overthrow of a recalcitrant and oppressive system such as slavery. The effects of Thoreau's courageous but controversial stance, not fully realized during his lifetime, were far reaching in the world of CD.

Civil Disobedience and Nonviolence for Justice

Four decades after Thoreau wrote his famous essay, Gandhi read "On the Duty of Civil Disobedience" while in law school and was so struck by it that twelve years later it remained one of his prime possessions in a South African prison and became an important tool in organizing his movement in using CD against injustice. Intrigued by Thoreau's insistence that people must conscientiously object to unjust laws that are injurious to a sector of society, in 1906 Gandhi mobilized thousands of Indians in his first mass nonviolent act of CD, to resist South Africa's Transvaal Asiatic Registration Act No. 29, labeled the Black Act. Inspired also by the Jainist moral principle *ahimsa*— "Do harm to no one"—Gandhi modified Thoreau's idea of CD with an embrace of complete nonviolence and became the first person to fuse an organized mass struggle with nonviolent direct action; his was a nonviolent noncooperation with unjust government actions in South Africa and later British rule in India.

Gandhi was imprisoned several times in South Africa and suffered the same fate later in India while leading his country's struggle for complete *swaraj* (responsible self-rule) from Britain. After he returned to India in 1914, he readily applied against British colonialism the ideas of mass CD he had used effectively in South Africa. In 1920, he coformulated India's first *satyagraha* movement that supported mass CD; he urged Indians to boycott British institutions, including its schools, courts, and businesses, and to consume their own locally produced goods. He also encouraged supporters to quit their government jobs, reject British taxation (following the example of Thoreau), and abandon British titles and honors. In 1924, he was imprisoned again, for two years, but upon his release, he worked untiringly to unify and free his country from British rule through organized acts of CD.

Though committed to fighting a peaceful battle for freedom and justice, Gandhi did not completely rule out the possibility of violence if he had to use it. On one occasion he said, "I do believe that where there is only a choice between cowardice and violence I would advise violence." However, he called off a political action in 1922 because of violent acts committed against police. In 1930, Gandhi led his most historic march, on foot from his commune in Ahmidabad to Dandi, approximately 200 miles (320 kilometers) away on the coast; it took him and over 100,000 marchers, whom he gathered along the way, just under a month. When he arrived on the coast, he made one of the most famous gestures in CD: he scooped up a handful of sea salt and advised his followers to do the same—an act in complete violation of British salt tax regulation. He and many followers were arrested promptly and incarcerated for their defiance.

For over three decades, Gandhi and his millions of supporters agitated for Indian independence and social change. Many satyagrahists were fined, beaten, and imprisoned repeatedly and had their property confiscated, but they did not offer the slightest hint of physical resistance. Through nonviolent CD, Gandhi put his country on the path to true swaraj but not before witnessing extreme religious and political violence that fractured India into three sovereignties—India, Pakistan, and Bangladesh. In the end, Gandhi paid the ultimate price of his own life; the most nonviolent conscientious objector and leader of peaceful CD of modern times met a violent death while fighting for national freedom and peace between Muslims and Hindus. He was shot three times in the chest by a Hindu extremist on January 30, 1948.

From Gandhi came some of the most commonly used techniques in nonviolent CD: resisters should bear the anger of the opponent but should harbor none in return; they should not retaliate verbally or physically when assaulted; even at the risk of punishment, resisters must not willingly surrender property in their keeping as a trustee; resisters must voluntarily submit to arrest by authorities and release personal property when required to; resisters should not insult the opponent or participate in anything that contradicts the spirit of ahimsa; a civil resister will risk his or her life to protect an official being assaulted or attacked during a CD struggle.

Peaceful CD did not die with Gandhi. The United States has a history of nonviolent CD: U.S. women won their suffrage through actions of CD; and U.S. labor unions have led many peaceful protests via strikes, as with the auto industry and the agricultural workers in the 1930s. In the 1950s, civil rights activists led nonviolent mass CD in social protest against segregation and injustice. The Congress of Racial Equality (CORE) organized freedom rides and sit-ins and collaborated with the Montgomery bus boycott. In the 1960s, the Student Nonviolent Coordinating Committee (SNCC) organized sit-ins at lunch counters and other forms of CD, and the Southern Christian Leadership Conference (SCLC)—an organization of church leaders of different Christian denominational backgrounds—took a stand in CD against segregation and white violence in the South, especially in Alabama and Mississippi. Their famous March on Washington in 1963 drew over 250,000 people to the civil rights cause and touched the heart of America through the voice of spokesperson Martin Luther King Jr. when he gave his famous "I Have a Dream" speech.

A little over a decade after Gandhi's death, King emerged as the world's leader of peaceful CD in the cause of justice. As a supporter of the nonviolent tradition, King was intrigued by his reading of Gandhi's life and work and even visited his mausoleum in India. Gandhi's grassroots movement and satyagraha philosophy had a direct impact on the formulation of King's nonviolent direct-action techniques in the fight against segregation, racial discrimination, disenfranchisement, and Ku Klux Klan violence. King said, as the days unfolded, "The Christian doctrine of love, operating through the Gandhian method of nonviolence, was one of the most potent weapons available to the Negro in his struggle for freedom." King's first organized movement in mass CD took place in Montgomery, Alabama, in 1955. It was sparked when Rosa Parks was arrested for her individual act of CD against the discriminatory law in public transportation and inspired African Americans to unite in boycotting the segregated city buses. The boycott, originally planned for a few days, lasted for a year and ended with the Supreme Court ruling in December of 1956 that buses in Montgomery must be desegregated. This was the first major African-American gain in CD, and it greatly energized the peaceful fight for civil rights.

King said he gave serious thought to Thoreau's revolutionary theory and method in CD, but his civil rights movement's greatest influence came from religion and Mahatma Gandhi's use of nonviolence. Until his own violent death, King insisted that the civil rights movement be peaceful and completely nonviolent. He confessed, "The experience in Montgomery did more to clarify my thinking in regard to the question of nonviolence than all the books I had read. Nonviolence became more than a method to which I gave intellectual assent; it became a commitment to a way of life." The nonviolent commitment called for organized and calculated actions such as boycotts, marches, crowding of jails, and other acts in CD by the freedom fighters. In the late 1950s and 1960s, King and many others were arrested and imprisoned several times fighting for freedom and dignity through CD. He was assassinated on April 4, 1968, in Memphis, Tennessee, where he was supporting the cause of sanitation workers. The movement, however, gained the support of millions of nonviolent activists who suffered intimidation by lawless white Klan organizations; the southern judicial system; governments; and police with attack dogs, assault rifles, and fire hoses. The mass arrests, mob beatings, and killings by whites were so brutal they stunned and infuriated even white America and galvanized support from unlikely sources to dismantle segregation.

Civil Disobedience and Religion

Religion is one of the most commonly known grounds for acts of CD, and it is protected under U.S. First Amendment. As a source of moral consciousness, however, religion is not always adequate to justify a person's right to practice CD in cases of contested legality. A religious claim can be disingenuous, and some religious actions put the lives of many at risk. Since the 1970s, this has been the case with groups like the People's Temple in Guyana, the Branch Davidians in the United States, Aum Shinrikyo in Japan, and Muslim extremists claiming religious justification for their violent actions. A few members of Operation Rescue, a Christian organization exercising CD against abortion, have taken some uncivil actions against medical clinics under the spell of religious enthusiasm (or fanaticism). Others of like faith have murdered physicians in the name of God. Even in legitimate cases, religious claims to CD can be open to question and must be transparent and rational in their objectives. In 1964, heavyweight boxing champion Cassius Clay (Muhammad Ali) objected to the draft on religious grounds, but the legitimacy of his newly acquired (in 1957) Islamic faith was called into question by military officials, and Clay was stripped of his title until a higher court overturned his suspension from boxing in 1970.

In spite of their limitations, religious and moral objections have supported some of the most important acts of CD in modern time, as religion and politics clash in people's response to laws of contested legality. The same way Gandhi used teachings, ideas, and practices of Asian religions to bring people of various castes and classes together in the cause of freedom, King made Christianity a platform for his message of justice and inspired Americans to acts of mass CD. The civil rights movement brought together people from different educational, social, economic, religious, and political backgrounds through the formation of interreligious, political, and racial alliances to fight injustice. The black church was the cornerstone around which King and other prominent church leaders built their mass movement in CD for civil rights from the 1940s to the 1960s. "The clergy and black church were at the center of the conflicts. Movement participants were meeting on a systematic basis, planning strategy, collecting funds, encouraging protest, and confronting local white power structures. For their efforts, many were paid with bombed homes, burnt crosses, threats, and beatings" (Smith-Christopher 1998). In 1957, SCLC drew up an agreement that officially changed their methods to the new forms of CD to the many oppressive practices and laws under which they suffered. The leaders declared, "We must realize in this time that direct action is our most potent weapon. We must understand that our refusal to accept Jim Crow in specific areas challenges the entire social, political, and economic order that has kept us second-class citizens since 1876." Their religious stance and unity in CD were essential for the dismantling of segregation laws.

South Africans also used religion as one of their many tools to motivate masses of the people to practice CD during the anti-apartheid

campaigns of the 1980s. Racial unity and pressure from the international community were essential in the struggle against apartheid, but religion played an important role in bringing together native Africans to fight for their rights against the policies of the Afrikaans. The South African Council of Churches (SACC), led by Bishop Desmond Tutu and Alan Bosack, two of Africa's strongest anti-apartheid voices, led supporters in protesting oppressive discriminatory race laws. Religious conflict ensued between SACC and the Afrikaans' Christian League of South Africa (CLSA), which justified apartheid on religious grounds. SACC encouraged a nationwide boycott of segregated businesses, public transportation, and schools and had a significant impact on South Africa's economy and white merchant community. It took a marriage between religion and CD and pressure from the international community, especially the divestment of companies doing business with South Africa, to bring an end to apartheid's reign of terror and almost daily beatings and murder of protesters throughout the country. Remaining peaceful in the face of such violent oppression was as great a challenge in South Africa as it was in India and the United States, but ultimately the perseverance of the black Africans paid off. They toppled the apartheid regime; gained the freedom to vote, live, and work in segregated cities; and under the leadership of the freed activist Nelson Mandela, sought a new South Africa.

Historic instances of strongly organized religious CD took place in Burma in 1988 and again in 1990. The Buddhist community in Burma makes up about 85 percent of the population, and the Buddhist leadership is by far the most respected body in the totalitarian state. In 1988, thousands of monks marched through the streets in a prodemocracy campaign, in CD of the military regime's ban on local criticism of the government. The military of Burma reacted swiftly and brutally to the actions of the monks by killing, beating, disrobing, and imprisoning thousands. In 1990, Buddhist leader Aung San Suu Kyi, leader of the National League for Democracy, won the first parliamentary election held in Burma in thirty years but was not acknowledged by the military junta, which refused to step down. The resulting protest against this injustice was repressed brutally and crushed the people's hope for democracy. Aung San Suu Kyi was awarded the Nobel Peace Prize in 1991 for her efforts to free her countrymen, but in 2010 she was still under house arrest. In 2007, at least ninety monks were still being held as political prisoners as a result of their peaceful actions. In the fall of 2008, thousands of Burmese monks marched in the streets for the first time in twenty years to agitate for democracy and peacefully protest fuel hikes that placed the masses in dire economic straits. After a week, the military regime violently suppressed the protests; they killed 8 people (including 5 monks), injured dozens, and hauled about 300 monks to prison in shackles to join their comrades. The junta put martial law into effect, placing a ban on assemblies of 5 or more people; arrested prominent antigovernment critics such as poets and comedians; shut down the Internet; and issued a curfew.

China's repression of religious-political dissent in Tibet is the most recent case of the clash of religion and politics of people's CD in the cause of peace and justice. China invaded and occupied Tibet in the 1950s, during which time, up to 86,000 Tibetans were killed and much of their cultural heritage destroyed. Since then, Tibetans have suffered from human rights abuses. They formed the organization Free Tibet around the Buddhist faith—the official religion of Tibetans—and Tibet's spiritual leader in exile, the Dalai Lama, who was awarded the Noble Peace Prize in 1989 for his tireless efforts to redeem his people. In March 2008, about 350 monks and 400 lay persons marched on government buildings in peaceful protest of the arrest of two fellow monks imprisoned for possessing a picture of the exiled Dalai Lama. Reportedly, dozens of protesters were killed by Chinese security forces in Lhasa as the protesters began to disperse, in what the Chinese government called "uncivil rioting." During the 2008 Summer Olympics, the Free Tibet movement found support around the world against the military repression in Tibet. As the Olympics torch passed through about a dozen metropolises, it was met by thousands of protesters and was extinguished three times while attempting to pass through Paris. Thirty-seven people were arrested in London on the British leg of the flame's journey. Rallies and protesters denounced the Chinese government as the torch passed through San Francisco. The veteran civil rights leader Desmond Tutu called for an international boycott of the games and pleaded, "For God's sake, for the sake of our children, for the sake of their children, for the sake of the beautiful people of Tibet—don't go [to the games]." His plea fell on deaf ears, and China continues its policies of abuse of human rights.

Civil Disobedience in Law and Punishment

In times of CD, people ask, if social protest is important to democracy and as a means of discouraging tyranny and political abuse, to what extent should government punish protesters when, out of conscience, religion, or overriding moral or religious principles, they refuse to obey a state law? Lawmakers who equate CD with encouraging anarchy and lawlessness contend that although citizens in a democratic society are free to disagree with a law, they have an obligation to obey it as long as it remains in force. Government must punish dissenters for breaking the law, whether the dissenter is

Mahatma Gandhi, a member of Solidarity in Poland, or a Tibetan monk. During the Vietnam War, some intellectuals and lawmakers, such as U.S. Solicitor General Erwin Griswold, held such a view based on the primacy of law. They accept that active resistance to a law "may be *morally* justified, but they insist that it cannot be *legally* justified" because "it is of the essence of the law . . . that it is equally applied to all . . . irrespective of personal motive. . . . One who contemplates civil disobedience out of moral conviction should" expect "a criminal conviction" (Dworkin 1971). But can law alone determine people's patriotism or CD on all moral and ethical decisions?

A law itself and its framers are neither altruistic nor infallible. Someone may be guilty of a crime for breaking a law only in a particular country of domicile, and laws are only authoritative in specific countries. A government policy in one country may be immoral or even criminal in another. Civil objectors say there must be a limit to obeying laws of the state of dictators like Adolf Hitler, Idi Amin, and Mussolini—especially when a law is aimed at destroying a group or class in society. In some cases, the law may not be enforceable, may be enforced unfairly or maliciously, may violate a law of greater fundamental import such as a First Amendment right, or may have unintended consequences. Prosecutors in the United States may not fully enforce a criminal law when the lawbreaker is a juvenile, is the sole support of a family, turns state's witness, or is repentant or plea bargains or in cases where the law is politically unpopular (for example, desegregation laws in the 1950s South) or of contested legality. There are "at least some good reasons for not prosecuting persons who disobey the draft laws out of conscience. One is the obvious reason that they acted out of better motives than those who break the law out of greed or a desire to subvert government" (Dworkin 1971). A law

may support injustice in one sector of the society and thus spark acts of CD. That was the case with the infamous 1907 Transvaal government's discriminatory Asiatic Registration Act No. 29, which abridged the rights and privileges of tens of thousands of productive, law-abiding Indians in South Africa; it exposed them to deportation, disfranchisement, exploitation, and public abuse with impunity.

The primacy of morality to law in acts of civil dissent has long been recognized as valid, but moral absolutism can lead to questionable CD and chaos. Moral acts of conscientious objection should be balanced by reason and good judgment, without which a people can be blinded by self-righteousness. It may not be morally wrong to lie to save a human life in a precarious situation. Also, it may not be immoral to kill someone in self-defense, or in CD for the greater good. (e.g., Who would condemn German clergyman Dietrich Bonhoeffer for attempting to assassinate Hitler in order to save millions from being murdered?) It does not follow that basic moral principles, such as proscriptions against lying and killing, are rendered void just because intelligence supports killing or lying. Moral justification of an action must not be left to the absolutism of conscience, as the voice of conscience may conflict with both the law and the conscience of others.

Samuel Murrell

See also: Gandhi, Mohandas K.; King, Martin Luther, Jr.; Quakers.

Further Reading

Bay, Christian. "Civil Disobedience: Prerequisite for Democracy in Mass Society." In *Civil Disobedience and Violence,* ed. Jeffrie G. Murphy, pp. 73–92. Belmont, CA: Wadsworth, 1971.

Byrnes, Rita M., ed. "Religion and Apartheid." *South Africa: A Country Study.* Washington, DC: Government Printing Office for the Library of Congress, 1996.

"China Confirms New Tibetan Riots." BBC News (online), April 4, 2008. Available: http://news.bbc.co.uk/2/hi/7330827.stm.

Dworkin, Ronald. "On Not Prosecuting Civil Disobedience." In Civil Disobedience and Violence, ed. Jeffrie G. Murphy, pp. 112–30. Belmont, CA: Wadsworth, 1971.

Gandhi, Mohandas K. "Non-Violence." In Civil Disobedience and Violence, ed. Jeffrie G. Murphy, pp. 93–102. Belmont, CA: Wadsworth, 1971.

Hook, Sidney. "Social Protest and Civil Obedience." In Civil Disobedience and Violence, ed. Jeffrie G. Murphy, pp. 53–62. Belmont, CA: Wadsworth, 1971.

"The Lost Legacy of Mahatma Gandhi," BBC News (online), January 29, 1998. Available: http://news.bbc.co.uk/2/hi/51468.stm.

Macan-Markar, Marwaan. "Monks vs. Military Hike Myanmar Tensions." Asia Times (online), September 8, 2007. Available: http://www.atimes.com/atimes/Southeast_Asia/II08Ae04.html.

"Monks Killed in Myanmar Crackdown." Al Jazeera (online), September 26, 2007. Available: http://english.aljazeera.net/news/asia-pacific/2007/09/2008525124541931636.html.

Murphy, Jeffrie G. "The Vietnam War and the Right of Resistance." In Civil Disobedience and Violence, ed. Jeffrie G. Murphy, pp. 64–72. Belmont, CA: Wadsworth, 1971.

Shepard, Mark. Gandhi Today. Washington, DC: Seven Locks Press, 1987.

Smith, Christian. Disruptive Religion: The Force of Faith in Social-Movement Activism. New York: Routledge, 1996.

Smith-Christopher, Daniel L., ed. Subverting Hatred: The Challenge of Nonviolence in Religious Traditions. Boston: Research Center for the 21st Century, 1998.

Smock, David R. Perspectives on Pacifism, Christian, Jewish, and Muslim Views on Nonviolence and International Conflict. Washington, DC: United States Institute of Peace Press, 1995.

Snodgrass, Mary Ellen. Civil Disobedience: An Encyclopedic History of Dissidence in the United States. Armonk, NY: M.E. Sharpe, 2009.

Thoreau, Henry David. "On the Duty of Civil Disobedience." In Civil Disobedience and Violence, ed. Jeffrie G. Murphy, pp. 19–38. Belmont, CA: Wadsworth, 1971.

Tracy, Jones. Direct Action: Radical Pacifism from the Union Eight to the Chicago Seven. Chicago: University of Chicago Press, 1996.

Zinn, Howard. "A Fallacy on Law and Order: That Civil Disobedience Must Be Absolutely Nonviolent." In Civil Disobedience and Violence, ed. Jeffrie G. Murphy, pp. 103–11. Belmont, CA: Wadsworth, 1971.

Colonization and Christianization

Ever since the ascendancy of Constantine I as Roman emperor and his legalization of Christianity through the Edict of Milan (313 C.E.), the conquest and control of other people's lands and goods and the establishment of Christendom have worked in synchronicity. Christendom emerged as the weaving together of the pursuits of Roman empire building and Christian church expansion as they worked at common tasks of expanding territory, theo-political domain, and sociocultural influence. The symbiotic relationship between religious zeal and the expansion of state control was not unique to Constantinian Christianity. The mythologies and histories prior to the life and teachings of Jesus Christ and in other religions also express a close relationship between various kinds of deities and the conquest of other lands and peoples. However, the relationship between colonization and Christianization fostered the many kinds of violence that ensued.

The practices of colonization (control by one power over a dependent area or people) and empire building (acquisition of outside lands and resources to expand influence and power) from the 1400s to the present essentially involved the establishment of control or influence over other lands and resources by countries or coalitions with superior military and economic might. Efforts of this nature involved the extension of a usually European nation's sovereignty over an area outside of the colonizing nation's borders, be it near or distant. Since 1400 C.E. there have been fourteen major colonizing powers: the Austro-Hungarian, Belgian, British, Danish, French, German, Italian, Japanese, Ottoman, Portuguese, Russian, Spanish, Swedish, and United States. It is not possible to quantify even the direct violence (actions that harm or kill individuals or groups) of this period. Nevertheless, by the late 1800s nearly

A group of Chiracahua Apaches before their first day at Carlisle Indian School, in Carlisle, Pennsylvania, in November 1886 (above); the same group is pictured four months later (facing page). Residential schools, such as Carlisle, served to assimilate and Christianize the children of indigenous peoples by isolating them from their families and cultures. *(Both images by John N. Choate/MPI/Getty Images)*

every continent had experienced colonization in concert with Christianization (adaptation or conversion to Christianity or to a particular denomination of Christianity). Of these empires, twelve saw themselves as Christian, and two—the Japanese and Ottoman empires—did not. The British Empire alone was so large that it was said that the "sun never set" on it, and the same could be said about the violence and coercion that took place in colonizing widely disparate lands.

Taking just one example, the colonization and Christianization of Native Americans, while estimates range considerably, it has been

claimed that approximately 100 million native people died because of colonization. The figure includes both those killed by fighting and those who died as a result of diseases that were brought by the colonizing forces. Such death toll claims are always disputed, and there is no way to come to definitive amounts. However, the worldwide number of deaths arising out of the coupling of colonization and Christianization is at least in the hundreds of millions. This figure points only to direct and indirect violence due to disease but does not include other forms of violence such as structural violence (slow harm to life as a result of social, political,

and economic systems), cultural violence (the justification of violence by cultural-religious means), and lateral violence (acts of an oppressed people directed laterally at their own people rather than the oppressor and rooted in rage, anger, and frustration from being constantly oppressed). These are all significant factors in the process of colonization by nations who considered themselves as Christian.

Both direct and structural violence arise out of the relationship between the expansion of state control beyond its borders and the efforts to make the world Christian, particularly during the period from the 1400s to the present. While many historians refer to the twentieth century and beyond as the postcolonial period (particularly following World War II), current

events indicate that certain vestiges of colonization have not entirely diminished. Understanding this violence requires understanding the features of colonization, of Christianization, and of their relationship that has led to such levels of violence.

Features of Colonization

Colonization basically consists of seven factors. First, it is always intrusive. The colonizers brought with them beliefs and attitudes that were rooted in notions of the superiority, or universal goodness, of their civilization. Although many indigenous peoples of the Americas were initially willing to share the spacious lands they occupied when the Europeans arrived, the demands of industrialization and certain notions of European progress and supremacy always resulted in invasive interaction between colonizers and indigenous populations. Often domination was accomplished by military conquest (e.g., in Portuguese Mozambique and the Belgian Congo), but sometimes little or no bloodshed took place nor even any extensive military operations (e.g., in the British Dominion of Canada). Sometimes initial contact was followed by settlement of the new territory by citizens of the conquering state (e.g., the British in New Zealand and the Dutch in South Africa); at other times a small group or rulers supported by missionaries would extend colonial rule over the dependent people (e.g., the French in Niger, the Russians in Alaska) without settlement. In any case, the coercive element of the colonizing nation's intrusion, along with the preparatory work of missionaries (be it intentional or not), allowed it to establish administrative dependencies in which the indigenous population was ruled directly or displaced.

A second feature of colonization is that colonizers would exploit the labor power of the territory and extract resources from the land as required by the needs of the colonizing country. Often colonial powers would restructure the economy of these territories in such a way that they shifted the local economy from modes of subsistence to the dependency on export economies. Inequality was characteristic of the political and economic relationships between colonizers and indigenous populations. Furthermore, the mother country would usually impose its sociocultural, religious, and linguistic structures on the conquered or dependent population. This type of cultural imperialism was beneficial to the colonizing country in that it aided the efficient extraction of resources and the effective management of the labor force. The imposition of this kind of domestic colonialism involving the establishment of European institutions (e.g., hospitals, schools and universities, sometimes prisons) usually took place at the hands of missionaries and other representatives of the church.

A third basic feature of the colonizing group's impact upon non-European ways of life was the destruction of social, cultural, spiritual, and ecological norms and customs established among the groups to be colonized. Some call this "cultural violence" because it uses various ideologies, traditions, and systems of legitimization that are foreign to the colonized population to destroy indigenous ways of life. Sometimes such destruction was deliberate, but often it came about simply due to notions of natural superiority or even the "rightness" of the European way of life. Whether by design or ignorance, the political, economic, kinship, learning, and spiritual structures of indigenous populations were undermined by economic and legal arrangements imposed by the colonizing nation. Colonizing powers ignored and violated well-developed ethical and cultural norms among colonized populations. For example, in Canada, British and French authorities went as far as making certain traditional customs such as the potlatch, the sundance, and sweat lodges illegal.

A fourth feature of colonization is the interrelated processes of external political control and economic dependence of colonized peoples. Once the dominant power has established control over the territory beyond its borders, the mother country sends representatives to this newly "conquered" territory through whom it rules the lands and people. These representatives set up institutions through which the colonial power takes over or has indirect influence over all the affairs of the colonized population. For example, in Fiji, the Great Council of Chiefs, or Bose Levu Vakaturaga, was established by the British colonizing power in 1876 so that the diverse and sometimes conflicting groups within Fiji could be ruled more effectively. Such measures mandated foreign ways of governance, dispute settlement, education, and health. Some consider this a form of structural violence, because it harms life systemically, through the ways that social, political, and economic structures are organized.

In general, a pattern of passive-aggressive response on the part of colonized peoples has been noted in the process of colonization. Usually upon initial contact, the indigenous populations being colonized more or less accept or tolerate the intrusion of the colonizing nation. Agreements based on ideal notions of friendship, peace, and mutual respect are formed, as was often the case in North America, particularly Canada. Sometimes, however, initial contact has been met with warfare, as in the case of the Maori and the New Zealand Wars of 1845–1872. Nevertheless, once the colonizing powers reveal their true character and the interrelated processes of political supremacy and economic dependence are better understood by those being colonized, many indigenous populations reject their powerless condition and start to take steps to restore their previous existence, only to find that not much can be done. What follows, sometimes over a process of many decades, is either surrender to general apathy and dispiritedness or settling for unobtrusive ways of resistance that are within their means. Either way, the colonized peoples remain economically dependent on the colonizing power, and their land and communities are viewed by the powers as geographical and social hinterlands, useful only for purposes of exploitation by the dominant society. This then allows, at least for a while, industrialized countries to extract nonrenewable primary resources such as furs, forest products, minerals, and eventually, oil and ship them to urban industrial centers for processing.

A fifth feature of colonization is the provision of low-quality or poorly funded services in education, justice, health, housing, and child and family services. Some scholars have noted an international pattern of indigenous people ending up in poverty and that poverty, when prolonged, turning into lateral violence—violence directed toward other members of the oppressed group rather than the oppressor (Eversole, McNeish, and Cimadmore 2005). Lateral violence takes many forms: sexual abuse, murder, physical abuse, and harassment, among others. Economic dependency and the destruction of social, cultural, and spiritual structures within the colonized population always result in social problems such as disease, crime, poverty, suicide, family breakdown, unemployment, and many other such factors. Once the social fabric (network of societal roles, norms, structures, and expectations held together by culture) of indigenous populations has been destroyed, the dominant power can enter the resulting social chaos and provide a helping role in rescuing the dependent people from their difficult social conditions. The colonizers, however, view those conditions as an indication of the inferiority of the culture they are trying to help, not as a result of colonization. From a Christianizing perspective, abject social conditions are also an indication of the sinfulness of colonized populations and their need for salvation, which the church can offer.

In fact, these social service types of effort have clearly been viewed by the colonizing forces as attempts to civilize the "savages," which leads to a sixth feature of colonization: the systemic establishment of the superiority of the colonizing group and subsequently the inferiority of the group being colonized. This sense of superiority by the colonizers was overtly expressed in public statements and even in educational settings in times past. Although it is now politically incorrect to express such notions of superiority, it must be remembered that these values and sentiments were built into the social, political, economic, and cultural institutions established to govern society in the conquered lands. Much of the structural violence continues even as the political rhetoric of those in power changes. Although the institutions evolved over time, the values on which they were built and shaped are largely intact.

A seventh and final feature of the process of colonization is the ongoing effort to weaken resistance of colonized populations in order to allow the colonizing nation unencumbered control of the society. This can be accomplished in a variety of ways, some of the more obvious mechanisms being the law, regulations, economics, and the establishment of social institutions. However, undermining the worldviews and perspectives of indigenous populations through soft measures should not be underestimated as a way of controlling resistance. For instance, many people in the dominant society rationalize their dominance and control over indigenous populations as being benevolent, fair, and helpful—the "Christian" thing to do.

Features of Christianization

Two definitions typically emerge for Christianization: (1) to take over or adapt in the name of Christianity; (2) to convert to Christianity. The first definition requires no persuasion or volitional acceptance of the beliefs involved in various forms of Christianity. The second definition may be based on conscious choices made by human beings who have the maturity and capacity to exercise their will. However, it must be recognized that such choices may also be subject to coercion, manipulation, fictitious premises, or seduction. Both processes are open to violence; indeed, in many places, the whole process of becoming Christian in relationship to other religions, paganism, or indigenous spirituality has a history of violence and brutality. Sometimes Christians have even tried to violently Christianize other Christian denominations. Six key features within some Christian understandings have led to this propensity to enter into violent arrangements with colonial powers.

The first such feature of Christianization is equating a good Christian with a good citizen. When Constantine I developed the first Christian state, the church had to transform itself from a religion of love and forgiveness to one of order and judgment. After some centuries of church and state battling for supremacy, they formed a kind of partnership in which the colonizing state depended on the spread of Christianity to extend its control. The missionaries also believed that the spread of colonial rule would assist their work. Some challenged the violence of the state, but they were usually sidelined. Church and state were allies in trying to "civilize" the world.

The legwork of such social and cultural destruction among peoples in the colonies was largely left to missionaries and other representatives of the church. Although some traditional practices were considered an economic threat to colonial powers, most traditional customs were objected to by the church because they were seen as heathen or some other threat to the church's understanding of appropriate spirituality. Aside from advising state officials what social, cultural, and spiritual practices should not be acceptable, the key way in which church officials attempted to assimilate colonized populations was through the setting up of schools and hospitals. Such programs and institutions were seen as tools or instruments by which they were doing the will of God. Yet some of the most destructive impacts of colonialism came exactly through such instruments as the residential schools in the United States and Canada. One of the goals of those schools was to separate the children being taught from their families and from indigenous culture, which was seen as heathen or pagan. The schools were a significant factor in crushing the cultural fabric of indigenous peoples and making them ripe for government programs of assimilation. Worse yet, the schools became the setting for widespread physical and sexual abuse of children at the hands of church representatives.

A second feature of Christianization is an authoritarian and hierarchical understanding of Christianity and of human relationship to the universe. The King James Bible was designed in 1604 by a colonizer, King James I of England, to fit his goals of reunifying and expanding the kingdom. For example, Genesis 1:28 says, "And God blessed them, and God said unto them, 'Be fruitful, and multiply, and replenish the earth, and subdue it: and have dominion over the fish of the sea, and over the fowl of the air, and over every living thing that moveth upon the earth.'" The English word *subdue* is not an adequate translation of the Hebrew word used in this account of the Old Testament creation story. The Hebrew word translated as *subdue* can also mean "do what a caretaker would do" and the word for "dominion over" can also mean to be "a steward or trustee." Certainly, the language chosen by the King James translators and repeated by most common Western revisions of the King James Version serves the purposes of empire building and authoritarian control, but it does not adequately convey what was intended.

A third feature of Christianization is the development of a theology to justify violence. Christianity has within it various schools of thought or denominations that have justified violence and death in dealing with each other (e.g., Catholic and Protestant or Protestant and Anabaptist). Some of these theologies predate modern colonialism. For example, the Celtic theology of innate goodness of creation was slowly displaced by the Mediterranean church's focus on original sin, starting already in the seventh century. By focusing on original sinfulness, the Mediterranean tradition developed a theology relating to a God of judgment. Over time, judgment, which the early Christians said should be left to God, became the prerogative of the state, with the blessing and urging of religious leaders. For hundreds of years, various churches have developed theologies that have supported the colonializing state's authority to act as violent judge.

A fourth feature of Christianization is the belief that the truth can be owned by one group. With this kind of ownership of the one and only true way, combined with the state's sense of supreme sovereignty, spreading truth became spreading European culture even if it required violence means. The Portuguese were known for being ruthless, destroying non-Christian temples and forcing conversion by threat of violence. When the truth becomes the property of one exclusive grouping, such as Christians or a denomination within Christianity, those who do not belong are seen as either apostate or less than human. For instance, during the fourteenth to sixteenth centuries, there was a debate among Spanish Jesuit theologians as to whether the indigenous populations "discovered" in the new world were actually human or not. This tendency to see and treat others as less than human is rooted in part in believing that truth can be owned and lorded over others by one group.

A fifth feature of Christianization since Constantine is the separation of spiritual and physical. When the spiritual is fragmented off as one realm of existence, distinct from the physical realm, the potential for violent theologies unfolds. If that which is considered sacred is separate from the earth or humanity, one can treat the earth or humanity in profane ways. Some indigenous authors have claimed that a significant part of why Europeans tend to dominate wherever they go is because they have the wrong relationship with the land (Battiste and Henderson 2000).

A final feature of Christianization is the missionary zeal to make the world Christian. Clearly, one of the last instructions left by Jesus to his disciples was "Go therefore and make disciples of all the nations, baptizing them in the name of the Father and the Son and the Holy Spirit, teaching them to observe all that I commanded you" (Matthew 28:19–20). While multiple translations of this passage are possible, the institutionalized expression of Christianity uses it as a mandate to collaborate with colonizing powers to expand their control and influence.

It is also important to understand how the church's attempt to do good became so oppressive to colonized populations. The early Christians always had extra bread, water, and a candle stored away in their homes. They did this because of the teaching that Christ, in the form of a homeless person, might come to their door and it was their loving duty to provide him with food and shelter. After Constantine declared Christianity the official religion, the bishops, with money provided by the state, set up a bureaucracy and management structure required for hospices, which attempted to meet the need of homelessness and poverty. This displaced the practice of Christians freely responding to needs on a personal and voluntary basis. This so-called corruption of Christianity demonstrates how, when Christianity is institutionalized on a mass basis, the focus shifts and the original intention can be lost.

Not all Christians or Christian traditions support the efforts to Christianize the world. Some point out that Jesus showed people a new way of life, not a new way of exercising governance. Instead of laws that could be "written on stone," he spoke of laws that could only be "written on the heart." However, it seems that, however imperfect, more work has been done in decolonizing the colonizer and colonized than has gone into de-Christianizing the Christianizers and the Christianized. It is important to note that while Christianity is losing influence in many colonialized countries, it is still growing in many colonized places such as South and Central America.

Dynamics Feeding the Coupling of Colonization and Christianization

The coupling of colonization and Christianity between the 1400s and the 1900s can be traced back to three spheres of influence: (1) views of creation, (2) age of reason, and (3) industrialization. Examination of these three formative impacts will also clarify the relationship between colonization and Christianization.

Views of Creation

Usually, the most fundamental area of difference in the worldviews of the colonizing European nations and the colonized indigenous nations is in how each group sees its relationship with the universe and in its understanding of a creator—God or a transcendent power of some sort. The notions to subdue and dominate the land and its peoples is based on a particular interpretation of the biblical creation story. These assumptions that humans' proper role was to subdue and dominate was a common assumption among the European colonial powers. Such a view, however, is in stark contrast with indigenous worldviews. A Canadian Cree view of creation follows:

Creation came about from the union of the Maker and the Physical World. Out of this union came the natural children, the Plants, nurtured from the Physical World, Earth, their Mother. To follow were Animalkind, the two legged, the four legged, the winged, those who swim and those who crawl, all dependent on the Plant world and Mother Earth for succour. Finally, last in the order came Humankind, the most dependent and least necessary of all the orders. (Ahenakew, King, and Littlejohn 1990)

In the dominant Euro-Christian view, humans are the ultimate creation and were meant to be dominant over all other aspects of creation, whereas in the indigenous perspective, humans are the most needy and lesser of all creatures. It makes sense that the former perspective would lead to greater conflict, violence, and destruction. One is based on control, and the other is based on humility.

Age of Reason

The Age of Reason was an influential period in the formation of the diversity of European worldviews starting in the seventeenth century and continuing as the Age of Enlightenment (1660–1800). The school of thought emanating from this period used positivist reason or logic (knowledge based on the five senses as confirmed by science) to challenge knowledge based on theology or doctrine as established by the church-state union. However, colonization and Christianization expanded immensely during the Age of Reason, as proponents of the age contended that human needs could be met through mastery over nature.

This idea of mastery over nature led to an expansionist worldview, shared over time by church, state, and rationalist philosophers. The perspective is clearly human centered with a focus on classifying, compartmentalizing, and fragmenting science and management into separate disciplines and specialties. In this perspective, progress means satisfying human needs, and to that end nature makes available a storehouse of resources that have utilitarian and economic value.

The Age of Reason also brought with it a particular orientation to time. A fundamental difference of almost all indigenous populations from their colonizers is that European worldviews are based on linear thinking, and indigenous worldviews are based on cyclical thinking. The European tendency is to understand hu-

mankind on a forward-moving trajectory toward betterment of individuals. In this view, some peoples can be seen as more primitive and in need of enlightenment. This rationalist logic of time underpinned the efforts of colonization and Christianization.

Industrial Revolution

The Industrial Revolution of the eighteenth century displays the most dramatically observable change in how the world's resources were exploited. Whether the expansionist perspective mentioned above led to making industrialization possible or simply rationalized it is not entirely relevant except to point out that the control and domination interpretation of the Judeo-Christian creation story lends itself well to what transpired in the Industrial Revolution.

Industrialization created wealth and markets as well as environmental degradation and the need for more raw materials. Even agriculture was affected. For example, the possibility of selective breeding of livestock meant that there could be more production. Furthermore, the creation of private land with fences around the perimeters meant that individual owners were then more willing to invest in mechanization and more modern agricultural technologies.

The resulting growth in agricultural production led to a corresponding jump in the population, which in turn led to concentrated areas of habitation, which we now refer to as cities or urban sprawl. As people began to produce more food, they settled down and married younger. The increase in childbearing years and the resulting population growth meant that more people's efforts could be diverted from agriculture and be exploited in manufacturing. New technologies were based on iron and coal. Industrialization caused the switch to coal as an energy source. Coal mining required pumping capacities, which was done by steam engines, the fabrication of which required iron, and the production of iron required coal. This became a continuous cycle of exploiting the earth's resources, requiring ever more raw resources to feed the process.

Both the process of industrialization and its consequences spurred colonial powers to find lands beyond their borders with more natural resources to exploit. Eventually, no part of the planet was left untouched by the Industrial Revolution. In fact, as machines were adapted and made to be more efficient, the pace of change was accelerated and the resulting pressure to colonize new lands was intensified. It should be noted at this point that the willingness of industrializing European nations to violate the environment (nature and resources) has a correlation to the violence imposed upon colonized populations.

Conclusion

The power and authority offered by the modus operandi of the state have a seductive influence on those who are captivated by the vision of an approaching new order based on peace, justice, compassion, and sharing. The colonizing perspective means (the mechanisms of the state) justify the ends (peace, justice, and compassion). The most powerful Christian colonizers—from the Romans to the British to the current world superpower, the United States—have sanctified the violence of the state as a tool to achieve better ends. The first settlers of the United States were clearly imbued with the notion that a new, better, and more Christian or godly way of life could be implemented in the New World, and they clearly invoked God and Christian principles as they understood them in their formation of governance and the Constitution. The violent clashes between those settlers and the indigenous peoples of the Americas and the settlers' later readiness to accept or tolerate slavery can

be seen as a consequence of using the vehicle of the state to inculcate Christian values.

Once Christianity becomes the state religion, it has a vested interest in the existing order and tends to use the cultic means at its disposal to legitimize that order. The Christian Church then shows little interest in a gospel of repentance, in judgment, in being distinct from the "world," or in making any statements that would be ethically challenging to the powers that be and holding them accountable. A common tendency of church-state alignments is to believe that history is on their side and that the opposing system is the incarnation of evil.

When the church and state are aligned, there is little talk in the church of the new order coming ("Thy kingdom come") because this previously anticipated realm is being realized empirically through the existing order of the state. The state now becomes the agent of God's defeat of evil, and the will of the ruler (emperor, king, president, etc.) as advised by the church leadership is the will of God.

In conclusion, where church and state partnered in the mission to colonize and Christianize the world, various kinds of violence inevitably ensued: direct violence, indirect violence, cultural violence, structural violence, and lateral violence. Although it is not fair to stereotype church-state alliances as a conspiratorial collusion of greedy and power-hungry despots, the fact remains that over the last 600 years the outcome of such alliances has always produced conflict leading to violence. It is safe to assume that the missionary efforts that characterized colonization were often grounded in sincerity and attempts to do good and be of service. However good the intent, the services performed by the church were nevertheless provided in the context of conquest and occupation by the state and notions of supremacy, paternalism, and exclusivity. Furthermore, conflict and violence usually follow whenever Christians feel obliged to implement their understanding of "God's plan" by means of the available political, economic, and military tools of the state. Colonization and Christianization leave imprints that endure over several generations, and therefore, the violence does not end when colonized countries become independent. Such a violent orientation is not innate to Europeans or Christians. It comes from various factors, choices, and interpretations of what it means to be Christian, to be human, and to be a citizen.

Len Sawatsky and Jarem Sawatsky

See also: Christianity; Ghost Dance and Sun Dance; Victims.

Further Reading

Ahenakew, Freda, Cecil King, and Catherine I. Littlejohn. "Indigenous Languages in the Delivery of Justice in Manitoba." Research paper prepared for the Aboriginal Justice Inquiry. Winnipeg: Government of Manitoba, 1990.

Armitage, Andrew D. *Comparing the Policy of Aboriginal Assimilation: Australia, Canada, and New Zealand.* Vancouver: University of British Columbia Press, 1995.

Battiste, Marie Ann, and James Youngblood Henderson. *Protecting Indigenous Knowledge and Heritage: A Global Challenge.* Aboriginal Issues series. Saskatoon, Canada: Purich, 2000.

Belich, James. *The New Zealand Wars and the Victorian Interpretation of Racial Conflict.* Auckland: Penguin, 1998.

Benart, William. "Southern Africa." In *Encyclopedia of World Environmental History,* ed. S. Krech, J. MacNeill, C. Merchant, and S. Krech III, pp. 18–19. New York: Routledge, 2004.

Eversole, Robyn, John-Andrew McNeish, and Alberto Cimadamore, eds. *Indigenous Peoples and Poverty: An International Perspective.* London: Zed Books, 2005.

Gorringe, Timothy. *God's Just Vengeance: Crime, Violence, and the Rhetoric of Salvation: Cambridge Studies in Ideology and Religion.* Cambridge, UK: Cambridge University Press, 1996.

Lujan, Carol Chiago. "U.S. Colonization of Indian Justice Systems: A Brief History." *Wicazo Sa Review* 19:2 (Fall 2004): pp. 9–23.

Page, Melvin E., and Penny M. Sonnenburg. *Colonialism: An International, Social, Cultural, and Political Encyclopedia.* Oxford: ABC-CLIO, 2003.

Royal Commission on Aboriginal Peoples. *Report of the Royal Commission on Aboriginal Peoples.* Ottawa: Canadian Government Publishing, 1996.

Satzewich, Vic, and Terry Wotherspoon. *First Nations: Race, Class and Gender Relations.* Regina, Canada: University of Regina, 2000.

Selengut, Charles. *Sacred Fury: Understanding Religious Violence.* Lanham, MD: AltaMira Press, 2003.

Stannard, David E. *American Holocaust: The Conquest of the New World.* New York: Oxford University Press, 1993.

Weber, M. *The Protestant Ethic and the Spirit of Capitalism.* London: Unwin Paperbacks, 1985.

Zehr, Howard. *Changing Lenses: A New Focus for Crime and Justice.* Scottdale, PA: Herald Press, 1990.

Conflict Theory

Conflict theory is a social theory that focuses on the ability of an individual or group to exert influence over others and affect the social order within a culture or society. Under conflict theory, the struggle of the individual or group to better its condition will ultimately lead to social change and innovation, sometimes but not always resulting in violence. Conflict theory is generally thought to be connected to the ideas of Karl Marx and his economic theories of social organization. For some scholars of social theory, calling Marx an economic theorist shortchanges his contributions and severely underestimates his continuing influence on social structures such as politics, cultural institutions, philosophical debates, and even how religion is incorporated into social orders. Marx's theories analyzed the relationship between those social structures and the means of production resident in a given society at a given time and place. Marx was generally concerned with how the economic order of a society or culture determined its social structures. For hunting and gathering societies the expression of social structures such as religion was very different from those found in advanced industrial societies, primarily because the underlying economic foundations of the society were very different.

Marxist sociological thought focuses on how best to interpret social events, such as a global jihad movement, in conjunction with how those events are associated with economic conditions. To simplify the theoretical arguments, it is not the consciousness of people that determines their existence; it is the social structures they live under that determine their consciousness. For Marx, the struggle is one based on class society; it is a struggle between the owners of the means of production and the workers who inhabit the factories where those means are employed. Society in this perspective is a class-based social circumstance for the generation of conflict, since those polar opposites would be in perpetual conflict. It is that conflict that is the underlying reason for social discord. To summarize: conflict is the very soul of modern life and social interactions.

Marx was more than a social philosopher; he was an empiricist who used facts to support his arguments; he was a moralist intent on changing the working lives of the poor; and he held a utopian vision of the future, in which socioeconomic arrangements such as capitalism could be revised for the betterment of social conditions. He embodied the hope for the future, and he confronted the despair of the present; in much the same way religion embodies the collective fears and personifies the best social intentions of believers.

Marx was not the only social theorist who wrote on conflict, and over time other social theorists have updated his ideas. The updates generally are referred to as conflict theories (or conflict schools) and typically focus on macro sociological issues. Marx's class conflict analysis has morphed into many varieties: power-elite models of explanation; analysis of hierarchies of power and influence; and specific analysis of the state's influence on all aspects of social life, especially the political arena. These are just a few of the many ways macro sociological interest groups were identified and analyzed from a conflict perspective.

Power-Elite Model

C. Wright Mills's power-elite model represents one variety of conflict theory, and his later work focused on how the state represents corporate interests, specifically those of the military and industrial concerns that seemed to be most prominent during this time frame (1950s) and which also apply today. Mixing theoretical ideas from prominent sociologist-economist scholars such as Max Weber, Thorstein Veblen, and Vilfredo Pareto with those of Karl Marx, Mills attacked what he saw as the significant social problems of his day with zeal and passion. He published *The Power Elite* (1956), a research endeavor that conducted class-conflict analysis with a specific focus on social stratification and interest-group politics. Like Marx, he looked at class conflict, but rather than the worker and factory owner being the primary social actors in social conflict, Mills focused on those class conflicts that had become more prominent over the last century. Large corporate interests were dominating social life more than ever by the mid-twentieth century, and that corporate dominance had ramifications that required a specific focus for social scientists, at least in Mills's theoretical perspective. Contemporary debates about the role of such corporations in the dominance of other cultures and their cultural beliefs (i.e., religion) show the relevance of his arguments for the understanding of religion-inspired violence.

Hierarchies of Power and Influence

Ralf Dahrendorf's work on hierarchies of power (1959) represents a different form of conflict analysis, one with ties to Marxist theory but with some distinctive analytical flavors garnered from other theoretical traditions as well. Dahrendorf tried to create a grand theoretical narrative that focused on how all of human existence is about power struggles. For Dahrendorf, social structures (e.g., education, government, religion) are the enforcers of conformity for the masses. It is this conformity that enables the powerful to dominate society. Those who hold power and influence in any social order use these social structures to coerce—chief among his theorized means for enforcing conformity—the less powerful into acting submissive and in many cases unknowingly bowing to the latent and manifest will of the powerful. For Dahrendorf, power and control are scarce resources, resources that are fought over and that are never far from the surface. Such conflicts are never resolved, since the struggle for power begets new forms of struggle and new constellations of power that have their own ongoing conflicts.

Dahrendorf's theory demonstrates how hierarchies of power exist in social orders, cultures, and societies. He also offers some sense of resolution to current politically violent conflicts. He notes that class conflict (or by proxy, intrastate conflict) can be channeled away from the more violent forms, but it will persist, no matter what. For Dahrendorf, conflict is a natural part of social organization and perhaps one of the most prominent features of modern social orders. In short, while he offers some philosophical "solutions" for contemporary violent religious conflicts, he also forces one to recognize that those troubles will be replaced by new and different forms of conflict on the world stage.

State Conflict Theory

Conflict is a complex social phenomenon and requires that theorists do more than just limit the analysis to conflicts between localized interest groups. Contemporary religion-based violence can involve clashes of large-scale social orders or what could be termed "meso conflicts." These social-order conflicts are not clashes of civilizations but may be rather more closely aligned with clashes of nation-states or quasi-nation-state entities with aspirations to become nation-states in the more traditional sense. The study of state theories is a branch of conflict theory that is helpful in understanding these meso conflicts.

In the state conflict perspective, the state (what many would call government) is what should be studied when talking about all things political, even political violence with religious overtones. The argument, as it relates to religious terrorism, can be explained as follows: if the state is beholden to one religious bias and is in conflict with another state entity or quasi state entity with a differing religious bias, the conflict between these groups will be on the surface about state-on-state differences (i.e., traditional reasons for wars). Underlying such struggles may well be religious motives, religion-inspired social norms, or religious conflicts promoted by powerful interest groups in the states.

It is critical to understand who controls the state in such conflicts, since these social actors (elites) are directing the conflict inherent in social order. This argument has been used by Islamic observers when discussing how the current conflict is being framed by radical interests in the Muslim world. Some Islamic radicals argue that the nation-state of the United States is controlled by a radical right-wing religious base and is seeking to control Islamic countries and crush their religious freedom and identity.

From this perspective, the current conflict is based on religion on both sides—an argument that does not readily resonate with those in the West, since they profess to have a separation of church and state, but does resonate in Islamic societies since the former president of the United States, George W. Bush, openly professed his religious bias and even used the term "crusade" in reference to the current conflict. Perceptions of such an American-based religious bias may well be part of the underlying party politics in which, of late, the Republican Party has had a profound connection to the religious Right and its fundamentalist politics. According to state theory, modern nation-states or their emerging postmodern equals are controlled by groups of powerful class interests, some of which are religion based (or to some degree beholden to religious groups for their power). For state theorists, these elite groups dominate the process for their own interests and do not share power in a pluralistic fashion (Carnoy 1984).

One such theory is posited by G. William Domhoff (1967) in his "power structure research" (which builds on the work of C. Wright Mills). For Domhoff, the upper class is a governing class that owns the means of production and controls the means of governance. The state acts on its behalf, since the upper class makes the state bend to its will and do its bidding. Conflict is normally between groups of elites and their sometimes opposing interests (e.g., international business vs. domestic corporate concerns). In Domhoff's theory, the state is beholden to those interests and represents only the needs, desires, and will of a small class of elites who control the masses. If that class of elites has a bias, the bias is generally economic, but it would be possible to extend this to a religious argument. Likewise, using this theory, it may be possible to understand meso conflicts, since the threat of religious violence is an economic threat to elite interests.

Other forms of state conflict theory exist and either support Domhoff's argument or run counter to it. In one articulation of state conflict theory, the proponents posit that the state is a mediator between powerful interest groups and in its mediation role sometimes the state

has autonomy in its decisions. Here the state acts to quell class conflict, and while its decisions generally support the economic interests of elites, it may run afoul of certain groups in exercising its autonomy. This theory could be used to help understand current conflicts and perhaps even posit state-based solutions to the conflicts between global interest groups, even religious interests.

Another articulation of state conflict theory has the state as a powerful interest group in and of itself. Here agencies within the overall state apparatus achieve some relative level of autonomy because of their enormous size in modern governmental structures and because they achieve a sense of societal gravity or mass by means of their own interest in preserving their separate identity. For example, state agencies such as the U.S. Department of Homeland Security work for their own interests and their own organizational good. Here, the generalized argument is that the military-industrial complex is such a large part of government that it can dictate priorities for the country. It has power in the overall social order, and, while it can come into conflict with other parts of government—perhaps taking resources away from social programs, for example—its relative power allows it to dominate the social discourse, perhaps more so during the current religion-inspired conflicts in the Middle East, since they are framed as a war.

State theory is a powerful way to see how the role of government is controlled by factions in society, sometimes even those that exist inside the government itself. Such theoretical perspectives allow one to look at how one segment of society can come to dominate the state and its actions. Besides some of the suggested connections previously mentioned, such perspectives could even allow one to theorize how religion could come to dominate the state and how religious interests could control the power of the state.

Religion, Theory, and Current Conflicts

One of the critical issues facing countries dealing with contemporary political and religious conflict is how to understand the conflicts currently being engaged in by many cultures, state governments, and organizations. Perhaps from one social perspective (say the Western, democratic perspective) the conflicts seem simple: a perceptual ethnocentrism born from cultural, economic, and social hegemonic dominance. However, to analyze the issues in a more systematic fashion, the analyst needs a more holistic perspective—which may be achieved by applying conflict theory to these contemporary conflicts. This requires one to look at both sides of the issues and find some explanatory value in a synthesis of the differing perspectives. In the case of contemporary political and religious violence, an understanding of both sides of an area of conflict is needed in order to find solutions to the social problems that arise from the violence.

Conflict theory, as a body of theoretical perspectives, offers one set of solutions. This does not mean the application of such theory is easy or will not be fraught with mistakes, miscues, and errors. For social scientists the application of theory is a trial and error process whereby ideas are tried, tested, discarded, and reconsidered. The bottom line is that applying the traditional models of conflict theory to the contemporary problems of a global Islamic jihadist, for example, may yield some positive results or may yield masses of paper ideas.

In conclusion, state theories seem to help scholars better understand the puzzle that is contemporary political and religious violence. A single conflict theory may not exist that explains the totality of the conflicts currently under way, but theorists are okay with partial answers—politicians and the public perhaps less so. To connect conflict theory to religious violence requires that those who attempt that analytical effort be willing to live with partial answers, to engage in long-term theory development on the topic, and to embrace the creation of alternative explanations for the conflicts at hand. It is just such a back-and-forth interplay that will help social science to eventually find theoretical explanations for social phenomena. However, the question remains as to whether societies will wait for that development process or conflict will overtake the social order we crave.

James David Ballard

See also: Just War Theory.

Further Reading

Althusser, L. *For Marx.* London: Penguin, 1969.

Boyns, D., and J.D. Ballard. "Developing a Sociological Theory for the Empirical Understanding of Terrorism." *American Sociologist* 35:2 (2005): 5–25.

Carnoy, M. *The State and Political Theory.* Princeton, NJ: Princeton University Press, 1984.

Coser, L.A. *Continuities in the Study of Social Conflict.* New York: Free Press, 1967.

———. *Masters of Sociological Thought: Ideas in Historical and Social Context,* 2nd ed. San Diego, CA: Harcourt Brace Jovanovich, 1977.

Cuzzort, R.P., and E.W. King. *20th Century Social Thought,* 3rd ed. New York: Holt, Rinehart and Winston, 1980.

Dahrendorf, R. *Class and Class Conflict in an Industrial Society.* Stanford, CA: Stanford University Press, 1959.

Domhoff, G.W. *Who Rules America?* Englewood Cliffs, NJ: Prentice Hall, 1967.

Gerges, F.A. *Journey of the Jihadist: Inside Muslim Militancy.* Orlando, FL: Harcourt, 2006.

Marx, K. *Capital: The Process of Capitalist Production as a Whole.* New York: International, 1967.

———. *A Contribution to the Critique of Political Economy.* New York: International, 1970.

Mills, C.W. *The Power Elite.* New York: Oxford University Press, 1956.

Poulantzas, N. *Political Power and Social Classes.* London: New Left Books, 1974.

Skocpol, T. *States and State Revolutions: A Comparative Analysis of France, Russia, and China.* New York: Cambridge University Press, 1979.

Stetter, Stephen. *Territorial Conflict in World Society.* New York: Routledge, 2007.

Confucianism

Confucianism and Daoism are the indigenous religious philosophies of China. (In this context, China refers to a geographical and cultural region, rather than a political state.) Buddhism, while not indigenous to the region, was imported from India and is practiced in some areas. Chinese culture and religion rest upon the pillars of folk religions and Confucian teachings. Confucianism was the preferred philosophy of the scholar officials who administered the dynastic bureaucracy. Daoism offered an alternative to the state Confucian ideology. The peasant farmers practiced their local clan customs, which freely borrowed from Confucian, Daoist, Buddhist, and other traditions. The down-to-earth, worldly character of Chinese philosophies and religions provides a practical approach to the search for value and meaning in human life. Chinese religions and philosophies emphasize the nondual or correlative interaction and interpenetration of complementary opposites. The Chinese worldview stands in contrast to the monistic (the belief that all is one) and dualistic (the belief that reality is split between two opposite forces— good vs. evil, spirit vs. matter) tendencies of the monotheistic religions (e.g., Zoroastrianism, Judaism, Christianity, and Islam).

In Confucianism one important correlative pair of opposites that account for the development of society and culture are *wen* and *wu*. *Wen* refers to literate culture, and *wu* denotes the martial arts. These concepts are also employed in the honorific titles bestowed upon the founding kings of the Zhou dynasty (1122–221 B.C.E.).

The founder of the Zhou dynasty, Wu Wang (the Martial King), bestowed the honorific title of Wen Wang (the Civilized King) upon his father and made him the hereditary founder of the Zhou. The violence of martial arts is pivotal to establishing a dynasty and promoting the civilized, literary culture. The opposing forces of wen and wu operate in a fashion similar to yin and yang in that they are interrelated, complementary opposites that interact and transform things and people. Chinese culture has permitted various forms of violence, such as warfare, corporal and capital forms of punishment, hunting, sacrifice, and revenge killing. Generally speaking, the teachings of Confucianism accept violence as a fact of life. The Confucian texts generally attempt to sanction violence by allowing only the ruler or emperor to promulgate war and to commission judges who punish criminals.

The term *Confucianism* is used to refer to three related but different systems of thought. First, in its narrow sense, Confucianism denotes the teaching of Confucius (551–479 B.C.E.). It is also used to refer to the beliefs and practices of the followers of Confucius. In this sense Confucianism is used as a translation of the term *rujia*, which refers to the Literati school of philosophy. Finally, the term is used very broadly to refer to the Chinese dynastic system, because the Chinese dynasties accepted Confucianism as the state religion.

Confucius

The name Confucius is a transliteration of Kongfuzi (which means "grand master Kong"). The man referred to as Confucius was originally named Kong Qiu, stylized as Zhongni. Despite his importance, we know very little about him. Most of the alleged biographical material, written centuries after his death, is not trustworthy, and only a few facts are clear. He was born into a minor aristocratic family in the state of Lu (located in modern Shandong Province). He was three years old when his father died.

By the age of seventeen, he was supporting his mother. He married at nineteen, though we know nothing about his wife. The couple had two daughters and one son. He held a minor office in Lu. He was promoted to be a magistrate at the age of fifty-one and then minister of justice in the same year. Discouraged in Lu, at the age of fifty-six he and his closest disciples traveled to other states in search of a worthy ruler who would implement his teachings. After twelve years, he returned to Lu and began to teach there. Because his teachings rely upon the six classics (the books of *History, Poetry, and Changes; Spring and Autumn Annals; Record of Rites;* and the *Book of Music,* which is now lost), it has been incorrectly assumed that he edited or wrote them. It is claimed that he had 3,000 students. Seventy-two of them mastered his teachings, and only twenty-two were close disciples. His immediate disciples compiled a record of his teachings known as the *Analects* (*Lunyǔ*), and later disciples and followers added to that text. Confucius loved to study and learn from ancient documents, and he expected his students to be just as dedicated to learning as he was. He hoped to reform the Zhou dynasty, but he did not find a worthy ruler who would implement his teachings. He probably died thinking he had failed.

After his death, Confucius underwent a process of apotheosis (being made into a god). By the time of Mengzi (372–289 B.C.E.), he was referred to as a sage. Emperors of the Han dynasty (206 B.C.E.–208 C.E.) sacrificed at his tomb, which became a shrine and later a temple. In 1 C.E. the imperial title of duke was bestowed on him. In 637, he was given the title foremost teacher. He was called king in 739 and perfect sage in 1013. By 1906, the ritual for the emperor on high was performed in the name of Kongfuzi. Though he could not save the faltering Zhou dynasty, the school of thought that emerged around him and his followers continues to shape Chinese culture, society, and politics.

Confucian Teachings

Confucius organized his curriculum around the six arts: ritual, music, calligraphy, mathematics, and two martial arts—archery and charioteering. In his time, war was still primarily an aristocratic adventure. His teachings are practical in nature. He emphasized the moral virtues that would solidify a community, a society, and a state, such as human kindness, ritual action, rightness, moral wisdom, trustworthiness, filial piety, and so on. Empathy (*shu*)—defined as "never doing to another what you do not desire"—is the one-word summary of his teachings (*Analects* 12/2 and 15/24). Confucius's main project was to stop the spread of political chaos by conserving the noble traditions of the early Zhou dynasty. Ritual action was the panacea to end the violence of political chaos.

By his own admission, Confucius did not study military affairs (*Analects* 15/1), but he proposed that before engaging in battle an efficacious person should train the troops for seven years (13/29) and that to send people into battle without proper training is betrayal (13/30). When asked about effective government, Confucius proposed that sufficient food, sufficient troops, and the people's confidence in their leaders were important. When asked to rank these, he replied that the troops were the least important, food was next, but without the people's trust in their leaders, there was no hope (12/7). He said warfare, illness, and ritual fasting were to be approached with caution (7/13).

Confucius praised the prime minister of the state of Qi, Guan Zhong (d. 645 B.C.E.), who served under Duke Huan of Qi (r. 685–643 B.C.E.), first for assisting Duke Huan in serving as the lord protector and maintaining peace in the empire (14/16), and then for taking military action against and repelling the Di tribe

(14/17). Confucius proposed that when the people of the empire possess the Way, ritual propriety, music, and punitive expeditions are initiated by the emperor (16/2). In this regard Confucius followed an ancient concept of sanctioned violence, namely that a virtuous ruler may have to resort to violence to maintain or reestablish peace and order in a community or empire.

The concept of sanctioned violence is embedded in the practices of the Shang (1766–1122 B.C.E.) and Zhou dynasties and in the ancient literature that Confucius drew upon. The basic idea was to maintain peace and order in the community, state, and empire by promoting close interpersonal relationships that are managed by codes of conduct and virtue ethics, especially ritual propriety and proper deportment. An analogy was drawn between the family and the state such that the ruler was referred to as "the father and mother of the people." Just as the family patriarch might have to impose punishment on the women and children, so too the ruler might have to punish the ministers and the common people when they did not behave properly. The emperor might have to deploy punitive expeditions against the feudal lords, rebels, or tribal peoples.

The ancient texts and documents that Confucius based his teachings upon, which were referred to later as the five classics (wujing), support the ruler's right to punish his subjects and to engage in warfare. The concept of sanctioned violence is tied to another Confucian concept concerning the interaction of heaven and humanity, later referred to as the unity of heaven and man (tianren heyi). The books of History and Poetry contain passages that promote the notion that the ruler is justified in punishing criminal subjects and engaging in warfare. These texts develop the concept of Heaven's Mandate (tianming), which was used to justify the right to rule. The Book of History relates how the tyrant Jie,

the last ruler of the Xia kingdom, was a vile and corrupt ruler and says that King Tang was justified in rebelling against him to establish the Shang dynasty. The dynastic cycle repeats itself, and King Zhou, the last ruler of the Shang, was an evil tyrant who had to be vanquished by the Martial King who founded the Zhou dynasty. The five classics accept violence as a basic fact of life and warfare as an inevitable fact of rulership. They seek to control such violence through clan and state sanctions.

In chapter two of the Book of Changes, an ancient divination text, there is an interesting passage about the lines of the Kun, or Receptive, hexagram, which describes the importance of not allowing ill will to develop because it can result in domestic violence, even murder. The Book of Changes was consulted before engaging in military campaigns in an attempt to ensure victory. The Spring and Autumn Annals is a historical record of the state of Lu. The Annals and its three commentaries—the Gongyang, the Guliang, and the Zuozhuan—were read for moral guidance in the art of rulership by following the examples set by good rulers and avoiding the mistakes made by tyrants. The Zuozhuan contains a number of interesting battle descriptions and expresses the importance of keeping one's word in military matters.

It is unlikely that the extant Record of Rites existed during Confucius's time, but the ritual sacrifice of animals was a long-standing practice that further sanctioned violence. Imperial mandates to punish criminals, oppress rebellions, and deploy punitive expeditions were extensions of the emperor's ritual action. The Record of Rites details the imperial rituals and contains essays on moral self-cultivation. Ritual and self-cultivation are offered as the civilized alternative to violence and warfare. These texts began the development of what can be called the calendar of violence, namely that the seasons, especially the autumn and winter, are the appropriate time for hunting, punishing criminals, and deploying troops. In an agrarian economy, it is important not to destroy the fields and crops before the autumn harvest. By analogy, just as the farmer cuts down the crop at harvest, autumn begins the season for criminal executions and punitive expeditions.

Confucius's son, grandson, and disciples carried his ideas forward and expanded them, and the school of thought called the Literati emerged from his teaching.

The Confucians

The last part of the Zhou dynasty, from the fifth century B.C.E. to Qin's unification of the empire in 221 B.C.E., is known as the Warring States period. During this time, warfare was no longer an aristocratic affair. Military achievement became an avenue for social mobility. The amount of bloodshed continued to grow. For example, in 363 B.C.E., 60,000 heads were taken in the battle between Qin and Wei. In 316, 80,000 heads were taken when Qin defeated Zhao and Han. In 311, 80,000 heads were taken when Qin attached Chu, and the lists go on.

A third-generation disciple of Confucius, Mengzi developed his teachings, expanding their humanitarian focus. Mengzi's disciples compiled his teachings in a book that bears his name. Mengzi was well aware of the increased suffering of the common people during his time. He stressed the importance of an equitable distribution of resources, especially food, and he emphasized the importance of the people's livelihood. He strongly criticized those rulers who did not care for and benefit their people as the foundation for a tranquil state. Mengzi argued that humans are basically good by nature and that the human heart cannot bear the suffering of others. He advocated that a worthy ruler base his policies on moral virtues, rather than the expectation of gain or profit seeking.

Going beyond Confucius, Mengzi proposed that the ruler serves the people and holds the throne because of the people. The people must support the ruler and his policy, or the state will collapse. Mengzi expanded the concept of the Mandate of Heaven to include the people's support. Hence, revolt was seen as evidence that the mandate had been lost. The ideal is that the heart that cannot bear the suffering of others would not perpetrate acts of violence unless such acts were sanctioned by the state and employed to rectify the people's suffering. Mengzi's teachings were canonized by the Song dynasty neo-Confucian Zhu Xi (1130–1200 C.E.) when he codified the four books, namely, the *Analects, Mengzi,* and two chapters from the *Record of Rites*—the *Great Learning,* and *Centrality and Commonality* (sometimes translated as the *Doctrine of the Mean*). In ancient times, the teachings of Xunzi (fl. 310–220 B.C.E.) were more widely accepted by the Literati.

The Warring States period is also known as the era of the Hundred Schools, because of the proliferation of various philosophies attempting to bring social harmony to the chaotic age. The Daoists sought to follow the way of nature to bring about harmony. The philosopher Mozi (c. 470–391 B.C.E.) advocated universal love and the use of defensive warfare. The Agriculturalists sought a return to a simple agrarian life. The Militarists offered their skills, tactics, and strategy. The Legalists acknowledged the importance of both agriculture and the military to stabilize a state, advocating the strict enforcement of rewards and punishments instead of moral virtue and self-cultivation. Xunzi advanced the practical character of Confucian thought by drawing on the various other schools. Borrowing from Daoism, he argued for a naturalistic interpretation of heaven (*tian*) as nature. Borrowing from the Agriculturalists and Legalists, he recognized the importance of managing agrarian resources. Borrowing from the Militarists and

Legalists, he placed greater emphasis on the importance of the military in protecting and managing the state than Confucius or Mengzi. Contra Mengzi, Xunzi argued that humans were basically socially deviant or selfish by nature. Hence, education, especially being well educated in performing the moral virtues and ritual action, was of the utmost importance for Xunzi. He demythologized the concept of the past golden age by arguing that the past and the present are basically the same. He argued that a contemporary ruler could not govern successfully by blindly following the alleged policies of the ancient sage kings. Although he gave more attention to the military, he maintained a moral or Confucian focus by advocating that the military must be led by a virtuous ruler and virtuous generals who deploy troops in a just or righteous war. He maintained the traditional concept of state-sanctioned violence.

Han Dynasty Confucianism

After Qin unified the empire in 221 B.C.E., the first emperor and his Legalist prime minister, Li Si, mounted a campaign against the moral teachings of the various schools, which were seen as a threat. In 213 B.C.E., the emperor issued an edict to burn books in private libraries that discussed morality. Among the Confucian classics only the *Book of Changes* was spared. The other classics were reconstructed from memory and fragments after the Han dynasty was founded. The third emperor of the Han, the Martial Emperor Wudi (r. 141–87 B.C.E.), was a patron of both Confucianism and Daoism. Under Wudi imperial colleges were established to promote the study of the reconstructed five classics. Although Wudi was attracted to Daoism and the quest for immortality, he sponsored a type of Confucianism with supernatural tendencies as the state religion. He revived and embellished ancient sacrificial rites to heaven and earth. He also led expeditions against the tribal peoples, expanding the boarders of the Han empire.

Dong Zhongshu (c. 179–104 B.C.E.) rose to prominence under Wudi. Dong specialized in the *Spring and Autumn Annals* and its *Gongyang* commentary. He authored a book entitled the *Luxuriant Dew of the Spring and Autumn Annals,* which promotes an eclectic social and political philosophy based on Confucian moral principles that are woven into a highly speculative and supernatural cosmology based on Daoist and especially Yinyang Five Phases (*wuxing*) theory. Dong correlated five Confucian virtues with the five phases. He sought to end the debates concerning the interactions of heaven and humans, especially the ruler, and his analysis placed some heavenly controls on the emperor's despotism. Employing the Yinyang Five Phases theory, he aligned virtue with the life-giving powers of yang and punishment with the yin. Following Confucius's agenda, he placed greater emphasis on virtue than on punishment. He correlated the Five Phases with the five offices, namely the ministries of agriculture, war, works, instruction, and justice. Dong revitalized the dialectic of the literary/martial (*wen/wu*) dynamic in Yinyang Five Phases terminology. His scheme accounts for violence as a natural outcome of the interaction of both cosmic and political-institutional forces. He also justifies the ruler's use of sanctioned violence in the form of punishments or punitive expeditions. Dong is famous for noting that it would be far better to have no wars, but there are just wars. After the Han, there was a period of political chaos, and Confucianism was threatened by Daoism and Buddhism. Confucianism was revitalized in the Song dynasty (960–1279 C.E.).

Neo-Confucianism

After the Tang dynasty (618–907), China entered a short period of political chaos known as the Five Dynasties (907–960). Various ethnic groups were vying for political control, especially in northern China and Central Asia. By the founding of the Song dynasty, the Liao controlled parts of the north. Then the Jurchen began to apply pressure, and they forced the Song to move south of the Yangzi River to what became the southern capital in Nanjing. The sustained military conflict affected neo-Confucian thinkers. Military prowess was a means for social mobility, and many young men were attracted to a military career. For example, as a young man the neo-Confucian Zhang Zai (1020–1077) was developing a career in the military until a scholar official, Fan Zhongyuan (989–1052), encouraged him to focus on the transmission of the Confucian teachings. Neo-Confucianism absorbed concepts and practices from Daoism and Buddhism. Zhu Xi (1130–1200) was the great synthesizer of Song neo-Confucian thought. He systematized the teachings of Zhou Dunyi (1017–1073), Zhang Zai, Cheng Hao (1032–1085), and his brother Cheng Yi (1033–1107) into a comprehensive philosophy. Because his philosophy relied heavily on the Cheng brothers' teachings, it is referred to as the Cheng-Zhu philosophy.

Zhu revitalized interest in the five classics, and he codified the four books, which then served as the basis for the civil service examinations until the twentieth century. Zhu was an official himself, and so he was drawn to practical solutions. He countered the common academic view that scholars should not concern themselves with economic and military matters by proposing that the scholars were the people best prepared to manage such affairs. Following the teachings of Confucius and Mengzi, he maintained that moral training and self-cultivation were of the utmost importance. He also maintained the traditional view that only state-sanctioned violence in the form of punishing criminals and punitive expeditions commanded

by the emperor was permissible. Zhu's intellectual and rational approach was countered by that of Lu Xiangshan (1139–1193). Lu taught a more experiential, less scholastic, approach that emphasized the unit of mind. It was the Cheng-Zhu teachings that influenced the subsequent development of Confucian thinking in China as well as in Korea and Japan. However, Zhu Xi's strategy for strengthening the Song and negotiating with the Jurchen was not applied, opening an opportunity for the Mongols to invade a century later.

After the Mongol Yuan dynasty (1271–1368), the ethnic Han Chinese regained the empire by establishing the Ming dynasty (1368–1644). The founder of the Ming, Zhu Yuanzhang (1328–1398), was an able military leader and a practical administrator who valued education and schooling. He stabilized education and the civil service exam system. Before Zheng He (1371–1435) was commissioned to embark on his ocean voyages to Southeast Asia, India, and Africa, he was assigned to quell revolts in western China. Zheng employed typical espionage tactics: he would infiltrate a rebel group, gain their trust, breed resentment and distrust among them, and even assassinate a leader. He was not a disciple of or advocate for the Confucian teachings. He was a Ming dynasty official, and his military approach displays the expedient approach of a military mind. Wang Yangming (1472–1529) was the great neo-Confucian scholar of the Ming period. He was a Confucian with Buddhist influences. Borrowing from Confucianism, he argued for the fundamental unity of nature and humanity, and he placed emphasis on human kindness. Like many Confucians of his day, he was influenced by Buddhism and practiced meditation, and the concept of mind played a major role in his philosophy. He maintained the practical focus of Confucian teachings, arguing for the unity of knowledge and action. Wang was a controversial figure and held a checkered career. From 1516 to 1519, he was ordered to suppress several rebellions. He was well acquainted with the military treatises, and he quoted them in his writings. In part, his success in quelling revolts was due to his humanitarian efforts. He rehabilitated the rebels, built schools, and generally improved the economy in the areas affected by the rebellions, thereby stabilizing those regions.

During the Manchu Qing dynasty (1644–1912), Confucian scholars were carefully monitored, controlled, and even imprisoned. At the founding of the Qing, a young Confucian scholar, Wang Fuzhi (1619–1692), organized a small army and attempted to restore the Ming when the Manchu began to invade his native province of Hunan in 1648. He was defeated and withdrew into the mountains to spend his life writing philosophy. He developed a philosophical materialism and opposed Song and Ming Confucianism for not being practical enough. Another Confucian scholar, Yan Yuan (1635–1704) studied fencing and military arts as a young man. He criticized Song and Ming Confucianism, especially attacking Zhu Xi. He promoted a type of learning by experience and also attacked scholarship and book learning. His thinking was not very profound, and he did not leave a lasting impression. Perhaps the greatest neo-Confucian of the Qing was Dai Zhen (1723–1777). Dai rejected the intellectual speculations of Zhu Xi and the introspection of Wang Yangming. He focused on objective evidence gained from the study of natural, everyday phenomena. Kang Youwei (1858–1927) attempted to apply Confucianism for much needed reform at the end of the Qing dynasty. He attempted to petition the emperor not to accept a peace treaty with the Japanese in 1895. After the Qing collapsed, Kang attempted to have Confucianism accepted as the state religion. He also attempted to restore the deposed Xuantong

emperor (r. 1909–1912) to the throne in 1917. Kang wanted to apply Confucian teachings to the practical political problems of his day. In his *Book of Great Unity,* he revitalized an ancient concept from Dong Zhongshu: that human history develops through three ages. Kang argued that the Confucian concept of human kindness is the basic material of the universe as ether or electricity. He said that history progresses from an age of chaos and disorder to the age of small peace. Out of the age of small peace will come the age of great peace and unity, in which all nations will be united and peace and harmony will prevail. In the age of great unity, all human suffering will cease.

The Confucian State

For well over 2,000 years, Confucius was praised as the great sage teacher. Many scholars aligned their ideas with his. After Wudi institutionalized the Confucian academy in the Han dynasty and promoted Confucianism as the state ideology and religion, many subsequent dynasties made Confucianism the state ideology and religion. The scholar officials who served as ministers in the dynastic bureaucracy were for the most part Confucians. They were schooled in the five classics and the four books according to the interpretations of one of the various schools of Confucianism. At first scholars were recommended by high officials or summoned by the emperor to serve as ministers because they had a reputation for practicing one or more of the Confucian virtues, such as loyalty or filial piety. After the Han dynasty, passing the civil service examination became the common method for entering government service. The civil service exam consisted of writing essays interpreting the Confucian classics. However, this dynastic or state Confucianism was removed from the humanistic ideals of Confucius. A large, multiethnic empire cannot operate successfully based on humanistic ideals alone. The ideal of Confucius and Mengzi served as the model for the dynasties—of the utopian values they hoped to promote, but the day-to-day operations of the dynastic government required more mundane practices. State Confucianism was a hybrid, eclectic system of theory and practice that drew upon the various other religio-philosophies and technologies available. As noted above, the type of Confucianism promoted by Dong Zhongshu that became the Han dynasty ideology was an amalgamation of various aspects of Confucianism blended with Daoist, Yinyang, and Legalist concepts. In addition to the challenges of human aggression and violence, the Confucian ministers had to control the hydraulics of the Yellow River floods. They had to manage trade, iron and salt production, distribution of grain and other commodities. The Confucian state could not adequately stabilize or defend itself with moral values alone. The dynastic system depended on legalist and militarist concepts and practices as much as on Confucianism.

The above-mentioned espionage methods employed by Zheng He were the state norm. As young men, many of the Confucian ministers had been attracted to martial arts. Many of them studied the military classics, such as Sunzi's *Art of War*. The ancient military text, called the *Wuzi*, advocates that just or righteous warfare is the highest form of military action. The *Wuzi* employs many Confucian concepts in developing its art of war. The ancient legal codes originated in the military camps, where strict adherence to rules of order was required. Each dynasty developed a legal system with severe forms of torture, corporal, and capital punishment, such as blinding by piercing the eye; branding the face; amputating the nose, hand, foot, or leg; and various forms of execution by slicing, burning, hanging, strangulation, decapitation, drawing and quartering, and so

on. Militarily, the Chinese developed various forms of offensive and defensive warfare. From ancient times an array of military weapons was developed—for example, all types of long and short swords, daggers, spears, halberds, compound bows, and trigger-operated crossbows. The ancient Chinese were masters in developing lightweight body armor. They employed fire and water in military tactics and were known to burn or flood a city to conquer it. Although Chinese gunpowder was primarily used in fireworks to frighten away hungry ghosts at folk ceremonies, the Chinese did use rockets and early rifles, or fire sticks, in battle. Confucian moral values were needed to restrain their use in perpetrating violence.

State Confucianism ended with the Qing dynasty. Because Confucian values shaped East Asian cultures for over 2,000 years, they continue to inspire political order in Singapore, Korea, and Japan. In the twentieth century Chinese intellectuals began to focus more and more on democratic and republican forms of government as opposed to the traditional "Confucian" monarchy. They were also attracted to science and technology. Mao Tse-tung (1893–1976) founded the Communist Party in 1921 and united the country in 1949. The Communist Party seriously critiqued Confucianism and all traditional forms of class oppression and domination. Confucian temples were turned into Communist Party buildings. During the 1960s and 1970s intellectuals were reeducated in Communist Party ideology. In the 1990s, however, party members began to restore the significance of Confucius. The Confucian ideology had been preserved in Korea, Japan, Taiwan, Singapore, and other places. After World War II, Chinese scholars began to refer to twentieth-century interpretations of Confucianism as New Confucianism to distinguish it from the neo-Confucianism of Zhu Xi and the Song, Ming, and Qing. Because Confucian philosophy acknowledges violence as a basic fact of human life and offers peaceful forms of conflict resolution and state-sanctioned and controlled violence in the form of criminal punishments and warfare, it is likely that New Confucianism will continue to contribute to global philosophy.

James D. Sellmann

See also: Asia, Central; Buddhism; Daoism/Taoism; Jainism; Shintoism.

Further Reading

Allen, Douglas, ed. *Comparative Philosophy and Religion in Times of Terror.* Lanham, MD: Lexington Books, 2006.

Ames, Roger T., and Henry Rosemont Jr. *The Analects of Confucius: A Philosophical Translation.* New York: Ballantine Books, 1998.

Chan, Wing-tsit. *A Source Book in Chinese Philosophy.* Princeton, NJ: Princeton University Press, 1963.

Legge, James. *The Chinese Classics.* 5 vols. Hong Kong: University of Hong Kong, 1960.

Lewis, Mark Edward. *Sanctioned Violence in Early China.* Albany: State University of New York Press, 1990.

Nylan, Michael. *The Five Confucian Classics.* New Haven, CT: Yale University Press, 2001.

Thompson, Kirill O. "Confucian Perspectives on War and Terrorism." In *Comparative Philosophy and Religion in Times of Terror,* ed. Douglas Allen, pp. 195–209. Lanham, MD: Lexington Books, 2006.

Conscientious Objection

On the basis of his research and experiences as a member of a tribunal during World War II, the philosopher G.C. Field concluded that "conscientious objection is not one single simple creed, but a number of creeds, based on widely different and sometimes diametrically opposed general principles. This obviously makes the task of critical evaluation particularly difficult" (Field 1945). This task is even more challenging today because of the increasingly differentiated uses of the "conscientious objector" label. While in Field's time the term was understood to refer to someone who refused participation in armed combat, today the term is applied to ever more diverse instances of informed noncompliance.

Although there are primordial examples of pacifist beliefs interacting with military systems prior to modernity—such as between pre-Constantine Christianity and the Roman Empire or in the case of over 2,000 years of nonviolent traditions in India—it took a special confluence of factors to create the conscientious objector proper. Those conditions were present at the time of the Reformation in Europe as the state building project, with its imperative for mass military mobilization, interacted with diverse expressions of religiosity. In particular, due to the manner in which they defined their identity outside of the emerging "state backed by force" dichotomy, select groups of radical reformers can be considered the first conscientious objectors.

Post-Reformation Christian Denominations and Peace Witness

The earliest written form of the Anabaptist peace witness (one who addresses the issues of violence with the tenets of Christian faith, such as worship, prayer, and prophetic direct action) is traced back to the first known Swiss Brethren joint document, the Schleitheim Confession of 1527, which extolled both nonresistant pacifism and the separation of church and state. Although former Dutch Catholic priest Menno Simons himself was not always consistent in the duty to refrain from combat, once he was rebaptized (c. 1536) his Anabaptist followers, who due to his significant influence in the Low Countries became known as Mennonites, soon made nonviolence a tenet of their faith. In the wars associated with Dutch nation building, the Mennonites were able to gain exemptions to conscripted service by such actions as making large "free gifts" of money to the House of Orange, paying for substitutes, and performing civil defense functions like digging trenches.

Across the North Sea, in 1660–1661, the

Society of Friends (the Quakers) presented a declaration to the English king. Their collective position was clear: as part of their belief in the innate equality of human beings, tools of violence were never to be employed by a Quaker. Expulsion from the religious community was, henceforth, the consequence for any Quaker, or Friend, who embraced violence. In that period, when Quaker conscientious objectors were detained by the infamous Royal Navy press gangs, anger and punishment were often directed against Friends by commanding officers. On board ships, nonviolent resistance by Quakers ranged from total noncompliance to helping the wounded in times of battle. Quakers who persisted in their noncompliance and endured a certain amount of punishment from Royal Navy captains and crews were often eventually let off the ships by commanding officers who viewed them as bad for morale.

The American Civil War—cast as it was by the Unionist side as a battle for emancipation—proved morally problematic for many Mennonites, Quakers, and other would-be conscientious objectors due to their intense commitment to egalitarianism. Even members of those traditional peace churches were tempted to bear arms to fight for the end of slavery. At the same time, other churches were forced to come to clear conclusions about the nature of their peace witnessing. Emerging as a distinct denomination in the 1850s, Seventh Day Adventism, with its geographical distribution in the northern U.S. states and its deep abolitionist roots, debated the validity of declaring itself a pacifist church. By 1864, the issue was settled, and the church leadership sought to gain guarantees from various levels of government that their church membership would be recognized as pacifist and thus eligible for conscientious objector status, along with the historic peace churches. Previously, a movement had been under way to pool the resources of the Seventh

Day Adventist membership to pay the $300 fee to exempt a member from the Unionist draft. This system broke down due to lack of financial means in the church at the time. However, the legacy of the Seventh Day Adventists' campaign in the 1860s was a new argument for conscientious exemption based not just on the Bible's sixth commandment prohibition against killing but also on the fourth commandment, because Sabbath keeping was an important element of their faith.

Even the Quakers, who held a strong claim to being among the most effective peace advocates in the United States at the time of the Civil War, faced dissension in regard to all their male members seeking conscientious objector status. Indeed, many Quakers felt that their informed conscience told them to support the war as a means to free the slaves in the southern states. It followed that even while their leadership was engaged in a campaign for total exemption, many Quakers elected to pay the commutation fee when drafted, which, strictly speaking, was against their principles of peace witness; after 1864 legislation provided another option, to work with emancipated slaves behind Unionist lines in an active form of conscientious objection or even enlist in the medical corps. The peace witness of the Quakers was further fragmented by the fact that many male members chose to voluntarily enlist in the Union army. In Indiana, for example, 1,212 Quakers volunteered for combat duty. After the fighting had ended, 238 of those men were dead, 220 apologized for their actions and were allowed to rejoin their communities, 148 were disowned, and it appears that the remaining 608 quietly returned to Quaker life. The peace testimony of the Quakers had been transformed by the Civil War. In the main, the Society of Friends was no longer willing to use the full force of disciplinary action against dissenters. As a result, assent to the peace testimony was increasingly considered a matter of individual conscience to be respected by the larger Quaker community.

Rights to Conscientious Objection in Law and Policy

With the turn of the century, Australia became the first country to enact permanent conscientious objector legislation. As a result, in 1903, the norm of allowing members of the historic peace churches special consideration in obtaining conscientious objector status based on religious belief first received the sanction of enduring codified law. During the next decade, World War I marked the institution of mass tribunal systems in the Western democracies. In the United Kingdom, whether or not to include conscientious objector clauses in the conscription legislation had been a matter of some debate. The tribunal mechanism was meant to verify claims of conscience that could in theory include secular motivations, such as a belief in the pacifist imperatives of international socialism.

Despite this liberal framing of their duty, tribunal members were most often selected on the basis of their patriotism (prowar Quakers and Labour Party members who supported the conflict were a "hot commodity" in this regard). When thousands more applications for conscientious objector status than had been expected were received, many tribunal members began to fear that if they did not stem the tide of men being exempted from combat, Britain might lose the war. The result was that despite their ability to grant total exemptions, that outcome was rare in a tribunal ruling. Many Quakers who could demonstrate lifelong commitments to their faith had their conscientious objector claims denied. The interchange that took place at these meetings often betrayed a bias of the tribunal members against pacifist Christianity. Conscientious objectors were quoted passages from the Bible such as Matthew 10:34 in which

Jesus is reported to have said: "I come not to bring peace, but to bring a sword" and then asked to respond. In one case a claimant was asked if he believed that Jesus's blood forgave sins; when he answered in the affirmative, he was asked why he did not, therefore, believe that he would be forgiven if he participated in the war.

Working within more communitarian dynamics during the Russian involvement in World War I, Mennonites were able to convince the czar's government to allow their community to fund and organize alternative service. For 8,000 Mennonite men, this took the form of a frontline medical corps supported by medical trains that transported the wounded from the front to fully staffed hospitals in Moscow and Ekaterinoslav. Continuing a tradition dating back to 1881, another 4,000 Mennonites worked in self-funded forestry camps. The transformation of the Russian Empire into the Soviet Union brought an end to those arrangements and caused many in Soviet Mennonite communities to immigrate to North or South America, where they were resident when the next global conflict erupted.

New Tensions in the Context of World War II

The discord between a country's domestic policy, recognizing a right to conscientious objection, and allowing individuals to avail themselves of that right is evident in the case of World War II conscientious objectors who were citizens of the Western Allied powers. For the most part, the days of blanket amnesties from conscription had passed. During the period of the war, an apparently able-bodied male walking down the street in a Western democracy without a uniform would have been viewed with suspicion. The fact that the war was cast as a battle between good and evil did not help matters when tribunal members sub-

A religious leader pickets outside the White House on October 1, 1946, protesting the imprisonment of conscientious objectors during World War II. Among other groups, Quakers, Mennonites, and Jehovah's Witnesses refused conscription on religious grounds and were either arrested or forced into alternative service to the state during wartime. *(Marie Hansen/Time Life Pictures/Getty Images)*

scribed to such a framing of the conflict. For instance, Jehovah's Witnesses, who were often absolute in their conviction that they could not aid the war in any manner, clashed with the point of view that sincere conscientious objectors had to avoid charges of laziness by giving some form of service to the state. The Jehovah's Witnesses' case was further complicated by the fact that it was state-sanctioned violence and not all violence that their faith condemned. For this reason, Jehovah's Witnesses posed a major problem for government conscientious objector programs based on alternative service and often faced long prison terms and discrimination while serving their sentences.

Also during this time, Canadian Menno-

nites—groups of whom had been granted exemption from military service in perpetuity as a condition of immigration in the 1870s—found that community-based exemptions, including those to participate in essential agricultural production, were difficult to obtain when surrounded by a mass English-speaking society that supported conscription. Such exceptions had been granted routinely during World War I. The fact that many of their educational and faith organizations used a form of the German language did not help matters when individual Mennonites were brought before certain conscientious objector tribunals. Of the 126 Mennonite conscientious objector claims that were heard by the Saskatchewan tribunal during 1941, 70 were refused. The official record reveals that those rejections were often based on affirmative answers to what today would be considered entrapping or even irrelevant questions. For instance, one application for conscientious objector status was rejected on the basis that the claimant could not be a pacifist because he had once participated in a schoolyard "scrap."

A generation later, the Vietnam War was noteworthy for the way it brought to the fore the issue of selective conscientious objection—conscientious objectors were allowed to weigh the merits of an individual war and determine their participation based on those merits. In 1967, three years after winning the Nobel Prize for Peace, Martin Luther King Jr. connected issues of peace, civil rights, conscientious objection, and social justice in calling for an end to the Vietnam conflict. By 1970, most Christian denominations were advocating for a principle of selective conscientious objection. However, the example of the churches and other arguments based on the Constitution failed to convince the United States Supreme Court, which upheld the principle that a conscientious objector must be opposed to all wars. It is in that struggle for the recognition of a right to selective conscientious objection that the activist debates continue in Western democratic countries.

Emerging Trends in International and Domestic Norms

In terms of international norms, the United Nations Humans Rights Commission (UNHRC) believes that article 18 of the *International Covenant on Civil and Political Rights* establishes a right of conscientious objection. As such, it insists that conscientious objectors cannot be discriminated against either for their refusal to perform military service or for the basis of their beliefs. In 1987, when the UNHRC passed its first resolution recognizing a universal right of conscientious objection, the votes cast were indicative of a divide between Western democracies, who almost all voted in favor of the resolution, and more totalitarian regimes such as Iran, Iraq, and the People's Republic of China, which were adamantly opposed to the idea. The vote distribution mirrors the expansion of domestic law–based norms that support the principle of conscience-based objections to military service.

An example of jurisprudence at the junction of religiosity and conscientious objection is found in the European Court of Human Rights' recent ruling that a Jehovah's Witness who had refused military service in Greece and served two years in prison as a result could not be barred from the accounting profession in that country because of his conviction. That ruling was made on the grounds that no other option for service was made available to the petitioner that would have allowed him to effectively exercise his religion at the time of his sentencing.

Casting conscientious objection in that manner places the issue in the realm of individual human rights and thus, in a real sense, divorces such exemption for pacifist witness from its original religious and communitarian roots in the traditional peace churches. It should

be noted, however, that the "just war" tradition, in so much as it advocates judging the merits of each case, could be deemed a form of selective conscientious objection when it results in a pacifist conclusion in any given instance of moral deliberation. Accordingly, for example, the principles of Roman Catholic morality hold that resistance to unjust wars (discerned as such by an informed conscience) is mandatory. This is a form of peace witness in a mainstream denomination that is buttressed by the shift to individual human rights methodology when reviewing cases. This shift allows adherents of mainstream denominations to cite instances of noncompliance with violence from within their own traditions as part of their individual justifications for a given case of conscientious objection. Since the end of World War II, the task of discernment in this regard has been made easier by the existence of faith-based peace organizations such as the Roman Catholic Pax Christi and the Anglican Peace Fellowship— both of which support individual decisions to conscientiously object and which take a formal stance against involvement in war.

Conscientious Objection in Non-Christian Faith Traditions

Although most of the academic literature on the subject focuses on conscientious objection in terms of Christian and secularized conscience, the term can also be applied in other religious contexts. For instance, the existence of the State of Israel and its military policies has made conscientious objection an issue for Jewish scholars. In Israel only Haredi Jews (commonly identified as "ultraorthodox") are exempted from mandatory service on religious grounds for reasons similar to those for which Palestinian and Negev Bedouin citizens of Israel are also excluded: either ambivalence or hostility to the state itself. There is no officially recognized right of conscientious objection for other Jews. Further, despite Haredi Jews' historic mistrust of the State of Israel, the Israeli Defense Force is now looking to actively attract segments of the Haredi population who are not studying in yeshivas (religious schools) with the programming of the *Netzah Yehuda* Battalion. According to their Web site the Netzah Yehuda Battalion was founded to "provide the Haredi community with a unique opportunity to share the nation's military burden as well as bridging the social gap between the secular and religious populations in Israel"

Earlier, during the war against Lebanon in the 1980s, some soldiers challenged the equation of military virtue with civic virtue through acts of conscientious objection, which called into question the validity of the conflict. In reviewing events surrounding the 2005 Israeli withdrawals from Gaza and northern Samaria, another inference can be made. That year, a former chief rabbi of Israel called on members of the Israeli Defense Force not to comply with disengagement from those territories. Relatively few soldiers heeded the call, while some seem to have negotiated alternative arrangements with their commanding officers. Yet the debate and the court-martial of sixty-three soldiers for noncompliance raised the specter of a significant number of soldiers considering their participation in the specific military actions conditional upon the Israel Defense Forces' order being in accord with Jewish law. This is a noteworthy example because it demonstrates how selective conscientious objection is not necessarily based on a pacific alternative.

Another interesting example of conscientious objection in practice is found in the Nation of Islam in the United States. When the United States had policies of conscription in World War II and the Vietnam War, black Muslims were encouraged by their leadership not to accept a duty to fight in what were deemed racist wars. Famous in this regard is the case of heavyweight boxing champion Muhammad Ali (then Cassius Clay), who refused to be drafted to fight in Southeast Asia on the grounds of conscientious objection.

Broadening Applicability

Perhaps as a consequence of the increasing acceptance of the proposition, implicit in the reasoning behind Ali's objection, that violence has structural and systematic features, there has recently been a broadening of the context in which conscientious objection is applied. Further, in principle, the methodology of conscientious objection could be applied to a variety of cases where the dictates of civil law and firmly held moral scruples conflict. The term itself can be traced to the 1890s, when it was applied to those who refused to participate in mandatory vaccination programs. Reviving the connection with biomedical ethics, for instance, some academic literature speaks of issues of conscientious objection in the provision of emergency contraception by pharmacists and late-term abortions by physicians.

Similarly, the United States Congress has recognized the right of conscientious objection for self-employed Old Order Amish to opt out of the old-age security programs because of their belief that the state should not care for the aged. Citing issues of government stability and functioning, the U.S. Supreme Court was unwilling to interpret this right as further permitting Amish employers to withdraw from the social security system. For similar reasons, the court has been reluctant to extend the principles of conscientious objection to a right to withhold tax revenues based on an objection to war or another moral issue.

This Old Order Amish example is representative of the current trend in the Western democracies in regard to conscientious objection. In this context, the movement has been toward broadening the concept of conscientious objection in both popular use and application. The main path forward in this regard has been through the institution of individual human rights norms, which open a space for conscientious objection based on diverse religious and moral perspectives. If one supports the broadening of the conscientious objection program through such means, a salient issue is how the principle is being applied around the world. Even allowing for a gap between law and practice in the Western democracies and the European exception, it is problematic that very few countries that actively practice conscription effectively recognize a right to conscientious objection with binding legislation. Until this situation is addressed, there remains a major structural barrier preventing the realization of a global order where international human rights norms supportive of principled conscientious objection receive fuller expression in state-based realities. However, it follows that a fuller incarnation of international human rights norms, backed by political will and effective programming, would allow both secular and religious conscientious objectors to remove themselves from armed combat, and perhaps legitimate authentic dissent in other areas.

Christopher Hrynkow

See also: Civil Disobedience.

Further Reading

Brock, P. *Against the Draft: Essays on Conscientious Objection from the Radical Reformation to the Second World War.* Toronto: University of Toronto Press, 2006.

Capizzi, J.E. "Selective Conscientious Objection in the United States." *Journal of Church and State* 38:4 (1996): 339–63.

Chambers, J.W., II. "Conscientious Objectors and the American State from Colonial Times to the Present." In *The New Conscientious Objection: From Sacred to Secular Resistance,* ed. C.C. Moskos and J.W. Chambers II, pp. 23–46. Oxford: Oxford University Press, 1993.

Cohen, C. "Conscientious Objection." *Ethics* 78:4 (1968): 269–79.

Cohen, S.A. "Tensions Between Military Service and Religious Orthodoxy in Israel: Imagined and Real." *Israel Studies* 12:1 (2007): 103–26.

Edge, P.W. *Religion and Law: An Introduction.* Aldershot, UK: Ashgate, 2006.

Field, G.C. *Pacifism and Conscientious Objection.* Cambridge, UK: Cambridge University Press, 1945.

Helman, S. "Negotiating Obligations, Creating Rights: Conscientious Objection and the Redefinition of Citizenship Rights in Israel." *Citizenship Studies* 3:1 (1999): 45–70.

———. "War and Resistance: Israeli Civil Militarism and Its Emergent Crisis." *Constellations* 6:3 (1999): 391–410.

Jackson-Peerce, J. *Minority Rights: Between Diversity and Community.* Cambridge, UK: Polity Press, 2006.

King, Martin Luther, Jr. "The Declaration of Independence from the War in Vietnam." In *Conscience in America: A Documentary History of Conscientious Objection in America, 1757–1967,* ed. L. Schlisssel, pp. 426–38. New York: E.P. Dutton, 1967.

Levi, M., and S. DeTray. "A Weapon Against War: Conscientious Objection in the United States, Australia and France." *Politics and Society* 24:4 (1993): 425–64.

Mellors, C., and J. McKean. "Confronting the State: Conscientious Objection in Western Europe." *Security Dialogue* 13:3 (1982): 227–39.

Moskos, C.C., and J.W. Chambers II. *The New Conscientious Objection: From Sacred to Secular Resistance.* Oxford: Oxford University Press, 1993.

Savulescu, J. "Conscientious Objection in Medicine." *British Medical Journal* 332 (2006): 294–97.

Standfield, J.H., II. "The Dilemma of Conscientious Objection for Afro-Americans." In *The New Conscientious Objection: From Sacred to Secular Resistance,* ed. C.C. Moskos and J.W. Chambers, II, pp. 47–56. Oxford: Oxford University Press, 1993.

Stewart-Winter, T. "Not a Soldier, Not a Slacker: Conscientious Objectors and Male Citizenship in the United States During the Second World War." *Gender and History* 19:3 (2007): 519–42.

Walters, L. "A Historical Perspective on Selective Conscientious Objection." *Journal of the American Academy of Religion.* 41:2 (1973): 201–11.

Coughlin, Father Charles Edward (1891–1979)

Father Charles Edward Coughlin was undoubtedly the first American to use the electronic media, national radio in his case, to spread a message of anti-Semitism and radical property rights. While he rarely appears as more than a historical footnote to the social and political history of the Great Depression and World War II, at its height Coughlin's weekly program commanded an audience of over 40 million listeners, roughly a quarter of the U.S. population. During the mid-1930s, Coughlin was the most widely heard Catholic clergyman in North America. Many of the ideas he espoused—such as the existence of a worldwide Zionist conspiracy, the invalidity of property foreclosures, and the dangers of the federal government— still resonate with a contemporary audience. While seldom quoted or acknowledged today, his sermons are an articulate and seemingly well-thought-out manifesto of right-wing religious extremism. His rise to fame was gradual, his fall quick, and his slide into obscurity an inevitable result of backing the wrong side in World War II.

Early Life

Charles Edward Coughlin was born October 25, 1891, into a solidly middle-class Irish Catholic family in Hamilton, Ontario. At that time Hamilton was the center of the Canadian steel industry and a thoroughly working-class town. When Coughlin was born, his father held a supervisory job at a large bakery. His mother was devoutly religious, and his father had once worked as sexton at St. Mary's Catholic Church in Hamilton. Coughlin's birth was followed fifteen months later by the birth of a sister, who died at three months. The effects of the sister's death are hard to gauge at a distance, but the events seem to have pushed a religious family deeper into religious belief, perhaps pathologically so.

The Coughlins moved to a house adjacent to their church, where the mother attended mass daily. While a student at the parish school, Coughlin frequently served as an altar boy. A good student, he seemed particularly gifted in mathematics. Upon graduation from St. Mary's in 1903, he was sent to St. Michael's College High School in Toronto and upon graduating attended St. Michael's College (part of the University of Toronto), graduating in 1911. His ambition at the time was to enter politics; his parents' goal for him was to enter the priesthood. His final decision was to become both a religious and a secular leader. Toward that goal he entered St. Basil's Seminary, headquarters of the Basilian order for the Archdiocese of Toronto. The Basilian order, which originated in France during the 1820s, was and is dedicated to service to the poor.

At St. Basil's he was drawn to the works of Pope Leo XIII—the so-called working man's pope—who was strongly identified with an early form of social gospel. The social gospel is based on the premise that true Christian charity is heavily vested with a call to action for the achievement of social justice. Having considered the effects of the Industrial Revolution and the early labor and socialist movements, Pope Leo argued that both socialism and capitalism contained major flaws relating to respect for human rights and human dignity. In his 1891 encyclical (a papal letter addressed to all Roman Catholic bishops) titled *Rerum novarum* (Of new things) he clearly delineated the Church's view of the obligations employers had to their workers.

Beginning the Priesthood

Coughlin was ordained a priest of the Basilian order of the Diocese of Toronto in 1916. Rather than entering a pastoral ministry, he was assigned to teach psychology, English, and logic at Assumption College in Sandwich, Ontario (near Detroit, Michigan). Due to an influx of Catholics into Detroit, Coughlin was sent there on weekends to perform pastoral duties. In 1918, the Basilian order was reorganized, and all priests were given the option of taking a vow of poverty or leaving the order. Coughlin elected to leave the order and thus came under direct control of the Archdiocese of Toronto. In 1923, he was incardinated into the Diocese of Detroit and assigned as assistant pastor to a church in Kalamazoo, Michigan. Kalamazoo was not a choice assignment. Coughlin used his growing influence with the hierarchy of the Detroit Diocese to arrange his transfer to St. Leo's in Detroit, a church of some 10,000 congregants. His duties there were primarily to stimulate attendance and giving, at which he excelled. He also developed a reputation for preaching.

In 1926, Bishop Gallagher of Detroit attended the canonization ceremony of Saint Thérèse, the Little Flower of Jesus. Gallagher returned to Detroit with the intent of building a shrine to Saint Thérèse in the Detroit suburb of Royal Oak. There were two problems with that idea. First, there were less than a dozen Catholic families in Royal Oak. Second, Royal Oak was a stronghold of the Michigan Ku Klux Klan. Gallagher handpicked Coughlin to build the Shrine of the Little Flower in Royal Oak as "a missionary oasis in the desert of religious bigotry." The irony is inescapable, as under Coughlin's guidance the new church was to become an electronic beacon of religious bigotry within a few years.

In the meantime he was able to show his flair for organization and publicity. When the Klan burned a cross on the lawn of the church, Coughlin used the headlines to create positive publicity. When a Klan-led funeral procession passed the church, Coughlin interjected himself and somehow ended up leading the graveside prayer. Using his status as a former college baseball player, Coughlin became friends with many players in the Detroit Tigers baseball club and persuaded several of them to attend mass at the shrine. When the New York Yankees came

to Detroit in midsummer of 1926, he persuaded Babe Ruth to attend Sunday morning mass. These actions increased church attendance and his personal celebrity. His next idea, a weekly radio program, was to have profound consequences not only for him and the shrine but for the country as well.

Radio

Coughlin had long been told he was an engaging speaker, and he believed radio could be a showcase for the shrine and his message of social justice. He knew radio was growing rapidly in popularity, especially among the newly prosperous blue-collar Americans of the mid-1920s. His bishop was enthusiastic, as was Leo Fitzpatrick, the Episcopalian station manager of WJR, Detroit's first and leading radio station. Coughlin was given a trial run Sunday afternoon, October 17, 1926. The program received a mildly enthusiastic response, and Coughlin was given the 2 P.M. time slot every Sunday. As the program grew in popularity over the next year, attendance increased at the shrine, as did monetary donations; perhaps more important, Coughlin was becoming famous. In the fall of 1927, his program was broadcast statewide. By the fall of 1929 his sermons were being broadcast in Chicago and Cincinnati, and a new building had been erected to house the shrine.

The foundation of Coughlin's early radio sermons was basic mainstream Catholicism. When economic depression hit in the wake of the stock market crash at the end of October 1929, he began to attack prohibitionist Protestant clergy who to Coughlin's thinking were unconcerned with the social impact of unemployment. He also began to call for government regulation to protect workers from exploitation. For reasons that remain unclear, Coughlin launched a heated attack on communism and socialism during his January 12, 1930, radio sermon, and in the main, the audience stated a clear enthusiasm for the new topic. The following Sunday his sermon was "Christ of the Red Fog," a scathing attack on those who had written criticisms of the previous week's sermon. As he continued his attacks on communism, his popularity soared. During the summer of 1930, he was invited to appear before a congressional committee as an expert on communism. At least in part as a result of his testimony, Coughlin was given a contract by CBS to take his program to a national audience. In the face of the growing economic depression, he returned to preaching the social gospel over CBS, but that soon changed.

The Uses of Economics and Politics

In January 1931, Coughlin began to concentrate his broadcasts on discussing the causes of the Depression. He stated that the major cause of the worldwide economic disaster was the Treaty of Versailles, which he decried as part of an elaborate plot by a group he vaguely identified as "international bankers." He also attacked President Herbert Hoover as an incompetent who was in no way qualified to lead the country. Apparently having read the work of British economist John Maynard Keynes, Coughlin proposed that the solution to America's economic woes was for the government to encourage inflation, which he believed would promote employment and stabilize the economy. Ironically, Keynes was a socialist, part of the group Coughlin associated with communists in his radio sermons. Through those sermons Coughlin soon came to be considered by many Americans an economics expert.

Roosevelt or Ruin!

In late 1931, Coughlin came to the belief that Franklin Delano Roosevelt was the best choice to replace Hoover as president. Using his growing political influence, he was able to meet Roosevelt on a few occasions and strongly supported Roosevelt's nomination as the Democratic presidential candidate at the 1932 National Convention. It is alleged that he originated the campaign slogan "Roosevelt or ruin." With Roosevelt's election, Coughlin was one of three men asked to collaborate in the writing of the president's inaugural speech.

By the fall of 1932, the Depression was at its worst, with roughly 25 percent of the workforce unemployed. Coughlin shifted the blame from international bankers more specifically to Wall Street bankers. Rather than the Treaty of Versailles being the crucible of depression, it was the Wall Street bankers' manipulation of the gold standard that had led to ruin. While he did not refer to those bankers as Jews, the context of his remarks made that implicit.

Anti-Semitism and Populism

Coughlin's subtle anti-Semitism, combined with allegations of personal financial impropriety and his incessant demands to advise the president on the economy, led Roosevelt increasingly to distance himself from Coughlin. While at first Coughlin seemed unbothered by Roosevelt's attitude, he soon began to use his radio program as a platform for attacking Roosevelt's economic policies. In addition, he organized the National Union for Social Justice in December 1934. The organization was strongly populist and nativist with a strong anti–New Deal platform. It was also opposed to property foreclosures against farmers and the urban working class. Much of what Coughlin and the union called for was echoed by the midwestern militia movement during the 1980s.

At the same time that he created the union, Coughlin began voicing his support for the populist Louisiana politician Huey Long for a possible run for the presidency against Roosevelt in 1936. When Long was assassinated in 1935, Coughlin shifted his support to another populist presidential hopeful, William Lemke of North Dakota, the short-lived Union Party's presidential candidate in 1936.

By 1936, Coughlin's radio program was a rant against Roosevelt, the New Deal, and the Jewish bankers. He identified the New Deal with communism and communism with Satan. At the same time, he linked Roosevelt with Jewish bankers, another force he identified as satanic. Eventually, he pointed the finger at both communism and Wall Street as an international Jewish conspiracy. He blamed both the Depression and the Russian Revolution on "international Jewish bankers." He openly praised the policies of Hitler and Mussolini and spoke sympathetically of Franco and his Nationalists and of the Falangists, a political party modeled on the Fascist Party of Mussolini. In addition to his weekly radio program, he launched an overtly anti-Semitic newspaper called *Social Justice,* which, along with various news items, reprinted speeches by Goebbels and other Nazis and excerpts from such anti-Semitic polemics as the *Protocols of the Learned Elders of Zion.*

Support for Hitler

Shortly after the November 1938 Kristallnacht—a night of Nazi-sponsored terrorism against Germany's Jews—Coughlin informed his radio audience that the Nazis were merely exacting vengeance for Jewish persecutions of Christians. As a result, radio stations around the country refused to broadcast his program. In Nazi Germany that action was decried as American persecution of someone telling the "truth" about the Jews. Coughlin quickly became a Nazi hero. The entire episode buttressed allegations that Coughlin was receiving funds from the Nazis.

The Christian Front, a Depression-era version of the militia movement of the 1980s, was organized about this time. The group claimed to have been inspired by Coughlin, and he actively supported it. A now obscure organization, it was perhaps allied with the German American Bund and William Pelley's Silver Shirts, which were active Nazi organizations in the United States at the time. Christian Front members were sometimes referred to as "Father Coughlin's Brown Shirts"—an allusion to Hitler's Brown Shirts, the infamous Storm Troopers. The Christian Front was involved in several protests in New York City, and members allegedly armed themselves for the purpose of killing Jews. The FBI took them seriously enough to raid the organization in January 1940 and jail several members. Coughlin was never implicated in any conspiracy or overt acts but continued to voice his support for the organization.

World War II and Coughlin's Fall into Obscurity

With the outbreak of World War II in Europe, the Federal Communications Commission (FCC) promulgated new regulations intended to curtail controversial political speech, specifically what is now known as "hate speech." Coughlin's last radio broadcast occurred a few weeks after the Nazis invaded Poland on September 1, 1939. Shortly thereafter, the Post Office Department revoked his mailing privileges and thus effectively stopped circulation of *Social Justice.* After the United States entered the war, in December 1941, Coughlin was investigated for sedition by the U.S. Attorney General's office. In 1942, Archbishop of Detroit Edward Mooney, wishing to avoid a scandal, ordered Coughlin to cease his political activity and return to his ministry at the Shrine of the Little Flower, threatening to defrock him should he refuse. Coughlin returned to the shrine and held that post and his peace until retirement in 1966. He died in Bloomfield Hills, Michigan, in 1979.

Legacy

Coughlin is little remembered today even by his political successors; however, his legacy is evident among the extreme Right. Opposition to property foreclosures and suspicion of a Jewish conspiracy controlling the economy were not new even in Coughlin's time, nor was identifying the Jewish people with Satan. Coughlin's contribution to religious extremism was to pioneer the effective use of mass media, both electronic and print, to disseminate his message. His efforts have matured into the widespread use of the Internet to spread messages of anti-Semitism and hate.

M. George Eichenberg

See also: Christian Identity Movement; Christian Right; Christianity.

Further Reading

Catholic Encyclopedia Online. Available: http://www .catholic.org/encyclopedia.

General Jewish Council. *Father Coughlin: His "Facts" and Arguments.* New York: General Jewish Council, 1993.

Levitas, D. *The Terrorist Next Door: The Militia Movement and the Radical Right.* New York: St. Martin's Press, 2002.

Marcus, S. *Father Coughlin: The Tumultuous Life of the Priest of the Little Flower.* Boston: Little, Brown, 1973.

Niebuhr, R. *Love and Justice.* Louisville, KY: Westminster John Knox Press, 1992.

Tull, C. *Father Coughlin and the New Deal.* Syracuse, NY: Syracuse University Press, 1965.

Warren, D. *Radio Priest: Charles Coughlin, the Father of Hate Radio.* New York: Free Press, 1996.

Creativity Movement and Church of the Creator

The Creativity Movement was founded in 1973 by Ben Klassen, a former Florida state legislator and chairman of George Wallace's 1968 presidential campaign. The ideology of this religion was achieved through a deification of Hitler, and his book *Mein Kampf* blended with Norse heroic warrior myths. Klassen considered the former Nazi Party and governmental organization a model structure for the future development of Creativity. Grounded in a kind of social Darwinism and core to Creativity's ideology is the belief that the white race is nature's finest creation. According to Creativity, this is evident in the fact that the white race is responsible for every social and cultural advance made in the world. Any civilization that is worthwhile, Creativity says, was created by the white race. Since the white race has risen to the top of nature's racial hierarchy, anything that threatens the white race's place in such a hierarchy is "unnatural."

Creativity sees white people's social ascension as predetermined by a creator who fashioned the other races before he created the white race. Afterward, the creator made his finest creation, the white race, and gave it dominion over all others. It should be noted that the creator is not an omnipotent being and adherents to this "race religion" reject Christianity as superstition. The white race has a soul, but it is not a soul that ascends to heaven after one dies. Rather, the soul of the white race is an intuitive and natural feeling or desire that the other races do not share. The white soul has an impulse to create (music, literature, law and order, architecture, etc.). The "inferior" souls of other races are said to lack this impulse, making them no more than animals. Anything that threatens the white race threatens this impulse toward creation and therefore threatens the world. Consequently, what is good for the white race is good, and what is bad for the white race is, by definition, bad. Anything that threatens the white race is bad. Anything that perpetuates the existence of the white race is good.

Klassen believed that the white race would soon be in a life and death struggle with the other, inferior races.

Klassen preached that the white race was threatened by a Jewish-inspired move toward greater and greater social integration of the races. This "race mixing" was a clear attempt to breed the white race out of existence and was no less than genocide. While he viewed Jews as the ultimate enemy of the white race, he voiced a disdain for African Americans, calling them "muds" or "mud races" for their dark skin tone, and spoke out against African Americans as a race.

Klassen believed that a Racial Holy War (RAHOWA) would eventually be the only way to save the white race. While he did not believe that the white man had reached the need for a Racial Holy War, he did claim RAHOWA as the Creativity credo. In his pamphlets and other literature, Klassen argued that white people should begin to prepare for RAHOWA by living a life clean in body, spirit, and mind. This would include heterosexual marriages that produced white children who would defend the white race in the coming Racial Holy War.

Klassen formed the Church of the Creator as a means to reawaken the sleeping white masses, who, according to Klassen, were deluded by "the Jew" and made comfortable by the "degenerate" capitalist. The Church of the Creator also provided Klassen with a religion that would "allow its followers to redefine the meaning of sin as it relates to violence. Through this redefinition process, the devotee conquers his moral self and comes to believe that violence is not a sin. Under certain circumstances, it is an exalted virtue" (Hamm 1994). Since, according to Klassen, the white race is nature's greatest creation and is threatened by the Jews and the "mud races," the ultimate good would be the eliminating of

those threats. Indeed, compassion for anyone who is not white is viewed as a weakness and evidence that one is morally lacking.

World Church of the Creator

After Klassen's death, Matt Hale claimed control of the Church of the Creator, in 1996, and declared himself Pontifex Maximus, or Supreme Leader. If Klassen had primed his followers to prepare for the Racial Holy War, Hale tried—and succeeded—in convincing Creativity adherents that the Racial Holy War was at hand. First, he renamed the church World Church of the Creator (WCOTC) to enhance its and his credibility among potential recruits. Second, he took advantage of the Internet to form a Web site that stated WCOTC was an extensive organization with thousands of members. Third, he recruited young racist skinheads into his church as reverends to enhance the actual number of Creativity adherents and to serve as the recruiters of foot soldiers for RAHOWA. Indeed, at one time, many skinheads viewed Creativity as the core of skinhead culture. Fourth, Hale was one of the first white supremacists to market his Web page and other forms of literature to two groups that have traditionally not had much agency in the United States hate movement: women and children. By carving out a place for women and children in the World Church of the Creator, he was preparing a future for his church.

While nurturing and expanding his church, Hale completed law school and sought certification to practice law in Illinois. Initially, he argued convincingly that he was opposed to violence and would seek the accomplishment of his social goals only through peaceful means. However in 1999, Illinois bar officials judged Hale unfit to practice law due to his racist beliefs. That outcome would provide the first glimpse of Hale's control of his church's ethnoviolent acts.

Benjamin Nathaniel Smith

In 1998 Benjamin Nathaniel Smith discovered a World Church of the Creator flier on his car with Matt Hale's telephone number. Smith grew up in Wilmet, an affluent suburb of Chicago, and attended one of the finest high schools in the country, New Trier High. After enrolling in the University of Illinois, he experienced a range of legal and interpersonal problems that threatened his friendships and his academic career. He retreated to the Internet, where he discovered a burgeoning hate industry. Smith learned that he was a member of the greatest race the world has known, a race Hale traced back to the ancient Romans. Smith found an ideology that increased his self-esteem and provided an explanation for all of his problems, an explanation that absolved him of personal responsibility for his problems. This ideology taught him to hate Jews and their "servants." When they met, Hale offered his church as a way that Smith could protect himself from his enemies while also playing an important role in an epic struggle between good and evil. Hale became Smith's mentor, and later that same year Smith became the 1998 "Creator of the Year." Smith said of Hale, "He's given me spiritual guidance."

After Hale's application to practice law was denied, on July 2, 1999, he wrote to his followers, "I have been denied my most precious rights of speech and religion. If the courthouse is closed to NON APPROVED RELIGIONS, America can only be headed for violence." Shortly after, Smith resigned from Hale's church through registered mail and began a two-day attack on Jews, African Americans, and Asian Americans at the beginning of the July 4 weekend. He began in Chicago, where he murdered the popular Northwestern basketball coach Ricky Birdsong, as well as a Korean doctoral student. He then traveled south, through the Illinois countryside and into Indiana. In the end, he murdered two people and wounded nine before shooting himself as police closed in to arrest him. In an interview with the *New York Times,* Hale confirmed that he believed Smith's actions were connected with the rejection of his application. Since Hale had spoken to Smith just two days before the murders, many suspected that Hale had surreptitiously manipulated Smith to commit terrorist acts, but there was no concrete evidence to hold him legally responsible for the murders. Underhanded and coded messages were Hale's preferred means of encouraging ethnoviolence among his followers. According to the *Southern Poverty Law Center Intelligence Report* ("Pontifex Ex" 2004), a young church member, house cleaner, and confidant to Hale, Jimmy Burnett reported, "Far from distraught at losing the man he called 'my protégé,' Hale seemed positively ebullient, telling Burnett the national attention brought on by Smith's rampage would bring more in membership and PR." Although concrete evidence of Hale's involvement in Smith's murder spree was lacking shortly after the murders, enough evidence existed for the FBI to infiltrate his organization.

Matt Hale's Deadly Persuasion

More information about Hale's tactics for promoting violence came to light in the midst of a copyright infringement case brought against Hale by the Te-Ta Ma Truth Foundation's Church of the Creator. This church was dedicated to the unification of mankind and claimed that it was being confused with Hale's church. Given the stark differences between the two churches, Te-Ta Ma found this to be unacceptable and sued World Church of the Creator for copyright infringement. Federal Judge Joan Lefkow eventually ruled against

Matt Hale, leader of the white supremacist group World Church of the Creator, uses an Israeli flag as a rug at the entrance to his office at the organization's headquarters in East Peoria, Illinois, in July 1999. Hale is currently serving a forty-year prison term for conspiracy to murder a federal judge who ruled against him in a copyright infringement case. *(Tim Boyle/Getty Images)*

Hale, barring him from using "Church of the Creator" on any documents or publications. Hale told his followers that a state of war existed between Lefkow and their organization. In an e-mail, Hale told an FBI informant who had infiltrated his organization to get the judge's home address. According to a *Southern Poverty Law Center Intelligence Report* (Beirich and Potok, 2003), the following exchange between Hale and the informant took place the following day (reported from trial transcripts):

Informant: When we get it [the address], we going to exterminate the rat?

Hale: Well, whatever you want to do basically.

Informant: The Jew Rat.

Hale: You know, my position has always been that I, you know, I'm going to fight within the law . . . but that information has been provided . . . if you want to do something yourself, you can.

In another tape, Hale told a member of his security team of a church rival, "If I was to tell you to go out and shoot this bastard . . . I know you would." Eventually, charges were brought against Hale for soliciting the murder of lawyers for the Te-Ta Ma Truth Foundation's Church of the Creator and the church director. Hale was also charged with and later convicted of conspiring to have Judge Lefkow murdered.

Hale's legal entanglements emboldened some in his organization to challenge him for control of the church. Jurors heard testimony from a close member of his security team, as well as tape recordings of conversations, about how to deal with those challenges. In a conversation about what to do about one particular challenger, the *Southern Poverty Law Center Intelligence Report* ("Pontifex Ex" 2004) described the following exchange:

Hale: You have to understand my position. I can't ever say anything illegal and nor can I ever encourage anything illegal and that's why I simply have to say or hope . . .

Security: You wouldn't mind him falling off the face of the earth.

Hale: No, I wouldn't mind at all. . . . All I can say is that I hope the guy, however, one day, shuts up. I mean, what else can I say?

Security: It'd be like that [snaps fingers]. . . . All I need is the cash to make it happen.

Hale: Let me think about it.

One of his followers who testified against Hale may have summarized Hale's tactics most succinctly when he testified, "In public . . . Hale would inveigh against Jews and 'mud races,' but also advise members to 'stay legal at all times.'"

But it was more of a darker tone at private meetings . . . more hinting at violence. Hale would talk, for instance, about having 'Jewish leaders hanged.' . . . He would have race traitors exterminated" ("Pontifex Ex" 2004).

Conclusion

While Hale remains in prison, convicted of conspiracy to commit murder and serving a forty-year sentence, his church, now known as Creativity, maintains a presence within the American hate community. Hale himself sustains some significance within that community as a "prisoner of conscience." It would be a mistake to conclude that Hale and his rhetoric are made less significant by the fact that he is in prison. His rhetorical style was adapted to cultivate "lone wolf" acts of ethnoterrorism, a phenomenon that is coming to be understood as a cultural practice in the American hate community. Lone wolves are individuals in the hate movement who do not join organized hate groups and who live "underground" lives while waiting for an opportunity to strike at the enemies of the white race on their own initiative. Benjamin Smith is regarded as one such lone wolf. John William King and Lawrence Russell Brewer exemplified this role when they dragged James Byrd to death in Jasper, Texas, in order to gain credibility among others in the hate movement. Lone wolf ethnoviolence will continue, and other orators will emerge to craft hateful messages that encourage such violence.

It has been observed, following Hale's decline, that Creativity was a much less substantial organization than he often implied. Such an observation misses the value of that or any other race religion. A race religion does not try to build membership roles in the same way that, for instance, the National Alliance might. A race religion is important to the American hate movement because it provides a set of cultural beliefs and practices that might be shared by a diverse set of secular hate groups—cultural beliefs and practices that build the esteem of white supremacists, create their enemies, and justify the killing of those enemies.

Michael S. Waltman

See also: Christian Identity Movement; Christianity.

Further Reading

Anti-Defamation League. "Extremism in America: Matt Hale" (online). Available: http://www.adl.org/learn/ext_us/Hale.asp?LEARN_cat=Extremism&LEARN_SubCat=Extremism_in_america&xpicked=2&item=mh.

Beirich, Heidi, and Mark Potok. "Creator Crack-Up." *Southern Poverty Law Center Intelligence Report* (Spring 2003). Available: http://www.splcenter.org/intel/intelreport/article.jsp?aid=23.

Berlet, Chip. *Eyes Right! Challenging the Right Wing Backlash.* Boston: South End Press, 1995.

———. "White Supremacist, Antisemitic, and Race Hate Groups in the U.S.: A Genealogy." Political Research Associates Report, 2004. Available: http://www.publiceye.org/racism/white-supremacy.html.

Berlet, Chip, and Matthew N. Lyons. *Right-Wing Populism in America: Too Close for Comfort.* New York: Guilford Press, 2000.

Blee, Kathleen. *Inside Organized Racism: Women in the Hate Movement.* Berkeley: University of California Press, 2002.

Guttentag, W., and V. DiPersio (writers and directors). "Hate.com: Extremists on the Internet." Television series episode. In *America Undercover,* produced by J. Anderson. New York: Home Box Office, 2003.

Hamm, Mark S. *American Skinheads: The Criminology and Control of Hate Crime.* Westport. CT: Praeger, 1994.

———. *In Bad Company: America's Terrorist Underground.* Boston: Northeastern University Press, 2002.

———. *Terrorism as Crime: From Oklahoma City to Al-Qaeda and Beyond.* New York: New York University Press, 2007.

Hightower, Nia. "What's in a Name?" *Southern Poverty Law Center Intelligence Report* (Winter 2002). Available: http://www.splcenter.org/intel/intelreport/article.jsp?sid=64.

Kaplan, Jeffrey. *Encyclopedia of White Power: A Sourcebook on the Radical Racist Right.* Walnut Creek, CA: AltaMira Press, 2000.

"Pontifex Ex." *Southern Poverty Law Center Intelligence Report* (Summer 2004). Available: http://www.splcenter.org/intel/intelreport/article.jsp?aid=476.

Crucifixion

Crucifixion is a method of painful execution in which the condemned person is tied or nailed to a large wooden cross of various shapes and left to hang until death and, in some cases, decomposition of the body takes place. This type of punishment was first reported and frequently used around 2000 B.C.E. Crucifixion is thought to have originated in Persia, and then spread to other ancient civilizations, including the Assyrian, Scythian, Thracian, Indian, Seleucid, Macedonian, Egyptian, Carthaginian, Roman, Celtic, German, and Britonian. Its proliferation took place from the sixth century B.C.E. to the fourth century C.E., and it continues, though rarely, in the twenty-first century. It was abolished in the Roman Empire by the emperor Constantine in 337 C.E.

The term *crucifixion* comes from the Latin *crucificere*, meaning "to fix to a cross" (*crux*: "cross"; *ficere*: "to fix"). It was very popular with tyrants and governments throughout the ancient world, and it was used for contempt and shame before the time of the Roman Empire. The process is one of the highest forms of sadistic punishment, and from the earliest accounts it was considered the most horrible form of death. The Roman statesman and writer Cicero described it as the most cruel and disgusting penalty, and Josephus, the Jewish historian, as the most wretched, horrific death. The Roman jurist Julius Paulus described it as worse than beheading or death by wild beasts.

During the Roman era, crucifixion was usually preceded by scourging or flogging. In flogging, a whip was used with leather thongs of different lengths, with small iron balls or pieces of sheep bones attached to the end of the thongs. The condemned was flogged repeatedly, up to hundreds of times, until he lost consciousness, by which time his skin was excoriated and the underlying flesh deeply traumatized and profusely bleeding. The prisoner, weakened by this torture, was then obliged to carry all or part of the cross, usually on his shoulders, up to the place of final execution. This is how the punishment suffered by Jesus Christ prior to his crucifixion is reported in the Bible.

Deuteronomy 21:22–23 describes a form of crucifixion as a hanging from a tree, because at times there was no real cross but just a pole or a tree available. Generally, however, a cross was made of wood and was formed of two parts: the vertical *palus* or *stipes*, often already fixed in the ground at the place of execution; and the horizontal crossbar, the *patibulum*, on which the condemned person's outstretched arms were placed with the hands nailed to it. The shape of the cross was determined by the level of intersection of the horizontal bar with the vertical bar. Shapes were of three types: the *crux commissa*, a large T shape; the *crux immissa* or *ordinaria* (Latin cross), in which the horizontal bar is slightly below the upper end of the vertical pole; and the X-shaped *crux*. It is uncertain where the nails were fixed—at the level of the wrists, between the radius and the ulna, or in the hands, which most likely would not be capable of holding the weight of the body of the condemned person. The nails also may have been driven in at an angle, entering the palms in the crease that delineates the bulky region at the base of the thumb, exiting in the wrist after passing through the carpal tunnel. The feet were nailed to the cross as well. Sometimes the body was tied to the cross by the wrists and ankles. A foot rest, the *suppedanium*, and a *sedile*, a small seating support halfway up the cross, were also used. At the top of the vertical pole of the cross there was usually a small wooden piece, the *titulus*, with the written charges for the crucifixion. At times people were crucified with their heads down, as in the reported crucifixion of St. Peter.

The purposes of death by crucifixion were multiple: punishment, deterrence for particular crimes, and sadistic pleasure. The condemned usually died a slow death, purposely prolonged for sadistic and exhibitory reasons. Death was generally by asphyxiation and heart failure due to the inability to breathe properly. Hypovolemic shock, in which blood loss makes the heart unable to pump enough blood to the body, has also been proposed as a reason for death. Although the condemned person was usually still alive at the time of crucifixion, occasionally a dead body (killed by flogging and mutilation) was crucified in order to set an example. Crucifixion was usually a punishment for robbers, rebels, slaves, and occasionally, for foreigners. Within the Roman Empire, Roman citizens could not be crucified except if found guilty of treason.

The Romans, the Slaves, the Jews, and Crucifixion

The Romans did not invent crucifixion as a method of execution; instead, it seems that they adopted it from the Carthaginians during the Punic Wars, possibly through some Arab mercenary troops. The writings of the Jewish historian Josephus, the Greek historian Herodotus, and the Roman historian Tacitus all contain evidence of this theory. Crucifixion was considered the most painful, dishonorable, and abominable of all types of punishment. The Roman legal codex, *Sententiae,* catalogs the crimes punishable by crucifixions as desertion to the enemy, betraying of secrets, rebellion or incitement to rebellion, murder, prophecy about the welfare of rulers, nocturnal impiety, use of magic, and falsification of wills and testaments.

Under the reign of the emperor Caligula (37–41 C.E.), crucifixion was part of popular entertainment. For example, it was used in Alexandria, Egypt, by the prefect Flaccus in the torture and subsequent public crucifixion of Jews. It was also often used to punish slaves or foreigners. A slave owner exercised *dominica*

potestas (ownership) over his slaves. If a slave owner was unable to assert his *potestas* (power) over his slave, he could request that the Roman army carry out punishment. An example of this occurred when M. Acilius Glabrius suppressed a revolt in Etruria by crucifying the leaders of a rebellion and turning over the other slaves to their rightful owners.

During the Roman Empire, slaves were not looked upon as persons but as property. They were objectified, and the legal speeches of Cicero and the descriptions of Tacitus and Levy in that regard are numerous. As reported by the Roman philosopher and orator Seneca, the law of obedience of a slave toward his owner was such that if a slave refused his orders (including giving him [the owner] poison with which to commit suicide), he could be liable for punishment by crucifixion. In the writings of most Roman authors, crucifixion appears to be reported as the normal punishment for disobedient slaves.

Plautus (250–144 B.C.E.), the famous Roman playwright, left a vivid description of crucifixion in his plays. In *Miles Gloriosus,* the slave protagonist expresses fear of being crucified by his master for his petty thievery, knowing quite well, as the satiric dialogue says, that the cross would be his grave, as it had been for his ancestors—father, grandfather, great-grandfather, and great-great-grandfather. In Plautus's *Bacchides,* the main character, a slave who had stolen gold from his master, envisions himself in the future not as a gold bearer but as a cross bearer.

High places such as hilltops were usually selected by the Romans for execution by crucifixion. The historian Livy reported that in 217 B.C.E. twenty-five slaves who were plotting an insurrection in Campus Martius in Rome were crucified on the Esquiline Hill. Tacitus reported that the Esquiline, one of the Seven Hills of Rome, was often used for crucifixions. Horace, the Roman poet, described the vultures on Esquiline Hill as *esquilinae alites (*Esquiline birds*).*

The Roman poet Juvenal, in *Satires,* described the horrible end of the crucified corpse. In *Dialogue* 6.20.3, Seneca described the gradual death of victims of crucifixion as wasting away in pain and dying limb by limb. The goal of Roman crucifixion was not just to kill a criminal but also to mutilate and desecrate the body (*supplicium servile*). The body was left on the cross until it rotted. Such a death was especially dishonorable for the Jews, for whom leaving a body on a cross without proper burial was a great humiliation. The control of one's own body was of utmost importance in Jewish society.

In addition to literary sources of information about crucifixion, the four Gospels describe in detail the agony of Jesus of Nazareth on the cross. Golgotha, the hill outside the walls of Jerusalem, was selected for crucifixion and was the site of the crucifixion of Jesus. According to the Gospels, Jesus was nailed to the cross, not tied with ropes, as people sometimes thought, and his legs were not fractured to accelerate his death, as was occasionally done. He died fairly quickly, and his death was soon recognized by a Roman centurion (John 19:31–33). Asphyxia because of difficulty in breathing due to pain and the position of the body was most likely the cause of his death. It is reported that upon the insistence of the Sanhedrin (the highest judicial and ecclesiastical council of the ancient Jewish nation), Pontius Pilate ordered the crucifixion of Jesus in order to abort any rebellious movement against Rome. The Romans often used crucifixion as a controlling force for state security.

Famous Crucifixions

Crucifixion frequently took place on a hill, in a city square, or in a place where people would gather or pass by, since its purpose was not only retributive but to give an exemplary deterrent message to those observing it. Quintillian, a Roman rhetorician, reportedly said that whenever the guilty were crucified, the most crowded roads were chosen so that the greatest number of people could see it and be moved by fear. Early historians make mention of several crucifixions:

- King Darius of Persia had 3,000 Babylonians crucified around 519 B.C.E.
- Alexander the Great, at the siege of Tyre, a Phoenician city on the Mediterranean coast, crucified 2,000 survivors along the shore of the sea in 332 B.C.E.
- Alexander the Great reportedly had Callisthenis, his official historian and biographer, crucified because he disagreed with him.
- Antiochus IV, king of Syria, had Jews whipped and crucified in Jerusalem in 175 B.C.E.
- Crassus crucified 6,000 slaves along the Via Appia; Via Appia is one of the roads that leads to Rome, and the slaves were the followers of Spartacus during the Third Servile Wars in 73 B.C.E.
- Pontius Pilate ordered the crucifixion of Jesus of Nazareth in 32 C.E.
- The Roman general Titus, at the time of the destruction of Jerusalem and the temple (70 C.E.), ordered that 500 Jewish people be crucified daily along the walls of the city.

The Religious and Social Aftermath of the Crucifixion of Jesus of Nazareth

Crucifixion was known to the Jews as an instrument of persecution of Jewish believers by non-Jews. Prior to crucifixion, the victims were given a choice between renouncing their faith or death. Martyrdom was accepted in Jewish law and was seen as permissible when one was confronted with a choice between death and apostasy. The commitment to die expressed an absolute devotion for the sake of God's unity, with self-sacrifice standing at the center of world-restorative action. Voluntary martyrdom was forbidden, however.

Judaism does not convey a ritual meaning to the cross, as does Christianity. Rather, it is seen as an implement of torture—a curse that Jews carried for centuries because they were blamed for putting Jesus to death on the cross. It was Christianity that conceived of crucifixion as the symbolic act of the redemption of the world, as the paramount sacrifice of an innocent victim—God's son, Jesus Christ—and as an act of enthronement as the king, God's son. The Crucifixion was the culmination of Jesus's life. In Christian belief, Christ was approved by God as his Son, made manifest to man as his lord, and perfected in his character as redeemer. The desire of the church has always been to exalt the Crucifixion because therein is to be found the atonement for sin. In Judaism, dying a martyr confirms the covenant with God, the firmness of the martyr's faith under terrible torture and torment.

In the fourth century C.E., the Doctors of the Church began to present the cross as the standard and symbolic memory of the foundation of a new world order. It is reported that on October 27, 312 C.E., as the Roman emperor Constantine prepared to battle the usurper Maxentius at the Milvian Bridge near Rome, a cross appeared to him in the sky, on which was written, "In this sign shall you conquer," and later Christ appeared to him in a dream. He took these as omens that he was fighting under the Christian God. Constantine seized power after the battle of Ponte Milvio, on the periphery of Rome, which he won with the Christians' help. He then converted from paganism to Christianity, and following the Edict of Milan (313 C.E.), Christianity became the state religion. State and religion were thus inextricably intertwined in the Roman Empire.

Crucifixion was eliminated by the church as a form of capital punishment, but it continued as part of the political program of the new world empire. As represented by the cross, it became the image that the new church-state was called on to create in the pursuit of Jesus's sacrificial teaching. After the downfall of Rome in 453 C.E., the western regions of the empire and the Church of Rome became the seat of the new imperial authority, established upon the divine mission entrusted by Jesus to his apostles. Jesus's death and resurrection were adopted as true historical proof of the Catholic dogmas, the key act of the Easter miracle, and the foundation of Christianity. Thus, a blood ritual, the crucifixion of Jesus, is celebrated in the rite of Holy Communion as the religious model of the sanctification of its doctrine.

The story of an atrocious act, a *crime absolute,* began to be reenacted each day in the liturgy throughout Christendom. The liturgy recalls a violent death inextricably tied to the cross, several times a day, at sunset and at dawn, as a perfect symbolic time-cycle. Christianity has since become a cultural language of cultural hegemony, organized through the church hierarchies. The church could not escape its dilemma: If Jesus was crucified, the most horrendous and terrific of all crimes, the narrative made it necessary to identify a murderer. Jesus's death on the cross was the root metaphor of the Christian creed. It implied a demarcation between God's people (those under his protection) and the "others" or "enemies," and this became the basis of much Jewish persecution.

An "Unworthy Superstition"

The Christian emperors referred to Judaism as "an unworthy superstition" and a "turpitude," and to the Jews as "a feral sect." The medieval church found the peculiar and inferior Jewish status highly acceptable. It continuously reminded the princes of their duty to restrain Jewish influence and enforce Jewish inferiority. Understandably, the church did not base itself on the presumed historical arguments of the legalists. It went back to the "crime" of the Crucifixion, which made the Jews the enemies of Christendom.

Early church doctrine assigned Christians supremacy over others, since only Christians were said to be descended from God or Christ. State power became the instrument of government and of the world religious community and a means for universal conversion. In Byzantium in the Eastern Roman Empire, the cross offered a justification for the ruthless, bloody politics of pillages, territorial expansion, forced conversions, and confiscations of lands and goods—especially in the Middle East. This policy marked the beginning of the Crusades, the cycle of wars in the Middle East that led to the establishment of the crusaders' Kingdom of Jerusalem. The Crusades were military campaigns, wars of conquest, rather than religious wars, although in the thirteenth century the papacy focused on the liberation of the Holy Sites. The popes did not hesitate to encourage armed violence in the name of the Holy Cross, the crucifixion of Jesus. It was a brief and bloody point in history that left a deep mark on Islamic memory.

In central and western Europe, in the Middle Ages, the papacy became the exclusive interpreter of Christian orthodoxy. In western Europe, in a complex policy of alliances with kings and princes, the church established its ecclesiastical courts beyond the walls of Rome. The clergy had its own jurisdiction as a separate field from royal and baronial justice. The ecclesiastical courts worked as special tribunals—the "blood courts"—investigating any suspicion of heterodoxy.

In the name of Jesus's sacrifice and the pains he suffered, church courts were free to torture and burn any suspect in the public square. In 1252, Pope Gregory IX established a court for the suppression of heresy, the Holy Office, which was entrusted with the duty to defend church doctrine. Those found guilty were handed over to the secular arm, a secret tribunal entrusted with the defense of the cross for investigation and trial. These blood courts were instruments of political terror until the eighteenth century. In 1542, the inquisition court was transformed into the Congregation of Inquisition, and thereafter it is best known for its prosecution of Galileo Galilei and Giordano Bruno, the latter burned in Campo dei Fiori, one of the main Roman squares.

In the sixteenth century, when the city-republic of Geneva fell under Calvin's rule, Protestants burned Michael Servetus, an independent reformer, alive in the main square, imitating the Roman church. In the seventeenth century, Oliver Cromwell's army burned down the churches in Ireland in the name of the true faith and doctrine. Crucifixion justified the persecution of freedom of conscience and religion even in Protestantism. In sixteenth-century England, arrests, imprisonments, interrogations, trials, and executions of "dissidents" who offended the cross took place.

In the Muscovite Empire, the Russian Orthodox Church became the official church of the imperial state. It was a pillar of the political establishment, while the emperor of Russia, the czar, was adored as a divine creature. Thus crucifixion sanctified one of the most despotic regimes in European history, based on the exploitation of the peasantry until the 1917 revolution. In the country, however, from time to time, among the lower order, powerful messianic movements announced a world renewal with a purifying blood bath, in the name of Jesus and the cross, as had happened in Central Europe with the Hussite movement.

In medieval Islam, the Dabistan-i Mazahib describes the crucifixion of Christ by consent of Pontius Pilate (*Filatas*) upon the insistence of the Jews. Pilate himself washed his hands of the deed, and the Jews were found responsible—a historical fallacy that persisted for centuries.

The Spread of Crucifixion

Crucifixion was introduced in Japan during the civil wars (1138–1560) after a 350-year period with no capital punishment. Scholars believe it was suggested to the Japanese as Christianity was introduced to the region. The condemned, usually a sentenced criminal, was hoisted upon a T-shaped cross, suffered spear thrusts, and left on the cross until burial. In 1597, twenty-six Christians were nailed to crosses at Nagasaki. Among them was Pedro Bautista, a Spanish Franciscan friar who had worked for ten years in the Philippines. That execution marked the beginning of a long history of persecution of Christians in Japan, which continued until the Meiji Restoration introduced religious freedom in Japan in 1871. Nevertheless, it was reportedly used as a punishment for prisoners of war during World War II, when three prisoners of war were crucified for killing cattle; one of the prisoners survived after sixty-three hours on the cross.

In China, Confucian scholars and officials regarded Christian missionaries as deceptive. It is reported that crucifixion was introduced in China by the missionaries. The idea of an incarnate god willingly submitting himself to crucifixion was unthinkable. Similarly, the idea of an intermediary engaged in supplicating a supreme deity on behalf of humankind would not have fit any traditional Chinese concept of Confucian or Taoist origin.

In 1869, at Amoy, a well-known thief who was convicted of abducting young girls and selling them for prostitution was executed. He prayed to be crucified rather than beheaded. The cross was of the Latin form, and his sentence was to remain on the cross day and night until he died.

Crucifixion played an important part in colonial history but was already known and practiced in precolonial Africa. Human sacrifices were of frequent occurrence, and the usual form was crucifixion. Benin City was the seat of a very powerful theocracy, and Benin was exposed to Islamic Arabic influence. Overall, the evidence is convincing for a substantial increase in the scale of human sacrifice in Benin from around the 1830s to the 1880s, including sacrifices for purposes not recorded earlier (to control the weather and to close roads), sacrifices in new forms (crucifixion on trees), and the sacrifice of female as well as male victims at the annual ceremonies. In 1893, crucified victims were reportedly observed in Benin City on the plain outside the king's residence. The accession of a new king, Ovonramwen, in 1888, appears to have been followed by a temporary decline in the scale of human sacrifice. But the practice attained a new height at the time of the British attack on Benin in 1897, when numerous British victims were killed in a desperate attempt to ward off foreign conquest.

In Saudi Arabia, crucifixion was reported for punishment for *hudud*, or "boundary crimes": crimes whose punishment and evidentiary procedural requirements are clearly and legally defined in the Koran. Punishment includes execution by crucifixion, and persons convicted cannot be pardoned. The Koran describes crucifixion as one form of punishment for those who fight Allah and his messenger. In Iran, according to current criminal law, crucifixion may be used as a punishment for *moharebeh*, a major crime committed against Islam and the Islamic Republic of Iran. In Yemen, at the end of the twentieth century, nonlethal crucifixion of criminals was allowed, although it was also used for those condemned to death.

In the United States, the cross has long been used by the Ku Klux Klan as a symbol of terror and persecution. Following the Civil War, former Confederate soldiers founded the organization with the purpose of restoring white supremacy in the South. Its violence was aimed at former black slaves and white sympathizers, and its victims numbered in the thousands. Lynchings were often accompanied by burning crosses, some placed high on hills, where they were visible to all. Ku Klux Klan meetings also included ritual burnings of the cross. Following World War II, Klan attacks were directed against Jews, Roman Catholics, socialists, communists, and foreigners in general. At the beginning of the twenty-first century, the Klan, even though less noticeable, continues to be active.

Crucifixion as a Counter-Model of the Religious Order

In Europe, the view of crucifixion has varied. Its semiotic message was construed differently according to social and historical settings and the interplay of traditions. Crucifixion was also interpreted as a countermodel of ecclesiastical and political power—as a model of human suffering and frailty rather than a triumph. In the German painter Matthias Grünewald's Isenheim altarpiece, the human truth of Jesus's cross can be observed: Jesus is depicted as nailed to pieces of wood, suffering torments that will bring about his death—a wretched figure, alone and forgotten. The mood of this crucifixion painting evokes knowledge of the countless, unnamed human beings who suffer and die on their crosses each day of the earth's history. In Grünewald's depiction of the Crucifixion there is no effort at softening, blurring, or using warm blues and soft pinks to idealize what is hard and real. There is no stretching and smoothing of the body to make it appear full and lovely, to give it that strangely erotic appearance that is often observed in crucifixion art. Here, crucifixion is the crushing truth of common suffering.

In addition to its use as a sociopolitical penalty, crucifixion was of supreme efficacy as a deterrent measure. At the same time, it satisfied the primitive lust and sadistic revenge that was proper of some rulers and of some people. It may be unconsciously a remnant of the human sacrifice of ancient times. As such, it was the construct of the crucifixion of Jesus of Nazareth—*agnus dei qui tollis peccata mundi* ("the lamb of God who takes away the sins of the world"), the solidarity of God with the innumerable people who died via crucifixion in past centuries. The crucified Jesus died like a slave or a common criminal, in severe torment on a tree of shame. Nonetheless, the symbolic meaning of his crucifixion—and responses to it—have prompted myriad crimes against humankind through the centuries.

Carlo Rossetti and George B. Palermo

See also: Christianity; Judaism; Roman Catholicism; Self-Immolation.

Further Reading

Abdel Haleem, M.A.S. *The Qur'an.* Oxford: Oxford University Press, 2004.

Fishbane, M. *The Kiss of God: Spiritual and Mystical Death in Judaism.* Seattle: University of Washington Press, 1994.

Gallewey, H.L. "Journeys in the Benin Country, West Africa." *Geographical Journal* 1 (1893): 122–30.

Hengel, M. *Crucifixion: In the Ancient World and the Message of the Cross.* Philadelphia: Fortress Press, 1977.

Jones, J. "On the Punishment of Crucifixion in China." *Transactions of the Ethnological Society of London* 3 (1864): 138–39.

Josephus, F. *The New Complete Works of Josephus,* trans. W. Whiston. Grand Rapids, MI: Kregel, 1999.

Law, R. "Human Sacrifice in Pre-Colonial West Africa." *African Affairs* 84 (1985): 53–87.

Loewe, M. "Imperial China's Reactions to the Catholic Missions." *Numen* 35:2 (1988): 179–212.

Odahl, C.M. *Constantine and the Christian Empire.* New York: Routledge, 2004.

Plautus and Terence. *Five Comedies,* trans. Deena Berg and Douglass Parker. Indianapolis, IN: Hackett, 1999.

Runciman, S. *The First Crusade.* New York: Cambridge University Press, 1992.

Danish Cartoon Crisis

In September 2005, the Danish daily *Jyllands-Posten* ran twelve cartoons that satirically depicted the Prophet Muhammad, offending many Muslims throughout the world. The Danish response was to assert that the cartoons were printed in the name of freedom of speech and not to proffer an apology for any offense. This engendered great anger among Muslims from Gaza to Jakarta who responded with demonstrations, death threats, and attacks on Danish embassies in Damascus, Beirut, and Tehran.

Trajectory

Kare Bluitgen, author of a Danish children's book titled *The Qur'an and the Life of the Prophet Muhammad* (2006), had been unable to find an illustrator to draw the Prophet. No one was willing to take the job out of fear of provoking the Islamists, but eventually an illustrator accepted on the condition of anonymity. Such fear was well grounded. For example, on November 2, 2004, Dutch filmmaker Theo van Gogh was killed in Amsterdam by a Muslim radical after directing the film *Submission* (2004), which was critical of the treatment of women in the Islamic world. Since van Gogh's assassination, the film's writer, Somali-born author and former Dutch politician Ayaan Hirsi Ali, has had to live in protective custody.

On September 17, 2005, the Danish newspaper *Politiken* published the article "A Profound Fear of Criticizing Islam," which expressed Bluitgen's difficulties and attributed them to self-censorship. Two weeks later, twelve carica-tures of the Prophet Muhammad were published in *Jyllands-Posten,* a conservative newspaper with the largest circulation in Denmark. According to *Jyllands-Posten*'s cultural editor, Flemming Rose, the caricatures were in response to the climate of fear that surrounds the criticism of some Islamist taboos. More specifically, Rose stated in 2006, "As a former correspondent in the Soviet Union, I am sensitive about calls for censorship on the grounds of insult. This is a popular trick of totalitarian movements." He had asked members of the Danish Editorial Cartoonists Union "to draw Muhammad as they see him." Twelve out of twenty-five cartoonists responded and were paid 800 Danish krone (US$122) for each cartoon.

On September 30, 2005, the cartoons were published in *Jyllands-Posten* as part of an editorial titled "Muhammeds ansigt" (The Face of Muhammad), which criticized self-censorship in Danish media. The central image was an illustration of the Prophet among other turban-wearing people in a police lineup and someone stating, "I don't know which one he is." Jesus Christ, as well as the conservative Danish politician Pia Kjaersgaard and Kare Bluitgen were also depicted in the lineup. There were eleven other cartoons, most of which showed the Prophet in an unflattering manner. However, not all the cartoons had an especially critical or derisive tone. For instance, one simply depicted Muhammad in the desert walking into the sunset. Another merged his face with the star and crescent, the symbols of Islam. The other cartoons, however, were much more contentious and provocative. The most controversial showed the Prophet Muhammad as a dangerous-looking man carrying a turban-shaped bomb on his head, inscribed with the Islamic testimony of faith in Arabic. In another, Muhammad was depicted as a jihadist with a sword while two women behind him were completely covered with the exception of their eyes.

Other cartoons in the series also focused on terrorism and women's rights in Islam. For example, in one, the Prophet was standing on a cloud with suicide bombers who were trying to enter heaven. The Prophet called out, "Stop, stop, we have run out of virgins." The focus of this particular cartoon hinged upon the supposed reward for martyrs of seventy-two virgins in heaven (although many Muslim scholars reject this belief). Another cartoon was an abstract illustration accompanied by a poem: "Prophet, you crazy bloke! Keeping women under yoke." The Prophet was illustrated in one cartoon with a crescent moon around his head, positioned as a pair of devil's horns. Finally, he appeared looking at a sheet of paper and holding back two assassins with swords, saying, "Relax, guys, it's just a drawing made by some infidel South Jutlander" (i.e., someone from the middle of nowhere), which was meant to imply that the drawings were not harmful.

According to Rose, the cartoonists treated Islam as they normally would other religions. In 2005, he was quoted as saying that "by treating Muslims in Denmark as equals they made a point: We are integrating you into the Danish tradition of satire because you are part of our society, not strangers. The cartoons are including, rather than excluding, Muslims." No matter the intention of the cartoonists, members of the Muslim community considered the tone of the cartoons hostile and offensive.

No substantial public reaction occurred in the first week after publication. However, two weeks later, 3,500 protesters from the Danish Muslim community held a nonviolent demonstration in Copenhagen and demanded a formal apology from *Jyllands-Posten*. When no apology was issued, tensions continued to escalate. On October 20, eleven ambassadors to Denmark from Muslim-majority countries (Egypt, Pakistan, Turkey, Iran, Indonesia, Saudi Arabia, Bosnia-Herzegovina, Algeria, Morocco, Libya, and the occupied Palestinian territories) sent a formal letter of grievance to Prime Minister Fogh Rasmussen and asked for a meeting to discuss the issue. However, the request was rejected on the basis of freedom of speech in Denmark. In his reply, Rasmussen stated that the Danish government had no means of influencing the media, but that any offended party could bring the issue to Danish courts. The refusal of the prime minister to meet the ambassadors was publicly criticized by the parliamentary opposition, including twenty-two Danish ex-ambassadors and the former minister of foreign affairs Uffe Ellemann-Jensen.

Due to this refusal to meet the ambassadors, a group of imams from Denmark toured the Middle East to attract attention to the cartoon conflict. In Egypt, they met with Grand Mufti Muhammad Said Tantawi, Foreign Minister Ahmed Aboul Gheit, and Amr Moussa, secretary-general of the Arab League. They presented a forty-three-page dossier that included the twelve cartoons, as well as three more satiric illustrations that turned out to be unrelated. The dossier stated that "this dictatorial way of using democracy is completely unacceptable" and complained about "the lack of official recognition of the Islamic faith." These visits to Arab countries also paved the way for calls for a boycott of Danish goods. On January 30, 2006, the Organization of the Islamic Conference (OIC), representing fifty-seven Muslim countries, and the Arab League jointly called for a United Nations resolution condemning Demark.

The UN became involved in December, when Louise Arbor, the high commissioner for human rights, commented on the affair. On December 7, Arbor stated that she understood the concerns of Muslims and condemned all acts that could be seen as a lack of respect for other religions. The United Nations Commission on

Human Rights asked the Danish government to explain its view of the case. Moreover, in a statement on December 29, the foreign ministers of the Arab League criticized the reaction of the Danish government, "which was disappointing despite its political, economic and cultural ties with the Muslim world."

The public outcry grew, and as the newspaper received countless e-mails, phone calls, and bomb threats, *Jyllands-Posten* felt the need to react. On January 29, Flemming Rose appeared on the Arab TV channel al-Jazeera and stated that the publication had involuntarily offended Muslims. On January 30, 2006, the newspaper published a public letter in Danish, English, and Arabic as an apology for the unintended results: "In our opinion, the 12 drawings were sober. They were not intended to be offensive, nor were they at variance with Danish law, but they have indisputably offended many Muslims, for which we apologize." The apology was not for printing the cartoons but for the hurt they caused. The letter also underlined the fact that the Danish legal authorities did not find the paper guilty of violating the law. Carsten Juste, the editor-in-chief, argued, "If we really went out and apologized, then the Middle Eastern dictatorships would be able to control what we put in our papers." This same attitude was apparent in the apology of Rasmussen on television when he commented, "I personally would not have depicted Muhammad, Jesus, or other religious figures in such a manner that would offend other people." Nevertheless, he did not apologize for publication of the cartoons. This type of apology was not sufficient for various Muslim communities and leaders, and the demonstrations and boycotts continued.

Violence Grows

On January 26, 2006, the Kingdom of Saudi Arabia withdrew its ambassador from Denmark. It also started a comprehensive boycott against Danish products. In a short time the boycott spread to Kuwait and Yemen, followed by the rest of the Middle East, North Africa, and Southeast Asia. The Danish Ministry of Foreign Affairs reported that it received about 750,000 protests from all over the world.

Throughout February, violent demonstrations occurred in several Muslim countries. The Danish and Norwegian embassies in Damascus and the Danish mission in Beirut were burned down. In Tehran, the Revolutionary Guard and Basij Militia attacked the Danish, French, and Austrian embassies with stones and firebombs. Assaults in Lebanon and Nigeria targeted Christian possessions and Western businesses, and in Benghazi, Libya, the Italian consulate was set ablaze. In Nigeria, the Danish and Norwegian flags were burned by members of parliament. Throughout the demonstrations, burning the Danish flag became a commonplace occurrence.

In 2006, Danish citizens had to be on guard while visiting Muslim countries. In Indonesia, for example, Danish tourists might be confronted by Indonesian students demanding an apology for the incident. The Danish government temporarily recalled its embassy personnel from Syria, Iran, and Indonesia and advised Danish citizens to leave those countries. The situation was even worse for the Danish cartoonists, as bounties were offered for their killing: A Taliban commander in Afghanistan promised a reward of 100 kilograms (220 pounds) of gold, while a minister in India offered $11.5 million to whomever killed one of the cartoonists. Ironically, the majority of those who died during the demonstrations were Muslims. By the end of February, almost two hundred people had died in different parts of the Muslim world in episodes related to the cartoons.

On September 9, 2006, it was reported that the boycott of Danish products had reduced exports to Muslim countries by 15.5 percent. The boycott had several other effects as well. For instance, Danish pastries were renamed "Rose of Muhammad" in Iranian bakeries. Also, many Saudi supermarkets posted notices over their cheese displays stating that they were not selling Danish products. Even the Middle Eastern outlets of the French Carrefour supermarket stopped selling Danish products.

Reactions from the West

In response to the anticartoon demonstrations, counterprotests escalated in the West, and were sometimes quite provocative, as exemplified by the headline of the French newspaper *France Soir*: "Yes, we have the right to caricature God." By February 2, 2006, several media outlets had reprinted the cartoons in order to show their solidarity and support for freedom of the press. Similarly, many Web sites also featured the cartoons. The most striking counterprotest, however, was when the Italian minister Roberto Calderoli wore a T-shirt displaying the cartoons.

Rasmussen described the crisis as Denmark's worst international crisis since World War II, and as it exceeded national boundaries, the Danish government began to seek help from its allies. The allies, however, remained silent. Most of the American papers, for example, refrained from reprinting the cartoons. The first official response from the United States came as late as February 3, after Danish Foreign Minister Per Stig Møller met with Secretary of State Condoleezza Rice. As violence against Danish embassies escalated, the United States more openly expressed its unconditional support for Denmark while underlining that freedom of speech should not negate certain responsibilities. Furthermore, Rice blamed the Iranian and Syrian governments for provoking the violent riots in their countries.

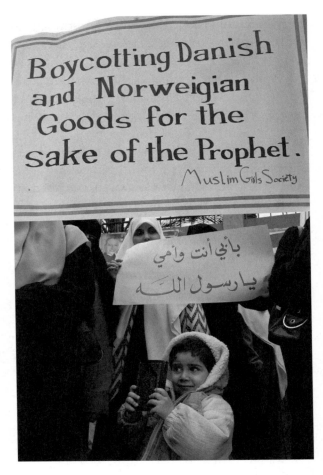

Palestinian women hold banners and copies of the Koran at a demonstration held in Gaza City on February 14, 2006, to protest the caricatures of the Prophet Muhammad published in a Danish newspaper. When no formal apology was issued by Denmark, Muslims worldwide reacted with varying degrees of violence, from nonviolent protests and the boycott of Danish products to death threats and attacks on Danish embassies. *(Mohammed Abed/AFP/Getty Images)*

The European attitude toward the conflict was also relatively deliberate. Initially, Norway sent its ambassadors to apologize to Muslim governments. On February 13, Javier Solana, the European Union's foreign policy coordinator, traveled to the Middle East in an effort to repair relations with the Muslim world. Two days later, the president of the European Commission, José Manuel Barosso, expressed his full support for Denmark. The European parliament also condemned the violence and called for respectful dialogue. That same month, the EU countries signed a joint statement, which underlined the responsibilities of freedom of speech and condemned the violence in the protests.

Causes and Effects

The violence that emerged at times during the anticartoon demonstrations, along with the attacks of September 11, 2001, and the Madrid and London bombings in March 2004 and July 2005, respectively, added to the mass public's view of Islam as a violent religion. Several explanations were raised as to why the printing of the cartoons created an international controversy. Specifically, the offense was related to the Islamic prohibition of depicting the Prophet and the equation of Islam with terrorism. The Islamic doctrine has strict limitations on figurative representation, especially in the case of Muhammad. This is evident in the miniature paintings of earlier centuries. However, it is also notable that in the Shi'a tradition depicting the Prophet or other religious figures is not problematic.

For many observers, the publication of the cartoons was neither an attempt to confront this Islamic prohibition, nor an exercise in freedom of speech. Instead, tensions arose along three major fault lines of Europe: Muslim immigration, fear of terrorism, and Islamophobia. The United Nations Commission on Human Rights also cited xenophobia and racism in Europe as the root of the crisis. The reactions to the crisis "served as a reminder of the gaping divide that still exists between the West and much of the Islamic world" (Graff 2006). This cultural gap also has hierarchical implications, as some believe that printing the cartoons had "a purpose of trying to achieve some kind of victory over Muslims, to bring Muslims into line" (Modood 2006). According

to that perspective, the ultimate aim could not have been an expression of freedom of speech, as the same newspaper had earlier rejected the publication of cartoons of Jesus Christ. In April 2003, a Danish illustrator, Christoffer Zieler, had submitted a series of cartoons about the resurrection of Christ to *Jyllands-Posten.* The paper's Sunday editor, Jens Kaiser, responded, "I don't think *Jyllands-Posten*'s readers will enjoy the drawings. As a matter of fact, I think they will provoke an outcry. Therefore I will not use them."

From a political perspective, the cartoon crisis was used by radical and isolationist groups on both sides. While autocrats in the Middle East could use the incident to dramatize the "evil" of Western democracy to their populations, European conservatives and far-Right extremists invoked the incident to demonstrate the "fanaticism" of Islam and the impossibility of living together with Muslim immigrants. It is telling that a poll published by Reuters in mid-February 2006 showed that the support for the Danish People's Party, which opposes immigration, increased to 18 percent of the votes in Denmark compared with 14.4 percent a month earlier. Thus, propagating the image of an enemy was advantageous for both sides to legitimize their own political stance and hide their unwillingness to compromise.

Hakki Tas

See also: Europe; Muhammad; Islam; Islamic Fundamentalism.

Further Reading

Asser, M. "What the Muhammad Cartoons Portray." BBC News (online), February 9, 2006. Available: http://news.bbc.co.uk/1/hi/world/middle_east/4693292.stm.

Browne, A. "Danish Cartoonists Fear for Their Lives." *Times* (UK; online), February 4, 2006. Available: http://www.timesonline.co.uk/tol/news/world/article726508.ece.

Dabashi, H. "Islam and Globanalisation." *Al-Ahram Weekly.*

March 23–29, 2006. Available: http://weekly.ahram.org.eg/2006/787/cu4.htm.

Graff, J. "A Right to Offend?" *Time,* February 5, 2006. Available: http://www.time.com/time/magazine/article/0,9171,1156573,00.html.

Heathcote, N. "Consumer Boycotts Sweep Middle-East." BBC News (online), February 6, 2006. Available: http://news.bbc.co.uk/1/hi/business/4685628.stm.

Karimi, N. "Iran President Lashes Out at U.S., Europe." *LA Daily News,* February 12, 2006.

Klausen, J. "Cartoon Jihad: Rotten Judgment in the State of Denmark." *Spiegel International,* March 8, 2006. Available: http://www.spiegel.de/international/0,1518,399653,00.html.

Larsen, H. "The Danish Mohammed Cartoon Crisis and the Role of the EU." Paper prepared for the BISA Annual Conference, University of Cork, Ireland, December 18–20, 2006.

Modood, T. "The Liberal Dilemma: Integration or Vilification?" *International Migration* 44:5 (2006): 4–16.

Powers, S., and A. Arsenault. *The Danish Cartoon Crisis: The Import and Impact of Public Diplomacy.* Los Angeles: USC Center on Public Diplomacy, 2006.

Rose, F. "Why I Published Those Cartoons." *Washington Post,* February 19, 2006.

Rynning, S., and C.H. Schmidt. "Muhammad Cartoons in Denmark: From Freedom of Speech to Denmark's Biggest International Crisis Since 1945." *UNISCI Discussion Papers* 11 (May 2006).

UN Commission on Human Rights. *Racism, Racial Discrimination, Xenophobia and All Forms of Discrimination.* January 18, 2006. E/CN.4/2006/16. Available: http://www.unhcr.org/refworld/docid/441182080.html.

Daoism/Taoism

The word *violence* is used to refer to acts of human aggression, acts of nature, and acts of God. Human violence occurs on various levels, from the intimate and interpersonal to less personal and more general acts of aggression, such as war. Damaging forces of nature range from the simple but deadly virus to the more complex but just as deadly typhoon or earthquake; other acts of God or nature are also described and experienced as violence. In exploring the relationship between Daoism/Taoism and violence, the word will be used to refer to any condition or experience that is not at peace, that promotes aggressive behavior, or that hurts or kills other creatures. From a Chinese perspective, construed broadly, violence is part and parcel with the cosmic forces. From the perspective of the Yinyang philosophy, which was integrated into both Daoist and Confucian thought, nature is composed of two complementary opposites, yin and yang. Yin denotes the dark, passive, female force that is associated with death and decay. Yang denotes the light, active, male force that is associated with life and growth. Violence is connected with the active and aggressive aspect of the yang energy. Generally speaking, for the Chinese tradition and specifically for the Daoist tradition, violence is accepted as a spontaneous aspect of both the natural environment and human culture.

Daoism is an ambiguous term that has been used to refer to various and even inconsistent belief systems. Scholars have applied the term to the political philosophy of Laozi; the self-cultivation philosophy of *Zhuangzi*; the religious beliefs, practices, and liturgy of the Celestial Masters, Spiritualized Treasure, Upper Clarity, and Complete Realization sects of Daoism; various meditative practices; acupuncture and herbal medicine; internal and external alchemy; gymnastics and breathing techniques; martial arts; sexual hygiene techniques; theatrical arts; music; painting; and poetry. Chinese Daoists often employ the expression "Daoist culture" (*daojia wenhua*) to capture the wide range of phenomena associated with Daoism. The term *Daoism* is used to denote a religion and a philosophy; an art form and a science; the foundations of both a systematic, rational understanding of medicine and chemistry and an irrational faith healing and magical system of beliefs. It also refers to a vast collection of various types of literature. More than 1,100 Daoist books are published in the Daoist canon (Daozang).

How Daoism Differs from Other Traditions

Along with Confucianism, Daoism stands as one of the two foundational pillars of Chinese culture. A common saying that captures their interdependent relationship is "Confucian by day, Daoist by night." This means that by day the average Chinese person abides by the beliefs and practices of the Confucian teachings—namely, to be a loyal and obedient member of the family, community, and state; and to be a filial child who becomes a loyal citizen and minister, abiding by ritual action, decorum, and other moral virtues that promote the public life. In the evening, when a person retires from the public eye, he or she can relax and focus on personal development, health, and personal concerns, recite or write poetry, paint or admire paintings, and enjoy music and the cool pleasure of the evening atmosphere and the moonlight. Daoists love to enjoy natural scenery.

Because the label "Daoism" is used to denote a wide spectrum of cultural phenomena, beliefs, and practices, it is difficult to define or describe. At the risk of overgeneralization or oversimplification, one common family resemblance that can be found in many of the belief systems labeled "Daoism" is that followers celebrate the spontaneous fulfillment and the natural enjoyment of living this life here and now. However, it would be an oversimplification to define Daoist religion and philosophy as mere hedonism. Daoists warn against overindulgence in and the pursuit of mere bodily pleasure while advocating the importance of engaging in self-cultivation that culminates in the enjoyment of a complete and long life. Daoist religion is unique among the world's great living traditions in that it advocates teachings that embrace the enjoyment and fulfillment of this life. Most of the great religious traditions propose that this earthly existence serves as a training ground for an afterlife. Many world religions teach that a person cannot achieve spiritual fulfillment in this body, in this life. According to the monotheistic traditions, a person must die and be resurrected before he or she can find eternal happiness in the afterlife. In the polytheistic and nontheistic teachings of Hinduism and Buddhism, a person must undergo countless reincarnations before he or she can be reborn in a paradise, such as the Buddhist Pure Land, or attain enlightenment—the Hindu *moksha* or the Buddhist *nirvana*. In contrast, the teachings of Daoism celebrate living this life to its fullest, being content with and finding fulfillment in this earthly existence, and an ultimate mystical union with the *dao* (cosmic way). Daoists embrace the present life and strive to prolong it, attempting to live a long life or even attain physical immortality.

Another interesting and major difference between Daoism and many of the other religions of the world is that Daoist priests take control over and command the spirits and gods; whereas in many religions it is believed that the spirits and gods have control over humans, and humans cannot or may not gain control over them. A third point of contrast is that where some of the major religions—such as early Judaism, Islam, Hinduism, and Confucianism—emphasize justice over mercy, Daoism, similar to Christianity and Buddhism, emphasizes mercy over justice. As the *Laozi* proposes, "Repay ill will with beneficence" (Poem 60), and "Do good to those who are not good" (Poem 49).

Origins

The origins of Daoism are shrouded in the prehistoric and early history of the geographical region known as China. Prehistoric humans were confounded by the problem of survival and death. The two perennial concerns they faced were confronting a hostile environment and group solidarity. If human aggression could be redirected so that people could work and live together in community, then managing the shortcomings of the physical environment could be better managed and survived. Confucianism focuses on keeping human social behavior in check, while Daoism offers guidance on controlling and harmonizing with the forces of nature. Daoism has its origins in the ancient tribal practices of the medicine man, the medicine woman, the shaman, and the warrior. The shaman is noted for undertaking spiritual journeys underground, underwater, or in the sky. The shaman communicates with and may even control the forces of nature or the spirit powers that control the forces of nature. The tribal shaman or healer discovers the medicinal and life-extending properties of minerals, herbs, animal by-products, and other materials. The shaman and warrior practice breathing techniques and gymnastics as part of their training to develop self-control and insight. All of these practices influenced the development of Daoist religion, philosophy, medicine, and alchemy.

According to Daoist belief and mythology, Daoism begins naturally with the dao, which generates the various energy fields and forces of existence. These forces or energy fields are usually anthropomorphized or conceived to be in human form, represented as gods or divine emperors, kings, rulers, and ministers of a spiritualized bureaucracy. The energy fields, conceived in human form as gods and spirits, structure the physical world and are responsible for the functions and operations of all of the forces of nature, from the galaxies and stars to the subtlest positive and negative charges of an atom. The anthropomorphized energy fields or forces of nature are depicted as operating by means of a bureaucracy for two reasons. First, the spiritualized bureaucracy is a reflection of

the imperial bureaucracy used to govern the dynasties. Second, the spiritual bureaucracy represents an organic synergistic process, which we might represent today in terms of organismic chemical transformations. One of the distinctly Chinese contributions to the development of human thought and science is the concept of a nonmechanical, organismic, systems approach. This approach was begun in Daoism, came to fruition in neo-Confucian philosophy, and was transmitted to Europe via Gottfried Wilhelm Leibniz (or Leibnitz; 1646–1716) and Jesuit missionaries. In Daoist mythology one of the earliest manifestations of the dao in human form was Lord Lao (Laojun), also known as Master Lao (Laozi) or "old master." According to one popular legend, Laozi was born after a sixty-year pregnancy. He did not experience a normal birth but walked out of his mother's abdomen with gray hair and the ability to speak. This story is partly derived from a pun based on the name Laozi, which according to one reading can mean "old son."

According to historical documents, the school of Daoist philosophy has its origins in a text attributed to Laozi. The text, like many ancient Chinese texts, is also referred to by the name of its alleged author; so it is called the *Laozi* (or *Lao Tzu*). Because the text is composed of two sections, namely the Power (*de*), and the Way (*dao*) chapters, it is also referred to as the *Classic of the Way and Its Power* (*Daodejing*). The early historians could not exactly identify who Laozi was. Modern scholars debate the historical authenticity of Laozi and whether or not he was the author of the *Daodejing*. Although the authorship and origin of the work are matters of scholarly debate, scholars and Daoist practitioners recognize that text to be a foundational literary source of Daoist teachings.

The *Laozi* and Violence

The *Laozi* consists of eighty-one short passages, most of which are rhymed poems, and the text has left a lasting impact on world literature. Such popular sayings as "The journey of a thousand miles begins with the first step" (Poem 64); "Without being last you cannot be first" (Poem 67); "Violent people will not die a natural death" (Poem 42); and "He who speaks does not know" (Poem 56) are derived from the *Laozi*. Historically speaking, after being orally transmitted for some time (possibly as long as two or three centuries), the text appears to have been written down by the middle of the third century B.C.E. by court ministers in order to provide guidance to other ministers and especially to the king or feudal lord, concerning the art of rulership. In 1973, two copies of the text were excavated from the Mawangdui tomb, which had been sealed in 168 B.C.E.

The basic idea of the text is that the person who masters the cosmic way, or dao, can master him- or herself and thereby become worthy to govern a state. Because the text has a political focus, it contains passages that deal with violence, the military, and war. For Daoist practitioners, the text is read as a manual for self-cultivation and to gain insights concerning the operations of the cosmic dao. Two related notions that are crucial for understanding the *Laozi* and Daoism in general are (1) the interchange of opposites, and (2) the return. The interchange of opposites refers to the experience of how opposites flip-flop—that is, how dry things become wet, hot becomes cold, soft becomes rigid, and vice versa. Related to this interchange of opposites is the notion that things return to their original source, the way of nature, or dao. Because the cosmic dao operates according to a pattern of reversal, the *Laozi* establishes a practice that pervades later forms of Daoism that entail rejecting conventional wisdom and practices by doing things backwards, so to speak. For example, because striving ends in failure and gain leads to loss, the *Laozi* advocates "acting by not taking action; managing affairs by not managing them" (Poem 63). Conventional wisdom has it that people must expend their energy to fulfill their desires. The *Laozi* proposes just the opposite: to fulfill the most basic natural desire to live well and long, a person must conserve energy. The return is also tied to another important aspect of Daoism—namely, the mystical union of returning to the dao, which is developed in the *Zhuangzi,* the second ancient text of Daoism. At first the claims of the *Laozi* appear to be paradoxes, but once the reader becomes orientated in the *Laozi*'s upside-down and backward way of looking at the processes of nature, the paradoxes are resolved. So although Daoists recognize that violence, aggression, and war are part and parcel of nature and human life, they seek to overturn them by living a softer, gentler, more peaceful form of existence. Consider the third poem of the *Laozi:*

> Do not exalt the talented, this will cause the people to stop fighting.
> Do not cherish things difficult to obtain, this will cause the people to stop robbing.
> Do not display desirable things, this will cause the people's hearts to be undisturbed.
> This is how the sage brings order to the state by:
> Emptying their hearts;
> Filling their bellies;
> Weakening their ambitions;
> Toughening their bones.
> Always cause the people to be without knowledge and without desire;
> Cause those who are wise to dare not take action.
> If they can practice the art of not taking action, then nothing will not be properly ordered.
> (Poem 3; original translations by the author)

This passage gives advice concerning the art of rulership. It contains three recurring themes: of being without knowledge, being without desire, and acting by not acting. The idea is to lead the people to live simple lives. Having sufficient food in their bellies and healthy bodies and not coveting rare and precious commodities, will stop conflict and robbery. What is valued is that the ruler and the masses live simple, peaceful, and tranquil lives.

The *Laozi* advocates that the key to living well and properly organizing a kingdom is to avoid conflict: "The only means is to stop fighting, thereby you will never be blamed" (Poem 8). The ruler must be at peace within himself to bring peace to the people. All people, but especially the ruler, are advised to avoid overindulgence, avoid dazzling colors, sights, sounds, and flavors, and avoid violent activities, such as hunting (Poem 8), to find their inner tranquility. A person who preserves inner tranquility attains the utmost void within and, through contemplation, makes the return (Poem 16). When such a person serves as the ruler, he or she can "dispense with shrewdness and dispel profit taking; robbers and thieves will no longer exist" in the state (Poem 19).

Violence is a part of nature, but even the sky and earth cannot make violence persist. Likewise, human violence cannot last long:

> To speak few words is spontaneous.
> Therefore, a whirlwind will not last the morning;
> A storm will not last the whole day.
> Who causes them? Sky and earth!
> If sky and earth are not able to make them last long,
> How much less can people?!
> So follow the dao in all endeavors. (Poem 23)

The burst of yang energy required to promote violent acts cannot last long or produce lasting effects. The Daoist ruler is advised to follow the way of nature. Such a ruler may have to resort to violence, but he or she knows that lasting results come from inner tranquility, being flexible and gentle. The vast powers of nature do not generate long-lasting violence.

For the most part the gentle breeze and morning dew are the norm, not the whirlwind and storm. The ruler who can abide by the example of nature can be entrusted with the state.

Images of avoiding aggression and violence abound in the *Laozi*. The ruler is advised to avoid excess (Poem 29), which includes violence. The ruler and general may have to resort to war, but they do not take pride in it, and they put an end to it quickly. As Poem 30 advises,

> Those who guide their ruler in the dao
> Do not run roughshod over the empire by force of arms
> Such actions return in kind.
> Thorn and thistle bushes grow, where armies camp.
> Poor harvests are certain, after a major campaign.
> The good achieve the outcome and stop;
> They dare not keep using force.
> After achieving the outcome:
>> Do not brag, boast, or feel proud;
>> Recognize that there was no other choice;
>> Do not force the issue.
> Things growing old in the prime of life is called going against the dao.
> Things going against the dao come to an early demise.
> (Poem 30)

This advice is continued in Poem 31, where it is made clear that the violence of war may have to be tolerated but cannot be celebrated:

> Strong troops are the instrument of ill omen.
> People despise them.
> Hence, those who comply with the dao do not abide by them.
> At home, the ruler respects those on the left.
> At war, he respects those on the right.
> Because troops are the instrument of ill omen,
> They are not the ruler's preferred instrument.
> He deploys them because he has no other choice.
> He values peace and quiet;
> He does not rejoice after a victory.
> To rejoice in it is to find pleasure in the slaughter of human life.
> Anyone who finds pleasure in the slaughter of human life will not

achieve his ambition in the empire.
On auspicious occasions, preference is given to those
    on the left.
On inauspicious occasions, preference is given to those
    on the right.
The Lieutenant Commanders stand on the left.
The Supreme Commander stands on the right.
This means that the Supreme Commander is associated
    with funeral rites.
When a multitude has been slaughtered, we mourn for
    them in grief and sorrow.
Victory in battle is associated with funeral rites.
    (Poem 31)

The Daoist ruler identifies with the pure simplicity of the uncarved block of wood, and thereby the masses spontaneously regulate themselves (Poem 32). Emphasis is placed on the ruler's self-mastery: "Power is to conquer others; / Strength lies in conquering oneself" (Poem 33). Because of the interchange of opposites, "The soft and the weak overcome the hard and the strong. Just as the fish should not be removed from the depths, likewise the state's sharp weapons should not be displayed before the people" (Poem 36).

In the context of the blood shed during the Warring States period (403–221 B.C.E.), the *Laozi* clearly advocates that the sage ruler must promote peace and tranquility within the nation and between nations. Poem 45 maintains that the empire is properly ordered through purity and tranquility. Poem 46 notes, "When the empire complies with the dao, fast horses fertilize the fields. When the empire has lost the dao, war horses are raised in the suburbs." The text sponsors gentle mercy rather than even-handed justice. Loving mercy is one of the *Laozi*'s three treasures (Poem 67). Contrary to the teaching of Confucius, the *Laozi* advocates repaying ill will with beneficence (Poem 63) and doing good to those who are not good themselves (Poem 49). The sage ruler is "a leader, not a butcher" (Poems 10 and 51, following Wu 1961). Note that

this passage can also be translated as "to allow things to grow and not dominate them."

One of the most profound statements concerning violence in the *Laozi* is "What others have taught, I also teach: 'Violent people will not die a natural death'" (Poem 42). Poetic images abound that describe death as a natural part of living; a few passages also suggest the possibility of extending life or overcoming death. The perennial predicament is that humans are confronted with the inevitability of death. In a sense, all of the religions of the world offer a solution to the problem of death, and Daoism likewise offers the hope of physical immortality. The *Laozi* proposes that those who live in harmony with the dao can enter battle without being harmed by weapons and that dangerous animals can find no place to sink their teeth or claws on such a person (Poem 50). This passage can be interpreted to mean that the person who lives in harmony with the dao is able to avoid such dangerous circumstances, but the passage has been interpreted literally by Daoists, martial arts experts, and various rebel groups, including those who led the Boxer Rebellion in 1909, believing that they could not be harmed by weapons, even bullets. Despite the *Laozi*'s teachings that seek to balance the excesses of violence, the text has been used to promulgate violence.

Legend has it that when Laozi was attempting to leave the Zhou dynasty (1040–256 B.C.E.) and travel to the West, Kuan Yin, the border guard, requested that he leave behind a text. Kuan Yin was the first adept to receive a text. The transmitting of texts from master to disciple has marked the historical development of Daoism. Historically, Laozi underwent a process of apotheosis and was defied as Lord Lao during the Han dynasty. Before Daoism developed as an organized religion, the *Laozi/Daodejing* was being chanted in ritual at the court of Emperor Han Wudi (141–87 B.C.E.).

Zhuangzi

The second early classic of Daoism is the *Zhuangzi*. Master Zhuang's personal name was Zhou. He is believed to have held a minor post as the official in charge of the lacquer tree park in Meng during the fourth century B.C.E. Only the first seven "inner chapters" of the thirty-three-chapter text that carries his name are believed to be his essays. This text develops a rich philosophy of language and meaning that scholars are still excavating. It also contains a number of poetic cosmological images of the dao, the Daoist sage, and the Sublime or True Person (*Zhenren*) that impact later developments of religious Daoism. The *Zhuangzi* is a composite text, containing a diversity of ideas and teachings from various different but related traditions. In the inner chapters, a profound nature philosophy is presented alongside stories of pale, soft-skinned, spiritualized, numinous beings who live deep in the mountains.

The teachings of the Daoist master Zhuang offer a nature mysticism—that is, a mystical experience of union with the cosmic dao. With the pervasive violence and bloodshed of the Warring States period as the background for the *Zhuangzi,* Zhuang Zhou's teachings provide self-cultivation techniques, meditation, and a philosophy of personal transformation as a means to attain a serene and tranquil life. The text provides stories that depict conflicts between Daoist masters and shamans, a theme carried on later in the historical development of Daoism. The *Zhuangzi* offers poetic images of free and easy wandering, carefree vacations floating down the rivers of life, aerial images of free flight, riding the winds, and charioteering the sun and moon to depict its nature mysticism. Passages from the later chapters of the *Zhuangzi* link Laozi and the Great Unity (*Taiyi*), an early divinity, which led to the deification of Laozi as Lord Lao.

The Celestial Masters and Violence

The Daoist religion was founded in violence—the physical violence of political rebellion and the spiritual violence of waging war against malicious demons and ghosts. Daoism grew out of and in turn rejected shaman practices. Ancient shamans in China, as elsewhere, danced themselves into trance, entered altered states of consciousness, and experienced states of ecstasy. These practices are evident in Daoist mysticism and religious practices, such as the ritual dance called the Steps of Yü, the Great. As the religion developed, Daoist priests vehemently attacked and criticized the beliefs and practices of village or clan cults and shamans. Toward the end of the Warring States period and during the short-lived Qin dynasty (221–206 B.C.E.) and the Former Han dynasty (206 B.C.E.–8 C.E.), popular religious beliefs and practices associated with exorcism, healing, and funerals were gaining popularity among both the common people and the aristocrats. The Yellow Emperor (Huangdi), the Yellow God of the Big Dipper, and a Yellow Old God (Huanglao) were very popular. There were also different but related movements associated with the Yellow Emperor and Laozi, also referred to as Huanglao, that affected political and medical thinking. Experts in methods (*fangshi*), who were independent practitioners of faith healing and shamanic arts, were the chief religious figures.

Two independent but related religious and political movements that developed at the end of the Later Han dynasty (25–220 C.E.) transformed some of the independent popular practices into an organized Daoist religion. In eastern and central China, a millenarian and messianic group named after their yellow headgear, the Yellow Turbans (also known as the Way of Supreme Peace), organized a rebellion against the Han in 184 C.E., which marked the first year in the sixty-year cycle. In the West, the Celestial Masters formed an independent state in Sichuan. Both groups focused on a text called *The Classic of Supreme Peace* (*Taiping jing*). Scholars debate whether there were two different texts with that title or one text that was used by both groups. Both groups shared certain practices, such as using talismans, holy water with the ashes of talismans, meditation, and confession to cure illness; reciting and chanting texts such as the *Laozi* and the *Taiping jing*; venerating the god Huanglao; organizing their ecclesiastical hierarchy on the three powers—namely, heaven, earth, and humanity—and honoring the sage-ruler as a religious and political figure. Both groups proposed that the Han would fall and a new world order would be ushered in by a moral state led by a religious-political leader. The *Taiping jing* refers to the spiritual sage-ruler as the celestial or heavenly appointed master (*tianshi*). The Yellow Turbans were defeated. The Celestial Masters survived the fall of the Han dynasty and formed the foundation of a public, organized Daoist religion that continues to exist to this day.

Around 142 C.E., Zhang Daoling claimed that he had begun to receive revelations from Lord Lao, encouraging him to prepare the chosen "seed people" who would inherit the empire and the world after an impending collapse of the Han dynasty. Lord Lao revealed to Zhang Daoling the new law known as the Sworn Oath Authority of the Orthodox Unity (Zhengyimengwei), which is another name for the Celestial Masters movement. Because its leaders collected a tithing of five bushels of rice, the movement is also known as the Way of the Five Bushels of Rice (Wudoumidao).

Unlike the Yellow Turbans, the Celestial Masters did not attempt to overthrow the Han dynasty directly. The Celestial Masters argued that they had been given the mandate to rule; so they founded an interregnum that would prepare the seed people for the transition to a renewed Han dynasty that would be governed by Daoist morality. Zhang Daoling's grandson, Zhang Lu, inherited the title of Celestial Master, but he apparently was not enthroned. Zhang Lu ceded political authority to General Cao Cao (155–220) in 215. In 215, Cao Cao formally recognized the Celestial Masters as an organized religion. Because the Celestial Masters maintained good relations with the Han imperial family, Cao Cao, and the founder of the Wei dynasty (220–264), the Daoist church established a firm root in Chinese culture during a period of political turmoil.

The Celestial Masters focused their attacks against the practices and beliefs of popular religion that have been associated with peasant farmers but were also practiced by aristocrats, especially in regard to funeral talismans and rites. The relationship between the Daoist church and popular, folk religion is a complex one. One of the reasons that the Celestial Masters have been able to persevere is their ability to incorporate practices and beliefs from popular customs as well as from Confucianism, Buddhism, and other organized religions. The Celestial Masters openly advocate that they share many of the values and goals of Confucianism and Buddhism. They vehemently oppose shamans (*wu*), extremist cults, and deviant teachings. They seek "to correct" and "unify" (*zhengyi*) humanity's relationship with the divine through the teachings of their Orthodox Unity (Zhengyi). They became the self-appointed priest-administrators of the Three Heavens (sky, earth, and water), who were expected to do battle against the evil Six Heavens. Basically, the program was to replace the worship of the local gods with worship of the Celestial Masters and their official hierarchy of the gods, spirits, and immortals as described in the revealed texts received by the masters.

As the Confucians of the Han dynasty created a complex bureaucratic administrative system to manage the empire, likewise the Daoists created an equally sophisticated spiritual bureaucracy to administer to the spiritual and physical needs of the people—namely, by practicing exorcism and curing the sick. One of the chief functions of the Daoist priest (*daoshi*) is to perform administrative duties similar to those of a bureaucrat in office—to issue edicts and to invoke by written commands the spiritual laws or Daoist gods and spirits to do his bidding in expelling demons, ghosts, and lesser gods or clan ancestor spirits. The demons are described as frightening creatures arrayed in armor and armed to the fangs with deadly weapons and magical powers. The malevolent demons and the Daoist gods are addressed by military titles such as soldier and general. The spiritual "weapons" wielded by the priests include handwritten talismans, holy water, the priest's spiritualized breath (*qi*), sacred writings and texts, and magical curses, along with battle assistance from the Daoist gods and spirits. To distinguish their system of belief from Buddhism and the popular practices, Celestial Masters' texts claim that they champion "loving life and despising death." While they appropriated the healing and exorcism powers and practices of the shamans, they criticized the shamans and engaged in spiritual battle against them and the spirits they commanded (Robinet 1997).

Later Daoist Sects

The Celestial Masters laid the foundation for the Daoist church. Ge Hong (c. 280–c. 343) authored *The Master Who Embraces Simplicity,* incorporating meditation and medical practices with alchemical and immortality practices. Between 364 and 370, Yang Xi received revelations and revealed texts from Lady Wei and other beings, and the Upper Clarity (Shangqing) sect developed. The gods of the Upper Clarity sect competed against the Celestial Masters and their gods while co-opting their battle against the folk cults. As the Upper Clarity sect attracted aristocrats, the prestige of the Celestial Masters declined. Around 400 C.E., the Spiritualized Treasure (Lingbao) sect's writings began to appear. The Spiritualized Treasure sect continued the divine battle by directly waging war against Buddhism, claiming that Buddhism was merely the teachings of Laozi that were disseminated after he left China and traveled to the West. The Spiritualized Treasure also generously incorporated elements from Upper Clarity texts. In opposition to the individualistic practices of the Upper Clarity teachings, the Spiritualized Treasure sect employed the Buddhist notion of universal liberation for all sentient beings.

During the Tang dynasty (618–907), Daoism enjoyed imperial sponsorship. During the Song dynasty (960–1126), internal alchemy was gaining in popularity, and the Complete Realization (Quanzhen) sect developed as a Daoist monastic response to Buddhist monasteries. During the Ming (1368–1644) and Qing (1644–1911) dynasties, the Upper Clarity and Spiritualized Treasure sects were reabsorbed into the Celestial Masters sect. To this day the Celestial Masters and the Complete Realization sects continue to wage battle against the ancestor spirits and lesser gods of the folk cults.

Daoism is a peace-loving religion that teaches people to be kind to those who hate them. The history of Daoism shows that Daoist movements became entangled in political rebellions in an attempt to fight for social justice. On the spiritual side, Daoist practices, especially exorcisms, and rituals are best understood as acts of spiritual warfare against the demons that cause illness.

James D. Sellmann

See also: Asia, Central; Asia, Southeast; Buddhism; Chinese Folk Religion; Confucianism.

Further Reading

Bokenkamp, Stephen R. *Early Daoist Scriptures.* Berkeley: University of California Press, 1997.

Ivanhoe, Philip J., trans. *The Daodejing of Laozi.* New York: Seven Bridges Press, 2002.

Robinet, Isabelle. *Taoism: Growth of a Religion.* Stanford, CA: Stanford University Press, 1997.

Watson, Burton, trans. *The Complete Works of Chuang Tzu.* New York: Columbia University Press, 1968.

Wu, John C.H., trans. *Lao Tzu Tao Teh Ching.* New York: St. John's University Press, 1961.

Yu, David C., trans. *History of Chinese Daoism*, vol. 1. Lanham, MD, and New York: Oxford University Press of America, 2000.

Death Penalty

At the beginning of the twenty-first century, an increasing number of countries had come to abolish the death penalty as the ultimate legal sanction applicable to one who has committed a crime. In the Western world, the legal abolition of capital punishment—a relatively late historical movement—has been supported in recent times by religious authorities. While death on religious grounds was historically prescribed for crimes, since 1958 most of the main religious groups in the United States and denominations and sects within them, have issued official statements opposing the death penalty, endorsing it, or refusing to take an official stance.

Today's religious assessment of the death penalty contrasts with the way it was conceived of as an acknowledged mode of punishment throughout the history of religion. To answer the question of how religion apprehends the death penalty, one must trace the evolution of the relationship between religion and capital punishment and examine certain significant historical stages in the development of this punitive practice.

The history of the death penalty is marked by the recurrence of the same set of arguments to justify its enforcement. One is whether society can give itself the right to sentence to death anyone who violated the law and made an attempt on another's physical integrity. Another is whether institutionalized killing is an appropriate response to illegal killing. Through the ages, the death penalty was regarded as the unique and appropriate means of either restoring the disrupted social order or preventing, through the fear of death, any future social disruption caused by criminal acts. Thus, the death penalty is meant to meet different ends. It is retributive, based on the primary principle of equivalence in punishment (one who killed must be killed); it is an obvious way of defending the society against the criminal (being put to death, the wrongdoer will not commit future crimes); it is a deterrent (executions will dissuade anyone else from attempting to commit similar crimes).

Biblical Accounts

While the Old Testament contains numerous dispositions, sometimes articulated as legal codes, the Gospel is virtually devoid of prescriptions except where Christ's message presents itself as a reinterpretation of the Hebraic laws. The Old Testament consists of quite a wide array of criminal measures, including the death penalty. These texts, which represent an interesting account of the original Jewish people's conception of law, would be incorporated later by Christian thinkers, including the fathers of the church, into their arguments up to the present time.

In ancient societies, where the only social structure was the family or the tribe, the leader exerted an absolute authority—that is, a right of life or death over the other members of the group. The absolute character of this kind of authority is best exemplified by the biblical passage in which Abraham acts as an executor of the divine judgment requiring that he sacrifice his son Isaac (Genesis 22:1–10). Revenge, as the individual action taken against one who committed a harmful act, appeared to be a prevailing practice among families or tribes (Genesis 4:22–23). As applied to homicide, the principle assumes the following form: "If anyone sheds the blood of man, by man shall his blood be shed; for in the image of God has man been made" (Genesis 9:6). Later, the settlement of the people in a territory and the emergence of an embryonic form of political organization would be coeval with a restricted use of revenge. This specific type of punishment came to be regulated by a legal principle, *lex talionis*, or talion, which authorized only a proportionate retaliation against the offender. The basic form of this punishment, which is found in the idea of "Life for life, eye for eye, tooth for tooth, hand for hand, foot for foot, burn for burn, wound for wound, stripe for stripe," repeatedly occurs in the Old Testament (e.g., Exodus 21:23–25; Leviticus 24:17–21; Deuteronomy 19:22). With respect to the biblical context, this formulation is open to various interpretations. Nevertheless, the talion principle unconditionally applies to willful crimes.

In the case of willful homicide, talion obviously calls for the death penalty, as shown in Exodus 21:12 and Leviticus 24:17. Yet the death penalty was prescribed for many other crimes, including idolatry, blasphemy, witchcraft, violation of the sabbath, adultery, incest, rape, and kidnapping. Stoning, the usual mode of punishment, was sometimes followed by the exposition of the condemned person's body and was regarded as fully achieving the sentence of death. The whole community participated in the execution of the judgment expressing God's wrath, which was directed against those who broke the obedience and service covenant. Idolatry, the worship of other gods, is a clear example of the collective character of such a traditional punishment: "Show them no pity or compassion and do not shield them. But you shall surely kill them; your hand shall be first against them to execute them, and afterwards the hand of all the people" (Deuteronomy 13:10–11). These prescriptions would later influence the Islamic law (sharia) that would endorse the stoning of women convicted of adultery—and still does, at least in the Muslim countries where it is implemented.

However, the idea of death as penalty, for which the Old Testament provides numerous cases, starkly contrasts with the imperative demand formulated in the Decalogue: "Thou shalt not kill" (Exodus 20:13). God, talking to Moses, asserted through this saying the intrinsic value of human life. Christianity would rely upon this fundamental teaching rather than on the set of precepts laid down by the Mosaic law.

With respect to the ancient code of laws, Christ's preaching carries with it a new commandment: "I give you a new commandment, that you love one another" (John 13:34). Far from abrogating the Hebrew legal code, it sheds some light on its very spirit. Charity accordingly becomes the shape to which social relationships conform, and communal life is conceived as peaceful. The faithful thus receive the Christian precept constituting this universal religion, *Pax et Charitas*: "Blessed are the peacemakers, for they will be called children of God" (Matthew 5:9). As a result, Christianity repudiates the older use of punishments, even codified ones such as talion: "You have heard that it was said, 'An eye for an eye, and a tooth for a tooth.' But I say to you, Do not resist an evildoer. But if anyone strikes you on the right cheek, turn the other also" (Matthew 5:38–39). Peace also implies forgiveness as an explicit moral requirement. Forgiving one's neighbor proves to be the very condition for the Christian believer to rightly expect God's forgiveness. This moral requirement will find its proper

Cardinal Theodore E. McCarrick, archbishop of Washington, DC, at a March 21, 2005, press conference to announce the Catholic Campaign to End the Use of the Death Penalty. The twenty-first century has seen a decline in support for the death penalty among American Catholics and an aggressive campaign by the Church to abolish the practice in the United States. (*Joe Raedle/Getty Images*)

juridical translation in the Christian medieval penal practice.

Not only did Christ formulate such moral precepts, he also revoked the earlier conception of penalty on at least two occasions, both of which illustrate the moral superiority inherent in forgiveness. The first biblical episode, that of the woman taken in adultery, concludes with a word underlining that such a crime can be forgiven: "'Woman, where are they? Has no one condemned you?' She said, 'No one, sir.' And

Jesus said, 'Neither do I condemn you. Go your way, and from now on do not sin again'" (John 8:3–11). Luke reports another episode in which Samaritans refuse to help Jesus and his disciples while on their way to Jerusalem. In order to take revenge for what they regarded as an affront, James and John then suggest to Christ, "'Lord, do you want us to command fire to come down from heaven and consume them?' But he turned and rebuked them. Then they went on to another village" (Luke 9:54–55). Medieval jurists, who were acquainted with this biblical source—in which Luke alludes to the book of Kings (Kings 1:12 et seq.)—through Saint Augustine, will see in this passage an illustration of the opposition between two codes of laws, the old and the new, dealing with punishment and forgiveness.

But for all that, one cannot conclude that Christianity gives priority to forgiveness over coercive penalty for offenses. Although certain Christian sects adopted such a stance, the Church remained more nuanced. By distinguishing two realms, the terrestrial and the celestial, Christ recognized the legitimacy of human justice: "Give therefore to the emperor the things that are the emperor's, and to God the things that are God's" (Matthew 22:21), which means that the state exerts its proper and legitimate authority over men even though political authority ultimately derives from God. This Christian political doctrine has penal consequences. When coming to terms with the lawfulness of the radical elimination of the criminal, Christ himself admits that the wrongdoer be slayed (Mark 9:42; Matthew 18:6; Luke 17:2). Finally, the words pronounced by the "good thief" on the cross next to Jesus eventually encapsulate the Christian principle of retributive justice: "And we indeed have been condemned justly, for we are getting what we deserve for our deeds, but this man [Jesus] has done nothing wrong" (Luke 23:41).

If the Gospel places the emphasis on a moral superiority inherent in forgiveness, that does not preclude the administration of punishment including the death penalty. Christianity can be said to be founded on the primary principle of forgiveness and the concomitant abandonment of revenge. But it makes provision for an exception to that principle in case of "public scandal," thus letting political authority adjudicate the crime. In his letter to the Christian ecclesia of Rome, Paul claims that political authority is divorced from the Christian community: "Let every person be subject to the governing authorities; for there is no authority except from God, and those authorities that exist have been instituted by God" (Romans 13:1). He acknowledges that a coercive human justice, as was Roman justice, is to be established: "But if you do what is wrong, you should be afraid, for the authority does not bear the sword in vain! It is the servant of God to execute wrath on the wrongdoer" (Romans 13:4).

The historical intertwining of Roman law and Christianity dampened to some degree the harshness of criminal practice. The fact that a larger number of subjects under the empire were granted Roman citizenship led the authorities to refrain from using death as penalty. Citizenship in itself constituted an impediment to the enforcement of capital punishment to the extent that such individual legal status required that the immunity it conferred upon citizens be removed. The extension of citizenship also paralleled the development of slavery as a substitute for capital punishment in order to meet the economic needs of the Roman Empire. But, by the end of that period, the death penalty was increasingly used to confront internal turbulences and external threats. From this view, it can be said that Christianity did not influence the Roman legislation. Before the reign of the emperor Constantine, when Christian worship was not tolerated, Christian communities usually provided assistance for prisoners and slaves alike. After Constantine, the whole penal system was reinforced to withstand the weakening of the social order. In this regard, Christianity approved of legal punishment, then seen as an anticipation of God's perfect justice (Romans 13:4); or did not leave out of account the possibility that violence often evokes more calls for violence—"All who take the sword will perish by the sword" (Matthew 26:52); or patiently endured injustice with hope (Peter 2:8–17). Christianity thus did not introduce any substantial change into the structure of the legal system, although the recollection of the crucifixion of Christ next to two wrongdoers could nurture compassion toward those who were found guilty. Only centuries later would compassion be part of a different understanding of criminal justice, which may be linked to the influence of secular humanism rather than to Christian theology.

The Fathers of the Church

Early Christian writers came to terms with criminal punishment, whether capital or other, and found in the Gospel the moral imperative of charity, from which stems forgiveness for offenses. In early Christian communities, one strived to adjudicate criminal cases without falling back on state power. Even in the wake of the Edict of Milan (313 C.E.), which put an end to the persecution of Christians, the fathers of the church still nurtured doubts about human justice and the reliability of the judicial institution. The Christian tradition tends to call into question our ability to judge our fellows insofar as human justice is subject to miscarriage. The church fathers' awareness of the potential defectiveness of human justice elicited their reluctance toward capital punishment. By the end of 408, Augustine wrote to the Roman proconsul of Africa, a Catholic layman, about the Donatist heresy—a dissenting movement within the Roman church that eventually resulted in a schism (which began in Africa in 311 C.E.) and whose members held in abhorrence all those who abjured their religion under the rule of Diocletian after the emperor proclaimed through an edict that Christians should be persecuted:

> We do not seek vengeance upon our enemies on this earth. . . . We love our enemies and pray for them. Hence, we desire that, by making use of judges and laws that cause fear, they be corrected, not killed, so that they do not fall into the punishments of eternal damnation. We do not want discipline to be neglected in their regard or the punishment they deserve to be applied. Repress their sins, therefore, in such a way that those who repent having sinned may still exist. (Letter 100)

The imposition of the death penalty would inevitably make impossible individual repentance for crimes as well as amendment. From this view, it is clear that the church does not intend to support the infliction of the death penalty but instead expects sinners to be converted. So the mandate "Thou shalt not kill" also applies to judges.

However, in the face of the spread of the Donatist heresy, Augustine moved to a different position and admitted that state coercion is required to restore some kind of civil order. By virtue of the separation between the terrestrial and ecclesial realms, the role of the state is to secure and preserve the stability of the social order. That is the reason Augustine eventually endorsed the sanctioning of the use of force by public law, not canonic law. In 413 or 414 C.E., Augustine wrote a letter to Macedonius, who was at that time a vicar in Africa, in which he explains why the state's power was instituted and Christian clemency does not interfere with it:

> Nor does it follow that the power of the sovereign, the judge's right over life and death, the executioner's instruments of torture, the weapons of the soldier, the discipline of the ruler, and the severity of a good father were instituted to no avail. All these have their limits, causes, reasons, and utility. When these are feared, the evil are held in check and the good live more peaceful lives among the evil. (Letter 153)

Thus, he enumerates in the *City of God* eight types of punishments, and following Paul's teaching (*Non sine causa gladium portat*—"For he bears not the sword in vain"), he considers that the state, whose role is to secure civil order, is legitimately allowed to resort to the death penalty. Judges would be able to prescribe and impose the death penalty on certain criminals without being accused of committing the sin of homicide.

The church of the time, which adopted Augustine's main lines of argument as well as that of the other fathers, posited the sanctity of human life as a defining principle. The death penalty, which then appeared to be an exception to such a principle, could be prescribed only by the legitimate authorities. Contrary to the state, the church does not have the power to visit the death penalty upon criminals. This view of the death penalty would later be refined by medieval canonists and theologians, and from the twelfth century onward civil jurists would draw upon the Roman law legacy at a time when it pervaded the Western world.

Thomas Aquinas

In the Middle Ages, Thomas Aquinas (1225–1274), the most influential thinker and theologian of that period, presented a rather sophisticated elaboration of criminal penalty as prescribed and administered by human justice. In his *Summa Theologica* (I-I, q. 48), Aquinas comes to terms with the basic distinction between good and evil. Evil may originate from either external causes or the human will. As one needs to assess the righteousness of individual conduct, then the following question arises: How can evil spring from human will? Man, Aquinas says, is subject to the human order (common good), to the individual order (morality), and to the divine order. By refusing to act in accord with his own reason or with the human or divine order, the wrongdoer disrupts the general arrangement of the human world. As a consequence, he incurs appropriate punishments, which are conceived as the payment of the debt he contracted through violating the ordered society, whether civil or ecclesiastical. Punishment therefore contributes to the maintenance or the restoration of the disturbed order (II-II, q. 68).

As penalty is clearly construed with respect to the common good, the problem is then one of defining the very nature of the retributive punishment that must be executed. What kind of punishment will enable the wrongdoer to pay his compensation for disrupting the human community? Contrasting divine and human punishments, Aquinas makes clear that, despite the commandment not to kill, the death penalty turns out to be an adequate means, especially when the wrongdoer threatens or endangers the whole community (IIa-IIe, q. 64. art. 2, concl.). It is thus lawful for judges to sentence a criminal to death: "The life of certain pestiferous men is an impediment to the common good, which is the concord of human society. Therefore, certain men must be removed by death from human society. . . . Therefore, the ruler of a state executes pestiferous men justly and sinlessly, in order that peace of the state may not be disturbed" (*Contra Gentiles,* III, c. 146).

This impressive endorsement of the death penalty, which occurs in a different form in the *Summa Theologica,* warrants further examination. In order to grasp Aquinas's view, one should pay attention to the status of the individual and his relationship with society. Aquinas, who never openly tackles the question of man's place within society, suggests that the community prevails over the individual. As suggested earlier, man is subordinate to both the social and divine orders. In any case, he is defined as being part of a greater whole, that is, society itself. Furthermore, he is entirely directed to society's use: "Every part is directed to the whole, as imperfect to perfect, wherefore every part is naturally for the sake of the whole" (*Summa Theologica,* II-II, q. 64, art. 2). Thus, it may prove necessary to put to death any member who imperils the integrity of the whole society. "Now every individual person is compared to the whole community, as part to whole. Therefore if a man be dangerous and infectious to the community, on account of some sin, it is praiseworthy and advantageous that he be killed in order to safeguard the common good" (ibid.). Such a position, which leaves no room for recognition of the individual as bearing specific rights, obviously stands in stark contrast with the later developments in the wake of the Enlightenment.

One should not think that such an impressive statement is Aquinas's last word since he does not advocate an unqualified endorsement of the death penalty. As punishments are held to be proportionate to crimes, robbery, for instance, stands beyond the scope of the death penalty since it does not involve the loss of life. Nevertheless, capital punishment as an appropriate and effective tool remains broadly approved because of the challenge posed by intractable religious dissent—that is, heresy.

Death Penalty and Modernity

The end of the Middle Ages, in a dramatic religious context, witnessed an increase in the use of force, which the penal practice reflected. The establishment of the Inquisition heralded the ever deeper involvement of the church in the sanctioning of violence, although the inquisitorial courts, just like the other ecclesiastical courts, were not authorized to exercise judgments of blood (mutilations or death), as stated in the adage *Ecclesia abhorret a sanguine* ("The church abhors blood"). Throughout Europe, the later centuries would be increasingly violent. In this respect, the sixteenth and seventeenth centuries represent a kind of climax of penal harshness. In England, under the reign of Henry VIII, who remained in power for thirty-seven years, 72,000 people were sentenced to death. In Germany, the criminal jurist Carpzov reports in his *Practica criminalis saxonica* (1635) that he imposed more than 20,000 death sentences within forty-five years. In the seventeenth century, trials followed by execution dealt with prosecuting witches and sorcerers, thereby extending the medieval criminal practice. The seventeenth century saw a gradual and steady process toward a more restricted use of capital punishment. Although this tendency was interrupted by the outbreak of the French Revolution and the ensuing political terrorism, it extended through the eighteenth century, which witnessed the rise of toleration. The modern dispute over the state's right to eliminate individual lives and society's responsibility for those condemned to death then begins with the release of Cesare Beccaria's *On Crimes and Punishments* (1764) and the inquiry by John Howard, *The State of Prisons* (1777).

Under the influence of the Enlightenment, the ancient conception of the common good and its preservation, based on the subjection of the individual to society, was reconsidered. Contrary to such a conception, the modern view of the relationships between these two entities emphasizes the central place occupied by the individual within the political organization in guaranteeing and securing his own fundamental rights, among them the right to life. The recognition of individual subjective and inalienable rights would eventually influence the teaching of religious authorities on the death penalty.

From a religious view, adhering to such a basic principle implies that the modern state can no longer be understood as holding and exercising the divinely delegated power to kill. Therefore, the role of the state cannot consist in protecting a divine order of justice. As a result, the retributive aspect of punishment, which is so fundamental to biblical teaching and faith, is undermined, and the death penalty can hardly be construed as expressing God's judgment on criminal acts. Since no one denies that public authorities have the right to punish offenders, just retribution, as distinguished from revenge, should be sought by secular courts. In addition to its retributive aim, criminal punishment pursues other goals, such as collective self-defense, deterrence, and rehabilitation of the convicted criminal.

Sébastien Viguier

See also: Christianity; Crucifixion; Honor Killing.

Further Reading

Aquinas, Thomas. *Summa Contra Gentiles.* New York: Benziger Brothers, 1264/1924.

———. *Summa Theologica.* Westminster, MD: Christian Classics, 1981.

Augustine. "Letters." In *Fathers of the Church,* vol. 20. New York: Fathers of the Church, 1953.

Coleman, J. *The Individual in Political Theory and Practice.* London: Clarendon Press, 1996.

Hood, R. *The Death Penalty: A Worldwide Perspective,* 4th rev. ed. New York: Oxford University Press, 2008.

Megivern, J.J. "Religion and the Death Penalty in the United States: Past and Present." In *Capital Punishment: Strategies for Abolition,* ed. Peter Hodgkinson and William A. Schabas, pp. 116–42. Cambridge, UK: Cambridge University Press, 2004.

The New Oxford Annotated Bible. New York: Oxford University Press, 1991.

Drugs

Many of the world's major religions have specific positions on alcohol and drug use. Some appear to completely prohibit any nonmedical substance use. Mormons, for instance, typically interpret their doctrine to prohibit use of any substance that is harmful to the body. They do not recognize a moral distinction between taking alcohol, tobacco, and coffee—all legal substances in the United States—and taking illegal drugs like marijuana, cocaine, and heroin. Muslims are prohibited from drinking alcohol, although there remains some interpretation regarding whether other drugs are prohibited. Debates continue over use of stimulants like coffee and *qat*, an amphetamine-like stimulant. People in the Middle East have chewed the leaves of qat for more than 600 years.

The religion-based prohibitions on substance use do not seem to be connected to concerns about violence, even though the link between many substances, alcohol in particular, has been well documented. Criminologists have repeatedly confirmed that people who are religious are less likely to engage in all forms of deviance, including both substance abuse and violence. One exception may be new religious movements (NRMs). Some have alleged that NRMs are more likely to be engaged in both substance abuse and violence than other religious groups, although this has not been confirmed through research.

"Collective violence" refers to acts committed by individuals in the name of the religion, or violence committed by agents of social control against members of a religious organization. Religious scholars David Bromley and Lorne Dawson, who have studied collective violence by new religious movements, have clarified a number of misconceptions about NRMs. First, it is not true that all NRMs are similar and can be easily identified. They come from all religious traditions (Christian, Buddhist, Hinduist, Neopagan, etc.) and vary according to their leadership, organization, and means of social control. Second, most NRMS are not violent.

Since the murders committed by the Manson Family in the 1960s, only twenty NRM groups have been implicated in multiple homicides or suicides. Third, it is not true that apocalyptic movements or those with millenialist beliefs are more prone to violence. Many groups throughout human history have been concerned with the end of time and convinced that the end of a millennium was the signal of doom. Of the groups discussed by Bromley and Dawson, the Peoples Temple, the Solar Temple, the Manson Family, and Aum Shinrikyo all used some kind of drugs (Bromley and Dawson 2004).

Jim Jones and the Peoples Temple

Reverend Jim Jones, a graduate of Indiana University and an ordained Disciples of Christ minister, was the leader of the Peoples Temple, which he founded in 1955. Initially, the Peoples Temple was set up as an interracial organization devoted to assisting the sick, homeless, and jobless. Jones moved his headquarters from Indiana to Ukiah, in northern California, and then to San Francisco during the mid-1960s and 1970s. When an exposé revealed possible illegal activities in 1974, Jones moved the cult to Jonestown, Guyana. There the group established an agricultural cooperative in which they raised animals for food, as well as assorted fruits and vegetables for both subsistence and sale.

In the later 1970s, rumors emerged that Jones was abusing prescription drugs and that physical and sexual abuse of members was widespread. Congressman Leo Ryan of California visited Jonestown in November 1978. During the visit, sixteen members of the Temple decided they wanted to leave the group. They, with Ryan, made it to the Port Kiatuma airport, but Jones did not plan to let them leave. Heavily armed members of the Temple's security forces arrived and began shooting, leaving Congressman Ryan and four others dead. Three of the people killed were with the press. Eleven others were wounded.

Reports differ regarding what happened next. Some say Jones discussed the issue with the Temple members, and they decided on group suicide. Other reports say he ordered his followers to drink grape-flavored Flavor Aid (similar to Kool-Aid) mixed with cyanide and other sedatives, including liquid Valium, Penegram, and chloral hydrate. A third of the group was infants and children, and a dog was reportedly given cyanide via a pipe. Some of the victims appeared to have been forcibly injected with the poison, as the Guyanese coroner found needle marks on their bodies. In all, more than 900 people died. Some sources put the number at 914, others at 911. This is because the bodies were in a state of decay when investigators arrived, and there was little time for a thorough investigation. Jones himself perished from a gunshot to the head. The Peoples Temple ended with this mass suicide, and its former headquarters in San Francisco was demolished by the Lorna Prieta earthquake in 1989.

A number of conspiracy theories have been offered to explain what happened with the Peoples Temple. Some believe the group was an experiment operated by the CIA to examine mind-control techniques. The theory contends that when Congressman Ryan found out, he and the 900-plus individuals involved in the experiment had to be exterminated. There appears to be no documented evidence of a conspiracy, but the U.S. government records about the case have never been made public.

Order of the Solar Temple

In 1994, a fire and apparent suicide at a farm outside the hamlet of Cheiry in Switzerland prompted what would end up being a multination investigation spanning many years, which some say was never concluded. Upon arriving at the farm, police found a secret chamber in which somewhere between twenty-two and thirty bodies lay, all draped in long robes and arranged in a pattern. Within a few hours, police had tied the deaths to bodies found in fires in homes in Granges-sur-Salvan, Switzerland, and Morin Heights, Canada. A total of fifty-three people, found to be members of the Order of the Solar Temple, had been stabbed, shot, poisoned, or suffocated to death. Most had drugs in their bodies; scholars believe this suggests that they had been forced to take tranquilizers. Immediately, a number of manifestos appeared in newspapers and on television proclaiming the deaths as a means of transit from this world to another on a higher metaphysical plane. The group's leaders, whose lavish lifestyle might have suggested foul play, had also perished while in "transit." More than a year later, sixteen Temple members committed suicide in a ritual in the countryside of France, and five others followed suit in Quebec, Canada, in 1997.

Joseph Di Mambro, a wealthy Swiss jeweler, founded the Order of the Solar Temple in Geneva, Switzerland, in 1984. In 1981 he had joined with a charismatic young doctor named Luc Jouret, who offered New Age spiritual ideas and homeopathic medicine to the group. Di Mambro soon garnered a large number of well-educated and affluent followers in Europe, the Caribbean, and Canada. In 1984 the group transferred its headquarters to Quebec. Members were convinced that natural catastrophes would end the world, and their apocalypticism drove them to an area where they thought the granite of the earth would protect them. The group was relatively obscure for many years but was involved in secret initiations, secret rituals, and lectures in Canada. In the early 1990s, however, some discontented members began to make embarrassing revelations about the group, discussing bizarre rituals encouraged by Di Mambro. In addition, Di Mambro and

Jouret had a major argument, and Jouret split from the group. Jouret had become increasingly dark and apocalyptic, while Di Mambro focused on the idea of transit. Initially, however, neither violence nor suicide was ever discussed as a means of transit; in fact, the spiritual elite were supposed to survive the coming crisis.

It is not entirely clear why violence and suicide came to be considered. In the fall of 1992, Jouret and another leader asked Quebec member Herman Delorme to find a pistol with a silencer. Delorme purchased three illegal handguns from a police informant and was arrested. His arrest led to a search of the Temple's grounds. Nothing significant came from the search, but the incident coincided with a series of anonymous threats against the Quebec minister of public security and other parliamentary deputies. The police somehow made the link between the Temple and the threats and launched an investigation in Quebec as well as in Europe and Australia. Rumors of gun trafficking and money laundering appeared in the media although those claims were never verified. In October of 1994, many members were invited to a meeting in Switzerland at which they thought they would be participating in a nonviolent and glorious transit. At the same time, however, two members in Quebec were sent to ritualistically stab defectors Tony and Nick Dufoit and their three-month-old baby because they had given their son a name reserved for the messiah. Ultimately, many members were murdered, while others took their own lives. It is unclear precisely what led the group to this end, but surely the internal debate coupled with paranoia about the investigations played a role.

Charles Manson and His "Family"

The Manson Family was an apocalyptic group not generally known as religious but notorious for drug use and the violent murders they committed in the summer of 1969 in Los Angeles, California. Charles Manson served as a prophet for his followers, known as the "Family," and they did virtually everything he commanded.

Manson was born "No name" Maddox in 1934. His mother, Kathleen Maddox, was a prostitute who was unable to care for her son. She married William Manson for a short time, and her son took the name Charles Milles Manson. Kathleen was in and out of prison; so young Charles was shuttled between relatives and various orphanages. As a youth, he followed his mother's lead and was repeatedly in legal trouble. In 1951, he committed his first federal offense—driving a stolen car across a state line. While incarcerated for violating parole after a series of crimes including check forgery, pimping, and grand auto theft, he began to study Scientology. He later combined that belief system with his own personal philosophy to forge the Family.

After his parole in March 1967, Manson was given permission to go to San Francisco. In the following few months he recruited his Family from drug-using hippies living in the Haight-Ashbury area. The group moved to Spahn Ranch outside of Los Angeles, where it continued to grow. There they lived much like a commune. Manson obtained tremendous control over his followers, although it is still difficult to understand precisely how he did so. According to one author, "Manson was able to see and understand what his Family needed: Security, faith, a father figure, and a leader" (Balfour 2004). Members said they thought of Manson as the second coming of Jesus Christ. Others said drugs were an important part of his influence. The group regularly used LSD, a drug known to reduce inhibitions and make a user more susceptible to suggestion.

On August 8, 1969, four members of the Manson Family—Charles "Tex" Watson, Patricia Krenwinkel, Susan Atkins, and Linda Kasabian—entered the property of film producer

Roman Polanski equipped with rope, knives, and a gun. They murdered eighteen-year-old Steven Parent, who was getting into his car as he was about to leave. They then went inside the home, where they murdered Polanski's wife, actress Sharon Tate, who was eight months pregnant. Tate was stabbed sixteen times. They also stabbed and shot Jay Sebring, an international hairstylist, and Tate and Polanski's friends Voytek Frykowski and Abigail Folger. Before they left, the killers wrote "PIG" on the porch door in Tate's blood. The next night, the murderous crew set out again, this time accompanied by Manson and some others. They scouted out and selected the home of Leno and Rosemary LaBianca. Manson stayed in the car while the others tied up and then murdered the couple, stabbing them both multiple times. A carving fork was found in Leno LaBianca's body and the word "WAR" was carved into his skin. The crew used blood to write "Death to pigs" on the living room wall, "Rise" near the front door, and "Helter Skelter" on the refrigerator door.

Initially, investigators presumed the murders at the Polanski property were part of a drug deal gone bad. Frykowski, Sebring, and Folger were all known for using a variety of drugs. Investigators had a tougher time trying to discern a possible motive for the LaBianca murders. Their investigations of another murder case, in which "political piggy" had been scrawled in blood, led the Los Angeles Police Department (LAPD) to Robert Beausoleil, a Family member who had been living at Spahn Ranch. Because Beausoleil was incarcerated at the time of the Tate-LaBianca murders, the LAPD dismissed the idea of his involvement. Not long after, Los Angeles Sheriff's Office (LASO) investigators looking into a string of car thefts raided Spahn Ranch and arrested almost forty Family members. Problems with the warrant resulted in their release, however. Several months later, a raid of Barker Ranch,

another Family enclave, for car thefts and arson, gave investigators a break. They found two young girls trying to flee the Family. One was Kitty Lutesinger, who was pregnant with Beausoleil's child. LASO officers interviewed her and obtained information connecting Susan Atkins and the Manson Family to the murder of Family acquaintance Gary Hinman, as well as to the Tate murders. Lutesinger provided the names of other Family members who had been involved, as well. Once Atkins was arrested and incarcerated at Sybil Brand Institute, she began to brag to fellow inmates about her involvement in the murders.

Eventually, Manson, Watson, Krenwinkel, Kasabian, Atkins, and Leslie Van Houten were indicted. Atkins initially cooperated with the prosecution in a deal intended to save her from a death sentence, but she later recanted, fired her attorney, and refused to cooperate. Kasabian became the prosecution's next best witness, as she had been present at the Tate murders and driven the car at the LaBianca murders. She was granted immunity and not charged for her involvement in order to secure her cooperation.

Throughout their nine-month joint trial, in which Manson, Krenwinkel, Atkins, and Van Houten changed defense teams multiple times, Manson repeatedly demanded to defend himself. According to author Marie Balfour (2004), "Whenever a lawyer would try to separate his client from the rest of the Family, by way of requesting a psychiatric examination or by utilizing a defense tactic not approved by Manson, within days the Family member would request a new lawyer." One of Van Houten's lawyers, Ronald Hughes, disappeared during the trial. Months later, his badly decomposed body was found in a creek bed. Many speculated that the Family had been involved, but that link was never clearly established. Because of Hughes's disappearance, Van Houten was granted a retrial. Manson, Krenwinkel, Atkins, and Van

Houten all received death sentences but were not executed. California law required all death sentences to be automatically appealed. While the automatic appeals were in process, the California State Supreme Court ruled that the death penalty as it was currently implemented in the state was cruel and unusual punishment (a decision that preceded a U.S. Supreme Court case deciding the same), and all of their sentences were commuted to life in prison. Tex Watson had fought extradition from Texas and was tried separately. He was convicted of seven counts of first-degree murder and one count of conspiracy.

Aum Shinrikyo

Aum Shinrikyo was founded in 1986 by Shoko Asahara, born Chizuo Matsumoto. Asahara had previously been part of Agonshu, a religion that stressed using meditation to free oneself from bad karma. Aum Shinrikyo also emphasized the release of bad karma, but by enduring various forms of suffering. According to some scholars, Aum members used this notion to justify the abuse of others. In some cases, new members endured a "nacro-initiation," in which they were given LSD or a similar drug and made to chant their allegiance to the group. *Aum* is Sanskrit for "the powers of destruction and creation in the universe," and *shinrikyo* refers to "the teaching of the supreme truth." The group first became known for its numerous protests and lawsuits, beginning in 1989 when it was denied permission to register with the government under the Religious Corporations Law (*shukyo hojin ho*), though the permission was later granted. The troubles for the group continued when a prominent Japanese newspaper, *Sunday Mainichi,* featured a seven-part series about the group that critiqued it for separating members from their families and for denying children formal education. There were also speculations of "blood initiations" and in-

voluntary blood donations from members. The series prompted great attention, and 200 former members and their families sent postcards expressing similar problems with the group. A victim's group was started called the Aum Shinrikyo Victim's Society (*higaisho no kai*). In November of 1989, Yokohama lawyer Sakamato Tsutsumi, who had been retained by parents to contest the child-parent separation practices used by the group, disappeared, along with his wife and child. Evidence pointed to the group, but Aum denied any involvement. The bodies were recovered from three separate locations nearly six years later.

In July 1989, the group formed its political wing, the Shinrito, meaning "Supreme Truth Party." All twenty-five candidates from the party lost, and the group became the subject of ridicule. Members felt persecuted and began to further isolate themselves from mainstream Japanese society. This prompted a shift in the group's goals, with Asahara now proclaiming that its primary mission was to prepare for Armageddon. Members began construction of nuclear shelters and communes in which they could escape worldly distractions as well as live when Armageddon came.

According to member Takahashi Masayo, in March 1993 Asahara chose a member named Murai Hideo to lead the group in manufacturing sarin gas; Hideo then put Tsuchiya Masami, who had a master's degree in chemistry, in charge of researching how to make the gas. In late 1993, Masami's group successfully made sarin. On June 27, 1994, the Kita-Fukashi district of central Japan was engulfed with clouds of sarin. Seven people died in the attack, and hundreds of others were injured. It was later revealed that Asahara had ordered the attack, which was in the vicinity of the three judges offices who were set to hear cases against the group and were injured in the attack. On March 20, 1995, ten Aum members boarded five trains at five different stations during the peak of morning rush hour. At a predetermined time, they punctured bags of sarin wrapped in newspapers and left the trains. The hardest hit was the Kasumigaseki Station, which is located under many government offices and the National Police Agency headquarters. Twelve people died, and thousands were hurt in the attack. Ten days later, the group attempted to assassinate Police Chief Takaji Kunimatsu. Other gas attacks followed as well. Asahara and 104 followers were indicted on multiple charges, including murder, in regard to the various sarin attacks, as well as illegal production of various drugs. Police reported that 33 Aum followers had been killed (or were missing and presumed dead) between October 1988 and March 1995; the causes of death included lynching, intense training, and suicide.

Conclusion

In sum, although drug and alcohol use is correlated with violence in general, it is not likely a major factor influencing religion-based violence. Its use is more likely, however, to be involved in violence perpetrated by apocalyptic groups and cults than other religious groups. Many times, drugs have been used for mass suicides. Although in some cases the drug use has been forced, more frequently victims have been persuaded to its use by charismatic leaders.

Laura L. Finley

See also: Aum Shinrikyo; New Religious Movements; Peoples Temple; Rastafari.

Further Reading

Balfour, M. "Charles Manson and the Tate-LaBianca Murders: A Family Portrait." In *Famous American Crimes and Trials*, vol. 4, ed. F. Bailey and S. Chermak, pp. 139–58. Westport, CT: Praeger, 2004.

Bromley, D., and L. Dawson. "Religious Movements and Violence: Incidents, Causes, and Policy Implications." In *Violence: A Contemporary Reader*, ed. S. Holmes and R. Holmes, pp. 367–82. Upper Saddle River, NJ: Prentice Hall, 2004.

Bugliosi, V., and C. Gentry. *Helter Skelter: The True Story of the Manson Murders*. New York: W.W. Norton, 1974.

Iadicola, P., and A. Shupe. *Violence, Inequality and Human Freedom*. Dix Hills, NY: General Hall, 1998.

Lamy, P. *Millenium Rage: Survivalists, White Supremacists, and the Doomsday Prophecy*. New York: Plenum, 1996.

Mullins, M. "Aum Shinrikyo as an Apocalyptic Movement." In *Millenniums, Messiahs, and Mayhem: Contemporary Apocalyptic Movements*, ed. T. Robbins and S. Palmer, pp. 313–24. New York: Routledge, 1997.

Reader, I. *Religious Violence in Contemporary Japan: The Case of Aum Shinrikyo*. Honolulu: University of Hawaii Press, 2000.

Sullum, J. *Saying Yes*. New York: Jeremy P. Tarcher/Putnam, 2003.

Eastern Orthodox Christianity

Eastern Orthodox Christianity, alongside Roman Catholicism and Protestantism, is one of the three major branches of Christianity. It numbers around 200 million faithful and largely spans from Eastern Europe to the Far East, though important diaspora communities are present in Western Europe, North America, Africa, and Australia. The *Oxford Dictionary of the Christian Church* defines *orthodoxy* as "a family of Churches, situated mainly in Eastern Europe: each member Church is independent in its internal administration, but all share the same faith and are in communion with one another, acknowledging the honorary primacy of the Patriarch of Constantinople" (Cross 2005). Orthodox Christianity means "correct belief" or "right thinking." The adjective "eastern" here refers to the eastern part of the Roman Empire and the Christian conversion of Eastern Europe under the political domination of Constantinople (fourth-fifteenth centuries). The Orthodox Church separated from the Catholic Church in 1054, with the mutual excommunication between Rome and Constantinople. This situation lasted until 1965, when the ecumenical patriarch Athenagoras (1948–1972) and Pope Paul VI (1963–1978) restored communion between their churches. Orthodox churches lack a systemized doctrine concerning the concept of violence; however, their theology and liturgical ceremonials suggest elements of violence that have symbolic meanings. This symbolism has had direct consequences on the political life of Orthodox communities.

Orthodoxy and Symphonia

The relationship between church and state in Eastern Orthodox Christianity is endorsed by the concept of *symphonia,* which dates back to the Byzantine Empire. The concept, also known as "the system of co-reciprocity," was developed in Byzantium and was at the core of church-state relations. The ultimate goal of Byzantine civilization was a collectively Christian society in which the emperor would control the administration and spiritual guidance would stem from the church. According to this view, the empire was considered a kingdom that would last forever and whose political and religious domination would be without competitor on earth, as it was the reflection of Christ's kingdom. Both the church and the state should collaborate, and there was no conflict between the means employed by church or state in promoting the welfare of their subjects. While there is a separation between the nonreligious character of the state and the religious status of the church, symphonia promotes equality and an intimate relationship between these institutions, albeit with different priorities and methods of operating. The state is interested in its survival within a system of states and the projection of its power within international politics; the church operates via religious methods that would lead the community toward the best way of achieving spiritual progress.

According to symphonia, both church and state use their own laws to promote their own purposes, and there is no confusion between them. The state does not rule itself according to church law, and vice versa. There is no interdependency, nor is there a complete separation. For this reason, in Orthodoxy religious leaders may be perceived as acquiring political roles in society, and political leaders may influence the church's position.

Both the church hierarchy and the emperor had special status in the Byzantine Empire. The emperor was considered equal with Jesus Christ's apostles. He fought for the right, or "orthodox," faith, while the patriarch was in charge of ensuring that the community was following the spiritual path toward salvation. The church-state relationship was influenced by the mutual cooperation between the emperor and the patriarch on their respective paths to achieving their individual salvation and that of their subjects. According to Orthodoxy, the emperor had a special place in the material and spiritual worlds as the chosen leader, considered "similar to God, who is over all, for he does not have anyone higher than himself anywhere on earth" (Pelikan 1974). The concept of symphonia acquired a stronger dimension during the reign of the Emperor Justinian (527–565), who, in the systematization of civil law, set out some aspects of the relationship between church and empire. The classical text that indicates the boundaries of the priesthood and imperial offices is Justinian's *Sixth Novel,* in which he states that the priesthood and the imperial authority are equal.

Justinian's model was followed by his successors and became the tenet of the relationship between Orthodoxy and government. His novels were developed in the ninth century in a document titled *Epanagoge,* most probably written by Patriarch Photius (858–867, 877–886). Even if that document was only a draft and was not officially adopted by the state, it was widely circulated in Orthodox territories and influenced the development of further legislation outside Byzantium through the Middle Ages to the creation of nation-states. *Epanagoge* states that state and church should cooperate, similarly to the relationship between body and soul.

The Byzantine Empire disappeared from Europe's map with the fall of Constantinople on May 26, 1453; however, its religious and political legacy for the predominantly Orthodox countries of southeastern Europe and Russia has remained. Through its religious ceremonies and jurisdictional organization, the church has continued to remind the faithful of the Byzantium model of symphonia regarding the relationship between church and state. Orthodox theology and the symbolic representation of violence have had an impact on the political emergence of nation-states and the transformation of national identities in this region.

Orthodoxy and Symbolic Violence

In Orthodoxy the body of the church is understood differently from that in Western Europe, where it is perceived as merely an ecclesiastical organization within the state. The Orthodox Church includes "the whole body of the faithful, the 'holy catholic church' of the Creed, or at least the faithful of his own persuasion" (Runciman 1971). According to Orthodoxy, Christ has redeemed the sinful nature of humankind through his crucifixion and remains the only one who defeated death. The separation between the spiritual and material worlds, Christ's death and resurrection are the underlying principle of the church and its appearance in history. The violent act of Christ's crucifixion is seen as marking the birth of the church. Orthodoxy explicitly emphasizes that the soldier's gesture of piercing Christ with a lance and Christ's blood and water can be seen as elements that brought the church into existence, from a completely spiritual realm into the material world. These elements are similar to the creation of Eve from Adam's rib, and consequently the church is metaphorically presented in the Orthodox liturgy as the "bride" of Christ.

In Orthodoxy's view, the church comprises both the living and the dead and will last until the second coming of Christ. By including in its structure both the living and the dead, the

Greek Orthodox priests carry a replica of Jesus Christ near the town of Messalogi, Greece, during a ceremony imitating Christ's removal from the cross. Solemn rituals that invoke the symbolic violence of the Crucifixion, which is considered the birth of the church, are performed during Orthodox Easter as a way for the Militant (earthly) Church to imitate the Triumphant (heavenly) Church. *(Dmitris Dimitriou/AFP/Getty Images)*

life according to the Orthodox precepts. Saints and martyrs are examples of individuals who achieved salvation and indicate the way toward the divinity and the heavenly world. Religious rituals are the visible means through which the Militant Church imitates the Triumphant Church and are necessary for the individual's spiritual progress. In this context, violence in Orthodoxy is a path characterized by the fight between flesh and spirit, having, on the one hand, the example of Christ, saints, and martyrs who sacrificed their lives for the church and, on the other hand, religious rituals through which the individual gains help and support toward his or her personal salvation.

The Seven Sacraments of Orthodoxy

Orthodoxy has seven sacraments that reinforce the spiritual progress of the faithful: baptism, the chrism or holy myrrh, the Eucharist, repentance or confession, the priesthood, marriage, and unction—all of which contain elements of symbolic violence. The most significant sacraments with violent representations are baptism, the chrism, the Eucharist, and the priesthood.

Baptism is the first sacrament of the church, through which the novice is included in the body of the church. According to Orthodoxy, baptism is a rebirth from death and represents victory against the original sin of Adam. During this ceremony the individual has to publicly renounce evil by reciting "excommunications." The novice claims that he renounces the kingdom of evil on earth, accepting to be in communion with the victorious Christ, who has absolute power over the damned and the good.

After the ceremony of baptism, the faithful is administered the sacrament of chrism (or the holy myrrh). The chrism is an oily substance composed of forty essences symbolizing the gifts of the Holy Spirit. These gifts have the

church is divided in two parts: a visible church on earth (the Militant Church) and an invisible church (the Triumphant Church). The Militant Church is composed of all living human beings and is in permanent conflict with evil, supporting the faithful in reaching salvation. The Triumphant Church is a heavenly church containing the souls of the virtuous and the saints of the church. Both Militant and Triumphant Churches form the universal Orthodox Church with Christ as its ruler.

Spiritual progress is achieved through participation in religious ceremonies and living a purpose of helping the faithful in his personal fight against evil, and they symbolize armor against temptation. The newly baptized person is compared to a soldier who faces the attack of sins and, following the church, engages on the path of salvation.

The most important sacrament in Orthodoxy is the Eucharist. The Eucharist is seen as being instituted at the moment of the Last Supper, when Christ consumed bread and wine with his apostles; it thus represents his body and blood and a remembrance of his life. The ceremony of the Eucharist is celebrated during the ritual of the liturgy, which symbolizes the life of Christ from his birth to resurrection. From a symbolic point of view, the table in the altar of the church represents the place where Christ is present in a continuous sacrificial moment. During Proscomidia, a liturgical rite in which the bread and wine are prepared, the priest uses a small knife called a lance to cut the leavened bread; its use symbolizes the centurion's lance, which pierced Christ after he died on the cross.

The priesthood is celebrated by a member of the upper hierarchy appointing someone to a leadership position in the church, such as a deacon, priest, or bishop, during the liturgy. According to the Orthodox doctrine, the priest and the bishop are seen as being similar to Christ and as having spiritual powers over the material world. In reinforcing his position, the clergy is dressed in special vestments that suggest authority. One vestment with violent symbolism is the epigonation. The epigonation is a diamond-shaped garment bound around the bishop's waist and hanging on one side to his knee. This cloth symbolizes the sword of the Spirit, which is the Word of God, and the ecclesiastical authority of the wearer as a so-called soldier of Christ in spreading the Word of God and countering heretical teachings.

As the symbolism of the aforementioned sacraments suggests, violence in Orthodoxy is the remembrance and actualization of a violent act: the crucifixion of Christ. The place for violence is inside the individual in the inner fight between the material and the spiritual. In addition to religious rituals, the iconography of the church reminds the faithful of the martyrs and military saints who sacrificed their lives for Orthodoxy. The violent symbolism expressed in the church's rituals, gestures, and iconography has a direct influence on the life of the faithful, as the imitation of the Triumphant Church on earth is the prime condition of the Militant Church.

Orthodoxy and Nation Building in Southeastern Europe and Russia

Bounded by religious symbolism with violent and political meaning, religious leaders assert the prime role of Orthodoxy in the construction of nation-states. The historical evolution of predominantly Orthodox states shows how politicians used the nationalist message of the church to induce national cohesion and gain support for their own political programs. Looking back in history, Orthodoxy influenced the nation-building process as its hierarchy saw the possibility of reviving the Byzantine dream of a Christian state. Thus, the dynamic between church and state presented in Justinian's *Novels* and Photius's *Epanagoge* has remained present in Orthodoxy's relationship with politics until today.

From the fall of Constantinople in 1453 until the nineteenth century, Orthodox churches of southeastern Europe were under the political control of the Ottoman Empire, recognizing the spiritual authority of the ecumenical patriarch. Differences between people were religious rather than ethnic, and following the concept of symphonia, the church sought accommodation with political leaders. The rise of modern nationalism brought significant challenges to the church. The Greeks, Serbians, and Romanians began revolutionary campaigns asserting independence from the government of the Ottoman

Empire, known as the Porte. Political revolutions were soon followed by religious actions. Local hierarchs embarked on political discourses and followed their leaders by disobeying the religious authority of the ecumenical patriarchate. Conflict between the Porte and the church reached dramatic tones in 1821, when Greece declared independence. Accused of treason and of supporting the insurgents, the ecumenical patriarch Gregory V (1797–1799; 1818–1821) was hanged outside the central gates of the Patriarchal Palace on April 10, 1821—Easter Sunday, the most important religious festival of the church. The execution of the patriarch had a great impact on the evolution of Orthodoxy. The faithful saw in the patriarch a martyr and a model for their nation-states, an example that would ultimately be embraced from mere priests to top clergy.

Greece

The rise of the first predominantly Orthodox nation-state in southeastern Europe had both political and religious overtones. In 1833, after the political elite proclaimed independence, the Orthodox Church of Greece also declared autocephaly (ecclesiastical independence) and to be outside Constantinople's jurisdiction, which was only recognized in 1850. Seeking political support from other European powers, Greece embraced monarchy. The new head of state, King Otto (1833–1862), was Roman Catholic and married an Evangelical wife from Germany. He was not forced to convert to Orthodoxy, but the 1843 constitution stated that his successors should be brought up in the Orthodox faith. The monarchy left its legacy on church-state relations by imposing a German style of ecclesiastical administration and transforming the church into a state institution.

Greece promoted the so-called Great Idea (*Megali Idea*), which advocated the expansion of frontiers and the incorporation of Greek-inhabited territories under Ottoman rule; in the long term, it aimed at the reestablishment of the Byzantine Empire. This policy started in 1864, when Greece included the Ionian Islands; subsequently included were Thessaly and parts of Epirus in 1881, Macedonia and Crete in 1912, and the Dodecanese in 1945. Greece's political ambitions led to military conflict with Turkey and the 1923 Treaty of Lausanne, which stipulated massive exchanges of population between the two countries. Belonging to and practicing the Orthodox faith were associated with being part of the Greek nation and were a condition of deportation from Asia Minor to Greece.

In the interwar period the church underwent a process of social reformation, while its top leaders became more actively engaged in political life. A prime political role was played by Archbishop Damaskinos Papandreou (1941–1949), who became head of state and opposed the expansion of communism. After World War II, Greece had an unstable political path culminating in the military dictatorship of the 1960s. The church was particularly affected by the dictatorship junta, which attempted to impose control over the hierarchy and to employ religion for political purposes. When the country returned to democracy in 1974 and joined the European Union in 1981, the church began to recuperate its previous political influence in society.

All post-1990 polls show that more than 95 percent of the population professes the Orthodox faith, although attendance of church services remains relatively low. Being Orthodox is perceived as being closely related to the Greek nation, and other religious minorities have constantly faced discrimination. Although the church does not incite the faithful to violent acts, the political reminiscences of the Great Idea have led some hierarchs to suggest the expansion of Greece's borders into Albania and Macedonia. The increasing influence of the church was recently evident in the dispute over eliminating religious references on national identity cards. Led by the charismatic Archbishop Christodoulos Paraskevaides (1998–2008), the church orchestrated mass demonstrations. Its pressure against the government indicated that the church continues to have a strong impact on the political trajectory of the state.

Serbia

Diplomatic discussions after Karageorge's First Uprising (1804–1813) and Milosh Obrenovich's Second Uprising (1815), when the Serbs rebelled against the Ottoman Empire, resulted in the proclamation of Serbian autonomy under Ottoman rule in 1830. The church paralleled the political situation and was granted autonomy from the ecumenical patriarchate in 1831, while Orthodoxy was declared as the state religion in the 1838 and 1869 constitutions. Serbia was recognized by the Congress of Berlin as an independent kingdom in 1878 and King Milan Obrenović (prince 1868–1882; king 1882–1889) and Metropolitan Mihailo Jovanović of Belgrade (1859–1881; 1889–1898) obtained autocephaly from Constantinople in 1879.

The establishment of the Kingdom of Serbs, Croats, and Slovenes after the First World War led to new status for the Serbian Orthodox Church. The church was raised to the rank of Patriarchate in 1919, and Metropolitan Demetrius Pavlovich (1920–1930) became its first patriarch. The patriarch occupied a position in the Royal Council, and the Orthodox clergy held seats in the National Assembly. The political unification of the South Slavs was perceived by the church hierarchy as the religious unification of the Serbian Orthodox Church; consequently, the church extended its influence in political affairs. This was especially true during the regime of King Alexander (1921–1934), when all significant ministerial positions were taken by Serbs. In addition, the political influence of the church was evident when its protests against the signing of a concordat between the state and the Holy See in 1935 led to withdrawal of the concordat two years later.

The German occupation of Yugoslavia during World War II had a deep impact on the church. Almost 25 percent of churches were destroyed and a fifth of the clergy killed, including six hierarchs; even Patriarch Gavrilo V Dožić-Medenica (1938–1950) was incarcerated in a number of Nazi concentration camps. Furthermore, the installation of communism was accompanied by religious persecution. This conflict remained acute until Josip Broz Tito (1953–1980) imposed Metropolitan German Đorić (1958–1990) as patriarch, a position he occupied until 1991. The church became subservient and was employed by the regime to support the nationalist stance of Yugoslav communism. During the communist period, the influence of the Serbian church greatly diminished after parts of its dioceses proclaimed autonomy: the Czechoslovak Orthodox Church in 1951, the American Canadian Orthodox Church in 1963, and the Macedonian Orthodox Church in 1967.

In the 1980s Serbian Orthodoxy more strongly embraced a political discourse. In 1989, during the celebration of the 600th anniversary of the Battle of Kosovo, religious icons were displayed together with photographs of Slobodan Milošević (1989–2000), and the relics of the most important Serbian saint, Sava, toured the country. The fall of communism and the political disintegration of Yugoslavia placed the church in a vulnerable position; the church was associated with Serbia's politics in the region, while Patriarch Pavle Stojčević (1990—2009) was accused of supporting Milošević's regime. Political violence followed religious lines, and the church's jurisdiction became limited to

Serbia's boundaries. The hierarchs distanced themselves from violent activities, while Serbian monasteries were perceived as centers of resistance in the predominantly Albanian-populated region of Kosovo.

Romania

The 1859 union between the principalities of Wallachia and Moldavia under the rule of Prince Alexandru Ioan Cuza (1859–1866) was closely connected to the rise of the Romanian Orthodox Church outside the jurisdictional authority of the ecumenical patriarch. Imposing control of the church, Cuza introduced the secularization of monasteries, declared Romanian as the only language spoken in religious rituals, and established a church council, or synod, that followed his rule. Comparable to Greece's political trajectory, Romanian political leaders sought support from European powers and elected the Catholic Prince Carol I from the Hohenzollern-Sigmaringen family (prince 1866–1881; king 1881–1914) as head of state. The Romanian Orthodox Church declared autocephaly in 1865 and was recognized by Constantinople in 1885. The proclamation of the Romanian independent kingdom in 1881 was accompanied by increasing control of the church by the state, which led to ecclesiastical instability.

The establishment of Greater Romania in 1918 with the incorporation of the territories of Transylvania, Banat, Bukovina, and Bessarabia was followed by the reorganization of the church. Parliament raised the church to the rank of patriarchate in 1925, and Metropolitan Miron Cristea was elected its first patriarch (1925–1939). Patriarch Cristea was actively engaged in political affairs, serving in the royal regency and as prime minister during three short-lived governments from 1938 to 1939. In the interwar period, the church was confronted with the rise of a Romanian version of fascism under the political coordination of the Iron Guard. Although the top hierarchs officially rejected the movement, some parts of the clergy combined religious values with political violence and advocated the exclusion of minorities and the association of Romanian identity with Orthodoxy.

After World War II, the church followed previous patterns of collaboration with the state, and the communist regime easily imposed its own people in the hierarchy. Patriarch Justinian Marina (1948–1977) supported the regime but also promoted an independent politics, which in the long term benefited the church. Due to its particular church-state relations, Romania was the only predominantly Orthodox country in the communist bloc that did not suffer mass religious persecution. Communist control of the church continued after Justinian's death in 1977, during the leadership of Patriarch Justin Moisescu (1977–1986) and Patriarch Teoctist Arăpaşu (1986–2007).

The fall of communism in 1989 led to the resignation of Patriarch Teoctist; however, he returned to the leadership in April 1990. The Orthodox Church enjoys the highest confidence of Romanians—over 80 percent of the population—followed closely by the army. Although Romania did not face the territorial disintegration of Yugoslavia, conflict between Romanians and the Hungarian minority resulted in sporadic violent clashes in the 1990s. The church distanced itself from violence, promoting unity and reconciliation. In the past few years, the church reentered political disputes over suggestions of directly engaging in electoral campaigns.

Bulgaria

Bulgaria offers a unique example of church-state relations in southeastern Europe, as the struggle for ecclesiastical independence from the ecumenical patriarchate took place before the emergence of the Bulgarian state. The first claims of autonomy came after the Crimean War (1854–1856) and resulted in the establishment of a Bulgarian exarchate in 1870. The exarchate was set up by the Ottoman government and comprised thirteen dioceses under Constantinople's jurisdiction. As Bulgarian hierarchs demanded a national church, in 1872 a synod under the leadership of the ecumenical patriarch Anthimos VI (1845–1848; 1853–1855; 1871–1873) rejected their request, condemning the doctrine of *philetism,* which asserted the emergence of ecclesiastical organization on ethnic lines. The synod refused to recognize the Bulgarian exarchate, declaring it a schismatic church. This position even continued after Bulgaria became an autonomous principality in 1878 and an independent kingdom in 1908.

Bulgaria's first constitution of 1879 stated that the church remained united with the ecumenical patriarchate. Due to its limited political role, the Bulgarian church was not involved in the election of Prince Ferdinand of Coburg-Gotha (prince 1887–1908; czar 1908–1918) in 1887, and conflict with political leaders remained acute until his abdication in 1918. The prince proclaimed himself czar, recalling the glorious past of the Bulgarian Empire, and claimed to be a descendent of the Byzantine emperors. In the Balkan Wars (1912–1913) he supported the idea that if his side won, he should be crowned in the Church of Saint Sophia in Constantinople. In the interwar period, King Boris III (1918–1943) lacked any interest in church affairs. After 1915 the church was ruled by a synod dependent on state finances, and the hierarchs were refused access to the court. This particular situation had an impact on the Bulgarian faithful, who were considered to probably be the least religious people in Europe at the time.

The Coburg dynasty lasted until 1944, when Bulgaria came under a communist regime.

The Bulgarian Orthodox Church was recognized by the ecumenical patriarchate in 1945, but that recognition had little effect, as the church strengthened its ties with the Russian Orthodox Church. Although the 1947 constitution declared freedom of religion and separation between church and state, top hierarchs were imprisoned and killed. In 1948 Metropolitan Stefan (1945–1948), the leader of the church, was forced by the communists to resign.

With the support of the Soviet Union, the Bulgarian Orthodox Church proclaimed itself to the rank of patriarchate in 1953. Metropolitan Kiril became the first patriarch (1953–1971), and the church became subservient to the communist regime. The church was given the role of a civilizing mission among the Slavs, suggesting that their common religion and similar languages should foster closer relations between the Soviet Union and Bulgaria. The political employment of the church continued during the leadership of Patriarch Maksim (1971–present). After the fall of communism, his close association with top communist leaders contributed to a major rift. In May 1992, part of the church split from the communist-appointed hierarchy and declared a separate church. Although the government did not intervene in the conflict, it continues to support Maksim's adherents.

Russia

The Russian Orthodox Church had a different historical trajectory than the other Orthodox churches of southeastern Europe. After the fall of Constantinople, Russia combined religion and politics and claimed to be the carrier of the spiritual mission of Orthodoxy. Peter the Great (1682–1725) abolished the Russian patriarchate in 1721 and transformed the church into a state department ruled by a holy synod and led by a procurator who was directly appointed by the government. Strict control of ecclesiastical affairs became the norm during the regime of Nicholas I (1825–1855), who declared the borders of episcopal sees the same as those of state provinces; clergy elections were eradicated, and parishes were inherited on genealogical lines.

The abolition of czarist autocracy and its replacement with a Marxist-Leninist government in 1917 had a fundamental impact on the church. The hierarchy declared the reestablishment of the patriarchate at the same time as the regime decreed the separation between church and state. The church was not allowed to control education and property, and those who opposed the regime were executed. Patriarch Tikhon (1917–1925) denounced those measures and anathematized the Bolsheviks, but he withdrew his condemnation in 1923. Tikhon died in 1925, and the following leader, Metropolitan Sergii (1925–1944) did not oppose the communists. Due to forced industrialization and collectivization, the church suffered intense persecution, especially between 1928 and 1932 and 1937 and 1938. Hierarchs were arrested, and their buildings were destroyed or given a different use. Figures for 1939 showed dramatic changes: only around 200 churches survived from around 46,000 before 1917, and only four bishops were free.

The start of World War II brought the church into a new situation. Metropolitan Sergii publicly announced support for the war effort and denounced the German invasion. Stalin (the leader of the Soviet Union at the time) realized that the church could play a significant part in the war and met Sergii in September 1943; four days later, Sergii was elected patriarch, a position he held until his death in 1944. His successor, Patriarch Aleksii (1945–1970), embarked on spreading Soviet influence in other Orthodox countries by traveling and organizing religious meetings on the propagandistic theme of peace. Churches were allowed to reopen, and the number of clergy

saw a significant increase until the end of the 1950s. The most significant antireligious measures were taken in 1954 and from 1959 until 1964 under the then Soviet leader Nikita Khrushchev's religious persecution. During this latter campaign, two-thirds of almost 20,000 churches were again closed.

In 1971 Metropolitan Pimen (1971–1990) succeeded Patriarch Aleksii and remained passive toward the atheist challenges of the regime; after his death in 1990, he was succeeded by Patriarch Aleksii II (1990–2008). The evolution of church-state relations remained unchanged until the beginning of Mikhail Gorbachev's regime in 1985. Gorbachev's slogans of *glasnost* (openness) and *perestroika* (restructuring) brought the church into a new position. It regained some of its previous property and was allowed to celebrate its millennium in June 1988. In 1990 a new law on religion removed previous restrictions and introduced the teaching of religion in schools. The church began rebuilding its demolished churches and monasteries, and the 1997 religious legislation offered the Russian Orthodox Church a prime position among other religions.

Conclusion

The evolution of Eastern Orthodox Christianity in southeastern Europe and Russia has been intrinsically linked to the emergence of nation-states and the trajectory of political regimes. Orthodox churches have followed the paths of political actions and have often been employed by political leaders. Control of the church spanned from collaboration between religious and political spheres, such as the situation in Greece and Romania, to religious persecution such as in Russia. In all countries, Orthodox churches have abstained from promoting direct violent actions, although, in some cases, Orthodox values have been employed to support violent actions, such as in Greece,

Romania, and Serbia. Furthermore, political regimes have taken advantage of the nationalist discourse of the church and benefited from the consolidation of the nation-building process.

The promotion of a symbolic violence with roots in Orthodoxy has been visible in most countries. For example, the Serbian Orthodox Church compared Serbia to a sacrificed nation, while reference to church history reinforced the mythical imaginary of the nation. The myth of the death of Prince Lazar, who, before the Battle of Kosovo in 1389, took communion with his soldiers, preferring to die and go to a heavenly world rather than to survive, was extensively used during the violent disintegration of Yugoslavia. Furthermore, after 1989 the church endorsed the so-called Jasenovac myth—the myth is named after the place where approximately 700,000 Serbs were allegedly killed during World War II—which emphasized the idea of a systematic persecution of the church and the Serbian people.

Similarly, from the first days of the revolution in Romania the church supported unity, and its religious symbols were displayed in places where people were killed. In 1999, when miners from the Valea Jiului region, dissatisfied with government policy, started a march to Bucharest, the government turned to the influence of Orthodoxy and organized a meeting with miners' leaders at the Cozia monastery. The conflict was settled with the support of the hierarchy, showing that the church could play a major role in the social and political reconstruction of the state.

In all Orthodox countries the nationalist discourse of the church is on the increase. This process is amplified by references to the tumultuous religious past and the canonization of saints, who are regarded as protectors of the nation. The Bulgarian Orthodox Church supports the idea of Bulgarians as martyr people who suffered under the Ottoman rule; it canonized

Cyril and Methodius as national saints, despite claims from Macedonia and Greece. Similarly, the Russian Orthodox Church is becoming more closely connected with the political transformation of the country; in 2000 it canonized Czar Nicholas II (1894–1917) and his family, who were executed by the communist regime in 1918.

Although Orthodox Christianity does not have a systemized doctrine related to violence, the trajectory of Orthodox churches suggests that employing symbolic violence and nationalism has an impact on politics. The church emphasizes the accomplishment of a "symphonic" agreement with political leadership and supports violent activities when the existence of the nation-state is under threat. For example, blessing the armed forces, providing logistical support during war, and working to attenuate social conflict may be part of a closer cooperation between church and state. Violence in Orthodoxy remains symbolic; however, the symbolism often extends from the religious to the political sphere.

Lucian N. Leustean

See also: Christianity; Roman Catholicism.

Further Reading

Angold, M., ed. *Eastern Christianity*. Vol. 5 of *The Cambridge History of Christianity*. Cambridge, UK: Cambridge University Press, 2006.

Bourdeaux, M. *Patriarch and Prophets: Persecution of the Russian Orthodox Church Today*. London: Macmillan, 1975.

Cross, F.L., ed. *The Oxford Dictionary of the Christian Church*. New York: Oxford University Press, 2005.

Ellis, J. *The Russian Orthodox Church: A Contemporary History*. London: Croom Helm, 1986.

Frazee, C.A. *The Orthodox Church and Independent Greece, 1821–1852*. Cambridge, UK: Cambridge University Press, 1969.

Hussey, J.M. *The Orthodox Church in the Byzantine Empire*. Oxford: Oxford University Press, 2004.

Leustean, L.N. *Eastern Christianity and the Cold War, 1945–91*. London: Routledge, 2009.

———. *Orthodoxy and the Cold War: Religion and Political Power in Romania, 1947–65,* Basingstoke, UK: Palgrave, 2009.

Lossky, V. *Orthodox Theology: An Introduction.* Crestwood, NY: St. Vladimir's Seminary Press, 1978.

Meyendorff, J. *Byzantine Theology: Historical Trends and Doctrinal Themes.* New York: Fordham University Press, 1987.

Mojzes, P. *Yugoslavian Inferno: Ethnoreligious Warfare in the Balkans.* New York: Continuum, 1994.

Pavlovich, P. *The History of the Serbian Orthodox Church.* Toronto: Serbian Heritage Books, 1989.

Pelikan, J. *The Christian Tradition: A History of the Development of Doctrine. The Spirit of Eastern Christendom (600–1700).* Chicago: University of Chicago Press, 1974.

Perica, V. *Balkan Idols: Religion and Nationalism in Yugoslav States.* New York: Oxford University Press, 2002.

Pospielovksy, D.V. *The Orthodox Church in the History of Russia.* Crestwood, NY: St. Vladimir's Seminary Press, 1998.

Ramet, P. *Eastern Christianity and Politics in the Twentieth Century,* Durham, NC: Duke University Press, 1988.

Runciman, S. *The Great Church in Captivity: A Study of the Patriarchate of Constantinople from the Eve of the Turkish Conquest to the Greek War of Independence.* Cambridge, UK: Cambridge University Press, 1985.

———. *The Orthodox Churches and the Secular State.* Auckland: Auckland University Press, 1971.

Schmemann, A. *For the Life of the World: Sacraments and Orthodoxy.* Crestwood, NY: St. Vladimir's Seminary Press, 1973.

Stan, L., and L. Turcescu. *Religion and Politics in Post-Communist Romania.* Oxford: Oxford University Press, 2007.

Ware, K. *The Orthodox Way.* Crestwood, NY: St. Vladimir's Seminary Press, 1979.

Ethnicity

In recent years, religion has merged with politics in different of areas and regions around the world: from the Buddhist monks protesting against the military junta in Burma to the demands for an independent Khalistan by radical Sikhs in India, from the consolidation of Islam as a moderate force in Turkish politics to its more radical impact in other areas, from Israel's self-legitimacy as a Jewish state to the active role played by religious organizations in antiwar demonstrations and various conflict resolution initiatives, to end with the ascendancy of religious neoconservatism in the United States at the turn of the millennium. The range spans from the positive impact of democratization to the negative collision of religion in politics, and finally war. Ethnic conflict varies from the involvement of religious organizations in "civil society building" to cases in which religious symbolism has been appropriated by the state for nonreligious ends. Yet none of the above cases or situations can be correctly described as an instance of religious conflict.

Ethnic Conflicts and Religious Conflicts

In the contemporary era, ethnic conflicts and so-called religious conflicts tend often to coincide and reinforce each other. Many religious conflicts might more prosaically be described as ethnic conflicts in disguise. In general, ethnic conflicts can be defined and circumscribed more easily than religious conflicts, as they articulate the defense of a specific ethnic group, rather than a religion. Moreover, ethnic conflicts tend to overlap with nationalism. Indeed, most scholars see the two as nearly synonymous, referring to the ethnic roots of nationalism or simply to ethnonationalism. Historically, the birth of political nationalism is commonly traced to the French Revolution. The influence of religion declined dramatically after 1789, with state structures becoming more secular. In turn, however, those structures were imbued with a kind of religious meaning and invested with sacral attributes. Indeed, scholars of fascism have increasingly identified extreme nationalism as a derivative form of secular religion.

Three very distinctive kinds of conflicts are

often confused: ethnic, ethnoreligious, and religious. The first two can be easily defined, while the latter is a more controversial term. However, all three types of conflicts are situated firmly in modernity, incorporating the sacralization of politics and encompassing radical nationalist movements, fascism, and Nazism.

Ethnicity is a collective identity, a sense of belonging, based on a subjective belief in a common origin and descent from common ancestors. This belief may or may not reflect historical facts or a true chronology. Although it is often accompanied by a discourse on culture, historical facts and chronologies should be kept analytically separated from ethnicity. Ethnic conflicts are thus conflicts whose protagonists are inspired by their own and others' ethnicity. Authors who conceive ethnicity in these terms are often inspired by Max Weber (1864–1920). For Weber, ethnicity and nationalism are both based on myths of common descent from distant ancestors. These myths have existed since antiquity, but the modern expansion of literacy has supplemented them with an extra layer of historical narrative. Both myths and history are built into nationalist discourse so that the demarcation line between them remains thin: The past provides a key inspiration for both historians and myth makers. These authors' work combines in the form of ethnohistory, or "history from below," initially devised to legitimize political goals by stateless ethnic groups aspiring to seize the state (Smith 2009). However, official history taught in standard school curricula can also be classified or understood as ethnohistory. It is sufficient to look at the Balkans, where the same event can be described in sharply different ways by each national school curriculum to the point of becoming unrecognizable.

The term *ethnie* is increasingly used in lieu of "ethnic group" and was only recently imported into English from the French. Some authors stress the continuity between ethnicity and nationhood, postulating premodern ethnic conflicts as primary forms of nationalism. In its original Greek connotation, *éthnos* was already associated with the idea of common descent and lineage. Classical authors used it to refer to contiguous peoples, while the *Oxford English Dictionary* renders it as "nation." The word *nation* derives from the Latin substantive *natio* (to be born) and has been used in the sense of common descent since at least the Middle Ages. It hence shares a stress on common origins with "ethnie" and "ethnic group" and even "race" (Fenton 2003). The main difference lies in the fact that the shift from "ethnic" to "national" indicates an aspiration to control political power and possess a sovereign state destined to shelter and protect a group's identity. Nationalism applies to both nation-states and stateless nations: it can refer either to a minority's aspiration to achieve statehood or to the enforcement of ethnic supremacy and domination within a nation-state. But while nationalism attributed to stateless nation does not control states, a nation-state is founded on the claim to embody or represent institutionally an entire nation—in Weberian terms, exercising the monopoly of legitimate violence within a specific and clearly demarcated territory. However, the term *nation-states* is a misnomer, as there are virtually no pure nation-states in the world—all of them contain ethnic minorities (Connor 1993; 2004).

Ethnic conflicts must be distinguished from so-called cultural conflicts. Both sociologists and race-relation scholars have warned against confusing culture with ethnicity; that is, cultural groups are not coterminous with ethnic groups. Indeed, conflicts are rarely cultural at all, except perhaps in a very superficial sense. On the contrary, the most violent conflicts tend to occur between highly similar groups sharing the same language and culture, yet with stringently opposed ethnicities. The most well-known cases include those of the Hutus and Tutsis in Rwanda and Burundi; the Serbs, Croats, and Bosniaks in former Yugoslavia; and the Protestants and Catholics in Northern Ireland. The last two cases include religious affiliation as a defining attribute, yet most scholars are reluctant to speak about religious conflicts, let alone about cultural conflicts. The only cultural linkage to ethnic conflict is generally subtractive: the perception of loss of one's own culture can inform the actions, justifications, and rationale of many radical confrontations. In other words, cultural elements become politically activated mostly when groups are threatened by assimilation, cultural loss, or dislocation. Indeed, cultural assimilation can often be more conductive to the diffusion of ethnic violence than cultural pluralism. Where and when assimilation has shattered local culture, violence can even replace culture as a binding mechanism. The model can be applied to the Hutus and Tutsis, who could be regarded as having coexisted for centuries within a common culture, while Serbs and Croats and Northern Irish Catholics and Protestants are good cases of cultural similarity where distinctive subcultures coalesce around ethnic membership defined on the basis of putative religious denominations.

The contrast between violent and nonviolent conflicts is particularly enlightening and can shed light on the causes of violence and civil wars. Few studies have systematically compared violent and nonviolent conflicts. In general, the literature on peaceful conflicts is quantitatively modest. This is paradoxical if one considers that they probably make up the majority of existing conflicts. Various studies have been produced on the struggles of the Tibetans, the Australian Aboriginals, and the Ogoni in Nigeria, while several other low-intensity claims have been studied little or not at all. Other underinvestigated nonviolent movements have emerged among the Batwa of Rwanda, the Hawaiians,

the Taiwanese (vis-à-vis mainland China), the Mapuche of Chile, the Rusyn (or Ruthenians) of Slovakia and Ukraine, Moldova's Gagauzs, the Crimean Tatars (in Ukraine), and other groups demanding autonomy within the Russian Federation: Bashkortostan, Buryatia, Chuvashia, Ingushetia, Ingria (or Ingermanland), Komia, Mariy-El (among the Mari), Sakha (or Yakutia), Tatarstan, Tuva, and Udmurtia. Religion has become a salient element in only a few cases: the aforementioned Tibetans, Iraq's Assyrians, the Buddhist tribes in Bangladesh's Chittagong Hills Tracts, the Lahu and the Palaung of Burma, and so on.

Nonviolent movements tend to be led by moderate autonomists aware that a secessionist agenda could damage their cause. For them, the search of a modus vivendi with the government is a priority and coexistence the preferred outcome. In general, the international community has upheld the integrity of the state wherever it has come under threat from secession. Each country has confronted the phenomenon in its own way with different outcomes: some brutal conflicts have been partially resolved through peace agreements, such as the accord reached between the Mon and the Burmese government in 1995. Less violent conflicts could be more easily resolved through bilateral agreements, including the regulation (*pacchetto*) offering an autonomy statute to Italy's South Tyrol in 1969 and the Saar plebiscite in 1954 Germany, when the *Saarstatut* attempt to establish an independent Saarland was rejected by 67.7 percent. However, when merged with politicized religion, other initially peaceful movements have degenerated into armed confrontations, for example the one pitting the Chinese government against the Muslims of Uighuristan.

Ethnic conflicts are the most common form of contemporary conflicts. As such, they are the catalyst of both internal and international wars. During the Cold War the prevailing illusion was that of a world forever freed from ethnonational conflicts. But the disintegration of multinational communist states led to a vindictive reaffirmation of repressed identities, often leading to civil conflict and even international war, as in the Caucasus and former Yugoslavia.

The amplifying influence of the media in a globalizing age may mislead people into believing that both ethnic and religious conflicts are intrinsically violent. In reality most conflicts are nonviolent, but the violent ones get the greatest attention. As Donald Horowitz (1985) put it: "The spilling of ink awaits the spilling of blood."

Secular Religion: Atheism and War

Most people would be surprised to discover that suicide bombing has been carried out mostly in nonreligious settings, particularly among Sri Lanka's Tamil Tigers, whose leaders were originally Marxists and atheists. Of the 186 suicide terrorist attacks that occurred between 1980 and 2001, the Liberation Tigers of Tamil Eelam (LTTE) accounted for 75. Among Islamic suicide attacks, one-third of attacks can be attributed to secular groups. Some scholars have insisted on stressing the religious character of nationalist self-immolation, while others see a two-way relationship between religion and ethnicity, stressing a latent religious dimension in ethnic identities.

Many modern secular leaders have been implicated in wars and mass slaughter, often in the name of nation building. Some of the most violent mass crimes perpetrated in the twentieth century have been carried out by practicing or former atheists—Stalin, the Khmer Rouge, Ataturk, Mussolini, and Milošević, to name a few, while Hitler's commitment to Christian principles was rather doubtful. The last two did not hesitate to appropriate religious symbolism to carry forward extreme nationalist programs when it suited their interests. Already by the

1950s, Nazism and fascism were described as totalitarian religions. The wars in former Yugoslavia exemplify the conflictual, boundary-building use of religious symbolisms by atheist leaders. Under Tito's reign (1945–1980), the official doctrine of atheism began to deeply affect individual beliefs. This occurred to different degrees within all dominant religions practiced there. In 1971, the Muslims of Bosnia-Herzegovina were officially transformed from a religious to an ethnic group; more specifically, they were elevated from national minority to constituent nation (*narod*)—a status fully enshrined in the 1974 constitution. At the same time, mass migrations, urbanization, deruralization, secularism, intermarriage, and the very autonomy enjoyed by Bosnia-Herzegovina as one of Yugoslavia's six constituent republics all contributed to reinforce the salience of territorial, civic, supraethnic, and suprareligious Bosnian identity.

By the early 1990s, local dynamics appeared to be contributing to the emergence of a new Bosnian identity, blending Muslims, Serbs, and Croats in a highly secularized society where intermarriage was increasingly the norm. A preexisting bridge-building tradition was thus being revived: each group was granted its cultural, ethnic, and historical rights but not religious freedom due to official discouragement and even persecution of religion. Although state-sanctioned atheism had a lasting effect in undermining the religious foundations of society, religiously based identities, rather than religion per se, were consolidated and began to violently reemerge in the 1990s. Forty years of atheist propaganda succeeded in substantially erasing religious belief: in its place, formerly religious boundaries now devoid of theological, moral, or normative content were being reinforced through ethnicity. The ensuing conflict can thus be described as a war between Catholic atheists, Orthodox atheists, and Muslim atheists. This postreligious, secularized form of belonging refers mainly to ethnicity and descent among groups that were formerly defined on the basis of religion. Descent on the basis of former religious affiliation had become the only shared and binding element used to differentiate Serbs from Croats and others after 1992. Exactly 500 years before, in 1492, Jews began to be expelled en masse from Spain. Over the next hundred years, those who had converted to Christianity from Islam and Judaism were still being hunted down and expelled on the basis of their ethnic descent rather than their actual religious beliefs.

In "atheist wars," ethnonational groups are essentialized as sacred and demand their members' ultimate loyalty. In the 1990s, Yugoslav atheist *apparatchiki* (loyal party members) coalesced around Slobodan Milošević by using religion as a building block for a "greater Serbia" project. However, important sections of the Serbian clergy have adhered to this policy by adopting exclusivist ethnic myths as religion was being ethnicized.

Both before and after the Dreyfus affair, anti-Semitism has periodically reemerged within French mainstream discourse. For modernization theory, future-oriented ultranationalist ideologies such as fascism and Nazism were fueled by a competitive drive to industrialize and rapidly modernize national economies. If so, questions remain as to why they needed to stress their adherence to a mythical past. Why, if their disruptive/regenerative impact turned out to be so radical, did they need to appeal to a Golden Age of national purity, and why did urban elites hypocritically invoke peasant values at the very moment when peasants were being uprooted, eradicated, and murdered? Some simply describe the nationalists' past-looking rhetoric as fraudulent. A further explanation can be found in a delayed response to the destruction of tradition or, as sometimes suggested, in a homeostatic reaction to dramatic social change.

More recently, democratization has also been linked to instability: Since the 1990s (the time of the supposed post–Cold War "disorder") and more dramatically since 2001 (the beginning of the so-called war on terror), the view that democratization can lead to an increase in ethnic conflict has become the dominant view. However, advocates of the doctrine of universal human rights tend to search for more elaborate responses and ways of accommodating conflicts by democratic means. Throughout modern history authoritarian rulers have used the opposite view, namely that authoritarian rule is necessary to hold in check ethnic conflict. In other words, they rejected full democracy on the basis that it could jeopardize state security. Politicians and media manipulators have used the potential threat of ethnic insurgency as a pretext to limit civil rights and democracy.

Language and Religion

Both linguistic and religious conflicts must in principle be distinguished from ethnic conflicts. Although language and religion can be used as markers of national identity, both work as bridges to cross the ethnic divide. Whereas ethnicity locks peoples and individuals into preordained categories, religion and to a lesser extent language can bridge that gap, bringing together peoples from different ethnic groups. The choice of a specific supra-ethnic language affiliated neither to tribal identities nor to the colonial past has been a hotly debated issue in postcolonial societies. In several countries the colonial language could be replaced only by selecting the dominant local language—an act that many feared would hasten interethnic rivalries. For instance, the "Sinhala only act" adopted by the Sri Lankan government in 1956 was allegedly one of the factors contributing to Tamil alienation.

Co-habitation among various ethicities is

easier when there are languages that are not associated with a particular ethnic group. For instance, the selection of alternative nonethnic languages like Swahili and Kiswahili in Tanzania, Kenya, and Uganda was designed to replace English without provoking ethnic rivalries. The Tanzanian statesman Julius Nyerere was a prominent advocate of this alternative. Tanzania has indeed been remarkably peaceful and devoid of intertribal conflict in comparison with neighboring countries. On the other hand, countries that have kept the colonial language as an administrative tool, such as the Democratic Republic of Congo (formerly Zaire), Liberia, Sierra Leone, and Ivory Coast, have experienced interethnic conflict and devastation in violent wars, although language may not have been the primary cause. Nyerere deliberately chose language as a unifying tool while tolerating a plurality of religious affiliations. Other cases of supra-ethnic languages include Bahasa Indonesian, invented from scratch by anticolonial intellectuals, and the similar Malay, which, despite being associated with ethnic Malays' ethnicity, tends to be seen as a unifying instrument by other ethnic groups. Each of these non-Western languages is spoken by a plurality of ethnic groups, providing a supplementary tool of civic society building.

Yet language continues to be most often associated with ethnicity. Some languages are exclusively associated with a specific ethnic group, and demands for linguistic rights are often perceived as a form of ethnic assertion. The term *ethnolinguistic conflict* can thus be used to describe ethnic conflicts with a preponderant linguistic component. For instance, in Belgium the Flemish language is often associated with the inhabitants of the Flanders region, while French is spoken by the Walloons inhabiting Wallonia. Both these populations share a well-defined sense of common origins and separate historical development. However, for about a century French remained the only official language, to the great disadvantage of most Flemish speakers. The latter's political demands were therefore framed in the idiom of language rights, and the resulting strife became a classical instance of ethnolinguistic conflict. Language can thus be a source of either conflict or pacification. In federal countries such as Russia and other former communist states and in India it has most often been accommodated, whereas in Yugoslavia the creation of a single Serbo-Croat language did not prevent (and was not really the cause of) the most violent ethnic conflict in postwar Europe.

Religious conflicts should be distinguished even more clearly from ethnic conflicts. Religion can play a sheer ascriptive role denoting mere group belonging rather than faith or belief. Ethnoreligious conflicts should thus be distinguished from religious conflicts. In the former, religion plays an identifying function secondary to that of ethnicity. In the latter, religious belief is preponderant, while ethnicity tends to be seen as accessory: Followers of cosmopolitan or apocalyptic sects may belong to a plurality of ethnicities and races. In such cases, ethnicity becomes irrelevant and may even be dismissed as distracting or antithetical to religious principles.

Therefore, religion in ethnoreligious conflicts is not a cause of conflict but an element of ethnic identification and national demarcation. However, this makes ethnoreligious conflict potentially more dangerous and destabilizing than other forms of more strictly ethnic or religious conflict. This is because religion confers a sacral aura to ethnic assertion: individuals carrying religious symbolism because of their ethnic belonging become ipso facto members of an "elected" nation by divine will, independent from their personal beliefs. Indeed, leaders manipulating religious symbols may be adherents, agnostics, or atheists, while displaying the passion of the faithful. For this reason, ethnoreligious conflicts can be particularly violent and difficult to resolve. Carlton Hayes (1960) warned that supreme loyalty could be easily commended "when national emotions meet with religious emotions." Ethnicity supported by religious affiliation and symbolism featured in the Armenian-Azeri War over Nagorno-Karabagh, in Bosnia, in Kashmir, in Mindanao, in Chechnya, in Sri Lanka, in Lebanon, in northern Nigeria, and in several other conflicts. Atheist leaders, well represented by Serbia's ex-communist apparatchiks are known for their unscrupulous use of religious symbology to legitimize their extremist deeds, which provides insight into the nonreligious nature of many conflicts ordinarily portrayed by the media as religious, ethnic, or ethnoreligious.

Religion also plays a founding role in secular nationalism. According to Adrian Hastings (1997), nationalism itself has Judeo-Christian roots: the translation of the sacred scriptures into the local vernacular helped to conceive the latter as a godly agency and divine medium. The people speaking the holy tongue were thus God-chosen. Accordingly, the first nation in history was Israel. But, with the translation of the Old Testament from Hebrew into other vernaculars, the mythical vicissitudes of the Jews became in turn associated with each people in whose language the Bible was translated. The Bible was often the first book to be translated into the indigenous languages of a population. Secularization does not imply desacralization. Nationalism has indeed turned the profane into the sacred. The object of the new idolatry is the people—that is, the nation.

The use of religious symbolism as a mobilizing tool has been appropriated by minorities and ethnies of disparate religious faiths: Catholics (Northern Ireland, East Timor, Bougainville, Croatia), Protestants (Moluccas, Nagaland, Karenni), Eastern Christians (Armenia, Georgia, Serbia), Muslims (Mindanao, Ache, Kashmir), Sikhs (Punjab), Buddhists (Tibet; Maghi, Mru, Tangchangya, and Tipera in Bangladesh's Chittagong Hill Tracts), Hindus (Tamil in Sri Lanka; Tripuri and Manipuri in Bangladesh), and pagans (southern Sudan, Jharkhand). Typically, conflicts have escalated in periods of deepening secularization. Despite the partnership between ethnicity and religious symbolism, many so-called ethnoreligious wars, such as the one in Bosnia, have been described as atheist wars, because of the parasitical use of religion for exclusively ethnic goals.

The Role of the State

It would be tempting to attribute the explosion of both ethnic and religious violence to primordial factors, such as ancient enmities or old prejudices. The "clash of civilization" thesis, for example, advanced by Samuel Huntington (1996) has been broadly attacked because it apparently shares many features of this shallow approach. However, the roots of conflict should be sought elsewhere. The most widespread cause of ethnic conflicts lies in the state and in specific governments' responses to ethnic claims. Draconian measures can momentarily silence them, but most often they simultaneously breed long-term negative reactions, which can then spiral out of control. Government repression has also the unintended consequence of discrediting more moderate ethnic leaders, inasmuch as extremists can play on a sense of grievance and threat: if the group's survival is thought to be at stake, some members may meet violence with violence. The long-term impact can be the very disintegration of state-society relationships. However, when local elites opt for a strategy of peaceful cultural maintenance or revival, the perception of threat may be diminished, making more likely the survival in turn of a moderate leadership concerned with cultural continuity rather than confrontational politics. Hence, cultural preservation and cultural renewal can inspire a concern for the maintenance of central aspects of a group's culture, which restrains a drift toward violence. Cultural revival has thus often been preferred to violent resistance, as well exemplified in the case of Tibet.

Alternatively, what can occur if the outcome is violence rather than cultural revival? And what happens if the state responds violently to ethnic demands? State repression can also lead to *ethnogenesis,* or the emergence of new collective identities. Eritrea is a nation made up of several religious and ethnic groups affiliated by the common experience of a thirty-year war that cut across class, race, tribe, religion, and language. A common sense of "Eritreanness" shaped by years of violent clandestine struggle has come to define a new sense of belonging that encompasses most other affiliations. The problem with such violence-based identities is their intrinsic precariousness, since the trend is to perpetuate the recourse to antistate violence as a community-building, solidarity-engendering tool. This partly explains the recurring conflict between Eritrea and Ethiopia over apparently trivial boundary disputes.

The state clearly emerges as the catalyst of conflict during transitions and political change, resulting in a decline of regime legitimacy. At least three reasons can be identified. First, there is a close relationship between discontinuity in the system of political representation and the emergence of ethnic movements. During periods of political transition, new opportunities open up for the emergence of new elites. Emerging elites can take advantage of dissatisfaction among unrepresented ethnic groups whose mobilization may provide them with effective support. Second, there is awareness among elites that crucial choices must be made during periods of political transition, as they shape political patterns for years to come—and the opportunity to influence them may not come again. Third,

ethnonational conflicts indicate a lack of state legitimacy, which is symptomatic of periods immediately preceding or accompanying political transitions. By entirely ethnicizing the existing Hindu religious boundary, Marxist-inspired Tamil radicals applied boundary-building principles in order to establish an independent Tamil Eelam in Sri Lanka's northeast. Ethnicity and language completely replaced religion as the core value of nationhood. Government repression disseminated the myth of armed struggle among the Tamil youth, generating an intergenerational schism that marginalized the more moderate and religious elements of Tamil autonomism. A similar development took place in Kashmir, with dire and baleful international repercussions. In Chechnya, the most extremist factions seized the initiative following the Russian army's fierce repression. The slow drift toward radical confrontation legitimizes brutal force and violence as likely rational avenues, but the brunt of repression is normally borne out by unarmed local populations. In most of these cases, religion has become a secondary marker, as the conflict rests upon strictly secular roots.

State repression has not always led to heightened conflict. But in most cases, the state's successes have been ephemeral and short term. On some occasions, the price has been the establishment of an authoritarian regime. Wherever an illusory peace was arrived at by coercion alone, its impermanent and provisional nature invariably emerged at a later stage. Following its 1975 invasion of East Timor (Timor-Leste), the Indonesian army, with full U.S. backing, conceived a "final solution" for the former Portuguese colony. For more than twenty years the region seemed to be pacified, only to openly explode at the first regime crisis, which led to East Timor's independence in 1999. Again, the East Timorese leadership was highly secular, despite the strong presence of Catholic activists and the fact that Catholicism was the main religion (around 90 percent). The Indian army's suppression of the separatist insurgency in Punjab (where a movement for free Khalistan operated) alienated a considerable part of the Sikh population, largely among the younger generations, while radical groups grew stronger among the Sikh diaspora in Britain, Canada, and the United States.

Globalization and Violence: From Ethnic to Religious Conflict

The triumph of Western-style "modernization" has been an often-cited cause of ethnic conflict. The trend has dramatically increased with globalization. The tangible sense of threat, instability, and lack of security in societies undergoing detraditionalization can become even more pronounced when accompanied by an intrusion and expansion of state powers. Since the 1980s, nearly every inhabitant of the world has been affected by globalization.

In the previous century, a faith in unlimited economic progress identified development as the panacea capable of extirpating ethnic conflict once and for all. Notwithstanding the exponential expansion of intercultural contacts and all sorts of transactions (economic, commercial, and cultural), ethnic sentiments are actually reinforced by international transactions. Homogenization of consumer behavior and the global destruction of material culture have not simultaneously led to a convergence in moral and ethical values, nor have they led to a transcendence of ethnicity and patriotism. Occasionally, ethnic movements coalesce to resist global homogenization, but their main target remains the state—indeed, often a specific state and form of rule, such as rule from Moscow for the Chechens and from Ankara for the Kurds. Moreover, these movements frequently assume violent forms once the moderating influence provided by traditional culture has vanished. In nationalism studies, modernist scholars broadly agree that radical changes in lifestyle deeply affect the values and structures of traditional societies, leading to a reawakening of ethnic identities and the explosion of conflict. In short, there is a strong mutual correlation between detraditionalization, nationalism, and violence.

Oliver Roy (2004) postulates that the rise of global Islam typically occurs among *déracinées*, or diasporas, against more moderate forms of traditional Islam. He argues that global Salafism, a broader umbrella movement encompassing al-Qaeda, is characterized by deterritorialization, deculturation, and a generational gap: The parents' ancestral culture is dying and no longer transmitted to the offspring. The correlation with specific ethnic conflicts may be casual or opportunistic. For instance, the Palestinians' confrontation with the State of Israel merely provides another arrow in the Salafist quiver to be used for the promotion of its "brand."

The diasporic dimension is shared by both ethnic and civilizational conflicts: Both ethnic wars and religious-political fundamentalism have received substantial support from émigrés, who are often less in contact with the traditions and heritage of their mother country. Indeed, a decisive role in the radicalization of ethnic conflict is played by those diasporic communities most exposed to Westernization. Historically, European nationalism also prospered among diasporic figures based in London and other Western capitals. The Liberation Tigers of Tamil Eelam access strategic resources through the support of émigré communities in Europe and the United States. The role of student groups for a "free" Khalistan (corresponding approximately to the current state of Punjab, in India) among the Sikh diaspora in Canada and the United States was pivotal in organizing international attacks, but the support for terrorism came often from secular, even nonreligious Sikhs. Independent groups have risen and declined among the 50,000-strong Ambonese/Moluccan community that has lived in the Netherlands for several generations, Christianity becoming a hallmark of identity despite near-complete assimilation into the host Dutch culture. Often stressing elements of secular religion, Kosovar, Irish, Kurdish, Chechen, Igbo, and other separatists have been in various ways championed by diasporic groups. Although diasporas can spawn peaceful and pacifist organizations, such as those among Tibetan and Ogoni refugees, the most radical elements tend also to be the most detraditionalized and assimilated into mainstream culture.

Conclusion

Although religion usually implies an adhesion to universalistic principles, ethnicity is an expression of societal particularism and solipsism. In the modern world, the two have often met and merged. In several cases, from the French Revolution onward, this fusion has been encouraged by the state. In the past century, the extreme consequences of secularization without desacralization have been reached under Nazi-fascism and state socialism, culminating with the rise of totalitarianism. Today, the ethnicization of religion has often led to the spread of conflict and the rise of interethnic barriers.

Daniele Conversi

See also: Genocide; Nationalism.

Further Reading

Armstrong, John A. *Nations Before Nationalism.* Chapel Hill: University of North Carolina Press, 1982.

Armstrong, Karen. *The Battle for God: A History of Fundamentalism.* New York: Ballantine Books, 2001.

Barber, Benjamin R. *Jihad vs. McWorld.* New York: Ballantine Books, 1995.

Brown, David. *Contemporary Nationalism: Civic, Ethnocultural, and Multicultural Politics.* London: Routledge, 2000.

Carmichael, Cathie. "Violence and Ethnic Boundary Maintenance in Bosnia in the 1990s." *Journal of Genocide Research* 8:3 (September 2006): 283–93.

Coakley, John. "Conclusion: Towards a Solution?" In *The Territorial Management of Ethnic Conflicts,* ed. John Coakley, pp. 293–316. London: Frank Cass, 2003.

———. "Religion and Nationalism in the First World." In *Ethnonationalism in the Contemporary World: Walker Connor and the Theory of Nationalism,* ed. Daniele Conversi, pp. 206–25. London: Routledge, 2004.

Cockell, John. "Ethnic Nationalism and Subaltern Political Process: Exploring Autonomous Democratic Action in Kashmir." *Nations and Nationalism* 6:3 (2000): 319–45.

Connor, Walker. *Ethnonationalism: The Quest for Understanding.* Princeton, NJ: Princeton University Press, 1993.

———. "Nationalism and Political Illegitimacy." In *Ethnonationalism in the Contemporary World,* ed. Daniele Conversi, pp. 24–50. London: Routledge, 2004.

Conversi, Daniele. *The Basques, the Catalans, and Spain: Alternative Routes to Nationalist Mobilization,* 2nd ed. Reno: University of Nevada Press, 2000.

———. "Cosmopolitanism and Nationalism." In *Encyclopaedia of Nationalism,* ed. Anthony D. Smith and Athena Leoussi. Oxford: Transaction Books, 2000.

———. "Democracy, Nationalism and Culture. The Limits of Liberal Mono-Culturalism." *Sociology Compass* (December 2007): 156–82.

———. "Demo-Skepticism and Genocide." *Political Studies Review* 4:3 (September 2006): 247–62.

———. "Dominant Ethnicities, Dominant Cultures and Cultural Resemblance." In *Dominant Nationalism, Dominant Ethnicity,* ed. André Lecours and Geneviève Nootens, pp. 57–72. Bruxelles: Peter I. Lang, 2009.

———. "Globalization and Ethnic Conflict." In *The Routledge Handbook of Globalization Studies,* ed. Bryan Turner. London: Routledge/Taylor and Francis, 2009.

———. "Homogenisation, Nationalism and War: Should We Still Read Ernest Gellner?" *Nations and Nationalism* 13:3 (2007): 371–94.

———. "Nationalism, Boundaries and Violence." *Millennium: Journal of International Studies* 28:3 (1999): 553–84.

———. "Reassessing Theories of Nationalism: Nationalism as Boundary Maintenance and Creation." *Nationalism and Ethnic Politics* 1:1 (Spring 1995): 73–85.

———. "Violence as an Ethnic Border. The Consequences of a Lack of Distinctive Elements in Croatian, Kurdish and Basque Nationalism." In *Nationalism in Europe: Past and Present,* vol. 1, ed. Justo G. Beramendi, Ramón Máiz, and Xosé M. Núñez, pp. 167–98. Santiago de Compostela, Spain: Santiago de Compostela University Press, 1994.

———. "'We Are All Equals!' Militarism, Homogenization and 'Egalitarianism' in Nationalist State-Building (1789–1945)." *Ethnic and Racial Studies* 31:7 (2008): 1286–314.

Edwards, John. *Language and Identity: An Introduction.* Cambridge, UK: Cambridge University Press, 2009.

Fenton, Steve. *Ethnicity.* Cambridge, UK: Polity Press, 2003.

Fenton, Steve, and Stephen May. *Ethnonational Identities.* New York: Palgrave Macmillan, 2002.

Fuglerud, Oivind. *Life on the Outside: The Tamil Diaspora and Long-Distance Nationalism.* London: Pluto Press, 1999.

Gallagher, Tom. *The Balkans After the Cold War: From Tyranny to Tragedy.* London: Routledge, 2003.

Gellner, Ernest. *Nations and Nationalism,* 2nd ed. Ithaca, NY: Cornell University Press, 2009.

Gentile, Emilio. *Politics as Religion.* Princeton, NJ: Princeton University Press, 2006.

———. *The Sacralization of Politics in Fascist Italy.* Cambridge, MA: Harvard University Press, 1996.

Ghai, Yash. *Autonomy and Ethnicity: Negotiating Competing Claims in Multi-Ethnic States.* Cambridge, UK: Cambridge University Press, 2000.

Gibson, Margaret A. *Accommodation Without Assimilation: Sikh Immigrants in an American High School.* Ithaca, NY: Cornell University Press, 1988.

Gray, John. *Al Qaeda and What It Means to Be Modern.* New York: Faber and Faber, 2003.

Griffin, Roger. *Modernism and Fascism: The Sense of a Beginning Under Mussolini and Hitler.* London: Palgrave, 2007.

Gurr, Ted Robert. *Minorities at Risk: A Global View of Ethnopolitical Conflicts.* Washington, DC: United States Institute of Peace Press, 1993.

Hastings, Adrian. *The Construction of Nationhood: Ethnicity, Religion, and Nationalism.* New York: Cambridge University Press, 1997.

Hayes, Carlton J.H. *Nationalism: A Religion.* New York: Macmillan, 1960.

Hill, Ronald J. "The Dissolution of the Soviet Union: Federation, Commonwealth, Secession." In *The Territorial Management of Ethnic Conflicts,* ed. John Coakley, pp. 199–228. London: Frank Cass, 2003.

Hooghe, Liesbet. "Belgium: From Regionalism to Federalism." In *The Territorial Management of Ethnic Conflicts,* ed. John Coakley, pp. 73–98. London: Frank Cass, 2003.

Horowitz, Donald L. *Ethnic Groups in Conflict.* Berkeley: University of California Press, 1985.

Huntington, Samuel *The Clash of Civilizations and the Remaking of World Order.* New York: Touchstone, 1996.

Knezys, Stasys, and Romanas Sedlickas. *The War in Chechnya.* College Station: Texas A&M University Press, 1999.

Kolstø, Pål. *Myths and Boundaries in South Eastern Europe.* London: Hurst, 2005.

Kostovicova, Denisa. "Republika Srpska and Its Boundaries in Bosnian Serb Geographical Narratives in the Post-Dayton Period." *Space and Polity* 8:3 (2004): 267–87.

Kriesberg, Louis. *Constructive Conflicts: From Escalation to Resolution.* Lanham, MD: Rowman and Littlefield, 1998.

Lieven, Anatol. *Chechnya: Tombstone of a Russian Power.* New Haven, CT: Yale University Press, 1999.

Malcolm, Noel. *Bosnia: A Short History.* New York: New York University Press, 1994.

McGarry, John. *Northern Ireland and the Divided World: The Northern Ireland Conflict and the Good Friday Agreement in Comparative Perspective.* Oxford: Oxford University Press, 2001.

Mitchell, Claire. "The Religious Content of Ethnic Identities." *Sociology* 40:6 (2006): 1135–52.

Murphy, Alexander B. "Linguistic Regionalism and the Social Construction of Space in Belgium." In *Political Geography: A Reader,* ed. John Agnew, pp. 256–68. London: Edward Arnold, 1997.

Nesiah, Vasuki. "Federalism and Diversity in India." In *Autonomy and Ethnicity: Negotiating Competing Claims in Multi-Ethnic States,* ed. Yash Ghai, pp. 53–76. Cambridge, UK: Cambridge University Press, 2000.

Pape, Robert A. *Dying to Win: The Strategic Logic of Suicide Terrorism.* New York: Random House, 2005.

———. "The Strategic Logic of Suicide Terrorism." *American Political Science Review* 97:3 (August 2003): 343–61.

Pateman, Roy. *Eritrea: Even the Stones Are Burning.* Lawrenceville, NJ: Red Sea Press, 1997.

Pettigrew, Joyce. *The Sikhs of the Punjab: Unheard Voices of State and Guerilla Violence.* London: Zed Books, 1995.

Qureshi, Emran, and Michael A. Sells. *The New Crusades: Constructing the Muslim Enemy.* New York: Columbia University Press, 2004.

Ramet, Sabrina P. *Thinking About Yugoslavia: Scholarly Debates About the Yugoslav Breakup and the Wars in Bosnia and Kosovo.* Cambridge, UK: Cambridge University Press, 2006.

Roy, Oliver. *Globalised Islam: The Search for a New Ummah.* London: Hurst, 2004.

Sacks, Jonathan. *The Dignity of Difference: How to Avoid the Clash of Civilizations.* New York: Continuum, 2002.

Schwartz, Ronald David. *Circle of Protest: Political Ritual in the Tibetan Uprising, 1987–1992.* New York: Columbia University Press, 1994.

Sells, Michael A. *The Bridge Betrayed: Religion and Genocide in Bosnia.* Berkeley: University of California Press, 1996.

Smith, Anthony D. "Dating the Nation." In *Ethnonationalism in the Contemporary World,* ed. Daniele Conversi, pp. 53–71. London: Routledge, 2004.

———. *Ethno-symbolism and Nationalism.* London: Routledge, 2009.

———. *Nationalism and Modernism: A Critical Survey of Recent Theories of Nations and Nationalism.* London: Routledge, 1998.

———. *Nationalism in a Global Era.* Cambridge, England: Polity Press, 1996.

Sprinzak, Ehud. "Rational Fanatics." *Foreign Policy* 120 (September–October 2000): 66–73.

Taylor, John G. *East Timor: The Price of Freedom.* London: Zed Books, 1999.

Tiruchelvam, Neelan. "The Politics of Federalism and Diversity in Sri Lanka." In *Autonomy and Ethnicity: Negotiating Competing Claims in Multi-Ethnic States,* ed. Yash Ghai, pp. 197–218. Cambridge, UK: Cambridge University Press, 2000.

Tololyan, Khachig. "National Self-Determination and the Limits of Sovereignty: Armenia, Azerbaijan and the Secession of Nagorno-Karabagh." *Nationalism and Ethnic Politics* 1:1 (Spring 1995): 86–110.

Tronvoll, Kjetil. "Borders of Violence, Boundaries of Identity: Demarcating the Eritrean Nation-State." *Ethnic and Racial Studies* 22:6 (November 1999): 1037–60.

Turner, Kathleen. "Myths and Moral Authority in Maluku: The Case of Ambon." *Asian Ethnicity* 4:2 (June 2003): 241–63.

Van den Berghe, Pierre, ed. *State, Violence and Ethnicity.* Niwot: University Press of Colorado, 1990.

Weber, Max. "The Nation." In *Nationalism: Critical Concepts in Political Science* (5 vols.), ed. John Hutchinson and Anthony D. Smith, vol. 1, pp. 5–12. London: Routledge, 2000.

Wilson, A. Jeyeratnam. "Sri Lanka: Ethnic Strife and the Politics of Space." In *The Territorial Management of Ethnic Conflicts,* ed. John Coakley, pp. 173–98. London: Frank Cass, 2003.

Zawadzki, Paul. "Nationalism, Democracy and Religion." In *Revisiting Nationalism: Theories and Processes,* ed. Alain Dieckhoff and Christophe Jaffrelot, pp. 165–90. London: C. Hurst, 2005.

Europe

Religious violence in contemporary Europe has been limited and on a fairly small scale. The violence that does occur is driven by several key factors and trends affecting Europe as a whole. First, increased perception of global conflict between the Muslim world and the Western world has made European countries targets of terrorist attacks and individual violence. Second, as populations of Western European countries become increasingly diverse, the struggle to become a religiously plural society has led to tensions. The influx of immigrants from North Africa and the Middle East in the last quarter of the twentieth century put pressure on traditionally Christian Western European countries to assimilate or incorporate large-scale Muslim migration while maintaining the traditions of separation of church and state and religious freedom. The result throughout much of Europe is significant anti-immigrant sentiment expressed both by political leaders and by extreme social movements.

Functionally, these immigrants are easy to distinguish from the majority through racial and religious differences. Religious doctrine and practice have become the spark around which anti-immigrant sentiment has developed. Ethnic self-determination is another factor behind contemporary religious violence. Northern Ireland demonstrates that religion as a marker of ethnic difference can have a profound impact on how a conflict is understood by the two sides. Anti-Semitic violence has continued to affect Europe, partly as a consequence of the renewed violence in Israel-Palestine and partly as a result of the legacy of European anti-Semitism. Anti-Semitic violence is carried both by Europe's neofascist movements and by other contending religious groups. Religious violence in Europe is driven by increasing contact between different religious communities that hold conflicting views of what religious pluralism in a liberal democracy should mean to its citizens and that have differential access to power and resources within their society.

There are two primary mechanisms through which violence arises in democracies. Radicalization occurs when a social group hopes to achieve change and has limited or no success using nonviolent means. A small group of activists splinters off the main group and chooses violence as a means to force the change they seek. Reaction occurs when a social group seeks to prevent specific change from occurring. When nonviolence means are not sufficient to block change, the group will split, with an extreme group adopting violent tactics and increasing the costs of change for the rest of the community (Gurr 2002). Religious violence in contemporary Europe is evidence of both of these mechanisms at work. Radical and reactionary groups have faced off over issues of freedom of expression and the rights of minorities and immigrants. In liberal democracies, mechanisms exist for the nonviolent expression of dissent, which account for the majority of religious conflict in Europe; both radical and reactionary groups have chosen at times to use violence as a mechanism for achieving their goals.

International Religious Terrorism

International religious terrorism has resulted in the highest casualty counts among religiously motivated violence in Europe. Contemporary European terrorists have primarily had affiliation with Islamic fundamentalist groups. The framing of religious jihad against the West has been a persuasive one in recruiting individuals to carry out terrorist attacks in European countries. The July 7, 2005, bombings on the London subway and bus system claimed 52 lives and injured more than 700 victims. On the 29th and 30th of June 2007, attempts were made in London and at the Glasgow airport to explode car bombs. Those two attempts succeeded in killing only the terrorists, but they were clearly intended to cause wider carnage. The attacks were known as the "Doctors' Plots,"

since Indian and Arab doctors residing in Britain were the organizers and perpetrators. The coordinated attacks on four commuter trains in Madrid on March 11, 2004, killed 191 people and injured more than 1,700. Of those tried for the train bombings, the large majority were Spanish or Moroccan.

France has experienced international terrorism in the form of the GIA, an Algerian terrorist group that in 1994 hijacked an Air France jet with the goal of crashing it into the Eiffel Tower. The GIA followed that up in 1995 with bombings of the Paris metro that killed 8 and wounded over 200 people. Strasbourg Cathedral was targeted during Christmas 2000, but the attack was thwarted by counterterrorism officials. In September of 2001 a plot was discovered, led by a French Algerian, to bomb the U.S. embassy in Paris. In February 2002, nine Moroccans were arrested by the Italian authorities for plotting to attack the U.S. embassy in Rome.

Although all of these attacks fall into a pattern of international terrorism that reflects a sense in the Muslim world that the West is engaged in a campaign to limit Muslim influence and power, the attackers in these cases were not foreigners slipping across borders to commit terrorist action. Rather, they were immigrants to the targeted country who expressed their frustration and sense of a global jihad through locally initiated acts of terrorism. Members of these terrorist cells represent a wide range of Arab and North African countries. North African Islamists forced to flee their homeland by security forces set up bases in Europe for their national groups, including the Algerian GIA, the Libyan Lift, and Egypt's Al-Jama'a. The Madrid train bombings, the attacks in France, and the cells in Europe were all connected to these North African terrorist groups. The press and counterterrorism officials have linked these terrorist groups to al-Qaeda, but it appears that these organizations are acting less out of a desire for an international Islamic power than out of desire to force change in their country of origin. Western European countries have been targeted by these groups due to the perception that European countries are backing the governments in power in North Africa. While attacks by North African groups may not have been formally supported or funded by al-Qaeda, the September 11, 2001, attacks on the United States may have provided inspiration for these national groups to step up violence against European targets. Al-Qaeda has also articulated an organizing ideology adopted by many of these groups.

Al-Qaeda remains a threat to Europe as a sponsor or perpetrator of or inspiration for continuing religious violence. Al-Qaeda as a top-down organization does not appear to have the ability to launch attacks, but small groups identifying themselves with al-Qaeda's ideology have shown their willingness and ability to target Europe. While most of the large-scale attacks have been carried out by affiliates of national Islamist movements from North Africa, counterterrorism officials in Europe have broken up al-Qaeda cells across Western Europe and aborted their planned attacks. In 2007 alone, al-Qaeda cells were broken up in France, Germany, Denmark, Spain, Belgium, and the United Kingdom. Al-Qaeda's framing of conflict between the Muslim world and the West as part of a religious jihad provides continuing potential for religious violence in Europe.

Tensions in Increasing Religious Pluralism

The liberal democracies of Western Europe enshrine in their political structures freedom of religion and equality of opportunity for all residents of their countries. But the increasing number of Muslim immigrants moving into majority Christian countries has challenged policy makers in Europe to provide for increased religious pluralism. Immigration in Western Europe has brought ethnic identity to the fore of European consciousness. With the exception of France and the United Kingdom, access to nationality for immigrants and their locally borne children is limited in Western Europe, placing immigrants in a permanent category of "other" in their adopted countries. Ethnic identity is primarily understood in Western Europe to have a basis in cultural distinctions. Recognizing cultural distinctions is often done through identifying religious difference as a marker of ethnic identity. The predominance of Islam as the religion of immigrants to Europe, in contrast to the Christian identity of native Europeans, has created a climate in which religious difference has become a primary marker of ethnic and immigrant identity. These markers of difference provide the boundaries at which resources, both economic and political, are distributed among the community. Radicalization of immigrant groups has occurred as immigrants have sought to achieve the same standards of living and political power as native Europeans. Immigrants' expectations of what they can achieve in Western Europe have been thwarted by their inability to gain legal status and the full rights of citizenship. Reactionary forces have gained strength in Europe as fears that the increasing numbers of immigrants will change the political and social structure of Europe have made anti-immigrant sentiment and violence toward immigrants increasingly common. Religious violence in Europe results from a complex mix of anti-immigration sentiment, religious difference, and discrimination.

All across Europe, reactionary groups have responded to the increases in Muslims by targeting Muslims for violent attacks. This trend was boosted following the September 11, 2001, attacks on the United States, after which there was a spike in the number of anti-Muslim attacks around Europe. In Britain, in the year following September 11, over 344 incidents of anti-Muslim violence were reported. Attacks have included vandalism and attacks on mosques. These anti-Muslim attacks have often corresponded with anti-immigrant sentiment in a community or country. Following the Madrid train bombings, increased anti-immigrant and anti-Muslim violence was witnessed in Spain. Muslims claim that crimes against Muslims are not being pursued vigorously in the courts and point to the acquittal of ethnic Spaniards for homicides of Muslim North Africans. The majority of anti-Muslim violence has not been organized or large scale but has consisted of individual confrontations between minority community members and reactionary forces. This trend is seen across Europe as suspicion has fallen on immigrant communities for terrorist attacks.

The Netherlands

A prime example of tensions between Muslim minority populations and the majority population of a country has been the rise in religiously motivated violence in the Netherlands. During the 1950s and 1960s, Moroccans were encouraged to immigrate to the Netherlands to fill a labor shortage. Fifty percent of Muslim immigrants in the Netherlands hold Dutch citizenship; Muslims make up approximately 6 percent of the population and have access to 30 Islamic schools and around 400 mosques. In 2002, prior to the election for prime minister, Pim Fortuyn, a populist and anti-immigration political leader, was assassinated after proclaiming Holland to be full and proposing that no more immigration should be allowed. His murderers were Muslim sympathizers. In 2004, Dutch filmmaker Theo Van Gogh made the documentary *Submission,* which attacked the treatment of Muslim women in Islamic society. Van Gogh was murdered and

a note pinned to his chest that proclaimed jihad against Holland, Europe, and the United States. The suspect in the murder, a Dutch Moroccan, was arrested along with seven other Muslims under antiterror laws and identified by authorities as the Hofstad group. The murder of Van Gogh and the subsequent arrests set off a series of retaliatory attacks against Muslims in the Netherlands. Anti-Muslim violence exploded with attacks on mosques and Muslim schools, followed by retaliatory strikes by Muslims on Protestant churches. In 2008, another Dutch filmmaker, Geert Wilders, produced *Fitna,* which sparked more violent protests by Muslims reacting to the film's presentation of Koranic verses with violent imagery of the September 11 attacks in New York and the Madrid train bombings.

While they are invited guests in the Netherlands, the Muslim population has not achieved parity with Protestant Dutch citizens. The unemployment rate among the Muslim population is high, and immigrants are required to attend Dutch language and culture classes. The religious violence in the Netherlands has been perpetrated by both reactionary and radical groups vying to achieve political goals within the Dutch system. In 2007, the Dutch government launched a large-scale initiative to combat rising radicalization among Muslim youth and far Right groups spurred by concerns about Islamic extremism in the Netherlands. The project supports local governments in education, child support, antidiscrimination, and employment projects to keep youth from turning against Dutch society and its values. The Dutch government is trying to maintain the ideals of liberal democracy by using social programs to limit the impact of radicalization and reaction on Dutch society. The focus of Dutch programs on providing improved social services to the minority communities indicates an understanding by government officials that discrimination and lack of opportunity are radicalizing members of the immigrant communities. This pattern of radicalization is seen throughout Europe among the immigrant and minority communities, especially from North Africa.

Denmark

Denmark has also been a flashpoint for Muslim-Christian violence across Europe. On September 30, 2005, the Danish newspaper *Jyllands-Posten* ran a feature titled the "Face of Muhammad" in which twelve drawings of the Prophet Muhammad were published. Several of the cartoons make a clear connection between the Prophet Muhammad and terrorism through depictions of him with weapons or welcoming suicide bombers into the afterlife. The cartoons generated a backlash from Muslim groups, both for breaking religious restrictions on creating representations of Muhammad and for what was perceived as anti-Islamic sentiment in the depictions. Telling of the existing tensions around the assimilation of the Muslim minority in Denmark, the cartoons' original publication was accompanied by the following words written by the editor: "The modern, secular society is rejected by some Muslims. They demand a special position, insisting on special consideration of their own religious feelings. It is incompatible with contemporary democracy and freedom of speech, where you must be ready to put up with insults, mockery and ridicule." The editors of *Jyllands-Posten* clearly felt that the tenets of freedom of speech and expression overrode any concerns for embarrassing the Muslim minority or breaking a Muslim taboo by depicting Muhammad.

Over the next six months, the cartoons were gradually reprinted in major newspapers across Europe. The reprinting was met with mass demonstrations, including embassy burnings and clashes with police in the Middle East, Africa, and Europe. Approximately 300 people died during the protests and counterprotests, with almost a thousand injured across thirty-five countries. The editor who had approved the article stated after the protests that it was incompatible with secular democracy for Muslims to ask others to respect their religious taboo against images of Muhammad in the public domain. He believed that while Muslims could expect others to respect their houses of worship, in public discourse it was not necessary to change the behavior of the majority to avoid offending the minority. This interpretation is consistent with the secular ideology of much of Europe, which believes the public space should not be influenced by religious matters. Muslim communities around the world continued to be enraged by the cartoons. Not only were the cartoons understood to be offensive, but also Denmark was perceived in the aftermath to be unwilling to enter into dialogue with Muslim governments about the issue.

Protests against the cartoons have not been the only religious violence in Denmark. In 2008 riots began in the immigrant neighborhoods of Copenhagen and spread to Denmark's other large cities. These riots were in response to changes in police procedures that Muslims perceived as allowing Muslims and Arabs to be specifically targeted by police. Arabs and Muslims make up 3.5 percent of the Danish population, and immigrants explained that police procedures allowed individuals to be targeted because of skin color or Arab features. There was speculation that the reprinting of the Danish cartoons during the riots may have exacerbated the violence among the minority youth. The publishing of the cartoons was a reaction against perceptions that assimilation of Muslims into Danish society would change that society. The cartoons radicalized elements of the Danish Muslim population into committing increasing violence when their demands were not met.

France

France has also experienced significant violence as it grapples with increasing religious pluralism. In France, "religion is considered a very private matter and proselytism is absolutely forbidden in the institutions of the French republic" (Limage 2000). France has the largest Muslim minority in Europe, and the relationship between public schools and religion has become a point of tension in the French Muslim minority community. Disagreement over the wearing of the traditional Muslim head scarves by French female students began in 1989. Initially school authorities required the removal of head scarves; students who did not comply were sent home. In 2003, a French commission recommended that all visible religious symbols should be banned in schools. This issue has become emblematic of the tension between Muslims and the French government over religious freedom and rights. Muslims view the ban on head scarves in school as limiting their right to freedom of religion. French officials believe allowing head scarves in schools threatens the core ideology of secularism and the separation of religion from political life. The debate over head scarves has also spread to Germany, where disagreement over the right of teachers to wear head scarves has contributed to increased religious tension. These tensions will likely strengthen and expand throughout the continent as countries struggle to accommodate increasing numbers of non-Christians into the social system.

In November 2005, large-scale riots overtook France and lasted for almost three weeks. The riots were sparked by the deaths of two North Africans who were attempting to flee from French police. The riots resulted in more than 9,000 cars being burned and more than 100 public buildings set on fire. Rioters felt that the North Africans had been singled out by police. Reactionary groups responded,

A Muslim man walks among gravestones vandalized with swastikas and SS symbols in a cemetery for France's Muslim servicemen in Strasbourg, France, August 7, 2004. Many factors have contributed to the increased violence against Muslim communities in France, including tensions created by the increase in religious pluralism and the threat of global jihad against the West. *(Cedric Joubert/Associated Press)*

and during the riots, Molotov cocktails were thrown at mosques in Lyons and Carpentras. Observers pointed to the long-standing racial barriers in French society that leave French Muslims less able to find jobs and education than other French citizens. These barriers have contributed to radicalization, particularly of young Muslims. As in the Netherlands, the government responded to the riots with plans to improve education and job prospects for poor immigrants and children of immigrants. By improving prospects for immigrants within the system, the government hopes to counteract the radicalization of immigrant youth.

Ethnic-Religious Separatism

A different kind of religious violence has plagued Northern Ireland. A dispute over the balance of power between ethnic groups, relationships between ethnic communities, and governance issues has been framed in terms of religious difference. In 1921, following a nationalist revolt in Ireland, the majority of Ireland gained independence from the United Kingdom. The Anglo-Irish Treaty of 1921 determined that the Catholic Irish Free State would control most of Ireland, while in Northern Ireland, the Protestant majority succeeded in remaining part of the UK. Republicans (those advocating Northern Ireland's separation from England) are typically Catholics and consider themselves Gaels or Celts—indigenous inhabitants of Ireland. The Unionists (proponents of maintaining a connection with the UK), are predominantly Protestant and ethnically Scottish or English. Even before the English arrived in Ireland, the short distance between Scotland and Northern Ireland meant that there was a significant Scottish presence in Northern Ireland. As English influence increased, Protestant settlers displaced Catholic landowners. This distinction between English and Scottish Protestants and Irish Catholics led to differential economic development, with Northern Ireland flourishing during the Industrial Revolution.

The violence between the two communities in contemporary times began in the 1970s with the Troubles. Marches and rioting in the streets became commonplace, and on both sides paramilitary groups became a part of the landscape. Peace campaigns have existed since the mid-1970s, and a series of peace agreements has been instituted. By the standards of civil wars, the total of fewer than 4,000 deaths

from the conflict in Northern Ireland is small, but the conflict generated intense international interest and intervention. Most notorious of the players in the Northern Ireland conflict was the Irish Republican Army and its offshoots. By the mid-1990s Sinn Féin, the IRA's political wing, was the primary party representing the Republicans.

In 1998, with the assistance of U.S. mediation, both sides to the conflict signed the Belfast Agreement, otherwise known as the Good Friday Agreement. The document included a Northern Ireland assembly with a power-sharing executive and cross-border institution linking the Republic of Ireland and Northern Ireland. The Republic of Ireland dropped its claim to the counties of Northern Ireland, and paramilitaries on both sides were responsible for decommissioning weapons. While the agreement received overwhelming support in referendums in both the Republic of Ireland and Northern Ireland, the provisions have taken almost a decade to enact. It took until 2005 for the decommissioning of Republican paramilitaries to take place and for the final power-sharing agreements to go into place. With the formation of a power-sharing agreement and decommissioning of paramilitaries, the stage appears to be set for peace to become the norm in Northern Ireland, but the peace is too new for complete success to be declared. While involving many more issues and identities than just religion, the conflict in Northern Ireland was framed by both sides as being between Catholics and Protestants, projecting an impression that the conflict was fundamentally about religion.

Neo-Nazi and Anti-Semitic Violence

Neo-Nazi or neofascist elements in Europe commit violence against Jewish communities and other ethnic and religious minorities. In France, a series of neo-Nazi attacks on Jewish and Muslim sites, including synagogues and mosques, raised fears about increased neo-Nazi violence. Neo-Nazi groups commit anti-Semitic violence because of an ideological opposition to Jewish communities in Europe. A second and separate source of anti-Semitic violence is anti-Israel sentiment, with violence against Jews in Europe committed by Muslims in response to Israel's actions toward Palestine and other Arab countries. Anti-Semitic violence is therefore both reactionary and radical, as different groups with different purposes single out Jews in Europe for attack.

The primary country afflicted with anti-Semitic violence has been France. The majority of the attacks there have been committed by Muslims of North African origin responding to their lack of opportunity in France and the situation of the Palestinians. The French government reports that approximately two-thirds of racist incidents in France are anti-Semitic, and most are perpetrated by Muslim youth. Anti-Semitic attacks in France have included the firebombing of synagogues, assaults on Jews, and the desecration of cemeteries. In 2004, Israel's prime minister urged all Jews living in France to move to Israel to avoid the rise in anti-Semitism. French Jews report that the anti-Semitism they experience is primarily a spillover from the Arab-Israeli conflict and the larger Muslim–Western world tensions.

In Britain, 2006 saw 594 reported incidents of anti-Semitism—the highest since recording started in 1984. These attacks have been focused on synagogues, individuals, and Jewish cemeteries. In 2000, Spain saw similar attacks, with rocks thrown at Jewish community centers. Among European countries, Austria and Hungary have the highest anti-Semitic sentiment throughout the population. In Denmark, police have placed renewed focus on groups like the Danish Front that represent the extreme right wing. Members of the Danish Front as well as White Pride in Denmark have been charged with several racial and politically motivated crimes.

Germany has been troubled by increases in neo-Nazi violence, as well. What concerns German officials the most is that neo-Nazi violence in Germany appears to be more organized and the groups to have a larger following than in other European countries. German neo-Nazis have attacked individual immigrants and Jews, as well as planting small bombs and firebombing immigrant and Jewish areas. The Internet has become a fertile recruiting ground for neo-Nazi movements throughout Germany and has allowed them to increase their reach across the country.

Conclusion

Religious violence in Europe is happening within liberal democratic structures that should allow political and ethnic minorities to express their grievances and concerns without using violence. But mechanisms of radicalization and reaction have allowed these groups to move from peaceful demonstrations and political expression to violence, both at individuals and using terrorist methods. Religious affiliation in Europe is closely tied with ethnicity; so while the issues of contention are generally not religious in nature, religious institutions and symbols have become the markers for difference and the nexus of contention. Perceptions of a global conflict between Islam and the Western world have encouraged small groups of Muslims in Europe to adopt the ideology of al-Qaeda and commit terrorist attacks in their adopted countries. This perception of global conflict has contributed to the increasing anti-immigrant sentiment and violence targeting immigrants across Europe. The resurgence of neo-Nazi and neofascist movements has been built on the foundation of distrust of all immigrant groups but most recently has been expressed in violence against both Jews and Muslims. The changes in demographic makeup of European countries have placed religion on the front lines of conflict in Europe. As traditionally Christian, avowedly secular nations are faced with increasing numbers of non-Christian minorities, the challenge to these liberal democracies will be to maintain their historical values and traditions without alienating minority communities.

Julie Shedd

See also: Cartoon Crisis; Ethnicity; Nationalism.

Further Reading

"Al Qaeda's New Front." *Frontline.* Public Broadcasting Service (PBS), January 25, 2005. Available: http://pbs.org/wgbh/pages/frontline/shows/front.

Bayoumi, Ayaa. "Religious Freedom: Muslims in Europe Face Widespread Abuse." *International Herald Tribune,* January 8, 2004.

Crowley, John. "The Political Participation of Ethnic Minorities." *International Political Science Review* 22:1 (2001): 99–121.

"Danish Police Official Rules Out Connection Between Youth Riots, Mohammed Cartoons." *Agence France Presse,* February 16, 2008.

"Dutch Government Launches Plan to Combat Radicalization." *Agence France Presse,* August 27, 2007.

"Germany's Neo-Nazis." *The Economist,* August 12, 2000.

Gilmore, Inigo. "Flee France, Sharon Urges Jews: Anti-Semitism Rising." *National Post* (Canada), July 19, 2004.

Giutta, Olivier. "Europe, Very Much on Al-Qaida's Radar." *Middle East Times,* March 3, 2008.

Goldstone, Brian. "Violence and the Profane: Islamism, Liberal Democracy, and the Limits of Secular Discipline." *Anthropological Quarterly* 80:1 (2007): 207.

Gurr, Ted. "Terrorism in Democracies: When It Occurs, Why It Fails." In *The New Global Terrorism: Characteristics, Causes, Controls,* ed. Charles Kegly, pp. 202–15. Englewood Cliffs, NJ: Prentice Hall, 2002.

Lichfield, John. "French Neo-Nazis Turn on Muslim Graves Attacks." *The Independent* (UK), June 21, 2004.

———. "Support for Sarkozy as French Rioting Subsides." *Belfast Telegraph* (Northern Ireland), November 14, 2005.

Limage, Leslie. "Education and Muslim Identity: The Case of France." *Comparative Education* 36:1 (2000): 73–94.

Madrid, Ed, and Peter Conradi "Spain Confronts Its Fascist Demons" *Sunday Times* (UK), November 21, 2004.

McGuire, Stryker. "Clash of Civilizations." *Newsweek,* November 22, 2004.

Pargeter, Alison. "North African Immigrants in Europe and Political Violence." *Studies in Conflict and Terrorism* 79:8 (2006): 731–47.

Sciolino, Elaine. "Attacks by Arabs on Jews in France Revive Old Fears." *New York Times,* December 3, 2003.

Sennott, Charles. "In France, Anti-Semitism Burns Anew." *Boston Globe,* December 21, 2003.

Ware, John. "The Price of Peace." BBC News, March 2, 2008. Available: http://news.bbc.co.uk/2/hi/uk_news/northern_ireland/7273611.stm.

Falun Gong

Falun Gong (Falungong), or "Law Wheel Qigong," is a Chinese spiritual movement based on ritual meditation exercises. Little is certain as to the background of its founder, Li Hongzhi, before he began teaching his system of physical and spiritual cultivation in China's Jilin Province in 1992. The movement, which is also known as Falun Dafa (Falundafa), or "Way of the Law Wheel," rapidly attracted millions of followers both in China and abroad. Though drawing upon traditional Asian spiritual practice and claiming to be nonpolitical, Falun Gong came to be viewed as a threat to Chinese Communist Party leadership. Following a massive demonstration by adherents in 1999, authorities attempted to eradicate the movement, using measures that drew international criticism. Presently, the Falun Gong is outlawed in China as a "dangerous cult." A well-organized community of globally linked followers, led by Li Hongzhi (now a U.S. citizen), continues to promote Falun Gong and to protest its repression.

The Origins of Falun Gong

Falun Gong began as a style of *qigong* (pronounced *chee-gong*), traditional breathing and meditation exercises that date back to the Jin dynasty (265–317 C.E.). Practitioners of qigong believe that by cultivating their *qi* (loosely translated as "life substance"), they could improve their health and elevate themselves spiritually. Qigong has roots in Buddhism, Confucianism, and Daoism (Taoism), but it also has been associated with past sectarian movements in China, such as the Yellow Turbans and the White Lotus Society, that focused on individual salvation. Qigong, as well as traditional religious groups, were suppressed by the Chinese Communist Party when it took power in 1949. But by the 1980s, the party endorsed qigong as a medical treatment and permitted a growing number of qigong masters and their adherents to practice freely.

Falun Gong's founder, Li Hongzhi, was born in 1952 in Changchun, Jilin Province. According to his authorized biography, Li was guided by both Buddhist and Daoist qigong masters from the age of four. In 1992, he began teaching his simplified system of qigong movements as a path to health and spiritual enlightenment. In speaking and television appearances, he projected a warm, everyman persona that attracted growing audiences (Leung 2002). Li taught Falun Gong in almost all major cities in China from 1992 to 1994, at the invitation of various qigong organizations. He then traveled abroad, introducing Falun Gong to other countries.

Core Texts: *Falun Gong* and *Zhuan Falun*

Li Hongzhi promoted his movement in two books that became instant best sellers. *Falun Gong*, published in 1993, is an introductory text that presents his five basic qigong exercises—four in a standing position and one seated. *Zhuan Falun* (Turning the Law Wheel), published in 1995 and updated in 2000, explains the spiritual dimensions of his movement. Li writes that Falun Gong is an advanced cultivation system in the Buddhist tradition, which formerly was handed down to only chosen disciples with extremely high *xinxing* (moral character). Cultivation of the self through Falun Gong entails the assimilation of Buddha Law's three qualities: *zhen*, *shan*, and *ren* (truthfulness, benevolence, and forbearance). Li claims that as *Dafa* (the Great

Law) judges each person in a process called *fa* (rectification), practitioners of Falun Gong can progressively attain wellness, supernatural abilities, and immortality. Li also states that Falun Gong is not to be used as a quick medical treatment. Instead, its purpose is to transcend illness by enduring pain, accumulating *de* (merit), and strictly following Li's teachings.

Zhuan Falun also elevates its author to god-like status. Li claims that his supreme level of cultivation enables him to control *fashen* (legal institutions) so that he can protect his followers and monitor their beliefs and actions from afar. He suggests that he is superior to any Buddha or god, since he alone, for the first time in history, can reveal the whole of Buddha Law to humanity. The publication of *Zhuan Falun* thus marked a turning point for the Falun Gong movement, from a health technique devised by a qigong master to a quasi religion led by a self-proclaimed supernatural being.

The Growth of the Movement

Li Hongzhi's message was spread through lectures, Web sites, books, videotapes, and DVDs. By 2000, Falun Gong had an estimated 10 million followers in China. An unpublished report on the Chinese government's investigation of Falun Gong states that devotees are typically over forty, and 60 percent are women. Lower- or lower-middle-income citizens, from both urban and rural areas, make up about 70 percent of the movement. Another segment of followers consists of middle-income professionals who are retired or marginalized by the newly privatized economy. The smallest but most influential component occupies China's upper echelons within the Chinese Communist Party, the military, civil service, and professional life. According to this report, these elite adherents either failed to find fulfillment in their careers or lost a power struggle within the new socio-political system, and so they now are antagonistic toward that system (Leung 2002).

Many of the older followers, facing borderline poverty and declining health, joined Falun Gong for its therapeutic benefits. The modest state medical services provided during Mao Zedong's regime (1949–1976) had been reduced under his successors' "self-responsibility" doctrines. Traditional family support had been undermined by Mao's social engineering programs, including the one-child policies of the early 1970s. Falun Gong, as a simple and widely marketed qigong practice, offered an affordable medical alternative.

For other adherents, Falun Gong filled a spiritual vacuum left by the collapsed ideals of Maoism. In the new free-market economy, these one-time supporters of the Communist Revolution felt financially marginalized and philosophically alienated. The rampant corruption and materialism of modern Communist Party officials added to their disillusionment. Simultaneously, the new economic climate freed them to associate outside government-controlled organizations. In Falun Gong and its spiritual leader, they could collectively find a new source of moral authority.

Falun Gong's growth was also due to Li Hongzhi's skill at keeping his disciples within the fold. He warned followers against the common Chinese practice of alternating qigong styles or switching masters, as this would "turn their bodies into a big mess," cause their cultivation to fail, and perhaps attract other masters' "evil spirits." He also discouraged defections by reinterpreting his followers' physical suffering as a source of merit that would accrue to their benefit in the future. Thus, Falun Gong made their ailments easier to bear, even when it was no better at relieving symptoms than a previously tried qigong system. Li also instituted rules to deter challenges to his leadership. Disciples were forbidden to speak of their own experiences or perspective or to use unauthorized teaching materials.

Antecedents to Repression

In the post-Mao era, Chinese authorities took a two-pronged approach to religious practice in China. They eased restrictions against the official, constitutionally recognized religions of Buddhism, Daoism, Islam, Catholicism, and mainstream Protestantism. However, they forbade outside missionaries and unsupervised worship in private homes. They also repressed those peripheral sects perceived as a significant challenge to state authority, such as Tibetan Buddhism and Islam in Xinjiang and Qinghai.

The Chinese government was slow to recognize the challenge posed by Falun Gong. As a qigong group, the movement had escaped the scrutiny of the Chinese government's Religious Affairs Bureau. However, by early 1998, the party-controlled China Qigong Scientific Research Association had removed Falun Gong from its list of registered cultivation groups, and the Chinese Academy of Social Sciences, also party sanctioned, had classified the movement as an illegal *xiejao,* or evil religious cult. This prompted protests in thirteen cities, culminating in a massive demonstration on April 25, 1999.

On that day, more than 10,000 Falun Gong practitioners quietly gathered for twelve hours outside Zhongnanhai, the headquarters of the Chinese Communist Party. Many carried the blue-covered texts of Li Hongzhi. The practitioners dispersed peacefully after they received word that their request for legal recognition would be granted. Nevertheless, many senior leaders, especially President Jiang Zemin, were greatly alarmed. These protesters had dared to directly challenge the leadership at its home base. They were not hot-headed youth but established, middle-class individuals—some

Communist Party members. The protesters had used elusive cellular and computer technology and a highly effective organizational structure to mount their demonstration. And they had caught China's security agencies completely off guard.

The regime had strong historical reasons to be wary of evangelical religious movements like Falun Gong. The Yellow Turbans and the Celestial Masters, two millennialist sects of the second century, had devastated the Han Empire. The Maitreya, or Buddha of the Future, was the messianic inspiration for centuries of insurgent movements, including the White Lotus Rebellion (1796–1804). The Taiping Rebellion (1850–1864), led by a self-proclaimed brother of Jesus Christ, overthrew the Manchu government. The Boxer Uprising (1898–1900) pitted a shamanistic, qigong-disciplined sect called the Harmonious Fists against Christian missionaries. Looking abroad, officials also saw a parallel between the exiled Ayatollah Khomeini's use of communication technology to orchestrate the overthrow of the Iranian monarchy in 1979 and Li Hongzhi's ability to mobilize his followers from overseas (Li had moved with his family to New York City in 1997). Jiang Zemin determined that Falun Gong must be nipped in the bud.

The Crackdown

Party leaders immediately mobilized the state's massive intelligence-gathering apparatus to address "the Falun Gong problem" both at home and abroad. Centrally based security agencies joined with their provincial and city counterparts to collect data on Falun Gong and its activities. Agents stationed in overseas diplomatic missions investigated foreign support for the movement. Within three months, a comprehensive plan was in place.

On July 22, 1999, Falun Gong was outlawed. An arrest warrant was issued for Li

Hongzhi, despite the fact that Li was now in New York City. Other top leaders were arrested, given show trials, and sentenced to long prison terms. Thousands of followers within the party underwent "rehabilitation" by renouncing the movement and coordinating anti–Falun Gong programs. Millions of average practitioners were "reeducated," often while detained in labor camps. In-custody torture, deaths, and organ harvesting were reported. In public squares and on national television, some 2 million Falun Gong books and instructional tapes were shredded or crushed with bulldozers. Over eighty Falun Gong Web sites were taken down. Harsh restrictions were imposed on other qigong groups who might shelter Falun Gong practitioners or pose a similar threat.

In January 2000, in reaction to these measures, five Falun Gong adherents set themselves on fire on Tiananmen Square—an incident the movement claimed was staged by authorities. This triggered a new wave of repression. Practitioners were sent to psychiatric hospitals, and there were more mass arrests. Officials stepped up their anti–Falun Gong rhetoric, charging that the movement undermines societal stability; betrays state secrets; purveys superstition; engages in mind control; and causes illness, insanity, and death. In a remarkably brief time, there were no more Falun Gong rallies in China. The millions of Falun Gong practitioners who congregated daily in parks and public spaces were gone.

The International Response

The international community promptly condemned China's suppression of Falun Gong. In December of 1999, the UN secretary general, Kofi Annan, appealed to China to adhere to the Universal Declaration of Human Rights and the Chinese constitution, which protects freedom of religion and assembly. The UN High Commissioner for Human Rights, Mary Robinson, made a similar plea in March 2000. Chinese officials were unmoved.

Both houses of the U.S. Congress passed unanimous resolutions criticizing China for its crackdown on Falun Gong. Then Secretary of State Madeleine Albright raised the issue in a commemoration of Human Rights Day in December 1999, prompting an open rebuttal from China's UN ambassador. The State Department continued to censure China in its annual *Country Reports on Human Rights Practices* and to reject China's requests for Li Hongzhi's extradition. But after September 11, 2001, the administration of President George W. Bush largely avoided the topic of Falun Gong as it sought China's support on matters of global security.

Chinese officials are able to counter foreign criticism by portraying it as a continuation of imperialist meddling. But China's best defense is its economic clout. Media conglomerates and Internet companies wishing to do business in China have been willing to withhold criticism, comply with censorship rules, and even supply user information to authorities in furtherance of repressive policies.

However, Falun Gong practitioners in New York, Vienna, London, Vancouver, Sydney, and other cities have kept the issue in public view. They regularly demonstrate, distribute literature, and stage graphic tableaux of Chinese persecution. Should any Chinese official venture abroad on global business, he is likely to encounter Falun Gong protesters. Even in Hong Kong, Falun Gong members rally without local interference despite objections from Beijing.

The Future of Falun Gong

Chinese authorities have little chance of eliminating Falun Gong in its current configuration. Spiritual leader Li Hongzhi is out of their reach. The group's organizational structure is fully intact. Members in over fifty countries render support to underground adherents, using communication technologies that elude monitoring. Followers in China blend readily into mainstream society, ready to emerge when it is safe.

Equally conducive to the movement's survival is the social climate of the "new China." The regime's Maoist methods of persuasion—labor camps, reeducation, hyperbolic propaganda campaigns—now seem crude and antiquated. The retroactive punishments imposed for newly criminalized activities strike many Chinese as illegal. Party policies, once colored by utopianism, are now devoid of ideals. In this environment, it is uncertain how the current leadership can rally the masses to crush Falun Gong and, more critically, how they can keep the masses from joining an enemy that offers a fresh moral vision.

According to Li Hongzhi, there are 100 million Falun Gong members worldwide, of which 80 million are in China. According to the Chinese government, the group has 2 to 3 million members. Whatever the true figure, Falun Gong has proven to be a vibrant and resilient movement.

Edith Linn

See also: Buddhism; Shintoism.

Further Reading

Amnesty International. "China: The Crackdown on Falun Gong and Other So-Called 'Heretical Organizations.'" March 23, 2000. Available: http://www.amnesty.org/en/library/info/ASA17/011/2000/en.

Ebrey, Patricia Buckley. *The Cambridge Illustrated History of China.* London: Cambridge University Press, 1996.

Lamb, Gregory M. "China Faces Suspicions About Organ Harvesting." *Christian Science Monitor,* August 3, 2006.

Leung, Beatrice. "China and Falun Gong: Party and Society Relations in the Modern Era." *Journal of Contemporary China* 11 (2002): 761–84.

Li Hongzhi. *Zhuan Falun.* New York: Universe, 1999.

Schirokauer, Conrad, and Miranda Brown. *A Brief History of Chinese Civilization.* Belmont, CA: Thomson, 2006.

Shamdasani, Ravina. "Falun Gong Eight Have Convictions Overturned; Top Court Says the Right to Demonstrate Made Arrests Unlawful." *South China Morning Post,* May 6, 2005.

"The Staged 'Self-Immolation' Incident on Tiananmen Square." Falun Dafa Clearwisdom.net. Available: http://www.clearwisdom.net/emh/special_column/self-immolation.html.

Stone, Alan A. "The Plight of the Falun Gong." *Psychiatric Times* 21:13 (2004): 1–5.

Tong, James. "Anatomy of Regime Repression in China: Timing, Enforcement Institutions, and Target Selection in the Banning of Falungong, July 1999." *Asian Survey* 42:6 (2002): 795–820.

Yunfeng Lu. "Entrepreneurial Logics and the Evolution of Falun Gong." *Journal for the Scientific Study of Religion* 44 (2005): 173–85.